STUDIES IN MUSLIM ETHICS

BY THE SAME AUTHOR

The Shi'ite Religion: A History of Islam in Persia and Iraq,
Luzac and Co., London, 1933

STUDIES IN MUSLIM ETHICS

By

DWIGHT M. DONALDSON
M.A., D.D., Ph.D.

American Presbyterian Mission, Iran and India
Formerly Principal of the Henry Martyn School of Islamic Studies, Aligarh, India

LONDON

S·P·C·K

1963

First published in 1953
Reprinted 1963
S.P.C.K.
Holy Trinity Church, Marylebone Road, N.W.1
Printed in Great Britain by
Fletcher and Son Ltd
Norwich

TO MY MUSLIM FRIENDS AND
CHRISTIAN FRIENDS OF MUSLIMS

CONTENTS

May the Divine Element Transcend Its Bounds? al
Ghazálí's Moral Cosmology: the *'álam al-mulk wa'l-shahádá*
and the *'álam al-jabarút*. Man's Consciousness of Freedom
of Choice. Psychological Determination of Action. Danger
in Associating Events as Cause and Effect. "Allah Alone Is
the Efficient Cause." The Significance of *tawḥíd*. al-
Ghazálí's Influence on Medieval Jewish and Christian
Thought. Analysis of the *Iḥyá'*.

PREFACE

AFTER PERIODS of warfare, when ordinary moral restraints have been set aside, Islamic thinkers have returned repeatedly to the study of ethics. As distinguished from Logic and Metaphysics, they call ethics "Practical Philosophy". But it is not a study that they have pursued independently. Always it has been considered in relation to the Qur'án, that unique book for Muslims in which their Prophet Muhammad set forth the way of life which he said had been revealed to him by Allah.

Muslim ethical literature, therefore, covers an exceedingly wide field. The general moral character of the pre-Islamic Arabs, the outstanding ethical teachings of the Qur'án itself, the portrayal of the Prophet as an example for the personal conduct of his followers, the theological efforts to limit the doctrine of determinism so as to provide for moral responsibility, the wholesome influence of Greek thought in the Muslim world, the ready acceptance of the attempted Neo-Platonic reconciliation between religion and philosophy, the Stoics' illuminating conception of a universal law of nature, the valuable contributions that were made by Christian ascetics and mystics, and the individual struggles of the Muslim mystics, or Ṣúfís, to master the inner life of man in relation to the will of his Creator, all these subjects belong to the ethics of Islam.

But in the narrower sense of systematic moral philosophy, Muslim ethics may be represented as the story of one remarkable book that was written in Arabic at the beginning of the eleventh Christian century by Ibn Maskawaihi (d. A.D. 1030), a man who is also distinguished for work he accomplished as a theologian and as an historian. This book is "The Correction of Dispositions and the Cleansing of Veins" (*al-Tahdhíb al-Akhláq wa Ṭaṭhír al-A'ráq*), It was written when Muslim scholars were most receptive to Greek philosophy, but it was after some two hundred years of almost incessant fighting between rival Muslim dynasties that it was brought to light again when it was translated into Persian, with amplification and adornment, by the astrologer and diplomat Naṣír al-Dín al-Ṭúsí (d. A.D. 1274), who was minister plenipotentiary between the chiefs of the "Assassins" and the great Mongol leader Khulugu Khan. Again, approximately one hundred and fifty years later, when the Timuríds had swept with ruthless destruction from Central Asia to Baghdad, at the court of the famous Uzun Hasan this work of al-Ṭúsí's was in turn revised and rewritten, with further literary ornamentation, as the "Flashes of Splendour Concerning Excellencies of Dispositions" (*Lawámi' al-Ishráq fí Makárim al-Akhláq*). The author was Jalál al-Dín al-Dawwání (d. A.D. 1501). This book, commonly called the *Akhláq-i-Jalálí*, was translated into English by W. F. Thompson in 1839 as *The Practical Philosophy of the Muhammadan People*.

It is my aim in this book to set forth examples of Muslim ethical thought in so far as it relates to personal conduct, exclusive of the separate fields of domestic economy and political science. A few years' experience in teaching ethics to Muslim college students, with textbooks that dealt solely with English and European ethical literature, suggested the need for something like a manual for the study of Muslim ethical literature. For naturally Muslim students desire to know what there is of permanent ethical value in the writings of their own theologians, philosophers, and poets, and to have examples of these teachings set before them in a convenient form and in the same language in which they are asked to study other systems of ethics.

The selections that appear in translation have been made with the hope that they will be recognized by Muslim readers as truly representative. Any system of ethics, especially any ethico-religious system, will have both its assets and its liabilities. The author hopes sincerely that he has not juggled the figures so as to magnify or to minimize either one or the other—"that in the balance ye should not transgress" (Qur'án lv. 6).

It will be shown that, in the ethical writings of the Greek philosophers, the Jews, the Christians, and the Muslims have been joint heirs in a precious heritage. It ill becomes western writers to depreciate Muslim ethics because there is so much in it that has come from the Greeks, to whom they themselves do homage.

Present-day scientific study of the development of moral ideas, the result of investigations in sociology and in modern psychology, presents to Islam, as well as to other religions of authority, many baffling problems. Great advance may well be made when modern Muslim writers on ethics undertake to answer these problems on broad constructive lines, with a readiness to set aside those religious preconceptions which they will come to evaluate as misunderstandings from ages gone by, that now serve only as barriers to further progress. Fundamentally, however, along with Immanuel Kant and T. H. Green, Muslims and Christians are on common ground in so far as they feel that they "are entitled to postulate the moral freedom of man, and the existence of God, as primary truths on which we can base our existence as spiritual beings" (A. C. Bradley, Introduction to T. H. Green's *Prolegomena to Ethics*, 5th edition, p. iv). Leadership may be expected from those individuals who consider it immoral to refuse to do what they know to be right, or to continue to do what they know to be wrong, on account of adherence to religious codes, customs, or taboos.

About half of the chapters in this book were delivered as lectures on Muslim ethics in several theological colleges in the United States, notably in Princeton Theological Seminary, in Western Theological Seminary, Pittsburgh, Pa., and in the Kennedy School of Missions, Hartford, Conn. In India also, at intervals since 1941, similar lectures were given in Serampore Theological College, in the United Theological College at Bangalore, in Leonard Theological College at Jubbulpore, and in the centres of the Henry Martyn School of Islamic Studies at Aligarh and Landour.

In the chapters that deal with the ethics of the Qur'án and the Traditions, and the Arabic and Persian books on ethics, the selections that are given in translation or analysis are for the most part my own work from the original sources, with the guidance of many suggestions from B. Carra de Vaux and others in the *Encyclopædia of Islam* and in the *Encyclopædia of Religion and Ethics*. I am largely indebted, however, in the chapter on early Arab virtues to Sir Charles Lyall's English translation of the *Mufaḍḍaliyát;* and in the study of the ethical values of Ṣúfí literature (chs. VII and VIII) I have been frequently grateful for the masterly studies of Professor R. A. Nicholson, Dr. Margaret Smith, Miss Gertrude Bell, and Dr. A. J. Arberry.

My belief that there is a considerable community of educated Muslim readers who will appreciate a convenient summary in English of the ethical teachings of their own literature has grown in the course of thirty-three years of association with Muslim friends in India and in Iran. It is confirmed by articles that appear frequently in the Hyderabad journal *Islamic Culture*, and by such books as Shushtary's two volumes on *Muslim Culture*. Also I have come to know personally of the desire of Western residents in Muslim lands, especially those who are Christian missionaries, to know and to appreciate the best that is to be found of high moral value in the literature of the people with whom they live.

1

EARLY ARAB VIRTUES

Outside Influences. We are not to think that the early Arabs lived a life that was wholly independent of foreign influence, for the recurring conflicts between the Persian and the Roman empires had repeated repercussions in Arabia. To obtain military and commercial advantages the Persians had seized ports on the eastern borders of Arabia; and to the north-west, on the Syrian border, the Arabs of the Ghassán tribe were under the recognized suzerainty of the Byzantine emperors. Similarly, in north-east Arabia the Persians had frequently protected and subsidized the Lakhmids of Hira. Each of the two great empires employed Arab tribes to defend its frontiers and incited them to make raids against those tribes that gave their support to its rival. Not only were these early Arabs dwellers on the edge round about a desolate and desert land, a people with loose cohesion and long-standing tribal divisions, but it must be remembered that in relation to their powerful neighbours they had the unenviable position of a buffer state.

When the Ghassán chief al-Hárith ibn Jabala had defeated the Lakhmid king al-Mundhir of Hira in A.D. 528, the Emperor Justinian recognized his supremacy and appointed him "lord over all the Arab tribes in Syria", and in Byzantium itself he was given the highest rank next to the Emperor. He reigned in this capacity from A.D. 529 to A.D. 569, and for the greater part of this forty-year period he was occupied in almost continuous warfare with his Persian-paid rival, al-Mundhir of Hira; until in the final battle at 'Ain Ubagh, on Ascension Day, A.D. 554, complete victory was gained for the Ghassánids and al-Mundhir was slain.

Reference is made to this final battle in verses by the poet al-'Algamah,[1] who interceded successfully with al-Hárith for the release of his friend Sh'as, who had been taken prisoner:

1. *Mufaḍḍaliyát*, cxix. 35–6. This famous *Anthology of Ancient Arabian Odes* has been edited and translated by Sir Charles Lyall, in two volumes, Oxford, 1918. The first volume is a carefully edited Arabic text and the second volume is an English translation with a valuable Subject Index. From this book, along with the same author's *Ancient Arabian Poetry*, which is composed of translations from the *Hamásah* and the *Mu'allaqát*, the English reader who is unfamiliar with the Arabic language can get a most vivid impression of the practices, beliefs, and moral conceptions of the early Arab tribes.

A man thou whose foes know well the marks that impact leaves: on these, scars of deadly wounds, but traces of bounty too.

Among men is not thy like, save only thy prisoner; yea, near is he, but none else of kindred can claim his place.

Thy favours on every tribe thou sendest in shower of boons: I pray thee, let Sh'as be one to draw from the flood his share!

It was in the courts of these rival kings that the principal Arab poets of the sixth century flourished, and along with their political differences there were some of them, however, who had Christian influences in common. While the kings of Hira did not themselves profess to follow the Christian faith, many of their Lakhmid tribe were Nestorians, especially from the clans that were called 'Ibád,[2] and the tribe of Ghassán were Syrian monophysites. Both people were familiar with the prolonged controversies between the theological schools of Alexandria and Antioch in regard to the person of Christ. There is record that the Christian churches in Arabia were established for the most part in districts in which there were citizens "of mixed Arab, Greek, and Roman population, where a higher form of culture was to be found".[3]

Note should be made also of the Christians from Abyssinia who had come into the district of Yaman in the South. When Abraha, the Abyssinian king, invaded the Hidjaz, he had with him chiefs of the tribe of Kinda, who "seem to have stood in much the same relation to their rulers as the people of Hira to the Persians and as the Ghassánids to Rome".[4]

Another point that should be remembered is that there were powerful tribes of Jews in Arabia for centuries before Islám, and when Muhammad finally abandoned his policy of conciliating these Jewish communities, some of them were numerous enough to meet the Muslim army in open battles. This was true of the Banu Qainuqá and also of the Banu Nadhir and of the Jews of Kaibar. Rabbi Geiger has observed that "the want of settled life, which continued in Arabia until the rule of Muhammad, was very favourable to the Jews, who had fled to that country in large numbers after the destruction of Jerusalem, in as much as it enabled them to gather together and to maintain their independence. A century before Muhammad this independence had reached such a pitch that among the Himyárites the Jewish ruler actually had jurisdiction over those who were not Jews; and it was only the mistaken zeal of the last

2. Rev. L. E. Browne, *The Eclipse of Christianity in Asia*, Cambridge, 1933, p. 13. Use can be made of the excellent sketch map in this book (frontispiece), which shows the general locations of the tribes mentioned.

3. Prof. Richard Bell, *The Origin of Islam in its Christian Environment*, p. 16.

4. *Encyclopædia of Islam*, art. "al-Kinda".

Jewish governor, Dhu Nuwás, which led him to a cruel attempt to suppress other creeds, that brought about the fall of the Jewish throne by the coming of the Christian Abyssinian king."[5]

Consequently, instead of thinking that the early Arabs lived in isolation from foreign contacts, we see that South Arabia was exploited by Abyssinia, with the co-operation of the tribe al-Kinda; and that for a much longer period North Arabia had been the scene of continuous rivalry between the Ghassánids from Syria, who depended on Byzantium, and the Persian Lakhmids who held sway at Hira.

Moral Stamina of Pre-Islamic Arabs. While modern Muslim writers usually recognize that there were foreign political and religious influences in pre-Islamic Arabia, still they are frequently disinclined to do justice to early Arab culture. They think that it is in the interest of the Islamic faith for them to magnify whatever they can of superstition or barbarity in the practices of the Arab tribes in pre-Islamic times, and ordinarily they fail to give enough credit to the ancient Arab chiefs for those stalwart qualities of character and real virtues that the poets assure us they possessed. They prefer rather to give an exaggerated idea of the practice of female infanticide, for example, and to speak of the "unlimited extent" of polygamy, and to deplore the way in which the Arab tribes had been "addicted to drinking, gambling, and music".[6]

While the Qur'án prohibits female infanticide,[7] as though it were a practice that was not uncommon, at the same time it is interesting to observe that Qais ibn 'Áṣim, who was the leader of the tribe of Tamím that came to visit Muhammad, is described as the man "who had revived in his family and tribe the evil custom of female infanticide, *which had almost died out among the Arabs*".[8] Near-famine conditions in Arabia did lead at times to refusal on the part of parents to allow their female infants to live,[9] because of the exacting demands of nomadic life. A similar practice prevailed, and for much the same reason, among tribes of North American Indians and among the tent-dwellers of Persia and Central Asia. Such nomadic peoples have regarded the burying alive or the exposure to quick starvation of a proportion of their newly-born girl babies as "a meritorious act on the part of a parent, done, as a precaution against famine, in the interests of the tribe".[10]

But aside from the hard demands of their desert existence, along

5. Rabbi Geiger, *Judaism and Islam*, pp. 4–5. Cf. also Torrey, *The Jewish Foundation of Islam*, New York, 1933.
6. Ameer 'Ali, *The Spirit of Islam*, ch. lxv.
7. al-Qur'án, vi. 152; xvii. 33.
8. Lyall, *Ancient Arabian Poetry*, p. 34.
9. *Encyclopædia of Religion and Ethics*, art. "Arabs" (Ancient), by Th. Nöldeke.
10. *Encyclopædia Britannica*, art. "Infanticide".

with the ignorance and superstition that was fostered by their idolatry, there was a moral stamina among the pre-Islamic Arabs which contributed in no small way to the later strength and progress of Islam, and which may be further appreciated by an examination of some of their virtues that were particularly outstanding.

Generosity. In so far as Arab ethical culture is indicated by references from the pre-Islamic poets, we find that hospitality was but a necessary aspect of the primary virtue of generosity; and that to express this virtue there were several words, such as *sakhá'*, *karam*, *muruwwa*, and *júd*. While each of these terms has its distinguishing shade of meaning, yet we may employ the word generosity in its most comprehensive sense, so as to include the ideas of liberal, hospitable, and noble conduct that these several words suggest.

The authorities relate that those of the Arabs who excelled in generosity were Ḥátim ibn Abdullah ibn S'ad of Ṭayyi', Harím ibn Sinán of Murrah, and K'ab ibn Mámah of the 'Iyád. But the proverb, "Ḥátim stands alone" marks him as by far the most celebrated.

The chief sources of information about Ḥátim of Ṭayyi' are two famous anthologies that were compiled in the tenth century. The first of these, the *Kitáb al-Aghaní*,[11] the "Book of Songs", is a marvellous treasury of Arabian folk-lore that was collected by Abu'l-Faraj of Isfahán (d. A.D. 967). The second is the *'Iqd al-Faríd*,[12] the "Unique Necklace", by Ibn 'Abd Rabbihi (d. A.D. 940). From these books that were written a thousand years ago a few instances of Ḥátim's generosity may be given.

But first it should be stated that there was a real Ḥátim, who lived from the middle of the sixth century into the seventh, and who was known both as a knight and as a poet. For a detailed study of his *Díwán* and for further explanation of the place he came to occupy in Persian and Arabic literature the valuable article on "Ḥátim al-Ṭá'í" in the *Encyclopædia of Islam* should be consulted.[13]

Ḥátim's father had died and the boy grew up under the protection of his grandfather. But when he reached manhood he developed the habit of giving his food to anyone with whom he might share it. This led his grandfather to plan for him to live at a distance from town associates. So he gave him a slave girl and a mare with her colt, and sent him to herd the camels. There he failed to find his friends, but he came across a group of strangers, men who were on their way to see the king of Hira. To their amazement Ḥátim killed

11. *Kitáb al-Aghaní*, vol. xvi. 96–110.
12. *'Iqd al-Faríd*, vol. i. 145–6.
13. Cf. *Der Díwán des arabischen Dichters Ḥátim Ṭej*, ed. transl. by Dr. F. Schulthess; *Kitáb Shu'ará' al-Naṣraniya* (ed. Cheikho), i. 98-134; Ibn Qutaiba, *Kitáb al-Shi'r wa'l-Shu'ará* (ed. de Goeje), pp. 123–30; and al-Mas'udi, *Murúdj al-Dhahab*, Paris ed., iii, 327–31.

three camels for them, and one of the men protested, "We needed only milk, but if you felt that you had to give us more, surely one camel would have been sufficient." Ḥátim told them that he knew that was true, but as he saw they were from different countries, it occurred to him that they might tell of his generosity when they would reach their respective homes. On hearing this they expressed their admiration so beautifully in verse that Ḥátim insisted that they should divide the remaining camels among them. So each poet received ninety-nine camels and went on his way, still praising Ḥátim. The grandfather, however, was irate, and "went forth with his family, and Ḥátim was left with his slave girl and the mare and the mare's colt".[14]

In the *'Iqd al-Faríd* (i, p. 145) we read how on one cold night in winter Ḥátim said to his servant, "Make a fire on the outer boundary of the land so that those who are travelling to-night may see it and come in."

Here also it is related that there was not anything that he retained as his own except his horse and his armour, and that he was not accustomed to show his generosity with his old clothes. Once when he had occasion to visit the 'Anza tribe he encountered a prisoner who urged him to set him free. Immediately he arranged to buy the prisoner's freedom from the people of 'Anza. But as he did not have the required redemption money with him, he himself took the prisoner's place in the chains until his own ransom would arrive.

It is said that Ḥátim's wife, Nawar, related this remarkable story: "There was once a year that afflicted us so terribly, when the earth was barren and the skyline was sombre dust, and the camels were doing no work because of their lameness. Even mothers were niggardly with their babes, and there could be no plumpness on a mere drop. That year killed the cattle and we ourselves feared destruction. Then one night, and I swear by Allah that this is true, it was bitterly cold and I had wrapped myself up with the family, when in their hunger our two boys greatly distressed me, as did also the girl Sifána. Then Ḥátim tried to divert my mind with a story, and I knew what he wanted and feigned to be asleep. After a while he said, 'You take the boys quickly, for Allah is about to feed them and you.' I took the boys, and as they clung to me I felt like an ostrich with her young about her. He then got up and went to his horse, and the means of (his) acquiring glory was a large knife, and when he came he said, 'Now it is your affair.' So we took the meat and roasted it and were all ready to eat. But first Ḥátim set out among the tribe, and as he invited neighbours from house to house he called, 'Awake, O people, there is a fire for you!' But when they had gathered about the fire he wrapped himself up so as to hold his cloak on the side facing us.

14. Cf. account given in the *Kitáb al-Aghaní*, xvi, 98, and Nicholson, *Literary History of the Arabs*, p. 86.

There he sat, and I declare he never even tasted the meat, though he had greater need of it than we had. When morning came there was nothing left of his good horse but bones and hoofs."

This story in the '*Iqd* is followed by a poem of Ḥátim's, in which he attempts to justify his unrestrained giving:

Be careful, for there is little credit in blame and censure,
And say no more to me than what is true:
Mention not that I am wasting property.
Be careful, for if I give cheerfully and naturally,
Remember the miser sees in wealth his way to fame,
And the generous man sees in wealth his blame.

Another of Ḥátim's wives was Máwiyya, and in lines he addressed to her he explained his principle of generous hospitality. These lines Professor Nicholson has translated from the *Hamása*:[15]

O daughter of Abdulla and Malik and him who wore
The two robes of Yemen stuff—the hero that rode the roan,
When thou hast prepared the meal, entreat to partake thereof
A guest—I am not the man to eat like a churl, alone—
Some traveller through the night, or house-neighbour, for in sooth
I fear the reproachful talk of men after I am gone.
The guest's slave am I, 'tis true, as long as he bides with me,
Although in my nature else no trait of the slave is shown.

There is record also in the *Kitáb al-Aghaní* of the pride that Ḥátim's daughter had in her father's reputation. In one of Muhammad's early raids she had been taken captive, and it is related that when she was led before him she said:

"O Muhammad, my sire is dead, and he who would have come to plead for me is gone. Release me, if it seems good to thee, and do not let the Arabs rejoice at my misfortune, for I am the daughter of the chieftain of my people. My father was wont to free the captive, and to protect those near and dear to him, and to entertain the guest, and to satisfy the hungry, and to console the afflicted, and to give food and greeting to all; and never did he turn away any who sought a boon. I am Ḥátim's daughter."[16]

As for the ethical character of the generosity that is typified in these somewhat legendary stories of Ḥátim al-Ṭá'í, it may be remarked that it would have been regarded by Muslim writers on classical ethics as a virtue that was exaggerated to the point of its becoming a vice, except as it may have been considered as an expedient to win fame. By the Arab poets its utilitarian motive is naïvely taken for granted.

15. Nicholson, op. cit., p. 87.
16. *Kitáb al-Aghaní*, xvi. 97, trans. Nicholson, *L.H.A.*, pp. 86–7.

Thábit ibn Jábir, the very first poet who is mentioned in the *Mufaḍḍaliyát*,[17] who flourished about the time when Muhammad was living in Mecca and whose poems are representative of that period, expresses clearly the calculating motive of such extravagant generosity:

> Use then the wealth that thou hast gained to stop
> Breaches round thy stead, till come the day
> When thou meetest what all mankind shall face.

The sixth-century poet, Zuhair ibn 'Alas al-Muṣayyib,[18] compared a generous man to an irrigation canal:

> Yea, thou art more generous than a brimming canal,
> With waves surging one upon another and dashing against the
> Banks: it seems as though with its piebald steeds in its sides
> It were charging the water-wheels of the husbandmen.

It was with a feeling of irreparable loss that al-Aswad, the blind poet who frequented the court of the last Lakhmid king of al-Ḥira, lamented the destruction of the 'Iyád princes by the Persian king Chosroes:[19]

> What can I hope, when Muharriq's house have gone to decay and left their palaces void? What better, after 'Iyád?—
> The folk who dwelt in Khawarnaq and Sáriq and as-Sadír, and the high pinnacled castle that stood beside Sindád—
> A land which Ka'b son of Mámah chose and Abú Du'ád to be the place where their father's stock should prosper and grow.
> Now sweep the winds over all their dwellings: empty they lie, as though their lords had been set a time and no more to be.
> Yea, once they lived there a life most ample in wealth and delight, beneath the shades of a kingdom stable, not to be moved.

Tranquillity. The highly esteemed virtue of tranquillity (*al-ḥilm*), which includes ideas of clemency, gentleness, and forbearance, is defined in the *Kasháfi Istilaháti Funún* ("Dictionary of Technical Terms") as "that virtue which requires that the soul (*al-nafs*) should be tranquil, so that anger will not move it easily, and thus it will not be disturbed on the occurrence of dire calamity, though it be long in duration". In the comprehensive Arabic lexicon, *al-Táj al-'Arús* ("The Bride's Coronet"), the same meaning is given, with the additional and special quality of "delay in requiting the wrong-doer".

17. *Mufaḍḍaliyát*, i, 25. Cf. *Kitáb al-Aghaní*, xviii. 214 ff.
18. *Mufaḍḍaliyát*, xi. 20, 21.
19. Ibid., xliv. 8–12.

There is not one of the virtues of later Muslims, or even of their prophet Muhammad himself, that is more firmly grounded in commendable qualities of the pre-Islamic Arabs than this virtue of *ḥilm*. Victory may not always be won, but for the honour of the tribe the spirit of heroic tranquillity must be constantly maintained.

In the battle of Shíb Jabala, the 'Abs tribe, with their allies of the Banu Ámír, had been routed by their enemies' use of a shrewd expedient. Their camels had been kept from water for several days, until they were mad with thirst. Suddenly they let them loose, and the whole troop of famished camels made a dash down a steep descent (*shíb*), at the base of which the 'Abs were encamped at the river's edge. The stampede that was created led to the defeat of the 'Abs, but nevertheless their poet Khurrashah was able to boast on behalf of his tribe:[20]

> There is not a tribe than which we are not better in discipline—both in the remnants that remain and in the fathers of old.
> Longer in our stand in the place of danger, in defence of all dear to us, or more settled in calm temper when the fresh springing pasture moves men to folly.

In a similar mood, Suwaid of Yashkur wrote of the tribe of Bahr:[21]

> The Merciful—praise be to Him!—wrote (in the Book of Destiny) that in us should be breadth of character and strength to bear;
> And stubborn resistance to all base things, what time he who is overborne by numbers has to accept wrong and bow before it.

The poet Salamah also, whom Ibn Qutaiba mentioned as "one who lived far back in the Ignorance"[22] (though his date is uncertain and he may have lived to become a Muslim), has celebrated the tribe of Tamím for their stalwart endurance:[23]

> A people they, when a year of famine presses, their tents bring strength to starvelings, and rest to wandering sons of the wild.
> When bites Calamity, sharp-toothed, cruel, patience is theirs to bear unflinching, and countless men to stand for the lost.

In the sense of *forbearance* we find that this ancient and inclusive virtue of *ḥilm* is illustrated in the lines of al-Muthaqqib, who lived during the same period as Salamah:[24]

20. *Mufaḍḍaliyát*, cxxi. 5–6.
21. Ibid., xl. 61–2.
22. Ibn Qutaiba, *Kitáb al-Shi'r wa'l-Shu'ará*, ed. de Goeje, p. 187.
23. *Mufaḍḍaliyát*, xxii. 25–6.
24. Ibid., lxxvii. 8–10.

Many the evil speech to which my ear has been deaf; and yet there is in me no hardness of hearing;
And I bear it patiently, for fear lest the fool should think that I am really as he said.
And in sooth some turning away of the face and ignoring of the evil-speaker is the safest thing, even though he be a wrong-doer.

Along with this ideal of tranquillity there was a notable mood of abstraction in contemplating the various vicissitudes of fortune:[25]

Yea, knowledge I have from Time, the best of all counsellors, the passing of days that brings to light wealth of hidden lore:
I know how the rich is served by riches, how fair the praise they gather with cunning hands, whatso be the blame his due;
And how lacking wastes and wears a man, though his heart be high—yea, sharper the sting thereof than falling of untanned scourge!
He looks on the steps of fame—the steps he can never tread—and sits in the midst of men in silence without a word.

As lovers, also, men are admonished that they should maintain an independent composure and not allow themselves to give way to distraction or subserviency. They are not to expect too much, "for when did rose-tinted finger-tips and binding pledges e'er agree?"[26] The teaching seems to be, as it is explained by Sir Charles Lyall, that "the ideal lover should be quick to cast off a love that has grown cold to him":[27]

Nay, but I, when a mistress grudges to grant me the boon I seek, and holds to me but by a bond already weak and frayed,
I fly from her straight, as I fled from Bajílah, when I put forth my utmost speed, on the night of the soft plain of al-Raht.

So said the poet Ta'abbata Sharrá, and Salamah held to the same general rule:[28]

I am one who gives love for love, and also one who can cut the bond if love wanes.

In the same vein a gentle warning is given to the foolishly inclined man of advancing years:[29]

Turn away from her, and let her not distract thee from business: verily love-longing, after grey hairs have come, is but to wander astray.

25. Lyall, *Ancient Arabian Poetry*, xxxiii, from the *Ḥamásah*.
26. Ibid., xli.
27. *Mufaḍḍaliyát*, i. 3–4. 28. Ibid., vi. 2. 29. Ibid., xxvi. 8.

There are beautiful pictures, however, that these early poets have left of persistent bonds of family affection that contributed to their spirit of tranquillity. For example, Ḥiṭṭán of Ṭá'í is remembered for this striking description of his children:[30]

Far would I roam and wide to seek my bread in Earth that
has no lack of breadth and length.
Nay, but our children in our midst, what else but our
hearts are they, walking on the ground?
If but the breeze blow harsh on one of them, mine eye says
"No" to slumber all night long.

It is gratifying to discover also the note of tender affection and genuine love that is expressed by Muwalik al-Masmúm at the time of the death of his wife:[31]

Take thou thy way by the grave wherein thy dear one lies
—Umm al-'Alá—and lift up thy voice: ah if she could
hear!
How art thou come—for very fearful wast thou—to dwell
in a land where not the most valiant goes but with
quaking heart?
God's love be thine and His mercy, O thou dear lost one!
not meet for thee is the place of shadow and loneliness.

And a little one hast thou left behind—God's ruth on her!
She knows not what to bewail thee means, yet weeps for
thee;
For she misses those sweet ways of thine that thou hadst
with her, and the long night wails, and we strive to hush
her to sleep in vain.
When her crying smites in the night upon my sleeping ears,
straightway mine eyes brimful are filled from the well of
tears.

The Vendetta (*th'ár*). But the most characteristic picture of the life of the early Arab tribes is stern and sombre. It shows, however, the bright lights of courage and loyalty against the dark shades of fear and hatred. We can stand aside and look at this picture in the poems that relate to revenge, for as Professor Nicholson has observed, "they show all that is best and much that is less admirable in the heathen Arab—on the one hand, his courage and resolution, his contempt of death and fear of dishonour, his simple-minded devotion to the dead as well as to the living, his deep regard and tender affection for the men of his own flesh and blood; on the other hand, his implacable temper, his perfidious cruelty and reckless ferocity in hunting down the slayers, and his well-nigh inhuman exultation over the slain."[32]

The moral quality that was demanded for the execution of the vendetta (*th'ár*) was a fearless readiness to accept it as a duty (*ḥaqq*),

30. Lyall, *A.A.P.*, p. 97. 31. Ibid., xxvii.
32. Nicholson, *L.H.A.*, p. 97.

and to carry it out, with patience and shrewdness, until full revenge had been taken. And so imperative was this sense of "duty" that not infrequently the second killing would exceed what the injured tribe or family had themselves been made to suffer.

Like generosity, this show of despatch and courage in taking vengeance was known as *murúwa* (manliness), a quality that the women demanded of their men as an index of their manhood. And as the vendetta is one of the pre-Islamic obligations that has been retained in Islam, though in a modified form, a number of instances may be cited to show how the early poets represented its inter-tribal acceptance as an unquestioned, almost religious obligation, in fact "comme la plus impérieuse institution de leur organisation traditionnelle".[33]

Vows would be made to abstain from wine and other luxuries until vengeance had been taken:[34]

> Forbidden was wine, but now it is lawful: hard was the toil that made it lawful.
>
> Give me not to drink if I bring not in Ghatafan by night the marching of a mighty and numberless host.

Likewise, at times they vowed that they would not pay court to women, nor play games; that they would not use perfume, nor wash their heads; and that they would not anoint their eyes with collyrium, nor eat food—until vengeance had been gained.[35]

Not alone did the bereaved parents consider that they were afflicted with a malady that could be cured solely by vengeance, but a rancour sickness for revenge was thought to cast its spell over a whole tribe. It was likened to a fever, and they employed the expression, "blood unavenged drips as dew", to express the idea that a man has died in vain, for they considered that the dew had no enriching effect upon the earth.

The early Arabs believed that when a man had been killed and his blood revenge had not been taken, then his spirit would come forth from his head as a bird that was like an owl. This bird was called *al-háma*, and as it hovered over a murdered man's tomb it would not cease to cry, "*isqúní!*" (Give me to drink!) until the blood revenge was taken.[36]

When there had been a murder or a general slaughter in retaliation, the event would be celebrated with a drinking bout, and on such occasions poets would sometimes give way to gloating over the

33. Bichr Fares, *L'Honneur chez les Arabes avant l'Islám*, Paris, 1932, pp. 72–5. Cf. also Lammens, H., *L'Arabie Occidentale avant l'Hégire*, Beyrouth, 1928, ch. iv. "Le caractère religieux du *ṭar* ou vendetta chez les Arabes préislamites."

34. Lyall, *A.A.P.*, pp. 49, 51; and *Mufaḍḍaliyát*, cix. 6.

35. Bichr Fares, op. cit., pp. 72–3.

36. Cf. *al-Mustaṭraf*, ch. 49.

dead. For example, we have the verses of the poet Ta'abbata Sharran as he gloried over those who had been killed of the tribe of Hudhail:[37]

> Reach me the cup, O Sawad son of 'Amir: spent is my body with grief for mine uncle.
> To Hudhail we gave to drink death's goblet, whose dregs are disgrace and shame and dishonour.
> The hyena laughs over the slain of Hudhail, and the wolf—see thou—grins by their corpses,
> And the vultures flap their wings, full-bellied treading their dead, too gorged to leave them.

One famous poem, by an aged poet and experienced warrior, suggests that he had lived to feel a kind of disgust or satiety at such killings, and that his mind had reached the stage of contemplating their futility. This is a short but important poem by al-Duraid (A.D. 535–630), the son of Ṣimmah (the "Viper"),[38] in which he bewails the killing that had occurred of several of his brothers, one after another, and then he meditates on the tragic lot of his family, the sons of the "Viper":

> Slaughter chose of all men born the race of Ṣimmah (the "Viper") for her own:
> They chose her, and would none other, so fate goes to fated end.
> Yea, and if our blood be ever end and aim of vengeful hands, striving day by day to spill it until the days shall be no more,
> Flesh to feed the sword are we, and unrepining meet our doom: well we feed him, slain or slaying, joyfully he takes our food!
> Hearts are cured of rancour sickness, whether men against us war, or we carry death among them: dying, slaying, healing comes!
> So we halve our days between us, we and all men else our foes: no day passes but it sees us busy with this deed or that.

At times proposals of peace were made by one side but were not accepted by the other, as when the sons of Ṣirmah had killed three of the sons of Ḥumais, and the poet al-Husain addressed the sons of Ṣirmah:

> Ye killed our client the Jew, and we killed a Jew in requital: then ye killed three of our friends of Qudá'ah, and we have killed three of your clients of Qudá'ah. Now do ye bid your Qudá'ites depart from among you, and we will bid ours. We are brothers together: let there be peace between us.

But the men of Ṣirmah would not listen and prepared for war.[39]

37. Lyall, *A.A.P.*, p. 49.
38. His father's name had been chosen for its deadly significance, as was frequently customary.
39. *Mufaḍḍaliyát*, p. 34, Eng. trans.

At other times a great chief is praised because he had brought to an end some devastating conflict between neighbouring (and often related) tribes by his willingness to enter into a final negotiation in camels for the price of the blood that had been shed. On this historical occasion when the tribes of 'Abs and Dhubyán made peace, after some forty years of warfare, the two outstanding leaders, who bore the burden of the price of blood, called forth the highest praise from the poet al-Zuhair:[40]

> The wounds of the kindred were healed with hundreds of camels good;
> He paid them orth, troop by troop, who had no part in the crime:
> Kin paid them forth to kin as a debt due from friend to friend,
> And they spilt not between them so much as a cupper's cupfull of blood.
> Among them went forth your gift, of the best of your father's store,
> Fair spoils, young camels a-many, slit-eared, of goodly breed.

A romantic story is told in explanation of this momentous conclusion of peace. A famous knight of Dhubyán had gone a-wooing, and the maid who agreed to marry him had shown such spirit and self-confidence, in contrast to her diffident sisters, that she said to her father, "As thou wilt." When her father protested, "But I offered this man's proposal to thy two sisters and they refused," she replied with assurance, "Not so in my case, for I am one who is fair of face, skilful with her hands, noble in nature, honourable in her father, and if he divorce me, God will bring no good upon him thereafter." But while she agreed to the match, she was not willing to become his wife at once. First she objected, "Not thus before my father and my brethren," and again on the journey she remonstrated, "Doest thou with me as with a woman slave or a captive woman taken in battle? First you must slay camels and sheep, and call the Arabs to a feast." But when he came and said, "I have made ready the camels and sheep as thou seest," she still held aloof. "I was told," she said to him, "that thou hadst a nobleness which I do not see in thee." "How is that?" he inquired. She then looked at him admiringly and asked, "Hast thou a heart to wed women while the Arabs are slaying one another?" And when he wished to know what there was that he could do she had her answer ready. "Go forth," she said, "to these thy kindred and make peace between them: then return to thy wife, and thou wilt not miss what thou desirest." For this reason it was, therefore, that he and his associates "came to the two tribes and walked between them with peace".[41]

40. Lyall, *A.A.P.*, p. 112.

41. Ibid., pp. 107–9.

2

THE ETHICS OF THE QUR'ÁN

FROM THE subject index of the contents of the Qur'án that is given in the large edition of the Urdu interlinear translation, which was prepared and published by Mulla Háfiz Nazír Aḥmad of Bombay in A.H. 1314, the references that are included under the head "Dispositions and Good Deeds" (*Akhláq wa Ḥusni Mu'ámalát*) afford a general view of the things that Muslims are most disposed to emphasize in the ethical teachings of the Qur'án. It is fitting that these references should be examined and arranged according to their subject matter.[1]

GENERAL PRINCIPLES

Duty to Allah. The general principles that are enunciated in the Qur'án to govern the conduct of the Prophet himself, and of all the believers, are based on the initial assumption that Allah created both men and women (iv. 1) and that He sees and hears and knows everything that they do (ii. 233, 237; xxiv. 28). These several principles are expressed in connexion with special admonitions. For example, the injunction "Be ye steadfast in justice" is associated with a reminder to the believers that they are "witnessing before Allah" (iv. 133). In the matter of the division of the spoils of war, they are cautioned "to fear Allah and to settle it among themselves" (viii. 1). Likewise unfaithfulness in keeping agreements is equivalent to being "treacherous to Allah and His Apostle" (viii. 27). It is Allah who enjoins them to "do justice and good, and to give to kindred their due", and to fulfil His covenant, "for ye thereby make Allah your surety" (xvi. 92, 93). In cases where there was opposition they were to "fight the party that has committed the outrage until it return to Allah's bidding", and when the recalcitrant party would return they were to "make peace between them with equity, and be just: verily Allah loves the just" (xlix. 9). And when victory came after great peril the believers were admonished, "Ye would have been timid, and ye would have quarrelled about the matter, but Allah

1. In all but a few instances where mention is made to the contrary, Palmer's English translation of the Qur'án has been employed, except that "Allah" is used sometimes in translations from Arabic books instead of "God".

preserved you; verily He knows the nature of man's breasts" (viii. 45). "Those who assent to their Lord" are those who "are steadfast in prayer, and whose affairs go by counsel among themselves" (xlii. 38).

Moderation. In fighting "in the way of Allah", with those who fought with them, they were "not to exceed the limits: surely Allah does not love those who exceed the limits" (M.A. trans. ii. 190). Similarly moderation is advised in the command "let not ill will against the people who turned you from the sacred mosque make you transgress (lit. "to exceed the limits"); . . . but fear Allah; verily Allah is keen to punish" (v. 2).

Forgiveness. It was because the believers could take refuge in Allah, "who both hears and knows", that they were to "take to pardon and order what is kind, and shun the ignorant" (v. 199). And when they are told that they should "pardon and pass it over", they are asked, "Do you not like Allah to forgive?" (xxiv. 22). Those who forgive when they are angry are counted among those who avoid great sins and abominations (xlii. 35). Though they are warned that there are some of whom they should beware, yet they are told, "but if ye pardon and overlook it, and forgive, verily Allah is forgiving, compassionate!" (lxiv. 14).

Retaliation. We find that in the Qur'án the principle of retaliation is made somewhat conditional and is restricted in its application. "And whoso transgresses against you, transgress against him like as he transgressed against you, but fear ye Allah, and know that Allah is with those who fear" (ii. 90). "Help one another in righteousness and piety, and do not help one another in sin and enmity; but fear Allah" (v. 3). "But if ye punish, punish (only) as ye were punished; but if ye are patient, it is best for those who are patient" (xvi. 26). In this kind of retaliation Allah's assistance is promised: "Whoever punishes with the like of what he has been injured with, and shall then be outraged again, Allah shall surely help him" (xxii. 59). It is gratifying to find, however, that there is this rule also, "Repel evil with what is better" (xxiii. 96), which is amplified in another reference, "Good and evil shall not be deemed alike; repel evil with what is best, and lo! he between whom and thyself was enmity is as though he were a warm patron" (xvi. 34).

Limited Liability. In two connexions the believers are instructed that "no soul shall be obliged beyond its capacity". On one occasion this rule is laid down in regard to the question whether a mother is required to nurse her child for two whole years or whether she may wean it or provide a wet-nurse (ii. 233). In another connexion the believers are assured that Allah himself observes this rule in the ordinances that he lays down for individuals among mankind: "We do not compel the soul save what it can compass" (vi. 153).

Oaths. "Fulfil Allah's covenant when ye have covenanted, and break not your oaths after asseverating them, for ye thereby make Allah your surety; verily Allah knows what ye do" (xvi. 93).

Rewards. "Allah's is what is in Heaven and what is in the Earth, that he may reward those who do evil for what they have done; and may reward those who do good with good; those who shun great sins and iniquities—all but venial faults—verily, thy Lord is of ample forgiveness" (liii. 31–2).

EXHORTATIONS TO PARTICULAR VIRTUES

Humility. "And walk not on the earth proudly; verily thou canst not cleave the earth, and thou shalt not reach the mountains in height" (xvii. 39). "And the servants of the Merciful are those who walk upon the earth lowly, and when the ignorant address them, say, 'Peace!' " (xxv. 64). "That is the future abode; we make it for those who do not wish to be haughty on the earth, nor to do evil, and the end is for the pious" (xxviii. 83). "And twist not thy cheek proudly, nor walk in the land haughtily: verily Allah loves not every arrogant boaster: but be moderate in thy walk, and lower thy voice; verily, the most disagreeable of voices is the voice of asses!" (xxxi. 18).

Honesty. "And give full measure when ye measure out, and weigh with a right balance" (xvii. 37). "And the heavens, He raised them and set the balance" (lv. 8, 9). "Woe to those who give short weight! who when they measure against others take full measure; but when they measure to them, or weigh to them, diminish" (lxxxiii. 2, 3).

Giving to the Poor. "And let not those amongst you who have plenty and ample means swear that they will not give aught to their kinsman, and the poor, and those who have fled their homes in Allah's way, but let them pardon and pass it over" (xxiv. 22). The believers were told clearly that there was to be "no hindrance to the blind, and no hindrance to the sick" in their eating from the houses of their fathers, mothers, brothers, sisters, etc. (xxiv. 61), and they were commanded also that they should not grant favours "in order to gain increase" (lxxiv. 6).

Kindness. "And to your parents show kindness, and to kindred and orphans and the poor, and the neighbour who is akin, and the neighbour who is a stranger, and the companion who is strange, and the son of the road, and what your right hands possess (of slaves)" (iv. 40). "Say, 'Come! I will recite what your Lord has forbidden you, that ye may not associate aught with Him, and may show kindness to your parents" (vi. 152). "Do not grumble at them, but speak to them a generous speech. And lower to them the wing of humility and of compassion, and say, 'O Lord, I have compassion on them as they brought me up when I was little!' " (xvii. 24–6).

Trustworthiness. "Verily Allah bids you pay your trusts to their owners, and when ye judge between men to judge with justice" (iv. 62). "O ye who believe! fulfil your compacts" (v. 1). "Be ye not treacherous to Allah and His Apostle; nor be treacherous to your engagement while ye know! Know that your wealth and your children are but a temptation, and that Allah—with Him is a mighty hire" (viii. 27, 28). "Prosperous are the believers . . . who observe their trusts and covenants, and who guard well their prayers" (xxiii. 2, 9). "And he who turns again and does right, verily, he turns again to Allah repentant. And those who do not testify falsely" (xxv. 72–3).

VICES THAT ARE CONDEMNED

Boasting. In Luqmán's advice to his son (xxxi. 11–17) we are assured that Allah does not love the arrogant boaster (verse 16), and that therefore a man's voice must be lowered and his walk should be moderate.

Blasphemy. "And those who annoy (speak against) Allah and His Apostle, Allah will curse them in this world and the next, and prepare for them shameful woe" (xxxiii. 57).

Slander. "And those who annoy (speak against) the believers for what they have not earned, such have to bear the guilt of calumny and obvious sin" (xxxiii. 38).

REGULATIONS FOR THE MUSLIM COMMUNITY

Orphans. "They will ask about orphans: say, 'To do good to them is best'; but if ye interfere with them—they are your brethren, and Allah knows the evildoer from the welldoer; and if Allah will He will surely trouble you" (ii. 219). "And give unto the orphans their property, and give them not the vile in exchange for the good, and devour not their property to your own property; verily that were a great sin" (iv. 2). "But do not give up to fools their (your) property which Allah has made you to stand by: but maintain them from it, and clothe them, and speak to them with a reasonable speech. Prove orphans until they reach a marriageable age, and if ye perceive in them right management, then hand over to them their property, then take witnesses against them; but Allah sufficeth for taking account" (iv. 4–7). "And draw not near to the wealth of the orphan, save to improve it, until he reaches the age of puberty, and fulfil your compacts; verily a compact is ever inquired of" (xvii. 36).

Nursing and Weaning. "Mothers must suckle their children two whole years for one who wishes to complete the time of suckling; and to him to whom it is born its sustenance and clothing are incumbent; but in reason, for no soul shall be obliged beyond its capacity. A mother shall not be forced for her child . . . but if both parties wish to wean by mutual consent and counsel, then it is no crime in them. And if ye wish to provide a wet-nurse for your children, it is no crime in you when you pay what you have promised her in reason. Fear Allah and know that Allah on what ye do doth look" (ii. 233).

Reconciliation. "And if a woman fears from her husband perverseness or aversion, it is no crime in them both that they should be reconciled to each other, for reconciliation is best. For souls are prone to avarice: but if ye act kindly and fear Allah, of what ye do He is aware. If ye are not able, it may be, to act equitably to your wives, even though ye covet it, do not however be quite partial, and leave one as it were in suspense: but if ye be reconciled and fear, then Allah is forgiving and merciful; but if they separate, Allah can make both independent out of His abundance; for Allah is abundant, wise" (iv. 128–9). "Men stand superior to women in that Allah hath preferred some of them over others, and in that they expend of their wealth: and the virtuous women are devoted, careful (in their husbands' absence), as Allah has cared for them. But those whose perverseness ye fear, admonish them and remove them into bedchambers and beat them; but if they submit to you, then do not seek a way against them; verily, Allah is high and great. And if ye fear a breach between the two (man and wife), then send a judge from his people and a judge from her people. If they wish for reconciliation, Allah will arrange between them; verily, Allah is knowing and aware" (iv. 8, 9).

Divorce Proceedings. To understand the stipulations in regard to divorce it is necessary to recall that marriage agreements are frequently concluded for the marriage of very young girls, of nine to twelve years of age, and that such agreements would sometimes be cancelled before the marriage had been consummated. This, too, is called divorce (*ṭaláq*) in the Qur'án.

"And if ye divorce them before ye have touched them, but have already settled for them a settlement, (*then pay them*) the half of what ye have settled, unless they remit it, or he in whose hand is the marriage tie remits it; and that ye should remit is nearer to piety; and forget not liberality between you. Verily Allah on what ye do doth look!" (ii. 237).

There is a chapter devoted to the divorce of actual wives, however (Sura lv), from which two stipulations may be cited: "When ye divorce women, then divorce them at their term, and calculate the term, and fear Allah your Lord. Do not drive them out of their houses unless they have committed manifest adultery" (lv. 1). "And if they be heavy with child, then pay for them until they lay down their burdens; and if they suckle the child for you, then give them their hire; and consult among yourselves in reason" (lv. 6).

Entering Houses. "O ye who believe! Enter not into houses which are not your own houses, until ye have asked leave and saluted the people thereof, that is better for you; happily ye may be mindful. And if ye find no one therein, then do not enter them until permission is given you; and if it be said to you, 'Go back!', then go ye back, it is purer for you; for Allah of what ye do doth know" (xxiv. 28, 29).

Debts and Accounts. "O ye who believe! If ye engage to one another in a debt for a stated time, then write it down, and let a scribe write it down between you faithfully. . . . Unless, indeed, it be a ready-money transaction between you, which ye arrange between yourselves, then it is no crime against you if ye do not write it down; but bring witnesses to what ye sell to one another, and let neither scribe nor witness come to harm, for if ye do it will be abomination in you; but fear Allah, for Allah teaches you, and Allah knows all things" (ii. 281, 283).

Wives. "But if ye fear that ye cannot do justice between orphans, then marry what seems good to you of women, by twos or threes or fours; and if ye fear that ye cannot be equitable, then only one, or what your right hands possess (i.e. female slaves). That keeps you nearer to not being partial. And give women their dowries freely; and if they are good enough to remit any of it themselves, then devour it with good digestion and appetite" (iv. 2, 3).

Inheritances. "Men should have a portion of what their parents and kindred leave, and women should have a portion of what their parents and kindred leave, whether it be little or much, a determined portion" (iv. 8). "With regard to your children, Allah commandeth you give the male the portion of two females; and if they be females more than two, then they shall have two-thirds of that which their father hath left: but if she shall be an only daughter she shall have the half" (iv. 11). "And your wives shall have a fourth part of what ye leave, if ye have no issue; but if ye have issue, then they shall have an eighth part of what ye leave, after paying the bequests ye shall bequeath, and debts" (iv. 14).

Relatives. "And when the next of kin and the orphans and the poor are present at the division, then maintain them out of it, and speak to them a reasonable speech" (iv. 9). "And let not those amongst you who have plenty and ample means swear that they will not give aught to their kinsman, and the poor, and those who have fled their homes in Allah's way, but let them pardon and pass it over" (xxiv. 22).

Privacy. "O ye believers! Let those whom your right hands possess, and those amongst you who have not reached puberty, ask leave of you three times (to come into your presence): before the prayer of dawn, and when ye put off your clothes at noon, and after the evening prayer: three times of privacy for you" (xxiv. 57).

Interceding for Others. "Whoso intercedes with a good intercession shall have a portion therefrom; but he who intercedes with a bad intercession shall have the like thereof, for Allah keeps watch over all things" (iv. 87).

Publicity to Evil. "Allah loves not publicity of evil speech, unless one has been wronged; for Allah both hears and knows. If ye display good or hide it, or pardon evil, verily, Allah is pardoning and powerful" (iv. 147–8).

Brothers in Religion. "Call them by their fathers' names: that is more just in Allah's sight, but if ye know not their fathers, then they are your brothers in religion and your clients" (xxxiii. 5).

Self-defence. "But what is with Allah is better and more lasting, . . . for those who, when wrong befalls them, help themselves. . . . And he who helps himself, after he has been wronged, for these—there is no way against them. The way is only against those who wrong men and are wanton in the earth without right; these—for them is grievous woe" (xlii. 40–3).

Forgiving Enemies. "O ye who believe! Verily, among your wives and children are foes of yours: so beware of them! But if ye pardon and overlook it and forgive,—verily, Allah is forgiving, compassionate!" (lxiv. 14).

It is obvious that the above list of references is insufficient, for anything like a complete summary of all that there is in the Qur'án that has to do with questions of moral conduct would make a book in itself. But even the most comprehensive treatment would be inadequate unless the underlying principles of the moral judgments could be determined. Three important questions arise as to the nature of any particular teaching: Is it confirmed by human reason and experience; is it exemplified in the conduct or approval of the Prophet; and is its authority by revelation from Allah?

The more modern Muslim is disposed to give primary importance to the test of reason. He is aware that this is the confirmation that is required by philosophy and science, and he has observed that in the Qur'án itself there are scattered instances where particular statements are brought before the court of human reason and experience.[2]

As a rule, however, the exhortations in the Qur'án are to obey Allah and His Apostle on a strictly authoritarian basis; and appeals to reason are occasional, exceptional, and rather by way of illustration than for necessary confirmation. This gives tremendous impor-

2. When believers were told to "take to pardon and order what is kind", the question followed, "Do you not like Allah to forgive?" (xxiv. 22). Observe that the duty of forgiveness is here put on a rational basis, which is similar to that which is found in the New Testament, Matthew vi. 14–15. It should also be mentioned that after the proclamation, "Retaliation is prescribed for you for the slain", there is the exclamation, "For you in retaliation is there life, O ye possessors of minds! It may be ye will fear" (ii. 173–5). The number of times that caution is given that a rule of action should be implied "in reason" is significant.

tance in Islam to the doctrine of divine revelation, and to the belief that the Prophet was directly inspired to give utterances that were written down and recited afterwards as the veritable words of Allah. Hence the supreme authority of the Qur'án among all Muslim peoples.

The student of ethics will wish to satisfy himself as to the truth of the ethical teachings of the Qur'án by processes of careful investigation, and this will necessarily include an historical survey of the circumstances in the life of the Prophet and particular situations in the community of believers which gave occasion for those declarations in the Qur'án which are most likely to be challenged on ethical grounds by non-Muslims. Such declarations, however, should not be singled out for isolated consideration, but should be studied along with the situations that led to them. An effort should be made to let the Qur'án speak for itself regarding the development of that ethical consciousness which the Prophet put into it, as Muslims believe, by divine authority, and in which he exhorted the believers to follow his example.

IN MECCA

The moral instruction which Muhammad gave his followers in Mecca was based on deep religious convictions. He was satisfied that in special ways he had been called by Allah, and that his revelations or declarations were Allah's own word. He insisted that Allah had created man with moral responsibility, and that therefore there must of necessity be a day of judgement for mankind, with rewards and punishments.

Men were admonished in the meantime to be appreciative of their proper place in the universe. Without disregarding the evidence of wisdom and far-seeing design on the part of the Creator, and while observing the wonders of everyday life, Muhammad was fully aware of the marvellous phenomenon of Man.

Professor Tor Andrae and others have considered that he must have heard Christian preaching, for he observes that "one often notices in Muhammad's revelations a fixed rhetorical scheme, with approximately the following outline: (1) a description of the blessings of God as revealed in His providence, especially in the wonderful creation of man, and the life-giving rain which brings about productive growth for the nourishment of man; (2) the duty of man, therefore, to serve God alone in faith and good works; and (3) the judgments and retribution which shall come upon all who do not fulfil this duty".[3]

It has been suggested that Muhammad may have heard Quss ibn Sá'ida preach at the fair of 'Ukáẓ, but it is generally considered that

3. Tor Andrae, *Muhammad: The Man and His Faith*, 1936, p. 126.

if Quss, whom we now know only as a legendary character, "really was an historical individual, he must have lived at a much earlier period than the generation contemporary with Muhammad".[4]

For the subjects that are included in Muhammad's "fixed rhetorical scheme or outline", however, it is not necessary to refer to any immediate Jewish or Christian influence. The materials which he used in his early preaching, "though they may remind us ever again of Jewish and Christian phrases and ideas, are in reality Arab materials. They may have been derived originally from outside Arabia, but they had by Muhammad's time become part of the Arab mind."[5] For before Muhammad's time the word *ḥaníf* "denoted the people, who, although influenced by Christianity, had refused both Christianity and Judaism in favour of a simpler and more primitive religion. But the historical development of such a movement is wrapped in an obscurity which cannot be cleared up with the material at present available".[6]

The tenth-century Muslim historian al-Mas'udí has stated that "there was a party among the Arabs, while they were still in the Time of Ignorance, who believed in the unity of God, who acknowledged the existence of a Creator, who held to the truth of the day of the rising and reviving (*al-ba'th wa'l-nushúr*) of the dead, and who were fully assured that God would reward the obedient (*al-muṭí'*) and punish the rebellious (*al-'áṣí*)". And al-Mas'udí goes on to explain that "among those who called men to God, the Great and Glorious, those who drew men's attention to His wonderful works, were Quss ibn Sá'ida, Riyáb al-Shanní, and Buḥaira the monk (*ráhib*), all of whom belonged to the tribe of 'Abd al-Qais".

"There were also among the Arabs", he further informs us, "those who acknowledged the Creator and proved the universe to be something originated (*ḥuduth*), who acknowledged the resurrection day and the repetition (*i'áda*) of life, but who denied messengers and continued in the worship of idols (*'aṣnám*) (cf. Qur'án xxxix. 4). They were those who went on pilgrimages to visit the idols, declared their intentions before them, slaughtered animals for them, devoted sacrifices to them, and in their name determined what was permitted or forbidden. Among these men there were some, however, who acknowledged the Creator, but who regarded the messengers and the day of resurrection as false. They were inclined to follow the opinion of the people of the time, 'It is only our life in this world, we die and we live, and naught destroys us but time!' (Qur'án xlv. 23)."[7]

As to the literary form of the utterances that are found in the

4. H. Lammens, *Encyclopædia of Islam*, art. "Quss ibn Sá'ida"; also *L'Arabie Occidentale avant l'Hégire*, Beyrouth, 1928, p. 21.

5. Richard Bell, *The Origin of Islam in its Christian Environment*, London, 1926, p. 69.

6. Cf. *Encyclopædia of Islam*, art. "Haníf", by Fr. Buhl.

7. Mas'udí, *Murúj al-Dhahab*, iii, p. 256 ff.

Qur'án, we have Brockelmann's excellent authority for considering that it "was probably not entirely new. The short clauses of the earlier revelations, borne on a free, gliding rhythm and connected together by a single rhyme, must have been closely akin to the *saj* of the old sooth-sayer (*káhin*). But their contents, the intimately personal struggle of the soul for its own salvation and that of mankind, was something that Arabia had never known before. Even when calm reflexion had taken the place of ecstatic emotion and the prophet strove to gain the attention of his people by means of stories, and finally when the revelation had become a mere form for laws and ordinances, its language must still have excited the admiration of the Arabs."[8]

The sacred book of Islám, *al-Qur'án*, "the Reading", contains a series of revelations that were "sent down" to Muhammad at intervals. Subsequently the Muslim theologians considered that if God had so willed "He would have inspired the prophets with quite a different preaching and a different law".[9] Moreover, this Qur'án was dictated from an original code, "the Mother of the Book", which is preserved in Heaven (xliii. 3; xiii. 39; iii. 5) as a "well-guarded tablet" (lxxxv. 22). The intermediary that brought the revelation to earth was "a faithful spirit" (xxvi. 93), later identified with the angel Gabriel (ii. 91). This revelation is to be "a guide for him who should do right" and "a decision on all matters" (vi. 155), because God has willed it.[10]

Muhammad was aware, as Professor Nöldeke pointed out a good many years ago,[11] "that the complete contents of the book were not communicated to him, as he expressly states, e.g. of the stories of the prophets: 'And we did send apostles before thee: of them are some whose stories we have related to thee, and of them are some whose stories we have not related to thee'" (xl. 78).

We should be prepared also to find in the Qur'án expressions of aspects of truth that appear to be contradictory. Sometimes a new emphasis is given, or the Prophet is dealing with a different angle of a broad subject. But it would be a serious mistake to consider that every apparent contradiction in the Qur'án is an instance of "abrogation".

Particularly in dealing with the problem of evil, in its origin and in God's relation to it, we will not be surprised to find the ardent prophet of Arabia feeling his way, first on this side and then on that. The teaching which predominates is that of fixed determinism,[12] though when Muhammad was faced with questions about the cause

8. Brockelmann, *Encyclopædia of Islam*, art. "Arabia".
9. Wensinck, *The Muslim Creed*, quoting Baghdadí, *Uṣúl*, p. 213.
10. Cf. Levy, *Sociology of Islam*, vol. i, p. 214.
11. Nöldeke, *Sketches of Eastern History*, p. 22.
12. Qur'án, liv. 49; lxxxvii, 2; liv. 52; xi. 8; ix. 51; vii. 17; xxxiii. 36; lxxvi. 29, 21; and vi. 107.

of man's wrong-doing, "on occasion he was compelled to the view that not God but man was responsible for the evil in the world".[13] Professor D. B. Macdonald came to the conclusion that "the contradictory statements of the Qur'án on free will and predestination show that Muhammad was an opportunist preacher and not a systematic theologian".[14]

As stated by Dr. Nadví in his recent book, *Muslim Thought and Its Source*,[15] "Every passage in the Qur'án must be studied with reference to the circumstances necessitating its revelation. When the nature of the divine power or the question as to the decisive factor in the disposal of human affairs was being discussed among the people, verses were revealed confirming the absolute power of God, such as the following:

xlviii. 12	He is powerful over everything.
xxii. 14	He does whatever He intends.
xvi. 77	God has all things at command.
xxiv. 45	God creates what He will.
ii. 49	And He pardons whom He will and punishes whom He will, inasmuch as God is a Supreme Sovereign.
liv. 49	Verily, I created everything with a (fixed) decree.

"Similarly when the question of human responsibility or irresponsibility was the topic of discussion among the people, verses were revealed, assigning to men some freedom of volition and discretion in the choice of actions, and imposing on them some share of responsibility for their actions, such as:

xli. 54	Whosoever acts virtuously does so for himself, and whosoever acts viciously does so for himself.
iv. 3	And whosoever gets to himself a sin, gets it solely on his responsibilities.
vii. 29	And when they commit a deed of shame they say, 'We have found that our fathers did so, and God obliges us to do it.' Say thou, 'Surely God requireth not shameful doing.'
xiii. 27	Verily, God changes not what concerns any people until they change what depends on themselves.
x. 108	So whoever follows the right path does so for his own good, and whoever goes astray bears on himself the responsibility (of going astray).

"By harmonizing these two sets of passages", Dr. Nadví observes, "the only right conclusion we arrive at is that God is undoubtedly the Supreme Sovereign, with very wide powers, but that human

13. Qur'án, v. 45; xxxiii. 72; iv. 81; vii. 27; and xviii. 28. Cf. Levy, op. cit., ii, pp. 36–7.

14. D. B. Macdonald, *Encyclopædia of Islam*, art. "Qadar", ii, p. 605.

15. *Muslim Thought and its Source*, by Syed Muzaffar-ud-Din Nadví, M.A., Ph.D., Lahore, 1946, pp. 14–16.

beings also have some hand in moulding their destiny, inasmuch as they can make choice between good and evil, right and wrong. Whenever God speaks of predestination or pre-arrangement of human affairs, He generally means that they must conform to the usual course of action, i.e. the law of nature. Man, within the limited sphere of his existence, is a builder of his character and an architect of his fortune, subject to the control and supervision of the Supreme Intelligence."

There is no question in the interpretation of the Qur'án that has had more discussion than that of man's responsibility for his actions in the light of God's sovereign decrees.[16]

THE MECCAN CODES

The ethical teachings of Muhammad, up until the time when he entered Medina, are summarized in three codes. The first of these codes, which is found in the chapter called "The Night Journey" (xvii. 23–40), distinctly resembles the Decalogue; and we note that it includes four positive commands and seven prohibitions. The commands are: to know one god only (23), to be kind to parents (24–8), to give to the poor (29–30), and to be moderate in spending (31–2). The things that are prohibited are: infanticide (33), adultery (34), killing unjustly (35), robbing orphans (36), cheating in trade (37), believing false reports (38), and showing pride (39).

The second code may be likened in form to the Beatitudes. It is found in the chapter called "The Discrimination" (xxv. 64–75), and the last verse of the passage declares that "these shall be rewarded with a high place (in Paradise) for that they were patient". The reference is to those who are lowly (64–6); to the discriminating (67–70), whether about spending or killing or personal chastity; to the penitent (71); and to the truthful (72–4).

The third code is in the style of an old Persian "paternal admonition" (*pand-i-pidar*), which repeats, "O my boy!" or "O my son!" It is found in the chapter Luqmán (xxxi. 11–17), which is named for the sage who has sometimes been identified with Aesop of the Greeks. Its admonitions are: to have gratitude to Allah (11); to associate no other with Allah (12); to observe duties to parents (13–14); to remember that Allah brings everything to light (15); to seek in prayer to be steadfast, reasonable, and patient (16); and to live so as to avoid pride and ignorance (17).

Other moral precepts that Muhammad reiterated to his followers were: to assist their fellow-countrymen, especially those in need; to free themselves from the love of delusive wealth; to avoid all forms of cheating (xxvi. 182 ff. and v. 8 ff.); to be chaste in their lives; and not to expose for death their new-born girls (vi. 152; xvii. 33).

16. Cf. ch. 4, "Philosophical Ethics in Islam".

Such were the ethical principles and admonitions that Muhammad included in his preaching in the early years of his mission as a prophet in Mecca. They were years of conflict and of opposition, when he had as yet no authority as a ruler, and they are generally regarded as his best years of religious aspiration and of ethical achievement.

Yet for Muhammad there were times of uncertainty as to how rigorous he should be in his demands of the new believers. One occasion for such uncertainty was before he left Mecca, when he was led to hesitate in regard to his protest against associating any other with Allah. The persecution that had fallen upon members of his family because they continued to protect him from the idolaters had been a constant source of annoyance. It has been suggested that it was in order to ease matters somewhat that he "proclaimed in one of his sermons that the favourite deities of the Meccans, al-Lát, al-'Uzzá, and al-Manát, might be regarded as divine beings whose intercession was effective with Allah".[17] By this means the much desired reconciliation with his Meccan neighbours appeared for a while to be accomplished; but it should not be forgotten that Muhammad was not satisfied with this compromise, for very soon he declared that these words of his must have been the interpolations of Satan, and in their stead there came the words that are now found in the Qur'án (liii. 19–23), the passage which declares that these old deities "are but names which ye have named, ye and your fathers! God has sent down no authority for them."

That suggestions had been made to Muhammad to compromise in his monotheistic preaching is confirmed by the record in the *Síra*, that at one time when the Prophet was making a circuit of the Ka'ba, al-Walíd ibn al-Mughaira and three of the older men of the Quraish accosted him and said:[18] "Look here, Muhammad, let us worship what you worship and you worship what we worship, and thus we will share in this affair of religion. If it proves that what you worship is better than what we worship, then we will take our advantage from your religion, and if what we worship should be better, then you can take your advantage from that." But to aid him in his reply we are told that the following revelation was sent down to Muhammad (ix. 1–5, Rodwell's trans.):

> Say, "O ye unbelievers! I worship not that which ye worship, and ye do not worship that which I worship; I shall never worship that which ye worship, neither will ye worship that which I worship. To you be your religion; to me my religion.' "

It may sometimes be thought that a more thorough-going icono-

17. Fr. Buhl, *Encyclopædia of Islam*, art. "Muhammad", with references to al-Ṭabarí, i. 1192; i. 1195; and to Ibn Sa'd, I, i. 187 ff.
18. Ibn Hishám, *Síra*, Cairo, 1938, vol. i, p. 386.

clast would have destroyed the Black Stone in the Ka'ba, for it too was part of the ancient superstition and idolatry. But until long after the time when Muhammad and his followers left Mecca for Medina he had no jurisdiction over the Ka'ba. He had even declared that the prescribed direction for prayer was towards Jerusalem, which was regarded as the sanctuary of the monotheists. And by the time the Prophet came back to Mecca as a conqueror, he claimed that he had received revelations to the effect that the original foundation of the Ka'ba had been laid by Ibrahím and Isma íl (ii. 121), and that as the "station (*maqám*) of Ibrahím", where his very footprint was to be shown on a stone in the court, the Ka'ba was worthy to be the direction for prayer (*ṣalát*). The idols were then abolished as desecrations, but the Black Stone remained as part of the building which was left unaltered. In later Muslim legend it was said that the Black Stone had been brought in the first place to Ibrahím by the angel Gabriel from a sacred mountain on the eastern frontier of Mecca, a mountain called Abú Qubais, where it was said it had been kept since the Deluge. Originally it is said to have been a white stone and "only received its present colour as a result of contact with the impurity and sin of the pagan period".[19]

IN MEDINA

In A.D. 622, on Monday, the 20th of September, Muhammad and Abu Bakr approached Kuba, a suburb of Yathrib. In their white cloaks they looked so much alike from a distance that at first the expectant observers were in a quandary as to which one was the Apostle of Allah, until someone noticed that one of them was holding his cloak so as to shade the other, "who must therefore be Muhammad". they thought, "for a prophet comes to be served".

In Kuba they were received with little demonstration and waited there until Friday. 'Ali and his companion, Suhaib ibn Sinan, had joined them as they anticipated on Thursday, and the next day they all went together to Yathrib, where they were welcomed with enthusiasm by the group of Emigrants.

The Prophet found temporary lodgings in the house of one of the most dependable of the Khazrajite converts. This man's name was Khalid ibn Zaid, and he was a close friend of Muhammad's special emissary, Mus'ab ibn Umair, who had been sent ahead to establish a place of worship. The town of Yathrib, to which Muhammad and his loyal followers emigrated as to a city of refuge, became the outstanding "city" (*madína*) of the Prophet.

In their invitation to Muhammad to leave Mecca and to cast his lot with them, the converts in Medina were not moved solely by religious convictions. They "did not so much want to attract an

19. Wensinck, *Encyclopædia of Islam*, art. "Ka'ba".

inspired preacher to themselves as to get a political leader", for their inter-tribal relations had become intolerable.[20]

The situation may be illustrated by the story of how the Jewish community in Medina had been caught in a maelstrom of hatred between two Arab tribes. The Khazraj tribe felt that they had reason to fear that the Jews were allying themselves with the Aws tribe, who were their enemies. The Jews denied any such alliance, but the Khazraj demanded that they send to them as evidence of their good faith forty of their young men as hostages. This was done, but afterwards an unscrupulous element in the Khazraj tribe gained the upper hand and persuaded their fellow tribesmen that it would be to their advantage to fight the Jews along with the Aws, for in case they were victors they would be in position to take over the coveted and fertile lands that the Jews occupied. They saw that they could at once start such a war by killing the hostages that had been sent to them.

One of the Khazraj chiefs, Abdallah ibn Ubaiy, condemned such treachery, and he may be mentioned appropriately as an Arab in the pre-Islamic period who dared to challenge the doctrine that might makes right. But the other Khazraj chiefs murdered the Jewish hostages that had been entrusted to them, which immediately brought about a state of war between the Khazraj on the one hand and the Aws and their Jewish allies on the other. The fighting that ensued culminated in the decisive battle of Bu'ath, when the Khazraj were defeated. But there was an aftermath, however, of inter-tribal hatred and eager desire for vengeance, which became so menacing throughout the whole region of Medina that the group of converts to Islam who were living there, a group which included men from both factions, were able to advance the idea of inviting Muhammad to come to be their prophet-governor, and thus restore confidence and peace between the tribes.

The task that lay before Muhammad, therefore, in Medina, was one that would require both character and skill. "The inspired religious enthusiast, whose ideas mainly centred around the coming of the last judgement, who had borne all insults and attacks, who only timidly touched on the possibility of active resistance (xvi. 127), and preferred to leave everything to Allah's intervention, with the migration to Medina enters upon a secular stage";[21] and afterwards, as may be observed from the traditions as well as from the Qur'án, "Muhammad's notions of prophecy seem to have been chiefly influenced by those cases in which the prophet also claimed to be the head of the community".[22]

20. Fr. Buhl, *Encyclopædia of Islam*, art. "Muhammad", vol. iii, p. 641.
21. Ibid., p. 648.
22. Margoliouth, *Encyclopædia of Religion and Ethics*, art. "Muhammad", viii, p. 174.

Numerous problems were inherent in the situation and difficulties arose in the organization of the newly formed and heterogeneous community, so that Muhammad had to make many rapid and momentous decisions. Always there was the danger also that a prophet would not be expected to feel his way by experiments like other men, and that he might lose followers if he made mistakes or showed hesitation. Unless circumstances should so shape themselves as to bind both the leader and the led in a common struggle for the necessities of life, and unless the leader's assurance of his divinely appointed mission should be wholly positive, there would be ample opportunity in Medina for complete failure.

The community that Muhammad needed to bring into some kind of working unity included several elements. First there were the Emigrants from Mecca, who, in their loyalty to him, had sacrificed their home-town connexions and resources, and had now come away without either capital funds or lucrative occupations. The second element in the new community were the Helpers, those converts in Medina who had shown themselves to be gracious hosts, but who would soon tire of the burden of an increasing number of non-paying guests. The Hypocrites were those Arab residents of Medina who, like most of the Jews also, were not genuinely or religiously in sympathy with Muhammad's coming and who had no inclination to join in an aggressive support of his cause.

The most pressing problem was to distribute the responsibility for providing the necessary means of subsistence for the Emigrants, and to this end Muhammad decreed "brotherhood" between individuals of their number and other individuals from the Helpers (xxxiii. 6). This plan was immediately useful as a temporary expedient, but before long it was evident that other means would have to be sought. The Emigrants were steadily increasing and were almost entirely dependent upon the help of others. The privations they suffered and the variety of menial tasks they accepted in order to earn their daily food, all these are fully elaborated in the traditions. For hewing wood, for watering palm trees, and for making bricks they would get a small daily allowance of dates. A few managed to make a modest living by trading. We are told that Abu Bakr sold clothes in the bazaar, that 'Uthman bartered in dates, and that 'Umar too was a trader.

Another means of possible relief that the Prophet saw for his followers was to enlarge the number of the Helpers. This he first sought to do by ingratiating himself with the Jews, or rather by persuading them also to accept his leadership and authority. The tenth of Tishrí was the Jewish "Day of Atonement", a twenty-four hour fast, and this custom Muhammad incorporated into Islam by adopting as a Muslim day of fasting the tenth day of Muharram, and this day he called by the Aramaic name *'áshúrá*, "the tenth". The *qibla*, or fixed direction of prayer, if it were first determined as towards Jerusalem when the Prophet was in Medina, as is probably true, marks a tolerant and practicable concession to the Jews. But Muhammad went too far when he sought to convince the Jews that an Arab could be their Messiah, or that his hearsay accounts about Abraham, Noah, Moses, and David were to be credited as equal or superior in authority to their own Scriptures. In fact the more they heard of the Qur'án, the more ready they were to ridicule the Prophet's claims, so that after a few months the effort to conciliate the Jews was abandoned.

It was at this time, when the Jews had grown unfriendly and when his own followers were restless on account of their impoverished living, that word reached Muhammad that a rich caravan from Syria was about to return to Mecca. If this caravan could but be captured their poverty would soon be relieved. How did the Prophet take this suggestion? He saw the force of its immediate material advantages more clearly than its ultimate implication for the ethics of Islam. We are told, however, that before committing himself he referred the whole matter to Allah, and prayed: "O Lord, they (the Muslims) go on foot, make them riders; they are hungry, satisfy them; they are naked, clothe them; they are poor, enrich them."[23]

For a little more than a year, however, there was no answer to this prayer, for though six efforts were made to capture passing caravans they were all of them unsuccessful. For so long a time the Emigrants had failed to make their economic blockade of Mecca effective. They continued also to live in poverty, and to make matters worse, many of their women and children had come to them from Mecca. It is not difficult to imagine that as their needs became more and more severe, their desire to retaliate upon the Meccans grew fierce and determined.

Out of regard for the fact that the Arab tribes abstained from warfare during the "peace of the sacred months", Muhammad's men had so far remained inactive during that time. The months that were reserved as times of peace were the first, *Muḥarram*, which was so called because war was then unlawful (*ḥarám*); the seventh, *Rajab*, the "honoured" month, when there must be peace; the eleventh, *Dhu'l-Qa'da*, the "month of truce"; and the twelfth, *Dhu'l-Ḥijja*, the "month of the pilgrimage".

It may well have been that at such times of inactivity, when they could all get together and talk things over, that there were discussions about the wisdom or propriety of their thus undertaking to live by the sword, and that such discussions may have led to the new revelations that came:

23. *Mudárij al-Nabuwat*, p. 559, reference from Canon Sell, *The Battles of Badr and of 'Uhud*, C.L.S., p. 10.

War is prescribed for you, but it is hateful to you; yet haply ye hate a thing which is better for you (ii. 212).

Fight for the cause of Allah (ii. 245).

And when the month of Rajab, the shorter season of peace, approached and Muhammad himself had returned from another fruitless raid in the direction of Yambo, since so many attempts had failed, he was now prepared to be less scrupulous about violating Arab tribal laws. As at this time the Meccans would be bringing another caravan through, Muhammad sent forth a group of seven men under the command of Abdallah ibn Jaḥsh, who were to go towards Nakhlah. Abdallah carried sealed orders that were not to be opened until after the second day's march. And when the orders were opened they revealed that he was not to compel his men to join him in disregarding the sacred month if they objected. So the account we have is that two of them managed to wander away, ostensibly seeking their camels. But with the five men who remained Abdallah attacked a caravan, which, because of the month of peace, was accompanied by only four men. One of these they killed and another fled. The remaining two they captured along with the caravan, and with the first success in acquiring booty for the community of Islam they hastened back to Medina.

It was at this time, when objections were doubtless raised about such a raid in the month of peace, that the Prophet received the following revelations:

They will ask thee of the sacred month, of fighting therein. Say, "fighting therein is a great sin; but turning folks off God's way, and misbelief in Him and in the Sacred Mosque, and turning His people out therefrom, is a greater sin in God's sight; and sedition is a greater sin than slaughter" (ii. 209).

Permission is given to those who fight because they have been wronged—who have been driven forth from their homes undeservedly, only for that they said, "Our Lord is God"; and were it not for God's repelling some men with others, cloister and churches and synagogues and mosques, wherein God's name is mentioned much, would be destroyed. But God will surely help him who helps Him; verily, God is powerful, mighty (xxii. 40–1).

There was now an additional consideration, for the blood of Amr ibn Hadramí, the one man who had been killed in the raid at Nakhlah, would have to be avenged by his fellow Meccans. There would be inter-urban war, and all parties would be committed to it; on the one side the Meccans, on the other side Muhammad, with his Emigrants and the Helpers who had given them protection.

Also a much larger caravan was coming, the one that had eluded them the previous November. It was returning to Mecca in March, which would not be in a month of peace. The Meccans would be on the alert and there would certainly be fighting. The booty, however, would be worth about one hundred thousand dollars. Hence Muhammad arranged for a force of three hundred to start out from Medina, two hundred and forty Emigrants and sixty Helpers. For transport they had two horses and seventy camels; and for rations they carried dates and strips of cooked meat, though they also expected to find locusts on the way.

Abu Sufyán, the leader of the Meccan caravan, had been warned of his danger, and by making forced marches and detours he managed not only to take the caravan to Mecca in safety, but also to arouse some nine hundred and fifty Meccans, equipped with seven hundred camels and one hundred horses, to come forth to meet Muhammad in open battle. By their better discipline, their unity of command, their steadfastness of purpose, and perhaps partly because the rain had made the ground slippery for camels, Muhammad's small force from Medina prevailed. This was the day of the Battle of Badr, which is called in the Qur'án the Day of Deliverance—"the day before which the Muslims were weak, after which they were strong. Its value to Muhammad himself it is difficult to overrate; he possibly regarded it as a miracle, and when he declared it one, most of his neighbours accepted the statement without hesitation."[24]

After the Battle of Badr a determined effort was made to nationalize the new religion, for it was in those early years after the migration that the independence of Islam became manifest, first to Muhammad himself and shortly afterwards to the rank and file of his followers. The Prophet preferred to describe himself, however, as the restorer of the religion of Abraham, the true *ḥaníf* (vi. 79), who was neither a polytheist, nor a Jew, nor a Christian (ii. 129; iii. 60, 89). It was Abraham, he declared, and his son Ismá'íl, the traditional ancestor of the Arabs, who had founded the sanctuary at Mecca (ii. 118; xxii. 27). Thereby opportunity was given to incorporate various customs from the worship of the Arab tribes in pre-Islamic times. The Ka'ba at Mecca, with its sacred Black Stone, was adopted in preference to Jerusalem as the *qibla* or fixed direction for prayer. The *ḥajj*, or annual pilgrimage to Mecca, was made obligatory for believers. The newly decreed custom of twenty-four hours of fasting on the tenth of Muḥarram was discontinued and in its stead the month of Ramaḍán was to be a complete month of fasting (ii. 281), but with the provision they should refrain from food and drink only during the hours of the daylight. Friday, the day of the week that was appointed for congregational prayer, was not to be considered "a day of rest" (lxii. 9; l. 37) like the Jewish Sabbath. Furthermore, until such time as the new community would be again able to make the *ḥajj* (pilgrimage to Mecca), provision was made for a special annual sacrifice on the tenth of the month of Dhu'l-Ḥijja at the

24. Margoliouth, *Muhammad and the Rise of Islam* (Heroes of the Nations Series), p. 269.

muṣalla, or place of prayer, that was just outside Medina. And there was to be no more imitation of Jews in the way they wore their hair or in the burial of the dead, and Jews were no longer to be consulted about doubtful points of faith and conduct.[25] Revelations came also that were definitely anti-Jewish, such as, "but God has made selling lawful and usury unlawful" (ii. 276).

It was also after the Battle of Badr that we find Muhammad asserting the authority of a prophet to rule in matters secular as well as religious. His idea of the functions of a prophet included much more than that he should be a medium of revelations. Now that he had the power of leadership, difficulties were no longer to be referred to soothsayers for settlement, but to him, and the heads of the tribes and the commanders of expeditions would hereafter be designated or deposed at his personal behest. "Say, 'If ye would love God then follow me, and God will love you and forgive your sins, for God is forgiving and merciful'"; "Say, 'Obey God and the Apostle; but if ye turn your backs, God loves not misbelievers'" (iii. 28–9). With such revelations Muhammad confirmed his demand that "all important matters were to be laid before Allah and himself".[26]

Two of the prisoners who had been captured in the Battle of Badr were killed on the way back to Medina. One of them, al-Naḍr ibn al-Ḥárith, had posed as a rival. He had "bought the books of the Greeks, Persians, and Arabs of Hirah, and recited their contents; and argued that if story-telling was the criterion of a prophet then he had as good a right to the title as Muhammad". And when Muhammad now gained this opportunity to destroy his literary rival, he appears to have done so without hesitation or compunction; though when he heard the dirge of the bereaved daughter for her slain father he is said to have been moved to tears and regrets.[27] The other one of these men, Ukbah ibn Abu Mu'ait, "had formally espoused Islam, but had afterwards withdrawn". We are told of his early connexion with the Jews, and that "he may have at some time helped the Prophet with information". Not unnaturally there are some who have asked the question, Did both of these men know too much about what might help explain the "revelations"? When he decided that it was well that these men should be put out of the way at once, it may be that Muhammad's sense of expediency was keener than his strictly ethical consciousness.

It is not surprising to find that Muhammad, like other Arab chiefs, treasured genuine power and authority more than the display of jewels and silken robes, but it is surprising and disappointing that we find no word of protest when ignorant and devoted converts

25. Ibn Sa'd, *Ṭabaqát*, iii. 157, 27; Ibn Hanbal, *Musnad*, iv. 263; references from Margoliouth, *Muhammad*, p. 250.
26. Fr. Buhl, *Encyclopædia of Islam*, iii, p. 650.
27. Margoliouth, *Muhammad*, p. 268.

"struggled for the honour of washing in the water which the Prophet had used, and then drank it. Ere long he took to bottling the precious liquid and sending it, after the style of the relics of saints, to new adherents. When he employed the services of a barber, the Muslims crowded round, and even scrambled for the hair, and nail-parings, which they preserved as charms and relics" (Ibn Sa'd, II, ii, 87).[28]

Very soon the people were no longer to approach the Prophet in the free-and-easy way in which they were accustomed to go to their own chiefs, nor were they to address him as they would one of their own number (lxxiv. 64). For a time it was required that anyone who wished to speak to him must first make an offering to the poor, though this requirement was withdrawn (lviii. 13). These stipulations were doubtless intended not merely to expedite business, but to enhance the personal dignity and authority of the Apostle of Allah. In the view of the difficulties that are often experienced among Eastern peoples by travellers who wish to maintain the privacy they consider necessary for their work and comfort, it is easy to sympathize with some of Muhammad's stipulations in this regard. "Verily, those who lower their voices before the Apostle of God, they are those whose hearts God has proved for piety, for them is forgiveness and a mighty hire. Verily, those who cry out to thee from behind the inner chambers, most of them have no sense; but did they wait until thou come out to them, it were better for them—but God is forgiving, merciful" (xlix. 3, 4); and "O ye believers! do not enter the houses of the Prophet, unless leave be given you, for a meal—not watching till it is cooked! But when ye are invited, then enter: and when ye have fed, disperse, not engaging in familiar discourse" (xxxiii. 52).

Any careful student of the records of the life of Muhammad in the early years of his work as a prophet in Medina, as it is portrayed by references in the Qur'án, will not fail to be impressed with the remarkable convenience with which "revelations" were obtained to serve as legislative decrees. In accord with the various questions that arose they came successively as they were needed. While they were usually in the form of communications from Allah, in their content they resemble the natural afterthoughts of Muhammad, as he met his personal quandaries with rapid and bold decisions.

The instances that have been cited of such declarations in the Qur'án during the Medina period had to do with occasions when it was necessary to have Allah's approval for fighting in the sacred months of peace (ii. 209); for changing the direction of prayer from Jerusalem to Mecca (ii. 135, 139); for terminating the "brotherhood" relationship between the Emigrants and the Helpers (xxxiii. 6); for encouraging the resort to force (ii. 212, 245 and xii. 40–1); for discriminating the true *ḥaníf* (right-doer) from the Jew and the Christian (ii. 129 and iii. 60, 89); for relating the sanctuary at

28. Margoliouth, *Muhammad*, p. 216.

Mecca with the monotheistic faith (ii. 118 and xxii. 27); for establishing the fast of Ramaḍán (ii. 281); for distinguishing Friday from the Jewish "day of rest" (lxii. 9 and l. 37); and for outlawing the taking of usury (ii. 276).

In Mecca unbelievers had objected that Allah should sometimes substitute one verse for another, and they would say to Muhammad, "Thou art a forger!" (xvi. 105). But in Medina, especially after the success at Badr, "it called forth the admiration of the faithful to observe how often Allah gave them the answer to a question whose settlement was urgently required at the moment".[29]

EARLY PROBLEMS

Circumstances of continuing human interest, that were due to extraordinary happenings or criticisms in which the Prophet was directly concerned, provided numerous occasions for comments in the Qur'án. In these utterances questions with an ethical bearing were frequently involved, and the explanations that are recorded afford excellent examples of problems that arose very early in the ethical interpretation of the Holy Book. For as Professor Tor Andrae has taken pains to reiterate, "the Qur'án itself is a source of immeasurable value for the understanding of Muhammad's inner life, of the motives which prompted his message, and of the arguments and objections which his countrymen raised against his preaching. It is quite remarkable that Western scholarship has been so reluctant to exploit adequately the sacred book of Islam as a first-hand source for the inner life of the Prophet, and to treat it as a *document humain*, that enables us to trace a soul which wrestles with its fate, and with naïve candour reveals its aims and hopes, as well as its faults and accomplishments, its weakness and courage."[30]

Attitude towards Opponents. As has been mentioned, a fellow townsman in Mecca, one Naḍr ibn al-Hárith, had incurred the hearty dislike of the Prophet because he had publicly declared that the narratives Muhammad recited, which were mainly derived from Jewish sources, were in no way superior to those that he himself was accustomed to relate about the ancient kings of Persia. The earliest authority, Ibn Isḥáq (d. A.D. 768), describes al-Naḍr's conduct as irritating and reprehensible: "He was one of those insolent men of the Quraish, who annoyed the Prophet and showed enmity towards him. Eager to attract public attention, he had learned stories of the kings of Persia, and recounted the adventures of Rustam and Isfandiyár. The Apostle would be seated in a meeting, and when speaking of Allah he would warn his people of chastisement that had befallen other peoples. At such times al-Naḍr ibn Hárith would rise

29. Nöldeke, *Sketches of Eastern History*, p. 28.
30. Tor Andrae, *Muhammad: The Man and His Faith*, p. 159.

and say, 'By Allah, O ye men of the Quraish, I am better at telling stories than he is, so come to me and I will relate to you still better ones.' He would then tell them about the kings of Persia, and about Rustam and Isfandiyár. Afterwards he would ask, 'In what respect is Muhammad superior to me as a narrator of stories?' "[31]

We find that al-Mas'udí refers to al-Naḍr as a poet-minstrel, who brought the lute from al-Ḥíra to Mecca.[32] But from the comments in the Qur'án it would appear that it was his pretension as a teller of stories that displeased Muhammad:

> And amongst men is one who buys sportive legends, to lead astray from God's path, without knowledge, and to make a jest of it; these, for them is shameful woe! And when our signs are recited to him, he turns his back, too big with pride, as though he heard them not—as if in his two ears were fullness. But give him glad-tidings of grievous woe! (xxxi. 5–6).
>
> When our signs are recited to him, he says, "Old folk's tales." We will brand him on the snout! (lxviii. 15–16).

At the Battle of Badr al-Naḍr was taken prisoner, and as the victors were on their way back to Medina, when they reached a place that was called al-Ṣufrá, the Prophet instructed 'Ali ibn Ṭálib to put him to death.[33] This 'Ali did *deliberately* (*ṣabran*), which signifies that he killed him slowly, by repeatedly piercing him with a sword or lance.[34]

A poem of lamentation, which is said to be one of the best of its kind in the Arabic language,[35] is ascribed to the sister of al-Naḍr; and in this poem there is direct reference to his "death by torture" (*al-maniyatu mut'aban*). The bereaved sister asks why the Prophet could not have shown magnanimity and at least have allowed her brother to pay a ransom for his life:[36]

> O Rider, if the place of honour is supposed
> To be reached from the morning cloud, and you are prospered,
>
> Bear my greeting to him who is dead,
> A sincere remembrance that will not pass away.
>
> Shall al-Naḍr hear if I call to him?[37]
> As though the speechless corpse could hear!

31. Ibn Hishám, *Síra*, ed. Cairo, 1927, i. p. 320.
32. al-Mas'údí, *Murúj al-Dhahab*, viii. 93–4.
33. Ibn Hishám, op. cit., ii. 286, 357; and Ibn Sa'd, *Ṭabaqát*, v. 331.
34. For the force of the expression *qatalahu sabran*, cf. Lane, *A.E.L.*, p. 1644; and for a confirming tradition, cf. Abu Dawúd, 15. 119.
35. Margoliouth, *Muhammad*, p. 268.
36. Zuhar al-Adab, i. 28. Ref. Margoliouth, op. cit., p. 269.
37. This refers in satire to Muhammad's having addressed the dead bodies of the Quraish that had been thrown into a pit after the battle of Badr, for at that time he is said to have asked them "whether they were now convinced, telling his astonished followers that the corpses could hear, though unable to answer" (Margoliouth, op. cit., p. 268, with reference to the *Musnad*, iv. 252).

The swords of his own people pierced him again and again,
With more mercy they would have split him in pieces!

By force he was led to a death of torment,
When taken captive and bound in chains.

O Muhammad, was not your mother exalted among her people?
Then from a nobleman more nobility was expected.

What harm could have befallen you, if you had but been gracious to him?
Often it occurs that a generous man is gracious, though he may be intensely angry.

And al-Naḍr, whom you killed, was close of kin,
And therefore more worthy to be set free from captivity.

Or you could have taken a ransom, for assuredly the one about to perish,
He would have given in ransom his most precious possessions!

The approval of Allah for Muhammad's obviously angry and vindictive attitude towards his personal opponents is claimed in the special revelation in the Qur'án in regard to the conduct and the ultimate fate of the Prophet's uncle 'Abd al-'Uzzá ibn 'Abd al-Muṭṭálib, for it fixed upon this uncle the opprobrious name of Abu Lahab, the "father of the flame". It is by this name that he has continued to be known in Islamic history and literature. This was because he had frequently scorned Muhammad openly. In the curse that is pronounced upon him in the Qur'án it will be noted that his wife was also included, for as the sister of Abu Sufyán, the leader of the Meccan adversaries, she had aided her husband and her brother in her ridicule and her opposition. In A.H. I, shortly after the Battle of Badr, when word came of the death of Abu Lahab in Mecca from small-pox, there was the additional and significant item that his two sons had refused to bury him. If Sura cxi was revealed at that time, both the past tense that is employed in the second verse and the general meaning may be readily appreciated. When it is literally translated, and with this idea in mind,[38] the comment in the sacred book on Abu Lahab is as follows:

Perish the hands of Abu Lahab and perish himself.
His fortune and all that he acquired profited him not.
He will roast in a glowing fire (*dháta lahab*),
And his wife carries the wood,
On her neck a rope of bast!

Conspicuous among those of Muhammad's fellow-townsmen in Mecca who resolutely refused to acknowledge his claims, was al-Walíd ibn al-Mughíra ibn 'Abd Alláh ibn 'Umar ibn Makhzum. He

38. J. Barth, *Encyclopædia of Islam*, art. "Abu Lahab".

too died in the first year after the Migration, and the commentators suggest that several passages in the Qur'án make reference to him. These references may be more readily understood if we keep in mind what the traditions have disclosed about him, which has been well summarized:[39] "He was one of the earliest and most decided enemies of Islam, but at the same time chivalrous and not without culture. He therefore laid more emphasis on dissuading his fellow citizens from the new religion than on nipping it in the bud by attacking the personal rights of the Muslims. Instead of using physical force, he gathered round him men of talent, knowledge, and experience, like 'Umaiya ibn Abi'l-Ṣalt and Naḍr ibn Hárith, and endeavoured to expose Muhammad's contradictions and deceptions and to make him ludicrous and despicable in the eyes of intelligent people, while he silenced the common people by his prestige and material advantages." That al-Walíd was a man of undoubted influence and importance is certainly suggested by the fact that when the Ka'ba was rebuilt in Muhammad's young manhood, al-Walíd was the "first one to apply the chisel to the stone".[40]

It appears also from the traditions that he went among the pilgrims and discussed with them whether Muhammad should be regarded as a soothsayer (*káhin*), or as "one possessed" (*majnún*), or as a poet (*shá'ir*); and he would then conclude that it would perhaps be truer to regard him as a magician (*sáḥir*). This situation explains the following remarks in the Qur'án:

> And when the truth came down to them they said, "This is magic, and we therein do disbelieve!" And they said, "Unless this Qur'án were sent down to a man great in the two cities"—i.e. Mecca and Tá'iff (xliii. 29–30).
>
> Then he looked; then he frowned and scowled; then he retreated and was big with pride and said, "This is only magic exhibited! this is only mortal speech!"—I will broil him in hell-fire! (lxxiv. 21–5).

Thus it would appear that Allah was in somewhat ardent sympathy with Muhammad's dislike for al-Walíd.

Another member of the Quraishite family of Makhsúm was a nephew of this same al-Walíd. His name was 'Amar ibn Hishám ibn al-Mughíra, but in Islamic writings he is known by a designation that was given him in contempt, Abú Jahl, or "father of stupidity". He, too, had been persistent in his opposition to the Prophet and had taken active part in conferences against him. Once he had threatened Muhammad, saying, "You had better cease defaming our gods, or we will most certainly defame the god you worship." To this threat the Prophet appears to have taken heed, for the following revelation

39. K. V. Zettersteen, *Encyclopædia of Islam*, art. "al-Wálíd ibn al-Mughíra", quoting Sprenger, *Das Leben und die Lehre des Muhammad*, ii. 111.
40. Yaq'úbí, *Táríkh*, ii. 17–18.

was sent down: "Do not abuse those who call on other than Allah, for then they may abuse Allah openly in their ignorance" (vi. 108).[41] As Professor Tor Andrae observed, on the authority of Baihaqí,[42] the Quraish did not show their enmity for Muhammad very actively until he began to attack their gods and to declare that their fathers who died in unbelief were lost.

In the assembly of the principal Meccans Abú Jahl continued his hostility towards Muhammad. Baiḍawi and other commentators relate that he is said to have declared that if he found Muhammad with his head prostrated to the ground in prayer to Allah, he would most surely set his foot upon his neck. It is generally considered that this was the occasion for the revelation of Sura xcvi. 9–17:

> Hast thou considered him who forbids a servant when he prays? Hast thou considered if he were in guidance or bade piety? Hast thou considered if he said it was a lie and turned his back? Did he not know that Allah can see? Nay, surely, if he do not desist we will drag him by the forelock!—the lying, sinful forelock! So let him call his counsel: we will call the guards of Hell! Nay, obey him not, but adore and draw nigh!

And not infrequently Muhammad was thoroughly provoked by the irreverent witticisms of his Quraish trouble makers. For example, al-'Ás ibn Wá'il was indebted to a man named Khabbá, who was one of Muhammad's followers. The debtor told the Muslim creditor that he would pay him if he would leave his new faith. This the Muslim declared "he would never do, alive or dead, or when raised again at the last day". To this the Quraish debtor made the facetious reply that this would be perfectly satisfactory to him, for as he himself expected to have plenty of wealth and children at the last day, if the Muslim would kindly come around then he would be very glad indeed to pay him. The reply must have provoked a certain amount of laughter among the Arab listeners, for when it was reported to Muhammad, this was the comment that came down from Heaven:

> Hast thou seen him who disbelieves in our signs, and says, "I shall surely be given wealth and children"? . . . Has he become acquainted with the Unseen, or has he taken a compact with the Merciful? Not so! We will write down what he says, and we will extend to him a length of torment, and we will make him inherit what he says, and he shall come to us alone (i.e. for special punishment) (xix. 80–4).

This supposedly divine rebuke may have brought the Prophet some satisfaction in his personal pique against al-'Ás ibn Wá'il.

There is another observation, however, that should be made from these instances in the Qur'án where Muhammad's conspicuous

41. Ibn Hishám, op. cit., i. 380, quoting Ibn Iṣháq.
42. Tor Andrae, *Muhammad: The Man and His Faith*, p. 163.

opponents are rancorously rebuked. Religiously his Quraish opponents were inexperienced and almost indifferent. They were unable to dissuade him by reason or explanation, while their use of contempt and ridicule to bring upon him the pressure of their tribal disapproval only made him more confident in his own vision and conviction. Muhammad was an individualist who had the disposition and the courage to break away from the crowd. It may be said that he had a really fanatical belief that Allah was guiding him in word and deed, and thus it was that he was ever ready to call down divine utterances in accord with his personal objects. But it must also be observed that he showed indomitable persistence in the face of long-continued opposition from his own people.

Divine Authority for the Qur'án. The first important fact to consider in an effort to estimate the influence of the teachings of the Qur'án on the ethical development of Muslim peoples is that this book itself claims to have divine sanction and authority.

> Say, "I only warn you by inspiration (*waḥy*); but the deaf hear not the call when they are warned" (xxi. 46).
>
> By the star when it falls, your comrade errs not, nor is he deluded! It is but an inspiration inspired! One mighty in power (Gabriel) taught him, endowed with sound understanding, and appeared, he being in the loftiest tract.
>
> Then drew he near and hovered o'er, until he was two bows' length off, or nigher still! Then he inspired his servant what he inspired him; the heart belies not what he saw! What, will ye dispute with him on what he saw?
>
> It is not for any mortal that Allah should speak to him except by inspiration, or from behind a veil, or by sending an apostle and inspiring, by his permission, what He pleases; verily, He is high and wise!
>
> And thus have we inspired thee by a spirit at our bidding; thou didst not know what the Book was, nor the faith: but we made it a light whereby we guide whom we will of our servants (xlii. 50).

For Muslims who seek a religious basis for the ethical requirements in their personal, social, and political relations the Qur'án affords precepts for their general moral instruction, as has been shown; but the Qur'án has also imposed lasting restrictions on the ethical development of Muslim peoples. Furthermore, in subsequent years it has proved to be exceedingly difficult, almost impossible in fact, for these restrictions to be outgrown or superseded, because they are thus fixed for all time by a rigid doctrine of divine inspiration.

"The revelation comes to me in two ways", the Prophet is believed to have said. "Sometimes Gabriel visits me and tells it to me as though one man were speaking to another, but then what he speaks is lost to me. Then sometimes it comes to me as with the noise of a bell, so that my heart is confused, but what is revealed to me in this way never leaves me."[43]

This tradition is in accord with Sura lxxv. 16, which purports to impart Allah's instruction to Muhammad to maintain a state of passive receptivity: "Move not thy tongue in haste to follow and master this revelation, for we will see to the collecting and recital of it; but when we have recited it, then follow thou the recital."

The distinction between revelation (*waḥy*) and inspiration (*ilhám*) has probably been over-emphasized in later doctrinal statements. Mystics may claim the latter, but the former is generally understood to be reserved for prophets, who see the angel messenger; but the word *waḥy* is used in the Qur'án to denote knowledge that comes "either by the tongue of an angel who is seen, or by hearing his speech without seeing him, or by having it cast into the mind while awake or in a dream".[44]

As an illustration of the complete authority that has been accorded to the teachings of Muhammad, whether in the Qur'án or in the Traditions, a statement may be cited from the thirteenth-century Muslim creed that was drawn up by al-Faḍali:

> That Allah has distinguished our Prophet in that he is the seal of the apostles, and this his law (*shar'*) will not be abrogated till time is fulfilled. And 'Isa (Jesus), after his descent, will judge according to the law of our Prophet. It is said that he will go to the glorious tomb (of Muhammad) and learn of him.[45]

It is most unfortunate, however, that the Qur'án itself furnishes undeniable precedents for types of conduct that the moral consciousness of modern times cannot condone—such as slavery, concubinage, polygamy, the enforced segregation of women, and aggressive warfare in the name of religion. From the purely historical viewpoint present-day opinion may show a tolerant understanding of the occurrence of such practices in that early period, but the principles that underlie them and that are discerned in the teachings and in the example of Muhammad must be impartially and honestly appraised from the viewpoint of ethics. And any such appraisal will necessitate a significant conclusion, as to whether these principles ought to be promulgated throughout the world as the highest possible moral standards for mankind, or whether they ought to be retained on the ground that they are peculiarly suited to Muslims, or whether they ought rather to be revised and amended, notwithstanding doctrinal obstacles and historic prejudices, so that approximately two hundred and fifty million Muhammadan people may no longer be held back from reaching the very highest ethical development of which they are capable.

43. Ibn Sa'd, *Ṭabaqát*, I, i. 131. Trans. Tor Andrae, op. cit., p. 66.
44. D. B. Macdonald, *The Religious Attitude and Life in Islam*, p. 253.
45. D. B. Macdonald, *Muslim Theology, Jurisprudence and Constitutional Theory*, p. 345.

Non-ethical Predestinarianism. One of these principles that is reiterated in the Qur'án, a principle that has often baffled and discouraged ethical thought, has to do with the doctrine of the nature of God. In the Qur'án and according to Muslim theology, God's *greatness*, in the sense of His unlimited power, is the central concept about His being. And this greatness of God must not be thought of as being modified or limited by even the perfection of any strictly moral qualities. According to Islamic doctrine, God is essentially too great, too unlimited to be inherently good. He need not always be *true*, for that would be a restriction on His freedom and thus curtail His greatness. Similarly His will must not be thought of as being limited in its operations to the sphere of what is ethically *right.* As a consequence we find in Islam the firm belief that Allah may be both arbitrary and changeable in dealing with mankind.

We are informed by orthodox Islam that "if Allah had willed, He would have inspired His prophets with quite a different preaching and a different law".[46] Accordingly, on this belief there is room for scepticism as to whether the right preaching and the right law has yet been sent, or at least for doubt whether the Qur'án is God's final word.

Because Muhammad had difficulty in understanding why it was that some men persistently refused to believe his teachings and because he could not think that Allah could be impeded by the resistance of mortals, he declared: "Allah makes to err whom He will and guides whom He will" (lxxiv. 34). Such a conception suggests that Allah's sovereignty is asserted in arbitrary decrees, and this is confirmed in the Qur'án by further statements:[47]

> He whom Allah wills to guide, he opens his breast to Islam; and he whom He wills to lead astray, he narrows his breast (vi. 125).
>
> But ye will not please except Allah please! Verily, Allah is knowing, wise. He makes whomsoever He pleases to enter His mercy; but the unjust, He has prepared for them a grievous woe (lxxvi. 30, 31).

These and other similar declarations in the revealed book have been used in determining and in successfully maintaining the orthodox opinion that Allah's relation to mankind is a harsh predestinarianism. As late a theologian as al-Ghazálí (d. A.D. 1111), writing in the fifth century after the Hijra, with full knowledge of efforts that had been made within the ranks of Islam to exalt divine righteousness and human responsibility, was able nevertheless to quote with approval the tradition that the Prophet had said that Allah himself

46. Wensinck, *The Muslim Creed*, p. 260, quoting Baghdádí, Uṣúl, p. 213.

47. It is noteworthy that all of these verses are from suras that were revealed in Mecca before the policy was begun in Medina of employing power-politics in the intimidation of neighbouring peoples. Other references from Meccan suras are: xxxv. 9; xxxii. 12; and x. 99.

had declared, "These are in the Garden and I care not; and these are in the Fire, and I care not." And furthermore, in his carefully worded statement of the orthodox position on this question, al-Ghazálí wrote in the *Iḥyá'*:[48]

> No act of any individual, even though it be done purely for his benefit, is independent of the will of Allah for its existence; and there does not occur in either the physical or in the extra-terrestrial world the wink of an eye, the hint of a thought, or the most sudden glance, except by the decree of Allah—of His power, desire, and will. This includes evil and good, benefit and hurt, success and failure, sin and righteousness, obedience and disobedience, polytheism and true belief.

Punishment. Difficulties in ethics are also encountered in any careful survey of the principles on which punishments are decreed in the Qur'án. Those punishments that are stipulated for particular offences show that Muhammad had a working conception of legal equity, and also that he sought at times to correct the extravagances of passionate revenge that frequently went beyond the point of exact retaliation. Yet a critical examination of these punishments from the point of view of practical legislation, or in quest of what is ethically right, shows that they left much to be desired.

To compensate for the deficiencies and ambiguities that were soon recognized on the legal side, in the first three centuries of the Islamic era hundreds of statements that were attributed to the Prophet were collected and arranged by the legists in great tomes of *Ḥadíth* (Traditions), which have served to supplement the declarations of the Qur'án. But if we direct our attention to the principles on which the punishments that are decreed in the Qur'án are based and if we attempt to appraise these principles from the ethical point of view, a number of significant difficulties will be observed—difficulties that have been only the more persistent in that they can be justified by both the spirit and the letter of the revealed book.

The first of these difficulties lies in the acceptance of the principle of retaliation (*qiṣás*) for homicide. It was one of the principles that had been retained from pre-Islamic Arab life. At that time also the injured tribe or family had the alternative of killing in retaliation or of accepting the blood-money. But, as Professor Juynboll has remarked, "usually on both sides an attempt was made to put to death as great a number as possible of enemies of high rank in return for each fallen tribesman; for many regarded as insufficient mere retaliation, by which no greater injury was done to the other party than had actually been suffered."[49]

48. al-Ghazálí, *Iḥyá'*, i. 103, ref. and trans. from Levy, *Sociology of Islam*, vol. i. 43. For the discussion of al-Ghazálí's ethics, see ch. 5, "Authors of Arabic Works on Ethics".

49. Th. W. Juynboll, *Encyclopædia of Religion and Ethics*, iv. 290.

It is to the credit of Muhammad that he rebuked this excessive rendering of evil for evil, for he announced as a revelation from Allah: "Retaliation is prescribed for you for the slain: the free for the free, the slave for the slave, the female for the female" (ii. 273). Evidently he sought to correct abuses with which the Arab tribes were all too familiar. Nevertheless, if this decree is to be considered from the ethical standpoint, seeking only what is essentially *right*, the very principle of retaliation is open to question, and we are not profoundly impressed with a command from the Almighty to mankind to the effect that they should observe absolute and exact reciprocity in killing one another.

This same principle has been extended in its application so as to give the right of retaliation to anyone who has been wounded. He may similarly injure the one who injured him or else he may accept the price of blood. "The full *diyá* (blood-price) is incurred when, because of the wound, a part of the body is lost (e.g. the nose) of which man has only one; he who loses a part of the body of which men have two (e.g. an eye, ear, hand, or foot) may obtain the half of the *diyá* as damages; in the same way one-fourth of the full price of blood is incurred for an eyelid, one-tenth for a finger, and for a joint of the finger one-thirtieth of the *diyá*. . . . And if anyone has been wounded simultaneously in several places, he may claim damages for each wound separately, and therefore in some cases may receive even more than the *diyá* for manslaughter."[50]

Sometimes Muslims have themselves been able to laugh at the idea of accepting exact retaliation as a legal principle, as when Mullah Nasr ud-Dín related that one of his neighbours came to him and said, "Mullah, to-day your dog bit my wife's leg, wounding her, so you must make due compensation." He said that he replied, "Any injury for which an equivalent may be given calls for no further compensation. You have therefore but to send your dog to bite my wife's leg."

For some crimes the Muslim law has exactly determined punishments (*ḥudúd*), which are fixed by declarations in the Qur'án, and they are therefore considered as resting on a "right of Allah". Because they are thus divine requirements, there is not anything that may be added to them or taken away, and the acting judge has no choice except to execute them. They are "for wrong acts which no believer can commit at a moment when he has faith": for "when an adulterer commits the act of *ziná* (adultery), he is not at that moment a believer; when a thief commits the act of theft (*sirqa*), he is not at that moment a believer; when a drinker takes intoxicating liquor, he is not at that moment a believer; and when a brigand openly seizes a gentleman's property, he is not at that moment a believer."

If such delinquents were to be considered as almost the same as

50. Ibid., op. cit., p. 292.

renegades from the faith, it followed in natural sequence that accusations of these offences could not be established without the most complete evidence. Moreover, the good name of the community of the faithful could easily be injured by publicity given to such misdemeanours. There is therefore a tradition to record the Prophet's precautionary advice: "Allah will forgive the sins of every believer except when the sinner makes them known to the public. Allah loves those of his servants that cover their sins."[51]

"On the ground of this tradition", as Professor Juynboll points out in his article on *Adháb* (Punishments) in the *Encyclopædia of Islam*, "there is a prescription in the Mussulman law books that when the punishment is to be considered as a *ḥaqq Alláh* (right of Allah) the transgressor should hide his guilt as much as possible and not confess it, and even when he did confess it to revoke his confession. He is supposed to turn himself much more to Allah in stillness, for Allah accepts his conversion when his intention is pure. Practically the decisions of the canonical law offer everybody the opportunity for escaping such punishments."[52]

Under this class of offences comes illicit sexual intercourse. For women who commit adultery the punishment that is prescribed by the Qur'án is lifelong imprisonment, though the stipulation, "then keep the women in houses until death release them, or Allah shall make for them a way", lacks legal precision. But an accused woman is not to be considered guilty unless there are four witnesses (iv. 19), and the accuser who fails to bring four witnesses is to be scourged with eighty stripes (xxiv. 4). This condition, which is obviously of improbable fulfilment, proved to be impracticable, and an exception was stated by the Qur'án itself:

> And those who cast imputation upon their wives and have no witness except themselves, then the testimony of one of them shall be to testify four times that, by Allah, he is of those who speak the truth; and the fifth testimony shall be that the curse of Allah shall be on him if he be of those who lie. And it shall avert the punishment from her if she bears testimony four times that, by Allah, he is of those who lie; and the fifth that the wrath of Allah shall be on her if he be of those who speak the truth (xxiv. 69).

There was little hope, however, for such a wife if, after she had been cast out by her husband, she came to be regarded as a fallen woman, for a command is given in this same Sura (xxiv. 2) in regard to the punishment of adulterers: "As for the whore and the whoremonger, scourge them each with a hundred stripes, and do not let pity for them take hold on you in Allah's religion, if ye believe in Allah and the last day; and let a party of the believers witness their torment."

51. al-Nasá'í, 46. 1.
52. Th. W. Juynboll, *Encyclopædia of Islam*, art. "'Adháb".

It is said that the Caliph 'Umar acknowledged that there was originally a verse in the Qur'án that prescribed the punishment of stoning for adultery: "If a man and woman who have reached years of discretion commit adultery, stone them in every case, as Allah's punishment." But after recent investigation, Joseph Schacht is of the opinion that "it is improbable that this verse is genuine, the tradition relating to it and the mention of 'Umar are clearly tendentious; and the stories that the Prophet punished by stoning are also unworthy of credence".[53]

There is one merit in this apparently bewildered and indeterminate legislation, and that is that it has discouraged the false accusation (*qadhf*) of married women, which is apt to be based on merely circumstantial evidence, such as that which threw suspicion on the Prophet's young wife A'isha. It was that incident in fact which led to the revelation of this *surat al-núr* (Chapter of Light), xxiv. As a contribution towards the solution of the problem of social vice, however, it would be hard to show that this Qur'ánic legislation has accomplished any more than to provide occasions for the exhibition of brutality with the object of general intimidation.

It is because of this that we are told that the full legal punishment for adultery has been exceptional, "in so much as *ziná* (adultery) can only be proved by the evidence of four male, competent witnesses". These witnesses "must report all the details of the incident", and if their evidence is not sufficient they are liable to the *hadd* (determined punishment) for *qadhf* (false accusation). The result is that the *ḥadd*, or prescribed punishment, for adultery can hardly ever be inflicted unless the culprit himself confesses his guilt. And for this very reason "the place of legal regulations was often taken by summary and usually secret action, either by the authorities or by the relatives of the guilty women; in this case drowning was a common form of punishment".[54]

High ideals of conjugal fidelity on the part of husbands are not held in a system in which the standards for the two sexes are so radically different. It must be remembered, however, that the Muslim law was evolved in a period when slavery was a common practice. It is written that the believing slave-girls "shall be chaste and modest and have no lovers" (iv. 29), but at the same time it was permissible for them to be persuaded by their Muslim owners to gratify their sexual desires. That sometimes the wives of Muslim men were disposed to object when their husbands were so inclined towards their slave-girls is shown by the attitude of Muhammad's own wives towards Mary the Copt, and also by the anger of Fatima when she felt that 'Ali had been neglecting her for slave-girls.[55] The greater

53. Joseph Schacht, *Encyclopædia of Islam*, art. "Ziná".
54. Ibid., op. cit., iv. 1227.
55. Ibn Sa'd, *Ṭabaqát*, viii. 16.

latitude of Muslim men in these matters is explained on the basis of their theory of property. Their wives and their female-slaves were their own property, and adultery was primarily objectionable because it was regarded as a case of one man trespassing on the property rights of another man.

The punishment for theft (*sirqa*) that is prescribed in the Qur'án is the cutting off of one or both of the hands of the thief. Here we have a survival of a purely animistic conception, the primitive idea being that the members of the body that did the stealing should be removed. But it is nothing short of astounding to find that such a decree appears in the Qur'án as a law that has been sent down by the Almighty (v. 42): "The man thief and the woman thief, cut off the hands of both as a punishment, for that they have erred—an example from Allah, for Allah is mighty, wise."

An instance of one occasion when this punishment was inflicted by the Prophet's own order is related by Ibn Sa'd in the *Ṭabaqát* (viii. 192). During the time of the Farewell Pilgrimage, when riders were dismounting at the stopping-place for the night, a woman who was known as Umm 'Amr had snatched a piece of their luggage. She had been seen and caught, and they had tied her firmly until morning. Then she was taken to the Prophet, where she sought to secure the intervention of his wife Umm Salmah, but Muhammad remained obdurate. He declared that if she had been his own daughter Fatima, he would have to inflict upon her the punishment prescribed by Allah. "So her hand was cut off, and she fled, with the blood dripping, to one of the women she knew, who gave her warm food. Afterwards the Prophet allowed her to go to her uncle, who was of the Bani 'Abd al-'Uzzá."

But in this connexion also, on account of the severity of the punishment that was prescribed, the legists carefully limited the kinds of *taking* that were to be considered as *stealing*. At times exemption was granted on account of the small amount that was taken. The minimum that is given by the different authorities varies from three dirhams to ten dirhams, which in either case would be less than one dinar. It was also necessary that the offence should be proved to be "the clandestine removal of legally recognized property in the safe keeping of another". It had to be shown further that the thief, mature and in his right mind, had acted on his own responsibility and that he had had the full intention of stealing. It made no difference whether the offender was a freeman or a slave, a male or a female. But simple household pilfering—as between husband and wife, or among near relatives, or as between a slave and his master or a guest and his host—this would not come under the head of theft. Similarly we read that "it is not theft to take articles of trifling value (wood, water, wild game) and things which quickly go to waste (fresh fruit, meat, and milk)". Furthermore the penalty for theft was not applicable in cases of the removal of "things which are not legitimate articles of commerce—like free-born children, wine, pigs, dogs, chess-sets, musical instruments, gold crosses, etc." Such misdemeanours would come under the head of usurpation (*ghaṣb*). Likewise amputation of the hands was not to be inflicted for a breach of trust (*khiyána*), as in the case of a shareholder in a joint property (booty, state treasure, or religious endowment).[56]

With all these carefully enumerated exceptions there is no doubt but that the decree in the Qur'án for the punishment of theft by the amputation of one or both of the hands of the thief has afforded one of the best examples in legal history of the fact that a law which is by its very nature impracticable and unjust soon proves to be worse than no law at all.

It should be added, however, that the full penalty of the amputation of the hands, and at times of the feet also, has not infrequently been given for highway robbery, the "greater theft" (*al-sirqa al-kubrá*), for in such a case the object of the punishment has been the intimidation of tribes of Beduin, or other robber bands, who were regarded as public enemies. However, if a robber or one of his associates had killed any of those who were attacked, then the death penalty has been in order, in accord with the principle of retaliation (*qiṣáṣ*), and ordinarily in such cases the bodies of the victims would be exposed in some public place for several days.

Abrogations in the Qur'án. Within the Prophet's lifetime the contradictions, corrections, and qualifications that occur in the Qur'án began to attract attention and to arouse discussion; and the Prophet appreciated that for further explanation or authoritative decision special revelations were required. So it is that verses like the following may be found:

56. Heffening, *Encyclopædia of Islam*, art. "Sáriq". It is noteworthy that in substituting the "Indian Penal Code" for the penal laws of the *sharia*, Sir Benjamin Lindsay wrote (cf. O'Malley, *Modern India and the West*, p. 136): "In taking this step the British in India were merely anticipating the action which has since been taken in other oriental countries in which the Islamic code has been largely superseded, and has been replaced by new systems, both of substantive and procedural law, that are based upon the model of one or other of the codes of continental Europe. In these countries too it has come to be realized that a body of law which was supposed to have reached the limits of perfection by the eleventh century, and was declared to be unalterable by human agency, has long outlived its usefulness." Cf. also an article by the present writer on "Modern Persian Law" in the *Moslem World*, 1934, pp. 341 ff., from which the following statement is quoted: "The book of common law, with its clearly stated provisions in regard to property, wills, partnerships, etc., the rules of order for court trials, legal ways of hastening decisions in particular cases, with special provision for the trial of government servants charged with criminal offences, all of these are systematically arranged and briefly stated. It is evident that foreign law codes have been freely consulted and frequently imitated."

And whenever we change one verse for another—Allah knows best what He sends down (xvi. 103).

Allah blots out what He wills, or He confirms; and with Him is the "mother of the Book" (*umm al-kitáb*) (xiii. 39).

Whatever verse we may annul or cause thee to forget, we will bring a better than it, or one like it; dost thou not know that Allah is mighty over all? (ii. 100).

At the time when al-Ṭabarí (d. A.D. 922) wrote his exhaustive commentary on the Qur'án there were numerous works on the subject of "The Abrogating and the Abrogated" (*al-násikh wa'l-mansúkh*), and eighteen of these books are mentioned by al-Nadím in the *Fihrist*.[57] Two of them are still extant, and date from the eleventh century, the first having been written by Abu'l-Qásim ibn Saláma (d. A.D. 1019), and the second by 'Abd al-Qáhir ibn Ṭáhir (d. A.D. 1038).

In the introduction to the former work[58] we read that in the Qur'án "is explained the permitted and the forbidden, the restrictions and the injunctions, the beginning and the end, the absolute and the limited, the varieties and the similarities, the concentrated and the diffuse, the particular and the general, and the *abrogating* and the *abrogated*—surely he will perish who destroys the testimony and he will live who acts according to it! Allah is undoubtedly the Hearing and the Knowing." The author then proceeds with this significant statement: "The very first point that occurs to me for anyone who wishes to be familiar with the Qur'án is the importance of an elementary acquaintance with '*the abrogating and the abrogated*', following what has come to us from the ancient *imáms*, and may Allah be pleased with them all! For assuredly no one should venture to speak authoritatively of this precious Scripture unless he is acquainted with the teaching in regard to *the abrogating and the abrogated*."

"It is related of 'Ali ibn Abu Ṭálib", the writer goes on to explain, "that one day when he entered the great mosque in Kufa, where the Friday prayers were said, he saw there a man who was known as 'Abd al-Rahmán ibn Dáb, a companion of Abu Musa al-Ash'arí. A large number of people had gathered around him and were asking questions. But in his replies he was confusing the ordinance for prohibition (*al-amr bi'l-nahy*) with the granting of liberty for what is forbidden (*al-ibáḥat bi'l-ḥaẓr*). When 'Ali perceived this he said to him,

57. al-Nadím, *al-Fihrist*, ed. Cairo, A.H. 1348, p. 56. Other books that were written to discuss the doctrine of the abrogation of some verses of the Qur'án by others on the strength of Traditions were: (1) *Kitáb al-I'tibar fí al-Násikh wa al-Mansúkh min al-Hadíth*, by Abu Bakr Md. b. Musa al-Khazimi al-Hamdání (d. 584/1188), cf. Brockelmann, i, pp. 356, 366; (2) *al-Násikh wa al-Mansúkh fí al-Hadíth*, by Abu Bakr b. Musa al-Kharazmi (circa 710-1310), cf. Brockelmann, ii, p. 195.

58. Abu'l-Qásim Hibat Allah ibn Saláma, *al-Násikh wa'l-Mansúkh*, published in Cairo, A.H. 1310, on the margin of al-Nishaburi's *Asbáb al-Nuzúl*.

'Can you distinguish the abrogating verses from those which are abrogated?' The man answered, 'No.' 'Ali then seized him by the ear, and as he twisted his ear severely he said, 'You are never to venture to speak in our mosque again!'

"And there is a tradition that Hanifa ibn al-Yamán once said, 'There are but three men who are authorized to speak to the people—the Amir himself, his deputy, and the man who can tell the abrogating verses from the abrogated—and a possible fourth is the man who opposes a fool.'"

There is one class of these abrogating verses, as has been pointed out in a recent Muhammadan apologetic work,[59] that may fairly be regarded as revelations that were given in further explanation or limitation of previous assertions. In this sense of further qualification in order to correct misimpressions, an example of abrogation may be found in Sura xxi. Several of the Quraish opponents had heard the Apostle recite verse 98: "Verily, ye, and what ye serve beside Allah, shall be the pebbles of Hell, to it shall ye go down." And according to Ibn Hishám,[60] Abdulla ibn al-Zabará then raised the objection: "Shall everything that is worshipped besides Allah be in Hell with the one that worshipped it? For instance, we worship the angels, and the Jews worship 'Uzair (Ezra), and the Christians worship 'Isá ibn Maryam." Muhammad saw the point of this objection, and accordingly a qualifying statement was made in regard to 'Isá ibn Maryam and to 'Uzair, and also with regard to "whomsoever the people worshipped from among the monks (*al-ahbár*) and the Jewish saints (*al-rahbán*), who had kept faith with Allah, and all of whom Allah had taken to himself; but showing that whoever worships them belongs to the people of destruction for regarding them as their masters rather than Allah". The qualifying statement that came thus conveniently as a further revelation in the Qur'án was the passage (xxi. 101–2):

> Verily, those for whom the good (reward) from us was foreordained, they from it [i.e. the fire of Hell] shall be kept far away; they shall not hear the slightest sound thereof, and they in what their souls desire shall dwell for aye. The greatest terror shall not grieve them; and the angels shall meet them saying, "This is your day which ye were promised!"[61]

A second class of abrogating verses may be distinguished, where commands to employ violence abrogate previous injunctions to toleration. The slogan "To us are our works and to you are your works!" (ii. 133) is said to have been abrogated by the verse of the sword (iv. 5): "Kill the idolaters wherever ye find them." It is considered that this verse abrogates also the opening verse of the same

59. Muhammad 'Ali, *The Religion of Islam*, Ahmadiya Press, Lahore, 1936, pp. 38 ff.

60. Ibn Hishám, *Sira*, . 283.

61. *al-Násikh wa'l-Mansúkh*, pp. 225 ff.

sura (ix. 1): "An immunity from Allah and His Apostle to those idolaters with whom ye have made a league." There is no verse in the Qur'án that is mentioned so frequently as abrogating other verses as this verse of the sword, for there are one hundred and twenty-four verses that it is said to have set aside or modified. At the same time we are further assured that the first part of this sword verse has been abrogated by the latter part. This may be understood when the passage is quoted in full:[62]

(*a*) But when the sacred months are passed away, *kill the idolaters wherever ye may find them*; and take them and besiege them, and lie in wait for them in every place of observation;

(*b*) but if they repent, and are steadfast in prayer, and give alms, *then let them go their way; verily, Allah is forgiving and merciful.*

It is largely because of passages that are contradictory or obscure or obviously open to criticism on ethical grounds that translations of the Qur'án into the languages of the non-Arab peoples have for so long been discouraged or forbidden. For only in comparatively recent years, after Western scholars had translated the sacred book of Islam into European languages, did translations begin to appear in Turkish, Persian, and Urdu. These eastern translations, moreover, have been so meticulously word for word that it may still be said with a considerable measure of truth that in many instances only a reader who knows the Arabic language can hope to get the meaning that is intended. That this has been the situation in Muslim countries is further evidenced by the fact that the translations that were permitted were required to be either interlinear with the Arabic text or the text and the translation were to be printed so as to appear on opposite pages. If much larger numbers of the followers of Islam were given opportunity to read and study the Qur'án in languages that they understand, and to appraise and criticize it freely in the light of their present-day knowledge and ethical consciousness, a series of modern books might well appear on "The Abrogating and the Abrogated".

Meanwhile the orthodox position has been summarized by al-Shahrastání as follows:[63]

62. Ibid., op. cit., pp. 44 and 184 ff. Cf. also Kulaini, *Furu al-Káfí*, where the following tradition is given on "the excellence of the *jihád*": "Good fortune (*al-khair*) is entirely dependent on the sword (*al-saif*), people are not able to survive without the sword, for in fact the sword holds the keys to Paradise and to the Fire!"

63. *The Summa Philosophiae* of al-Ṣhahrastání (*Kitáb Niháyat al-Iqdám fí 'Ilmi'l-Kalám*), ed. and trans. by Alfred Guillaume, Oxford, 1934, pp. 158–9. A convenient presentation of the abrogating and the abrogated verses, which is based on Abu'l-Qasim's work and the *Tafsír al-Jalalain*, was prepared by Rev. Anvar al-Haqq, and published by the Methodist Publishing House, Lucknow, 1926. It gives the verses in both Arabic and English.

"Islam abrogates all previous codes of which it is the perfection. Muhammad is the seal of the prophets, and with him we seal this book. . . . There is no doubt that Moses came after Adam, Noah, Hūd, Ṣāliḥ, Abraham, and many of the prophets in time. Were they bound by the law of Moses or only by part of it? If by all of it, then he did not found the law; he only confirmed an existing one. If he only laid down one law other than theirs the first was abrogated by his law, or we may say that the time of the first expired and the new one came into being and abrogation was established. We have only to think of marriages with sisters in Adam's time, circumcision on the seventh day which was not practised till Abraham, and so on, to see that abrogation is no innovation.

"The solution is that lawfulness and unlawfulness are not predications which belong to actions as if they were attributes of them, nor are actions to be classed as good or evil, nor does the law-giver cause them to acquire attributes which cannot be annulled or confirmed. But the predications (of right and wrong) belong to the speech of the law-giver (i.e. actions are not right or wrong in themselves, but because the legislator has declared them to be so). Thus the predication is verbal, not actual; legal, not intellectual; and one can abrogate another: e.g. divorce abrogates conjugal rights. If contemporary law is subject to constant alteration to meet changing conditions why is it impossible that laws given to one people at one time should be abrogated elsewhere at another time? The law corresponds to actions, and the active changes of death and life, man's creation and annihilation, sometimes gradually, sometimes instantaneously, correspond to the legal changes of permitted and forbidden. God orders men's actions as He pleases and must not be asked what He is doing. If we consider the formation of man from his pre-embryonic beginning to his full stature we see that each progressive form abrogated its predecessor. Similarly man progressed from code to code till the perfection of all codes was reached. Nothing lies beyond it but the Resurrection.

"Muhammad, the perfect man, is the climax of man's evolution, as Islam is the climax of successive laws."

Bible Characters as Examples. It may be observed that in the Qur'án, as has been pointed out frequently,[64] Abraham was Muhammad's chosen prototype. He turned to Abraham to find an example of his own faith, particularly his belief in Allah's unity (ii. 129; iii. 60; vi. 79; and xvi. 121, 124). He was impressed with the thought that Allah had made Abraham his friend (*khalil*), as shown in Sura iv. 24; and he related with only slight alteration the Rabbinical stories of Abraham's struggle against the idolatrous beliefs of his own people.

Narratives of others of the patriarchs and prophets of Israel were

64. Geiger, *Judaism and Islam*, p. 95 ff.

also employed by Muhammad in his sermons, which make up so large a part of the Qur'án. The principal examples of men whom God had uplifted to grades of wisdom according to His will are mentioned in the Qur'án in one passage (vi. 83–6):

> We uplift to grades of wisdom whom we will; Verily thy Lord is Wise, Knowing.
>
> And we gave him Isaac and Jacob, and guided both aright; and we had before guided Noah; and among the descendants of Abraham, David and Solomon, and Job and Joseph, and Moses and Aaron: Thus do we recompense the righteous.
>
> And Zachariah, John, Jesus, and Elias: all were just persons.
>
> And Ishmael and Elija and Jonas and Lot: all these have we favoured above mankind.

The expressions quoted, "thus do we recompense the righteous", "all were just persons", and "all these have we favoured above mankind", summarize very well the general use that Muhammad made of references to Biblical characters for the purpose of moral instruction. They are cited as instances of men whose faith in God was rewarded, and who found strength to resist particular temptations or to overcome their enemies by God's special favour. There is little attempt made by Muhammad to analyse the moral problems they met or to explain and develop their ethical teachings.

The story of Joseph is made exciting and interesting for Muhammad's Arab audiences by special elaboration of his encounters with the wife of the Egyptian prince who had bought him as a slave. In the time of most severe temptation Joseph exclaims, "God keep me! verily my Lord hath given me a good home: and the injurious shall not prosper" (xii. 23). "But she longed for him: and he had longed for her had he not seen a token from his Lord.[65] Thus we averted evil and defilement from him, for he was one of our sincere servants" (xii. 24).

Muhammad depicts Moses' struggle with Pharaoh, and recounts the plagues that came upon the Egyptians, shows how Moses was shocked at the defection and unfaithfulness of his own people, and in portraying the various circumstances in which he could easily sympathize with Moses he frequently makes Moses voice sentiments that are closely akin to his own:

> And none believed on Moses but a race among his own people, through fear of Pharaoh and his nobles, lest he should afflict them: For of a truth mighty was Pharaoh in the land, and one who committed excesses.

65. This reference is to the Jewish apocryphal suggestion that he was made to see an apparition of his father, who said, "Hereafter shall the names of thy brethren, engraved on precious stones, shine on the breast of the High Priest. Shall thine be blotted out?" Cf. Rodwell's *Koran*, p. 232, with reference to Tr. Sotah, fol. 36.

And Moses said, "O my people! if ye believe in Allah, then put your trust in Him—if ye be Muslims."

And they said, "In Allah put we our trust, O our Lord! abandon us not to trial from that unjust people and deliver us by Thy mercy from the unbelieving people" (x. 83–6).

And Moses said, "I take refuge with my Lord and your Lord from every proud one who believeth not in the Day of Reckoning" (xl. 28).

And he who believed said, "O my people! follow me: into the right way will I guide you. O my people! this present life is only a passing joy, but the life to come is the mansion that abideth. Whoso shall have wrought evil shall not be recompensed but with its like; but whoso shall have done the things that are right, whether male or female, and is a believer—these shall enter paradise: good things unreckoned shall they enjoy therein" (xl. 41–3).

David is referred to as being the inventor of coats of mail (xxi. 80; xxxiv. 10), and Burton has observed that on account of Muhammad's acceptance of this myth it is found that in most Muslim countries "the blacksmith is respected as treading in the path of David, the father of the craft".[66] Reference is made in the Qur'án to the way in which Allah led David to personal judgement against himself by sending him two pleaders (xxxviii. 20–5)[67] the one charging the other with having taken his one ewe when he already had ninety-nine ewes of his own. David replied, "Certainly he hath wronged thee in asking for thine ewe (to add her) to his own ewes: and truly many associates do one another wrong—except those who believe and do the things that are right; and few indeed are they!" And then we read in the Qur'án, as though Allah were himself giving the account of what happened: "And David perceived that we had tried him; so he asked pardon of his Lord, and fell down and bowed himself and repented. So we forgave him that (his sin);[68] and truly he shall have a high rank with us, and an excellent retreat in Paradise. O David! verily we have made thee our vicegerent upon earth. Judge therefore between men with truth, and follow not thy passions, lest they cause thee to err from the way of God. For they who err from the way of God shall meet with a grievous chastisement, for that they have forgotten the day of reckoning." The Qur'án says also that the mountains were constrained by Allah to join with David in praise at even and at sunrise, and that the birds would flock to him (xxxviii. 17, 18). The high gift that was given to him was the Psalter (xvii. 57), which is mentioned in the verse which has

66. Rodwell's *Koran*, p. 156, note, with reference to Burton, *First Footsteps in E. Africa*, p. 33.

67. For the Biblical account of this incident, cf. 1 Samuel, 12.

68. For discussion of the origin of the Islamic dogma of the sinlessness of the prophets and the *imáms*, cf. chs. xxx and xxxi of *The Shi'ite Religion*, by D. M. Donaldson, Luzac, 1933.

been said by Rodwell to contain the only scriptural text that is quoted in the Qur'án (xxi. 105):[69] "And now since the Law was given have we written in the Psalms that '*my servants, the righteous, shall inherit the earth*'."

Solomon is cited in the Qur'án as an example of a king who showed gratitude for divine favour, to himself and to his parents, and who sought Allah's assistance to do righteousness (xxvii. 17). When he had forgotten the hour of evening prayer, because he had been engrossed in the admiration of some captured horses—a shortcoming that was readily understood by the Arab gentry—his confession was: "Truly I have loved the love of earthly goods above the remembrance of my Lord, till the Sun hath hidden the veil of darkness."

Then the Qur'án goes on to state that he called for those horses to be brought before him again, and when they came "he began to sever the legs and necks" (xxxviii. 29, 38).[70] Thus it was that he met the first trial or temptation that Allah sent to him.

The second time that Allah made trial of Solomon was when he caused him to see a phantom placed upon his throne, whereupon he returned to Allah in penitence and said: "O my Lord! pardon me, and give me a dominion that may not be to anyone beside me, for thou art the liberal giver" (xxxviii. 33–8). In explanation of the fault for which repentance was necessary, there is a Muslim legend, which is borrowed from Jewish legends,[71] that says that one of Solomon's captured women, Jerádeh the daughter of the King of Sidon, continued so to mourn her father that Solomon resorted to the expedient of having an image of her father made. Before this image Jerádeh and her maids then paid homage. It was to punish Solomon for allowing this idolatry, we are told, that Allah sent a devil named Sakhar to secure Solomon's magic ring. With this power the devil was able to impersonate Solomon, so as to appear as a phantom on his throne, and in walking about the palace for a period of forty days. During this time he caused Solomon himself to be unrecognizable to his subjects. Afterwards the devil threw the magic ring into the sea, where it was swallowed by a fish, and this fish in turn was caught and brought to Solomon, so that thereby the ring was restored.

The legend of the lost ring, however, is not given in the Qur'án, which says only that after Solomon's repentance on account of the phantom on his throne, and in answer to his prayer for a form of dominion that would be unique, Allah subjected the wind to him,

69. The reference is to Ps. xxxvii. 29. Cf. Rodwell, *Koran*, p. 158, note.

70. As Rodwell's note on this passage points out, there is a Jewish legend about Solomon's love of horses (tr. Sanhedr. fol. 21), and that he determined to have a larger stud; yet not to send the people to Egypt (Deut. xvii. 16), but to have them brought to him out of Egypt (1 Kings x. 28).

71. Rodwell's *Koran*, p. 127, note, with reference to Sale's account, and to tr. Sanhedr. 20, b, and to Midr. Jalkut on 1 Kings vi. 6.

"so that it ran softly at his bidding, whithersoever he directed it". Moreover the djinn were made to do him service as builders and divers, and there were others that were bound in chains. This authority over the wind and the djinn was Allah's special gift to Solomon, with the injunction, "Be bounteous, or withhold thy favour, no account shalt thou render." And when the same story is told in another connexion (xxxiv. 11–12), the moral is drawn, "Work, O family of David, with thanksgiving! But few of my servants are of the thankful."

Such is the use that is made of references to Old Testament characters for the purpose of moral instruction. We would venture the opinion that Muhammad's purpose in repeating at length, and obviously from memory, the narratives in regard to Abraham, Joseph, Moses, David, and Solomon, was to set forth fundamental religious values for those of his followers who would heed their example. They were men of God, they were just, they were repentant, and they sought Allah's assistance to do righteousness. It was principally in the Mecca surahs that Muhammad had recourse to this type of preaching. It was there in Mecca that he had received the revelation, "And if thou art in doubt as to what we have sent down to thee, inquire of those who have read the Scriptures before thee" (x. 94).[72]

Within the compass of the Qur'án, however, only such material from the Old Testament was included as resulted from inquiries that were made in Muhammad's own lifetime. Unfortunately there is no mention of any of the great collections of the books of Isaiah, Jeremiah, or Ezekiel; with the result that the Qur'án has not been enriched by their great teachings about the personal relation of the individual to God, the development of ethical theology, and the philosophy of history. From the books of the so-called "Minor Prophets" also (Amos, Hosea, Joel, Micah, Nahum, Habakkuk, Zephaniah, Obadiah, Haggai, Zechariah, Malachi, and Jonah), all that the Qur'án recounts is the story of Jonah. No inquiry had been made in order to discover in the books of these prophets their discerning evaluation of sacrificial worship, their exacting ideals of social justice, their standards of faithfulness, their explanations of divine judgements in the history of Israel, their emphasis on the virtues of kindliness and reverence, their persistent belief in the final vindication of those who put their trust in God, their portrayal of the inexorable judgement and punishment of evil, and their confident hope for the future after the dark days of captivity.

Of New Testament characters we find that there are only four who are mentioned in the Qur'án in any connexion whatever. Of these the first two are Zacharias and his son John (the Baptist), who are

72. Cf. also similar statements in other Meccan surahs, e.g. xxix. 44, 45 and xlii. 14.

always described together. The father is represented as a man who was faithful in prayer: and when the angels foretold the birth of his son, whose name was to be John, they said that he would be "a verifier of the word from God" (iii. 32–4). In another reference we find that God is represented as declaring:

> We said: "O John! receive the Book with purpose of heart"—and We bestowed on him wisdom while yet a child; and mercifulness from Ourself, and purity: and pious was he, and dutiful to his parents; and not proud, nor rebellious. And peace was on him in the day that he was born, and the day of his death, and shall be on him when he shall be raised to life (xix. 13–15).

The other two New Testament characters that are named in the Qur'án are Mary and Jesus the son of Mary. As yet no one has been able to determine why it is that Mary is called in the Qur'án "the daughter of Imrán" (iii. 31 ff.), unless it was a case of confusion with the Maryam whom the Bible mentions as the sister of Moses and Aaron. Their father the Bible also says was Amram (Exodus vi. 18, 20; Numbers iii. 19; and 1 Chronicles vi. 2, 3, 18). A second anachronism, which is obviously consistent with the first, is found in a different sura (xix. 28–9), which speaks of Mary refuting an insinuation against her character that is explicitly stated:

> Then came she with the babe to her people, bearing him. They said, "O Mary! now hast thou done a strange thing! O sister of Aaron! Thy father was not a man of wickedness, nor unchaste thy mother." And she made a sign to them, pointing towards the babe.[73]

A more serious confusion occurs, however, when Mary, the mother of Jesus, is admitted to the Trinity in the place of the Holy Spirit (v. 76–9, and 116). It was this misconceived "Trinity", we should remember, that Muhammad repudiated. The unity of the spiritual character of the true Trinity he had not understood or appreciated.

From the ethical viewpoint the passages in the Qur'án that make reference to Jesus are disappointing in that they give so little importance to his moral teaching.[74] We read: "And we brought Jesus, son of Mary, the proofs, and strengthened him with the Holy Spirit" (ii. 81, 254). The angels are represented as declaring to Mary: "O

73. The attempts of Muslim commentators to explain away these anachronisms require that in the first instance there should be two Imráns in Bible history, the former the father of Moses and Aaron and Maryam, and the latter (of whom there is no record) the father of the New Testament character, Mary the mother of Jesus: and in the second instance, according to Baiḍawí, Mary may just have been called the sister of Aaron by way of comparison, or because she was of the Levitical race, or by way of derision in case there was a man by the name of Aaron who was renowned for either piety or wickedness.

74. Cf. Rev. James Robson, *Christ in Islam*, pp. 17–28.

Mary, verily God gives you good news of a Word from Him, whose name shall be the Messiah, Jesus, son of Mary, eminent in this world and the next, and one of those who approach God's presence. And he shall speak to men in the cradle and when he is grown up, and shall be one of the upright" (iii. 40).

"Verily Jesus in the sight of God is like Adam whom He created of earth, then said, 'Be,' and he came into being" (iii. 52). "And we brought him the Gospel in which is guidance and light; and (he was) verifying what was before him with respect to the Pentateuch, and was a guidance and warning to the God-fearing" (v. 50). "And when Jesus brought the proofs he said, 'I have brought you wisdom, and will make clear to you some of that about which you differ, so fear God and obey me. Verily God is my Lord and your Lord, so worship Him. Verily this is a straight path'" (xliii. 63–6). "And we caused Jesus, son of Mary, to follow in their traces [i.e. of the prophets], and we brought him the Gospel and put gentleness and compassion in the hearts of those who followed him. But as for the monastic state, they invented it. We prescribed for them only desire for the acceptance of God; but they did not observe it as it ought to be observed. So we gave their reward to those of them who believed and many of them were impious" (lvii. 26, 27). "O you who believe, be God's helpers, as Jesus, son of Mary, said to the disciples, 'Who will be my helpers towards God?'" (lxi. 14).

It will be observed that in the Qur'án there is no reference to any of Jesus' parables. That means that a Muslim who is familiar only with the Jesus of the Qur'án knows nothing whatever of the powerful ethical teachings in such parables as that of the Pharisee who thanked God "that he was not like this publican", or that of the Good Samaritan, or that of the Prodigal Son, or that of the Sower. If Muhammad knew these parables he must have failed to appreciate them. And the same comment may be made in regard to the Sermon on the Mount. There is no reference to it in any of the passages that mention Jesus. We are forced to conclude, it would seem, that Jesus as a great moral teacher is given but passing and summary recognition in the Qur'án—as one whom God strengthened with the Holy Spirit, and one in whose good news there is guidance and light.

It would be a grave error to conclude, as Weil did more than a hundred years ago,[75] that Muhammad "brought the most beautiful teachings of the Old and New Testaments to a people which was not illuminated by one ray of faith". Narratives of Old and New Testament characters are related in the Qur'án, and they are set forth as examples for God-fearing men of other ages to follow, but anything like a careful comparison of the narratives in the Qur'án with the records in the Bible will show not only historical discrepancies and

75. Cf. Weil, *Mohammed der Prophet, sein Leben und seine Lehre*, Stuttgart, 1843, quoted by C. Snouck Hurgronje, *Mohammedanism*, p. 24.

the addition of merely legendary material, but most important and significant differences in ethical insight and appreciation.

The most crucial of these differences for Christian readers of the Qur'án is found in Muhammad's failure to understand the meaning and purpose of Jesus' suffering and death on the cross. He takes the position rather that it would not be reasonable to consider that God would allow such a good and just man to suffer and die in that way. His repudiation of Jesus' death on the cross is found in Sura iv. 155 ff., in a passage in which he rebukes the Jews for their unbelief and for a grievous calumny against Mary:

> And for their saying, "Verily we have slain the Messiah, Jesus the son of Mary, an Apostle of God." Yet they slew him not, and they crucified him not, but they had only his likeness. And they who differed about him were in doubt concerning him: no sure knowledge had they about him, but followed only an opinion, and they did not really slay him, but God took him up to Himself.

But in the later development of Islam there came to be a vast number of *sayings* that were ascribed to Muhammad, and in these traditional sayings familiar Biblical phrases and well-known teachings of Jesus are found. Also in connexion with the meditations of the early Muslim ascetics, the speculations of theologians and commentators, and the more particular investigations of historians there is evidence of a desire for more knowledge of the Bible than the Qur'án provides, especially in regard to the capacity of the individual to come into personal relation with God. The ethical literature of Islam, therefore, while based primarily on the Qur'án, has been considerably broadened by important sources of influence in later times.

3

THE ETHICS OF THE TRADITIONS

FAITH (*imán*) in Islam involves more than doctrine. Whether the faith of the Prophet himself is studied, or that of his companions, or that of his followers of the present day, the findings will have in them more of practice than of theory. This is made particularly clear by an examination of the sources of the Muslim faith, namely, "Allah's Book" and the Prophet's "Sunna",[1] the latter of which is said to constitute a chronicle of Muhammad's action (*fi'l*), utterance (*qawl*), and unspoken approval (*taqrír*). For devout Muslims, therefore, faith means primarily the ordering of their lives according to a conscious imitation of the actions of their prophet Muhammad. Their highest desire, both ethically and religiously, is that their actions may be in accord with the teachings of Allah in the Qur'án and in harmony with explanatory sayings of Muhammad that are believed to have been preserved by oral traditions that were handed down from his companions to succeeding generations.

The inclusive term for all that has thus been handed down about the Prophet, all that is attributed to his authority by an accredited series of narrators, is *al-ḥadíth* (the Tradition). The meaning of the verb *hadatha* is "he narrated", and we find that in the Ḥadíth literature the narratives are exceedingly numerous and remarkably brief. It is enough to constitute a single tradition if a particular association, a casual remark, a definite action, or an acquiescing silence is ascribed to the Prophet with a series of authorities for the statement.

When it is taken as a whole, the Ḥadíth literature of orthodox Islam includes all that has been narrated of the actions and sayings of the Prophet and his companions. In so much as every believer is expected "to take the conduct of the Prophet and his companions as a model for himself in all the affairs of life",[2] these many volumes of traditions are regarded as of the utmost importance.

The method of oral narration, though it was revered and depended upon for nearly one hundred and fifty years, gave way at last to lists of traditions that were received on the authority of famous individual collectors and narrators. From these there came in due course several

1. Muslim, Ch. *Imán*, tr. 246.
2. *Encyclopædia of Islam*, art. "Ḥadíth", by Th. W. Juynboll.

compilations that were roughly classified into chapters, usually according to the subject matter that was covered in general by each chapter. Unfortunately there are none of the separate lists of the individual narrators that are now extant,[3] and the earliest of the classified compilations dates only from the latter part of the second hundred years after Muhammad.

Those compilations that set forth traditions as basic material which is to be taken along with the Qur'án for the determination of ceremonial duties, legal practices, necessary beliefs, etc., are called the *Sunna*; those that have been made for the purpose of accumulating everything that throws any light on the biography of the Prophet, presenting events in his life and the circumstances in which he lived and taught, are called the *Síra*; and those that are arranged with the object of teaching the requisites for good manners, education, and general culture are known as the *Adab*. From each of these points of view the customs and sayings of Muhammad and his companions have been regarded as second only to the Qur'án for the determination of all the affairs of human life. Much has been written about them as the material from which the Muslim legal system has been developed,[4] but an examination of them from the moral point of view reveals that they are also the life-blood of Muslim ethics.[5]

While it would scarcely be in place to discuss the historical value of the Ḥadíth literature in any detailed way in this connexion, yet there are several general aspects in which the question of its historical value does have ethical importance. On the one hand, it is obvious that in so far as this literature can be regarded as being true to the action, utterance, and silent approval of the Prophet, it represents his ethical as well as his religious consciousness. On the other hand, though it is said that there were thousands of instances in which traditions were falsely attributed to the Prophet, still these very traditions may have evidential value for the religious and moral syncretism that took place in the development of the Muslim community after the all-absorbing period of rapid expansion.

For we read that "after Muhammad's death the original ideas and usages, which had prevailed in the oldest community, could not remain permanently unaltered. A new period of development set in.

3. Reference is made to them, however, by Ibn Ḥanbal (d. A.D. 855) in the *Musnad*, which is arranged according to the contributions of a large number of narrators, and gives a good idea of the records the author had at his disposal in the early years of the third century after Muhammad.

4. *Encyclopædia of Islam*, art. "Sharí'a", by Joseph Schacht; Charles Hamilton's English translation of the Hidáya, 2nd ed., 1870, with preface and index by S. G. Grady; and Abdur Rahim's *Muhammadan Jurisprudence*, London, 1911.

5. This statement refers to the general ethics of the Muslim peoples, which must be distinguished from the books on ethics that were derived mainly from the later study of Greek philosophy.

The learned began systematically to develop the doctrine of duties and dogmatics in accordance with the new conditions. After the great conquests Islam covered an enormous area. New ideas and institutions were borrowed from the peoples conquered, and not only Christianity and Judaism, but Hellenism, Zoroastrianism, and Buddhism also influenced the life and thought of the Muslims of the day in many respects."[6] Accordingly, traditions that may be no more than pious fictions in so far as they relate to an historical Muhammad may yet have evidential value for the ethical consciousness of the people of Islam at particular periods in their history.

Moreover, there is a negative aspect that must also be considered. The deliberate practice of inventing traditions and of attaching to them lines of transmission that may be plausible enough in appearance but had no basis whatever in fact, a process of deliberate deception for propaganda purposes, was in itself essentially immoral. For this falsification of traditions, too often on the basis of sheer opportunism and in accord with what was thought to be expedient at the time for the interests of a particular group or a religious order, or perhaps in comparing Muhammad with Moses, Jesus, or Zoroaster, may be said to have robbed Islam of that unbiased historical perspective, that unswerving faithfulness to truth, which is requisite for the highest ethical development of any people. While it would be entirely wrong to suggest that Muslims alone have suffered from false traditions and from deliberate deception on the part of their religious teachers, or from far-fetched exegesis of passages of Scripture in order to bolster up questionable doctrines, or from the sanctioning of fabulous legends that has led to the veneration of tombs, yet it must be recognized that in so far as these influences have operated within Islam they have been detrimental to ethical progress. For wherever and whenever an intellectual and moral awakening has occurred, repudiation of what is manifestly false has had to go along with the acceptance of what is true before any substantial ethical reformation could take place.

THE SUNNA

A survey of the contents of the Sunna, to estimate its value as ethical literature, is facilitated by Wensinck's *Handbook of Early Muslim Traditions*, which is alphabetically arranged, and also by exceedingly valuable articles in the *Encyclopædia of Islam*.[7] In Wensinck's *Handbook* the names of the chapters in each of the great collections of the Sunna are given in separate lists.[8] When these lists of

6. *Encyclopædia of Islam*, art. "Hadíth".
7. Ibid. Cf. articles on "Hadíth", "Sunna", "Síra", "Adab", "Abu Hanifa", "Malik ibn Anas", "al-Bukhárí", "Muslim", etc.
8. Cf. *Early Muhammadan Traditions*, Introduction.

the names of chapters are grouped alphabetically they form a working harmony, which may then be reclassified under a few general headings. Under these headings a kind of bird's-eye view of the main subjects that are commented upon in the Sunna may be presented as follows:

Faith. The principal subjects that are included as matters of faith are the doctrines of creation, revelation, predestination, the oneness of Allah, the mission of Allah's prophets, that Muhammad was the last of the prophets, the sacredness of the Qur'án as the book of Allah —with its descriptions of Heaven and of Hell and of the Day of Resurrection and Judgement—and the authority of the Sunna.

Prayer and Sacrifice. Mention is made of ritual prayers for different occasions, of the *masjids* as places of prayer, of prayer in the sense of personal petition, of the public call to prayer, of the necessity at times for seclusion in prayer, of special stipulations for the prayers of travellers, with instructions also about stated times for prayer, how to begin a prayer, how one should pray when there is an eclipse of the sun or of the moon, and for praying when there is great need of rain or in times of special fear. As sacrifices and sacrificial ceremonies are closely associated with the Muslim conception of prayer, detailed directions are given about the victims that are to be killed and how they should be killed. The ancient custom of shaving an infant's hair to make a payment or sacrifice of the equivalent weight in gold or silver is also described.

Special Religious Duties. Numerous regulations are given for the ceremonial bath, for the dedication of property to pious uses, for the pilgrimage to Mecca, for the burial of the dead, and for the celebration of religious festivals. The merit of fasting is emphasized, with particular directions for observing the fast during the month of Ramaḍán. Rewards are promised for the giving of alms, for repentance, for doing penance for wrongs that have been committed, for going forth to war in the way of Allah, and for renunciation of the world.

Civil Regulations. Civil regulations cover a wide field, which includes the rights of freedmen and of slaves, rules for commercial transactions, the laws of inheritance, the tax of the obligatory "fifth", the custom of swearing allegiance, the taking of rent, the giving of bills of transfer, requirements in becoming surety, the *jizya* or tax on non-Muslims, the responsibilities of governors, the rights of farmers in the harvests, regulations regarding horses and camels, partnerships in land or in water-rights, marriage customs and restrictions, legal agency, and last will and testament.

Criminal Law. Traditions are grouped together to serve as precedents for restricting the custom of retaliation or revenge, to determine equitable compensation for murder, to estimate penalties, to deal with apostates, or for punishing thieves. And as Muslim law was martial law in the beginning, there are special provisions for the treatment of prisoners, sentries, and those besieged, and for quelling public disturbances.

Moral Admonitions. Attention is given to the great value of knowledge, of good dispositions, and of fleeing from evil to good. There is an enumeration of virtues, with descriptions of the moral character of the Prophet, and exposures of hypocrites. There are also discussions about poetry and its dangers, about works of supererogation, about obligations to the sick, about requirements in trade, and about borrowing and the payment of debts. Still other considerations under this heading are conversations with women, the question of obligatory giving to kindred, and the custom that had developed of introducing rational judgements in cases where precedents from the Sunna appeared to be insufficient.

Personal Habits. In addition to those sayings of the Prophet that have served jurists in making their decisions, the Sunna is rich in admonitions for the cultivation of acceptable personal habits. Advice is given that has to do with culture, with the usage of words that indicates good education, and with ways of living in general. There is direction about foods and drinks that are allowable, clothes and ornaments that may be worn, friendly salutations, and the proper procedure for nursing infants. Traditions are included to regulate in detail the performance of natural bodily functions, and they are to be found also on the hot bath, on sleeping soundly, and on the use of medicines and perfumes.

But along with these directions commendable virtues are advocated on the ground of the Prophet's example. For instance, when a party of Jews came and addressed Muhammad, substituting *al-sám* (death) for *al-salám* (peace) in the customary greeting, his young wife 'A'isha is said to have resented the insult, but the Prophet said to her gently, "Surely Allah loves kindness in all circumstances" (Bukhari, 78. 35).

On another occasion he said to his followers, "Do not hate one another, do not be envious of one another, and do not insult one another. Servants of Allah are like brothers and it is not permissible for a Muslim to forsake his brother for more than three days" (Bukhari, 78. 57 and 58).

Likewise double-heartedness is condemned (Bukhari, 78. 52), and quarrelsomeness is rebuked (Tirmidhi, 25. 58). On many occasions the Prophet himself showed self-restraint (Muslim, 45. 106–8) and calmness (Tirmidhi, 25. 66). Kindness (Tirmidhi, 25. 67) and the honouring of old age (Tirmidhi, 25, 15) were enjoined. One should aim to show a good disposition (*husn al-khulq*) (Tirmidhi, 25. 55, 62, 71), and reward is promised to those who remove stumbling-blocks (Bukhari, 10. 32, and Tirmidhi, 25. 36).

It would be most misleading, however, if such an outline gave the impression that the traditions that have to do with moral admonitions and personal habits were the only ones to have any particular ethical character or value. On the contrary, the whole of the Sunna is important for the study of Muslim ethics. The requirements of believers, in all their individual and collective capacities, were summed up in the expression, "holding fast to the Book and the Sunna" (*i'tiṣám bi'l-kitáb wa'l-sunna*). All that was permitted or prohibited was to be found clearly set forth, either in the Qur'án, which was accepted as the word of Allah, or in the Sunna, the traditional "use and wont" of the Prophet of Allah.

The ultimate ideal of Islam, whether in ethics or in religion, is "submission" to the will of Allah: but at the same time there is what may very truly be called *Muhammadan Ethics*, because of the continued belief that Muhammad's example furnishes the ideal standard of human conduct. Moral issues that arose in the Muslim state, legal questions that called for decisions, problems in social relations, difficulties in family affairs, and details in personal conduct—all of these matters could be determined solely by relating them to reported sayings or actions of Muhammad.

The outstanding question that confronts the student of ethics in the study of the Sunna, therefore, is this, *Can purely imitative conduct be ethical?*

While he may not always be aware of it, the devout Muslim will render obedience to some of the requirements of the Sunna from considerations that lie beyond mere imitation. For some of these requirements he will have confirmed in his own experience as being eminently useful for himself and his family, or for the Muslim community. He will have subjected them to a kind of rational synthesis in his own reflexion, until they are no longer right for him solely because he finds them in the Sunna. Examples of personal ethical consciousness of this kind, in confirmation of traditional moral sanctions, may be found readily by those who are living in natural and friendly relations with Muslim people. Respect for parents, moderation in spending, gracious hospitality to guests, steadfastness in adverse circumstances, faithfulness in keeping trusts—these and other praiseworthy qualities are not infrequently made their own, with a moral appreciation that is grounded in their experience in reflective living.

There are other requirements of the Sunna, however, which these same Muslim friends will have failed to confirm in their own experience, and to which they will not have applied any process of rational criticism or appreciation, but which they follow scrupulously as stipulations of their Prophet.

Instances of purely imitative conduct on the part of believers may be illustrated by a brief reference to the traditional customs that are connected with the pilgrimage to Mecca. Take the kissing of the

Black Stone, for example. Although 'Umar is said to have protested, "I know that thou art a stone that neither helps nor hurts, and if the messenger of Allah had not kissed thee, I would not kiss thee", yet with this understanding he too kissed the stone. It can hardly be for any different reason that prominent Muslim judges—from India, Egypt, Iran, or Syria—have kissed the Black Stone. But what does it mean ethically, or even religiously, for a well-read governor, Oxford-educated, to take pains to say a ritual prayer under the water-pipe (*math'ab*) of the Ka'ba, while he is being assured on the authority of the Sunna that for so doing he will be made as pure as he was on the day when his mother bore him? Or when a group of lady teachers from a modern Muslim university make the pilgrimage to Mecca, and stop on their way back from Arafat, each to throw seven stones at seven stone-piles there in the valley of Miná? In thus conforming to custom they give little thought to the ethical meaning or significance of their actions. But it is possible that when some of them are given Zamzam water to drink, that when they are told that it is useful for every remedial purpose, they may at least have momentary doubts about its value.

But there is no need to go so far afield as the pilgrimage customs for examples of actions according to the Sunna that are placidly taken for granted, and for which there is no conscious appraisement from the ethical point of view. The use of the rosary, the segregation of women, the wearing of prayer-talismans, the "cutting of the Qur'án" (*istikhḍra*), facing Mecca in prayer, visits to the tombs of saints for their intercession, magic rites against the Jinn, and various ideas of defilement and purification—these and many other practices and superstitions have been continued from one generation to another in conformity with the Sunna, and with little or no consideration whether they are worthy of rational approval.

However, in justice to Muslims in our own generation it should be said that there are many particular injunctions from the Sunna that they show a tendency to ignore in their own conduct, as though they were at least somewhat doubtful as to whether these regulations are practicable for present-day life. That deliberate falsehood is permissible for purposes of reconciliation or to avoid domestic turmoil, that a man may have as many as four wives at one time and treat them all justly, that women should wear the veil and not let their faces be seen by men who are not members of their own families, that Muslim men should not shave their faces, that the month of Ramaḍán should be observed by a scrupulous fasting in the daytime and extraordinary feasting at night—these commands and prohibitions, explicitly stated in the Sunna, are being ignored by rapidly increasing numbers of Muslims, both men and women, who are coming to demand sound ethical reasons for what is permitted or forbidden.

The development of reflective ethical consciousness among mankind is according to processes that are more uniform than otherwise. The modern Jew who thinks in the terms of ethics is not entirely at home when he reads the Talmud; and the modern Christian who has intelligently appreciated the revolutionary nature of Jesus' teachings is certainly uncomfortable when he encounters unquestioning traditional acceptance of obsolete Old Testament conceptions by individuals within his own Christian community. Likewise, the modern Muslim would scarcely be true to his own age and environment if he did not find difficulty in adapting his life and thought, and his ethical code, to the Sunna.

In the words of the author of a widely studied manual of ethics,[9] "universal principles, applicable to all times and peoples, become gradually substituted for the customs and laws of particular tribes and nations". In Judaism and in Christianity ethical development has not led to less dependence on divine precepts. "Among the Jews, for instance, it is easy to trace a development from the customary and ceremonial law, through the Ten Commandments, to the deeper and more inward principles represented by the Psalms and the later prophets. The idea of the 'pure heart' gradually substitutes itself for external observances; and, in Christianity, the *law* is quite definitely superseded by the idea of the inner principle of love. When this takes place, the purely national character of the Jewish morality is at the same time broken down, and it becomes morality that is applicable to all times and peoples.

"In the case of this line of development, however, it is to be noted that every step takes place, as it were, by a new enactment. The deeper principle is always formulated by the voice of some prophet, speaking more or less definitely in the name of 'the Lord'. The idea of a divine law remains fundamental throughout. Even when the inner principle of Christianity is set against the external rules of the older system, it still appears in the form of a definite enactment, a 'New Commandment': 'It was said by them of old time . . . But I say unto you . . .' The appeal is still to an authoritative law."[10]

We shall see that in Islam there have been movements in this same direction, particularly among those philosophers who came more in touch with Greek thought, and among the early Súfís.

THE SÍRA

The word *síra* is found in the Qur'án (xx. 22) in a reference to Moses' rod, which was changed to a serpent and then returned to its previous *state* or *form* (*síra*). In the same general period in which compilations of the oral traditions were being arranged in the Sunna, with the purpose of clarifying and supplementing the divine precepts

9. Mackenzie, *Manual of Ethics*, p. 100. 10. Ibid., p. 101.

with precedents from the sayings and actions of the Prophet, other collections were being made of traditions that were intended rather to provide material for the study of the life of the Prophet. The Síra may be said to contain all the data that could be found for the biography of Muhammad. In this data, whatever can be derived from the Qur'án is included, but with circumstantial explanation that serves a most useful purpose, both for later historians and for those who have written commentaries on the Qur'án.

There are two outstanding authorities whose works on the Síra are still extant. The first of these is Ibn Hishám, who wrote the *Kitáb Sírat Rasúl Alláh* ("The Character of the Apostle of Allah"), which has preserved for us valuable citations from the *Síra* of Ibn Isháq, "who was the first to place Islam and its founder in the scheme of universal history".[11] The second is Ibn Sa'd, who wrote the *Kitáb al-Ṭabaqát* ("The Book of Classes"), and who has preserved traditions from an older authority, the historian al-Wáqidi.

Ibn Isháq (d. A.D. 768) grew up in Medina, for his grandfather, a Christian who had been captured in the church at 'Ain al-Tamr in 'Iráq, had been brought to Medina and became a client of 'Abdulla ibn Qais. In Medina Ibn Isháq collected stories about the life of the Prophet, but to avoid casting his lot with the 'Umayyads he found it expedient to go to Egypt, and thence later on to Baghdad, where he died in A.H. 151 or 152. The traditions that he included in his Síra are accessible in part in the extended extracts that are quoted by the historian al-Ṭabarí (d. A.D. 923), and it is probable that they have been almost completely incorporated in the extensive work of his successor, Ibn Hishám.

Ibn Hishám (d. A.D. 833) was born in Basra and died in Egypt. "He has adopted the materials of Ibn Isháq extensively, in a complete and unaltered form, in his well-known *al-Sírat Ibn Hishám* (as this work is designated in modern printed texts). In view of the fact that on comparison his extracts are found to tally almost word for word with the quotations from al-Ṭabarí from the same passages of Ibn Isháq, we may reasonably conclude that they are faithfully and accurately quoted."[12]

Al-Wáqidi's (d. A.D. 822) grandfather was also a client to a Medinese family. When Harún al-Rashíd visited Medina, al-Wáqidi served as his guide, to show him places of historic interest; and when he later visited Harún al-Rashíd in Baghdad,[13] he received an appointment as judge (*qáḍí*). This appointment al-Ma'mun confirmed when he came to Baghdad as Caliph. It would appear that al-Wáqidi enjoyed exceptional friendship with al-Ma'mun, for shortly before his death he appointed the friendly Caliph as his

11. *Encyclopædia of Islam*, art. "Síra", by G. Levi Della Vida.
12. *Haidarabad Journal of Islamic Culture*, vol. ix, p. 39.
13. Ibn Sa'd, *Ṭabaqát*, V. i, pp. 314 ff.

executor. In confirmation of his friendship with al-Ma'mun, we are told that on one occasion, when he had appealed to him for money with which to pay his debts, the Caliph sent him the money and reminded him of a tradition that he had once taught him, i.e. that the Prophet had declared, "Whoso spends much will receive much, and whoso spends little will receive little." Al-Wáqidi's grateful and friendly reply was that he was far more surprised that al-Ma'mun had remembered this tradition than that he should be so generous.

Ibn Sa'd (d. A.D. 845), whose father was a client of the Banu Háshim, was secretary to al-Wáqidi. In his *Kitáb al-Ṭabaqát* ("The Book of Classes") he has shown exceptional skill in his clear arrangement of a vast amount of material for the history of the Prophet, and his Companions and Successors. In this work of nine volumes, an edited text of which was published in Leyden, 1904 ff., there are most valuable indices, and the first two volumes contain most of the traditions that are on the authority of al-Wáqidi.

There are earlier sources, however, from which all these men gathered traditions to make up the Síra. They were writers of monographs on the exploits or campaigns (*al-magházi*) of Muhammad. The most important of them was 'Urwa ibn al-Zubair, who lived during the period from A.H. 23 to A.H. 94. His mother was Asmá', the daughter of Abu Bakr, and his father was a cousin of Muhammad's first wife, Khadíja. He himself took part in battles during Muhammad's career, and he spent much of his later life in Medina. Most of the traditions he gathered are attributed to his aunt 'A'isha, or to one or other of his parents, or to 'Ali ibn Abu Ṭalib, or to Abu Huraira. Because of 'Urwa's exceptional opportunity to receive traditions from prominent individuals who had associated intimately with the Prophet, Professor Fr. Buhl, in his article on "Muhammad" in the *Encyclopædia of Islam*, has given particular importance to 'Urwa's account of Muhammad's early relations with the Meccans.[14] And mention should be made also of those who received traditions from 'Urwa, for in addition to his five sons—Muhammad, 'Uthmán, 'Abd Alláh, Yahyá, and Hishám—there were al-Zuhrí, Sulaimán ibn Yasár, and Ibn Abí Mulá'ika. Al-Zuhrí (d. A.H. 124), who was so called because he was a member of the Meccan clan of Zuhrá, was one of 'Urwa's pupils, and like him he went to the court of the Caliph 'Abd al-Malik, where he wrote down his traditions. His grandfather had fought against Muhammad at the Battle of Badr and is said to have inflicted a wound upon him at the Battle of Uhud.

In his summary of attractive characteristics in Muhammad's personality, as evidenced by the Síra, Professor Tor Andrae has mentioned "his unique kindliness, amiability, and friendliness". He says that Muhammad "greeted everyone, slaves and little children as

14. Cf. Ṭabarí, i. 1180 ff., 1224 ff.; also, through al-Zuhrí, in Ibn Sa'd, *Ṭabaqát*, I. i, p. 133.

well", also "that he had a remarkable gift for winning people. Often, as with a magic stroke, he succeeded in transforming dissatisfaction into surrender and dislike into attraction. . . . His tendency to yield as far as possible in respect of the regulations and laws which he himself had instituted bears witness to the same characteristics. . . . The good qualities which stand out are a strong social instinct, a love of personal friendship and accessibility."[15]

It is instructive to observe that these outstanding and attractive characteristics that are ascribed to Muhammad in the Síra resemble closely those virtues that were most praised by the pre-Islamic poets in their encomiums to their tribal chiefs. Such virtues as tranquillity (*ḥilm*), generosity (*sakhá*), courage (*shajá'a*), steadfastness (*ṣabr*), and good disposition (*ḥuṣn al-khulq*) are frequently mentioned, and many of Muhammad's traditional sayings are in praise of these same virtues.

Of those familiar sayings of Muhammad, which occur repeatedly in both the Sunna and the Síra and in all popular books of moral instruction, the following may be given as examples:[16]

> The three doors of good conduct are generosity of soul (*sakhá al-nafs*), agreeable speech (*ṭib al-kalám*), and steadfastness in adversity (*al-ṣabr 'alá al-'adhá*).
>
> The generous man who is ignorant (*al-sakhíyu'l-jahúl*) is more precious in the sight of Allah than the learned man who is miserly.
>
> Generosity is one of the trees of Paradise. Its branches extend to the earth, and whoever seizes one of these branches will be raised to Paradise.
>
> The generous man, surely he is generous because of his trust in Allah, whereas the avaricious man, surely he is avaricious because of his suspicion of Allah.
>
> The most worthy of you is the one who controls himself in anger, and the most tranquil (forbearing) of you is the one who forgives when he is in authority.
>
> The plague of courage is insolence, the plague of nobility is pride, and the plague of liberality is obligation.
>
> The bravest of men is the one who conquers his own passion.
>
> A good disposition wipes out offences as water melts ice, but an evil disposition spoils an act as vinegar spoils honey.
>
> The best of you are those who are best in disposition, who show kindness and who have kindness shown them.

But the Síra keeps the main emphasis on the characteristics of the Prophet himself. One of the best of the brief summaries of the personal qualities of Muhammad, as derived from the Síra, is one that

15. Tor Andrae, *Mohammed*, English trans. Menzel, London, 1936, pp. 262–3.

16. *Sukhanán-i-Muhammad*, published in Persian and Arabic, Teheran, 1938. Cf. also *Sayings of the Prophet Muhammad*, by Muhammad Amín, published by Muhammad Ahsraf, Lahore.

has been made by a present-day Muslim writer:[17] "As to his personal appearance, it is related that he was of medium stature, of light complexion, and naturally ruddy. His teeth were well spaced and he had a broad, comely mouth. His head was large, and his forehead was broad and shapely. The upper parts of his cheeks were smooth, and the bones of his aquiline nose were prominent. He had broad shoulders and good-sized hands, with big knuckles and thin wrists. His hair extended to his ears and his beard was thick.

"The 'seal of prophecy' was between his shoulders, and it appeared to be encircled by light. Drops of his perspiration were like pearls and had the odour of musk. He walked with an energetic sway, as when one makes a slight descent with the intention of ascending; and so quickly did he proceed that it seemed that the earth was being folded up for him. On meeting people he would take their hands in his, and ordinarily his hands had the fragrance of jasmine. Sometimes he would place them on a child's head, and such a child would then be distinguished by this fragrance.

"Muhammad's face shone like the full moon. One of those who described him declared, 'I never saw anyone like him, and neither has anyone else.' Yet in his exceeding modesty and humility he would repair his sandals, patch his clothes, milk his sheep, and at times he would serve his family like a slave. At other times, on behalf of Allah, he would become very angry, for it was in Allah's pleasure that he delighted. In explaining his custom of walking behind his companions, which is contrary to the usual practice, he would remark, Leave the place behind me for the angels.' He would ride a horse, a mule, or a donkey—and yet there were kings who sent him presents.

"As a precaution against hunger, now and then he would bind a stone against his stomach, though he held the keys to the treasure-houses of the earth. Once indeed the hills asked to be turned to gold for him, but he rejected the offer. Yet in spite of all this, when he met anyone he was always the first to say *salám.*

"Often he would pray at great length, but at the Friday services he would preach briefly. With the gentry he kept on friendly terms, and he made it a point to show special honour to the learned. He would joke with them occasionally, but in doing this he would take care not to depart from the truth."

This is a direct and fair statement of the details about the personal characteristics of the Prophet that may be culled laboriously, one after another, from the Sunna and the Síra. But it is interesting to contrast this more complete statement with the very brief mention of "what has come in regard to the qualities of the Prophet" that is

17. This statement is derived from a condensation of material that is gathered from the traditions in regard to the personal characteristics of Muhammad, which is given by Shaikh 'Abbás al-Qúmmí under the heading "*Ḥusn al-Athár min Makárim al-Akhláq-i-Saiyid al-Bashar*", which is included as a supplement in his "*Hadayat al-Ahbáb*", Najaf, A.H. 1349.

given by the earliest of the compilers of the Sunna, Malik ibn Anas (d. A.D. 795):[18] "that the Apostle of Allah was neither outstandingly tall nor short, was neither dead white nor brown, and he did not have abundant hair. Allah sent him (as a prophet) when he was forty years of age. He remained in Mecca for ten years and in Medina for ten years. Allah, the great and glorious, caused him to die when he was sixty years of age, and there were not on his head and his face more than twenty white hairs."

Another enumeration of the distinguishing characteristics of the Prophet may be cited from the *Kitáb Mufíd al-'Ulúm wa Mubíd al-Humúm* ("Book to Dispense Knowledge and Dispel Care"), Cairo, A.H. 1330, which has been attributed to Abu Bakr Khawrizmí (d. A.D. 933), but which is thought to have been the work rather of Muhammad ibn Ahmad al-Qazwíní (d. A.D. 1185). All the particulars in this statement have also been carefully summarized from the Síra:

"When the Almighty and Most High distinguished His prophet by revelation, He caused a separation between him and His creation. In order to add to his honour and greatness, He made easy for him what he had made difficult for others; and to still further his dignities, there were things that he made hard for him that he had made easy for others."

These latter things that were made particularly difficult for the Prophet are mentioned first: "Allah required him to give his wives their choice, whether they would accept Islam and be his wives or whether they would rather go free. He was expected to observe the ritual prayer at night (*ṣalát al-lail*). He was forbidden to take for himself the alms that were presented to him, whether they were those required (*faríḍa*) or those given spontaneously (*tatawwu'*). He was not allowed to indulge in the surreptitious look (*kha'inatu'l-'a'yun*) of passionate desire. Whenever he would put on his chain-armour (*láma*) he was not to remove it until he had met the enemy. It was imperative for him to contend against what was wrong (*al-nakír al-munkír*), and it was required that he should neither write poetry nor commit it to memory. He was expected to pay off the debts of any Muslims who died. He acquired by his own efforts more knowledge than the whole world had attained by working together.

"In regard to his personal habits he himself made several remarks:

'For my part, I will not eat reclining.'

'I have been commanded so positively to use a tooth-brush that I fear that it may be decreed for my people.'

'As for onions, garlic, and leeks, if the angel had not come to me especially to forbid them, then of course I would have eaten them.'

"He was called by his Lord to live with a vision of the Truth, but

18. *Muwatta*, ed. Cairo, A.H. 1348, part ii, p. 218.

at the same time to be in association with men. When it happened that a cloud of desire would cover his heart, he would then ask seven times for Allah's forgiveness. When the Spirit (*al-ruḥ*) demanded him, he would appear to be seized as it were from the world. At first he did not pray for the person who died in debt, though afterwards this restriction was abrogated.

"As for the things that were made easier for him than for other men, Allah had made it lawful for him to have more than four wives,[19] some of whom were presented to him, while there were

19. The early biographers were exceedingly candid, so much so indeed that they made no effort whatever to conceal the number of their Prophet's wives. Ibn Hishám (d. A.D. 833) names nine wives whom the Prophet left at his death (*Síra*, iv, p. 321), which agrees with the statement of al-Ṭabarí (d. A.D. 923) (*Ta'ríkh*, Cairo text, iii, p. 175). But whereas Ibn Hishám says that Muhammad had married a total number of thirteen women, Ṭabarí says that the total was eleven, except for four others whose marriages had been arranged but not consummated. Ibn Sa'd (d. A.D. 845) gives short biographical notes that he compiled from the traditions in regard to twelve recognized wives. They include the nine who are mentioned by Ibn Hishám and al-Ṭabarí, then three who died before the Prophet. He adds also two others, Fatima the daughter of Ḍaḥak, and 'Asma the daughter of al-Na'mán (Ibn Sa'd, *Ṭabaqát*, viii. 35–100, 156). Of this total number of fourteen he says that six were of the Quraish, six were of other Arab tribes, and two were "from what Allah had given him" from the spoils of war.

In explanation of the verse in the Qur'án (xxxiii. 38), "No blame attacheth to the Prophet where Allah hath given him a permission. Such was the way of Allah with those prophets who flourished before thee; for Allah's behest is a fixed decree", Ibn Sa'd relates two significant traditions. The first is on the authority of Ibn Ka'b al-Qarzí, and is to the effect that the "permission" referred to was that Allah had given permission "that he should marry what he wished from women" (cf. Qur'án, xxxiii. 49). The narrator of this tradition, as recorded by Ibn Sa'd, goes on to observe, "and this was indeed the custom of the prophets, for Solomon the son of David had a thousand women, seven hundred by marriage portions (*mahíra*) and three hundred as concubines (*surríya*), while David himself had one hundred women, among whom was the mother of Solomon, who had been the wife of 'Uriya, and David had married her after the rebellion. These were more women than Muhammad had." And according to the second tradition given by Ibn Sa'd, this reference to the numerous marriages of Solomon and David was used by Muhammad in reply to the Jews, who had criticized him on the ground of his numerous wives.

In so far as the number of the Prophet's wives exceeded the stipulated "four" that were permissible for other Muslims (cf. Qur'án, iv. 3), it was necessary that there should be a further revelation of "a privilege for thee above the rest of the faithful. We well know what we have settled for them, in regard to their wives and to the slaves whom their right hands hold, that there may be no fault on thy part: and Allah is Indulgent, Merciful!" (Qur'án, xxxiii. 49–50).

As an ethical question, polygamy, with its consequences in family life, should be faced as a plain matter of fact. Is it true in human experience that the husband of one wife, who by her intelligence, love, and confidence is his companion and helpmate, obtains a higher degree of personal satis-

others who were acquired by marriage, but without a negotiating representative and without witnesses. Allah made him more precious to the believers than their own lives. He made marriage lawful for him in the pilgrimage garb (*iḥrám*), and it was thus in fact that he married Safíya, granting her freedom from her status as a slave prisoner in lieu of her marriage portion (*ṣidák*).

"Likewise Allah made lawful for him the booty (*al-fai'*), i.e. one-fourth of the fifths (*'ikhmas*) of the property taken from unbelievers without fighting, and one-fifth of the moveable spoils (*al-ghaníma*). The interdicted pasture (*ḥiná*) was made his exclusive privilege.

"He could enter the sacred territory of Mecca, and this he could do without putting on the special pilgrimage garb. It was lawful for him to put a man to death inside the sacred area, for it was there that he killed Ibn Khatal, who was one of the guards of the Ka'ba. He was allowed also to kill a man after he had granted him safety, and he thought it lawful to kill anyone who reviled or satirized him, whether it were man or woman, and he decreed that the act of defaming such a person was not only permissible for the Muslims but also a means of obtaining mercy.[20]

faction throughout his life than a man who seeks rather for enhanced sexual gratification from multiple alliances with a variety of women? One Muslim writer has expressed the opinion that a man's sexual gratification reaches its highest degree only with new alliances, which he considers to be unfortunate, in so much as the number of these alliances is restricted by Muslim law (cf. *Talbís Iblís*, trans. D. S. Margoliouth, *Islamic Culture*, April 1945, pp. 180–81).

The man who is happily married to one wife, whom he honours and loves, is apt to consider that the master of a harem of several inmates, who finds his prototype in nature in the stud or the rooster, is incapable of appreciating the character of a true and ennobling marriage. Every young Muslim knows that in his teaching and in his example the prophet Muhammad did not adhere to monogamy. One young man who became a Christian, and whose father and mother had been reciprocally faithful, said that he first became discontented with Islam as a religion for himself when he had come to realize that his own father had observed standards in his marital relations that were superior to those that were taught and practised by his Prophet.

20. Cf. Ibn Sa'd's account of the separate expeditions that were sent forth for this purpose, *Ṭabaqát*, II. i, pp. 18–23: *'Aṣmá' bint Marwán*. Then there was the detachment (sariya) of 'Umair ibn 'Adí ibn Kharashat al-Khaṭmí against 'Aṣmá' bint Marwán, of the Bani Umaiya ibn Zaid, five nights before the expiration of the month of Ramaḍán, at the beginning of the nineteenth month after the migration of the Apostle of Allah. 'Aṣmá' was dwelling at the time with Yazíd ibn Zaid ibn Ḥiṣn al-Khaṭmí. She had been finding fault and annoying the Prophet. Moreover she had been inciting people against him and had been speaking poetry.

Accordingly 'Umair ibn 'Adí came to her at midnight, and when he came upon her in her house the one of her children whom she was nursing was in her bosom. He felt her with his hand, for he had defective vision, and took the child away from her. Then he put his sword in her breast and it came through her back. Then at once he went for the morning prayer with the Prophet at al-Medina. The Apostle of Allah asked him, "Have you

"The forty-eight-hour fast was lawful for him. Another concession was that he could sleep and the ceremonial ablution (*wuḍu'*) would not be necessarily repeated. For him the voluntary ritual prayer that he recited while he was sitting down was of the same value as if he said it standing.

"A notable exception in his case was that the line of progeneration was to be by his daughter—though indeed all relationships are to be abolished on the Day of Judgement except relationship to him.

"A particular one of his special privileges was that it was allowable for him to call to a person that was repeating the ritual prayer, and

killed the daughter of Marwán?" He said, "Yes, and what will be the consequences for me?" He answered, "Two goats will not butt their heads together on account of it."

(The narrator adds,) This was the first saying that I heard from the Apostle of Allah, who called 'Umair *Umair al-Basír*, i.e. "Umair the weak of sight".

'Abi 'Afak, the Jew. Then there was the detachment of Salim ibn 'Umair al-'Amrí against 'Abi 'Afak, the Jew. It occurred in the month of Shawwál at the beginning of the twentieth month after the Prophet's migration. 'Abi 'Afak belonged to the Bani Amra ibn 'Awf. He was a very old Shaikh, who had reached a hundred and twenty years, and he was a Jew. He had been inciting people against the Apostle of Allah and had been speaking poetry. He was one of those who caused his people to weep.

On the day of Badr, Salím ibn 'Umair had declared, "For me there is a vow", i.e. that he should kill 'Abi 'Afak or he should die with him. But he put off going to look for him until the darkness of the first month. It was a summer night and 'Abi 'Afak was asleep in the courtyard. Salím ibn 'Umair knew him, and he approached from the rear and struck his sword into his liver. Then he leaned upon it until it pierced through the bed-clothes, as he exclaimed, "Enemy of Allah!"

There came then a number of men from the people of 'Abi 'Afak's own speech, and they entered into the house and buried him.

Ka'b ibn al-Ashraf. There was also a detachment for the killing of Ka'b ibn al-Ashraf, the Jew. This was when fourteen nights remained of the month after the migration of the Apostle of Allah. The reason for his killing was that he was a poet, who was accustomed to satirize the Prophet and his Companions. He had been inciting people against them and had been annoying them. But when the battle of Badr occurred he was overthrown and showed himself contemptible. For he said, "Today it is better to be under the earth than outside it." Then he went forth until he came to Mecca, where he wept for the killing of the Quraish and incited them with his poetry. When he came also to al-Medina, the Apostle of Allah said, "O Allah, shield me from Ibn al-Ashraf however thou wilt, from his proclaiming evil and his speaking verses!" Afterwards he remarked, "Whom do I have for Ibn al-Ashraf, for indeed he troubles me?" Muhammad ibn Maslama said, "I am ready for him, O Apostle of Allah, and I will kill him." Then he (the Prophet) said, "Go ahead and do it, but consult with Sa'd ibn Mu'adh about the matter." Accordingly Muhammad ibn Maslama got one of the men from the Ibn 'Aws tribe, 'Abád ibn Bashar, and Abu Na'la Silkán ibn Samáma, and al-Hárith ibn 'Aws ibn Mu'ádh, and Abu 'Abas ibn Jahr, and they said, "O Apostle of Allah, we will kill him, only give us permission to speak as we wish?" He answered, "Speak."

Now Abu Na'la was the half-brother on the mother's side of Ibn al-Ashraf,

moreover that person could answer him. He could also enter the *masjid* when he had been ceremonially defiled (*jaban*). And when he pronounced judgement, he could give a decision on his own authority, personally accepting the witness of anyone who testified to him. He could also give judicial decisions in regard to his own children.

"It is related that his slave, Umm Aiman, drank his urine, and he did not forbid her, but remarked: 'Now no injury will occur to your abdomen (*baṭn*).' And on the occasion when Ibn al-Zubair drank his blood, he did not say anything to forbid him. Sometimes he divided

so he went to him. At first Ka'b refused to know him and was apprehensive of him. But he said, "I am Abu Na'la, and truly I have come to tell you that the approach of this man (i.e. Muhammad) is towards us, and that for evil. The genuine Arabs (al-Arab) would make war upon us and would shoot us with one bow (Lane, I, p. 2575). What we want is to get away from this man. I have with me men from my own people, who are of the same opinion with me, and I want to come to you with them. We will buy from you wheat and dates and will give what will satisfy you as security. Then Ka'b believed what he was told and replied, "Come with them whenever you wish." He then went out with him to the place appointed.

Then Abu Na'la went to his companions to inform them. When they came together he told them that they should come to him when it was evening. Then they came to the Apostle of Allah and informed him. He walked with them as far as the Baqí district and then turned to leave them, saying, "Proceed with the blessing and help of Allah!"

It is said to have been a moon-lit night and they went on until they came to Ka'b's fortress. Abu Na'la called to him and he jumped up (from bed). His wife seized him by his garments and asked, "Where are you going? You are like a man going to war, or is it a new wedding?" He answered, "I have an appointment, it is with my brother Abu Na'la," and he knocked the garment loose with his hand. Then he said, "If my friendship is sought I will reply with a taunt." He went down to the men then and talked with them an hour, until he was merry and quite at ease with them. Suddenly Abu Na'la put his hand into Ka'b's hair, then seized his head by the two side-locks and called to his companions, "Kill the enemy of Allah!" At once they struck him with their swords, but there was no certain result as one interfered with another, and Ka'b clung to Abu Na'la. Muhammad ibn Maslama narrates, "I managed to extricate my sword and placed it on his navel, then I bore it down upon it and cut him to the groin, and the enemy of Allah cried out, 'Now no Jewish fortress remains that fire has not consumed!' They then cut off his head and took it with them."

When they reached the district of the thorn trees, *baqí al-gharqad*, they offered the *takbír* (the prayer declaring Allah's greatness). The Apostle of Allah was standing there that night praying. When he heard them offering the *takbír*, he did so also, for he knew that they had killed Ka'b ibn al-Ashraf. When they came to the Apostle of Allah he asked, "Are the purposes accomplished?" They replied, "Your purpose, O Apostle of Allah," and they threw the head before him. He praised Allah that the man had been killed, and when morning came he said, "Whomsoever you get in your power from among the Jewish men, put him to death." Consequently the Jews were afraid, and not one of them appeared. They had nothing to say and feared to pass the night anywhere, lest they should suffer the same fate as Ibn al-Ashraf.

his hair among his companions, and they used it when they prayed. All of these things mentioned are distinguishing characteristics of the Prophet."[21]

This same writer, Muhammad al-Qaswíní, has also gathered together in a special section the traditions that show that the Prophet was at times accustomed to jest.[22] "He would come upon a man from behind him, and put his hands over his eyes and say, 'Who will buy this slave from me?' Or he would stop and watch a party of Abyssinians with their tambourines, or to observe a group of rough fellows at play. On one of these occasions he said, 'I am not of a sporting disposition, it is not natural for me.' By sport (*al-dad*) he meant amusement (*al-lahw*).

"At times he would say, 'I am appointed to a liberal attitude, and I am not burdened with the severity (*al-'aṣr*) and the manacles (*al-'aghlál*) that were put upon the Bani Isra'íl. No one can do more than to fulfil his own nature, and the natural inclinations are not to be restrained; for if a man does restrain them by overcoming the self (*al-nafs*), yet there is a return to the natural disposition (*al-tab*).' And again he would say, 'The natural disposition becomes fixed (*tamallaka*)', or as some report, 'Whoever undertakes what is not in accord with his own disposition invites and calls down destruction upon himself; for everyone returns one day to his own character (*shíma*), even though he take to himself other qualities for a while.'

"People were very friendly towards him and he wished them to think that he was without awe and sternness (*naẓar wa'l'ubús*). Had he abandoned this cheerful and gentle manner they would most certainly have withdrawn themselves from him. So he would jest in order that they should have a good time, and he would pause in order to let his companions stop to look at the rough fellows who were playing.

"Once he said to the Bani 'Arfida, 'In comparison with the teaching of the Jews and Christians, in our religion there is latitude (*fusḥa*).' He referred to the freedom there is in Islam in regard to weddings, and to the public notice that is required (among Jews and Christians) for marriage, and to their restrictions in regard to banquets and entertainments, and to warnings about manifesting pleasure. But he did not contradict the statement he had made, 'For I am not of a sporting disposition, for surely sport is something useless', but when he would jest he would not say more than was true."

These summaries by Muslim writers of Muhammad's personal characteristics show that in the primitive Síra, from which they have gathered all their biographical material, the picture of the Prophet is "a perfectly natural picture", as Professor Arthur Jefferey has written, "where we find him speaking and acting as we might

21. "*Mufíd al-'Ulúm*", Cairo, A.H. 1330, p. 30. 22. Ibid, p. 80.

expect an Arab reformer in that environment and at that date would do". It is a picture, moreover, of a figure "which claims our sympathy and frequently stirs our imagination".[23]

The development of "the mythical Muhammad" is seen to a limited extent in the primitive Síra, and it reaches most fantastic extremes in the glowing narratives of later biographers. There is little to be found, however, in this development that is of interest from the standpoint of ethics. Only a passing reference need be made to the gradual ascription to Muhammad of pre-existent conscious life, and to the idea that many thousand years before God created Heaven and Earth he created the "Light of Muhammad"[24]; to the tracing of his genealogy back beyond his great-great-grandfather 'Abd al-Manáf to Ishmael the son of Abraham, and then on back through Noah and "Mattushalakh" to Enoch (Idris) and thence to Adam[25]; to the statement that when Muhammad's mother, Amina, was pregnant, a spirit appeared to her and said, "Thou art bearing the Lord of this people, so say at his birth, 'I place him under the protection of the one God, that he may protect him against the envious', and call his name *Muhammad*"[26]; and to the story related by 'Urwa ibn Zubair[27] that one of the idols that was worshipped by the Quraish had fallen on its face, and that when they had twice put it back in position they heard a voice, which seemed to come from the idol, and which declared:[28]

> Rejoicing because of the child,
> And radiant with his light,
> Are all the mountain passes of the earth,
> Both in the east and the west.
> And bowing down to him are all the idols,
> And trembling are all the hearts of kings,
> Throughout the world from fear.

Usually these flights of imagination on the part of the traditionists, as they developed the mythical Muhammad, were without any ethical implication, though it may be noted that the infant's innate capacity to judge what is right is portrayed in the tradition that "having regard to justice, he halved his wet-nurses's breasts with his foster brother".[29]

23. Professor Arthur Jeffery, art. "Muhammad: Real and Unreal", in the *International Review of Missions*, vol. xviii, p. 395.
24. For this conception, elaborated from the Qur'án (xxiv. 35), cf. Tor Andrae, *Die Person Muhammads* . . ., 1917, pp. 318–26.
25. Ibn Hishám, *Síra*, vol. i, pp. 1–2.
26. Ibid., vol. i, p. 170.
27. Ibid., vol. i, p. 172.
28. Koelle, *Muhammad and Muhammadanism*, London, 1889, p. 260.
29. Ibid., trans. from the *Rawzat al-Ahbáb*. Cf. also Ibn Hishám, *Síra*, i, p. 174 and Ibn Sa'd, *Ṭabaqát*, I. i, p. 69.

ADAB

If we keep in mind the fact that in Islam religion includes all of life, we may say that in the beginning the *adab* books had to do with religious education, or moral instruction, with emphasis rather on cultural values than on legal requirements. Professor Goldziher has pointed out in his article on "Adab" in the *Encyclopædia of Islam* that in both the heathen and the Islamic times *adab* has signified "the noble and humane tendency of the character and its manifestation in the conduct of life and social intercourse". And he cites the tradition that "it can almost be asserted that *adab* equals two-thirds of religion".

First there was a grouping of the sayings of the Prophet and his companions with reference to recognized virtues, such as silence, humility, tranquillity, and steadfastness. Due attention was given also to what had been said about vices, such as envy, greed, frivolity, and prodigality. An excellent example of a book that contains a mass of traditions that are classified in this manner is "The Treasury of Workmen in Traditions of Sayings and Deeds" (*Kanz al-'Ummál fí Sunan al-Aqwál wa'l-Af'ál*), which was written by Alá 'al-Dín ibn Mutaqqí (d. A.D. 1567), and which is published on the margin of the Cairo six-volume edition of the *Musnad* of Ibn Hanbal.[30] To give an example of the way in which sayings that have been ascribed to the Prophet on the authority of his more intimate companions have been assembled on a particular subject, we may cite part of the passage in the *Kanz al-'Ummál* that emphasizes the importance of a good disposition (*husn al-khulq*):[31]

> The believers who are the most perfect in faith are those who are the happiest in disposition.
>
> A good disposition is a bond of friendship from the mercy of Allah.
>
> A good disposition melts offences as the Sun melts ice.
>
> A good disposition is the greatest of Allah's creations.
>
> He who has a good disposition will receive the same reward as one who has merit from fasting and prayer.
>
> The *summum bonum* (*'aḥsanu'l-ḥusni*) is a good disposition.

As European and American writers study the Ḥadíth literature more assiduously, it is becoming evident how wide Christian influence was in the development of Muslim thought. In an article on "The Growth of the Muhammad Legend" Professor Joseph Horovitz remarked on a tendency that is readily observed in Muslim theology: "Not naïvely, as did the popular imagination, but consciously and deliberately, the theologians transferred to Muhammad what they had heard in the miracle-legends related to those of other

30. Cf. Brockelmann, *A.L.G.*, ii. 151 (153).

31. *Kanz al-'Ummál*, ed. Cairo on the margin of the *Musnad* of Ibn Hanbal, pp. 130 ff.

faiths. This process of the assimilation of the miracles performed by earlier saints and prophets, which was made imperative as it were by the requirements of the popular faith and by compulsion of the theological propaganda, had at the time when John of Damascus held his disputations (*c*. A.D. 750) progressed so far that the vacuum in the story of the Prophet's childhood and young manhood was already quite filled in with typical saint legends, and his whole career embellished with signs and miracles."

At this point it may be well to mention that probably no Christian has had such a remarkable influence on Islamic thought as John of Damascus. His grandfather, Mansur ibn Sarjun, was the Christian financial administrator who aided in the capitulation of Damascus to Khalid in A.D. 635. He was accordingly retained in his position by the Muslims, and his son was in due time appointed as his successor. Eventually the grandson, the young John, who associated as an intimate friend of Mu'awiyah's son Yezíd, also succeeded his father as the financial administrator of Damascus.

In the meantime the capital city of Christian Syria had become the capital city of the Muslim Empire. John of Damascus, in his position of high honour, was respected for his devotion to his Christian faith, and from the debates that were held in the Caliph's court, in which he took a prominent part, we are fortunate in having surviving accounts from both sides.

Of the writings of John of Damascus, who retired from administrative work and gave his last years to contemplation and literary work, we have an apologetic trilogy—the *Dialectica*, the *De Haeresibus*, and the *De Fide Orthodoxa*. There is also the *Disputatio Christiani et Saraceni*, along with its counterpart, the *Disputatio Saraceni et Christiani*.

Richard Bell mentions that "we see, even in the first two centuries, the biography of Muhammad being decked out with all kinds of miraculous and legendary stories with which we are familiar in the case of the Christian saints and Jewish rabbis". Miracle stories "found their way so early into the accounts of the Prophet's expeditions", and "they gather numerously round his birth, his escape from Mecca at the Hijra, and round his call to the prophetic office".

Of the miracles that were ascribed to the Prophet's maturer years at this early period we may mention those that were cited by 'Ali Ṭabarí in his *Kitáb al-Dín wa Dawla*. This author, who gives the Muslim reports of the debates that were held at the court of the Umayyads as early as the caliphate of al-Muttawakil (A.D. 846–61), accepted the Night Journey of Muhammad as an actual event, and ascribed to him such other miracles as that Lahab was eaten by a lion at his command, that Walíd ibn Mughira had died of a wound in his foot to which Muhammad had pointed, that Muhammad had met Aswad ibn 'Abd al-Yaghuth and had made a sign towards his abdomen, whereupon he became dropsical and died, that a camel once addressed Muhammad intelligibly, that a wolf testified to his status as a prophet, that at times trees walked at his command, and that on occasion he would miraculously provide water.[32]

One of the primary contributions to Muslim ethical thought from this widespread and long-continued Christian influence has come through the ascription of sayings to Muhammad that are patterned after sayings of Jesus. "It is of course not an accident", as Brockelmann observes, "but is quite in keeping with the importance, which is becoming more and more evident, of Christianity for the intellectual life of ancient Arabia, that New Testament sayings are common among Arabic proverbs, notably from the Sermon on the Mount." From the seventh chapter of the gospel of Matthew, al-Maidaní[33] has recorded proverbs that are obviously derived from the following verses:

2. For with what judgement ye judge ye shall be judged: and with what measure ye mete it shall be measured unto you.
15. Beware of false prophets, who come to you in sheep's clothing, but inwardly are ravening wolves.
16. By their fruits ye shall know them. Do men gather grapes of thorns or figs of thistles?

Among other familiar New Testament quotations that are encountered in books of Arabic proverbs are these four[34]:

Matt. 9. 24:	"for the damsel is not dead, but sleepeth".
Matt. 17. 2:	"his face did shine as the sun, and his garments became white as the light".
Matt. 23. 24:	"Ye blind guides, which strain out the gnat, and swallow the camel."
Gal. 6. 7:	"Be not deceived; God is not mocked: for whatsoever a man soweth, that shall he also reap."

During the first three centuries of Islam the sayings ascribed to Muhammad were still in a fluid state and there were renegade Christians and others who wished to strengthen the Muslim polemic in Christian communities. They made their influence felt in the formulation of sayings which they ascribed to Muhammad that would not be ethically unlike those of Christ. The following examples are in point:[35]

32. *The Moslem World*, ed. S. M. Zwemer, vol. x, pp. 49 ff.; Richard Bell, *The Origin of Islam in its Christian Environment*, pp. 199–200; and *Islam and Christian Theology*, by J. W. Sweetman, vol. i, pt. i, p. 70.

33. Maidaní, *Majma al-Amthál*, ii. 67; i. 192; and i. 34. Cf. also the book of the same name by Abu Hilál Asharí, which is printed on the margin of the Cairo edition of al-Maidaní.

34. Maidaní, op. cit., ii. 113, 67, 259, 73.

35. *Sukhanán-i-Muhammad*, Nos. 14, 21, 63, 306.

(*a*) Those similar to the "Golden Rule"—"Therefore all things whatsoever ye would that men should do to you, do ye even so to them" (Matt. 7. 12):

1. Seek for mankind that of which you are desirous for yourself, that you may be a believer;
   Treat well as a neighbour the one who lives near you, that you may be a Muslim.
2. That which you want for yourself seek for mankind.
3. The most righteous of men is the one who is glad that men should have what is pleasing to himself, and who dislikes for them what is for him disagreeable.
4. Whatever you abhor for yourself, abhor it also for others, and whatever you desire for yourself desire also for others.

(*b*) The "Lord's Prayer" is changed into an incantation[36]:

If any man suffers, or a brother of his suffers, let him say: "Our Lord God, who art in heaven, hallowed by Thy name; Thy power is in heaven and on earth; as Thy mercy is in heaven, so practise Thy mercy on earth; forgive us our fault and our sins, thou art the Lord of the good men; send down mercy from Thy mercy, and healing from Thy healing, on this pain, that it may be healed again."

(*c*) Other instances:[37]

1. "The man who does good and keeps it secret, so that his left hand does not know what his right hand has done."
2. "My companions are in relationship to my community as salt is to food, for food without salt is of no use."

In connexion with the development of the "ideal" as contrasted with the "real" Muhammad, it is well to recall that there had been a thorough-going Muslim occupation of Syria, Mesopotamia, and Egypt long before the recognized collections of traditions were compiled. In the newly occupied countries the followers of Islam were not infrequently called upon to compare Muhammad with Christ, and the more the Muslims came to know about Christ the more Christ-like their ideal of Muhammad became. This idealizing of Muhammad, obviously on the model of the life of Jesus Christ, led to declarations about happenings in his lifetime which are not mentioned in the Qur'án.

"As pre-existence was ascribed to Christ, so it was to Muhammad. As Gabriel announced Jesus to the Virgin Mary, so he did to Amina, the mother of Muhammad. As the angel gave the name of Jesus before he was born, so in the case of Muhammad. As Jesus in infancy was presented in the Temple, so was Muhammad in the national sanctuary of Arabia. As Jesus in the beginning of his ministry had to

36. L. E. Browne, *Eclipse of Christianity in Asia*, pp. 126–36, with Goldziher's quotation from Abú Dá'úd, *Kitáb al-Ṭibb*, Delhi, 2nd ed., p. 187.

37. Goldziher, *Muhammadanische Studien*, ii, pp. 384, 391, 392.

pass through an ordeal of Satanic temptation, so did Muhammad. As Jesus chose twelve apostles, so Muhammad chose twelve companions. As Jesus ascended into heaven, so did Muhammad; and so on."[38]

In the more advanced examples of Muslim "Adab" writings each chapter begins with sayings of the Prophet on a particular subject, which are followed by confirmatory passages from the Qur'án and illustrative incidents in early Muslim history, and to this will be added apt quotations from the poets. The following selections from al-Máwardí's (d. A.D. 1058) *Kitáb Adab al-Dunya wa'l-Dín* ("A Book of Secular and Religious Culture"), which he is said to have written at the age of eighty-six, will be seen to conform to this accepted outline.[39]

Forbearance (al-ḥilm) and *Anger* (al-ghaḍab): Muhammad b. Ḥárith al-Halálí has related that Gabriel descended upon the Prophet and said, "O Muhammad, I come to you with the noblest ethical attainments (*mukárim al-akhláq*) in this world and the next. Take pardon (*'afw*) and the command to proclamation (*'amr bi'l-'araf*) and avoid the ignorant (*'i'ráḍ 'an al-jáhilín*)."

Sufyán b. 'Ayaina has related that the Prophet said when this verse came down, "O Gabriel, what is this?" He replied, "Do not inform anybody about it until I ask the Knowing One." Then Gabriel returned and said, "O Muhammad, surely your Lord commands you to pray for the one who casts you off, to give to the one who denies you, and to forgive the one who injures you."

Hishám has related from al-Hasan that the Prophet had stated, "Is it not permissible that one of you should be like Abi Ḍamḍam, for when he went forth from his house he said, 'O Allah, I will give alms in proportion to my profit to Thy servants.'" And it is related from the Prophet that he said, "Surely Allah loves the man who leads a life of forbearance and hates the obscene man of bad morals." And he said also, "From forbearance comes nobility and from understanding there is increase (*izdád*)."

One of the educationalists (*'udabá'*) has said, "Whoever plants the tree of forbearance gathers the fruit of peace." And one of the philologists (*al-bulaghá'*) has remarked, "Nothing wards off hazards (*al-a'ráḍ*) like the flat of the sword (*al-ṣafḥ*, i.e. restraint) and qualities of good repute (*al-a'ráḍ*)." And one of the poets has said, "My zeal was to seek the noblest ethical attainments; I loathed criticizing, even when men were at fault; I forgave slander with forbearance, the wickedness of the man who is quick to revile, who fears the one who is afraid of him, and who fails to esteem the one who fears not."

38. Professor Arthur Jeffery, "Muhammad: Real and Unreal", in the *International Review of Missions*, vol. xviii, pp. 395 ff.

39. Máwardí, *Kitáb Adab al-Dunya wa'l-Dín*, A.H. 1315, pp. 163–6, and 170–1.

At this point al-Máwardí defines *al-ḥilm* as "a restraint of self (*ḍabt al-nafs*) from the vehemence of anger", and for this self-restraint he names ten contributing causes:

1. Pity for people who are ignorant (*al-rahmat li'l-juhál*).
2. The exercise of power over vindictiveness (*al-qudrat 'ala'l-intisár*).
3. Holding one's self above using abuse (*al-tarfi' 'ani'l-sibáb*).
4. Making light of the evil-doer (*al-istihnát bi'l-musí'*).
5. Embarrassment in answering (*istiḥyá' min jazá' al-jawáb*).
6. Showing favour in spite of abuse (*tafaḍḍul 'ala'l-sibáb*).
7. Disdaining and stopping abuse (*istinkáf al-sibáb wa qaṭ' al-sibáb*).
8. The fear of requital in accord with the answer (*al-khawf min al-'uqubat 'ala'l-jawáb*).
9. Kind treatment because of former assistance and needful respect (*ri'ayat li yadi sálifati wa ḥurmati lá' imati*).
10. Circumvention and relying on opportunities of concealment (*al-makr wa ṭawaqqu' al-furasi'l-khifyati*).

Qazi Ahmad Mian Akhtár, who has written recently a sketch of the life and works of al-Máwardí (*Islamic Culture*, July 1944), has shown how he was esteemed for his moral courage. When in A.D. 1079 the Buwaihid prince Jalal al-Dawlah brought pressure upon the Caliph al-Qa'im to obtain the right to designate himself "King of Kings", al-Máwardí had manifested his disapproval by absenting himself from the court. In the end, however, Jalal al-Dawlah told him that he appreciated that his opposition had been free from any selfish motive, and assured him that he greatly admired him for his moral courage.

The importance that he assigned to reason has led some Muslim writers to consider that al-Máwardí had a definitely Mu'tazilite tendency. He certainly held Qadarite opinions, and the Qadarites and the Mu'tazilites had much in common, particularly in Basra, where, as von Kremer has observed, "for the first time the doctrine of Free Will, which had its origin at Damascus, was developed into a rationalistic school of theology, which subsequently played a distinguished rôle under the name of Mu'tazilite".

The second example of this type of moral discourse from al-Máwardí is on *al-sidq wa'l-kidhb* ("Truth and Falsehood"):

"Allah the Most High, who is the most truthful of all speakers, has declared (in the Qur'án): 'Then will we invoke and lay the malison of Allah upon those that lie' (3. 54, Rodwell trans.). The Most High hath said also, 'Surely they invent a lie who believe not in the signs of Allah' (16. 107, Rodwell trans.).

"And from the Prophet is it related that he said to Hasan b. 'Ali: 'Repel that which causes you to have suspicion with that which does not cause you suspicion; for surely falsehood (*al-kidhb*) is the ground of suspicion (*riba*) and truth (*al-ṣidq*) is the basis of assurance (*ṭuma'nína*).' From the Prophet also is related the saying, 'May Allah be merciful to the commander (*amír*) whose language is most conciliatory, whose contention is least, whose word adheres most clearly to the way of truth, and who does not report idle talk with his tongue.'

"Sufyán b. Salím has related that someone asked the Prophet, 'Is it possible that a believer may be a coward?' He answered, 'Yes.' Then he was asked, 'Is it possible that he may be a miser?' He replied, 'Yes.' Again he was asked, 'Is it possible that he may be a liar?' To this he said, 'No.'

"Ibn Abbás has remarked in regard to the saying of the Most High, 'And clothe not the Right (*al-ḥaqq*) with the Vain (*al-báṭil*)' (2. 39), that it is equivalent to saying, 'Do not mix truth with falsehood.'

"It is said in the book called *Manthúr al-Ḥikam* ("A Scattered Collection of Wise Sayings", a MS. of which is in the Yale University Library), 'Falsehood is a thief (*al-laṣṣ*), for a thief is one who steals your property, and falsehood steals your reason (*'aql*).' One of the learned scholars said, 'Dumbness (*al-kharas*) is better than falsehood and truth of speech is the best of good fortune.' One of the philologists said, 'The truthful man, though he be from those who are so avaricious as to suck their ewes, is still respectable (*jalíl*), whereas the liar, though he be from those who are favoured household servants, is contemptible (*dhalíl*).' One of the educationalists said, 'There is no sword like the Right and no helper like the Truth.' And one of the poets said, 'There is nothing, when you stop to consider, that takes away manliness and elegance like the lie (*al-kidhb*), which has no good in it, and drives away the confidence of men.' "

While al-Máwardí regarded the authority of the Qur'án and the Ḥadíth with respect, yet, like the Christian scholar John Scotus, who lived almost two hundred years earlier, he betrayed a basic belief that authority springs from reason, not reason from authority. Accordingly we find that at this point in his discourse on "Truth and Falsehood", he undertook to express the idea that reason demands veracity, and it is well to recall that this was nearly eight hundred years before Immanuel Kant's effort to demonstrate the rational necessity of truthfulness, in his *Critique of Practical Reason*. Like Kant, al-Máwardí also reasoned on practical considerations:

"The lie is the sum of all wrong, the origin (*aṣl*) of all blame, and this is on account of the evil of its results and the wickedness of its consequences. It leads to slander (*al-namímat*) and slander causes violent hatred (*al-baghḍá'*). Moreover, violent hatred accounts for enmity (*al-'adáwa*), and there is no security or rest along with enmity.

"It is said, 'he who has retained his veracity (*al-ṣidq*) has kept his true friend (*al-ṣádiq*)'. Truth and falsehood have to do with accounts that are given of things that have already occurred (*al-akhbár al-máḍiya*), whereas the accomplishment of a vow (*al-wafá'*) and a breach of promise (*al-khulf*) have to do with agreements for the future (*al-mawá'íd al-mustaqbalát*). Truthfulness (*al-ṣidq*) is the narration of anything as it really was, and falsehood (*al-kidhb*) is the narration of anything as different from what it was.

"Now for each one of these there is a motive (*dawá'*) : the motive for the truth is one that must be accepted (*lázima*), and the motive for falsehood is one that must be avoided (*'ariḍa*). In regard to the truth, we may say that reason requires it as a *cause* and that divine law demands it in corroboration. But in regard to falsehood, we recognize that reason seeks to avoid it and that law is in opposition to it. It is permissible, therefore, that true reports should be spread abroad, and that at intervals they should be repeated: but it is not permissible that false reports should be disseminated, because agreement of mankind is on the basis of the truth, whereas falsehood does not satisfy.

"With reference to the demand for the truth, it is very possible that a large number of people should be united in opposition to it until they really get the facts, and then a considerable number will separate themselves from those with whom they had (at first) agreed.

"A report will be accepted as true because men realize that truth (alone) affords advantage or profit (*nafi'a*). The general agreement of men on a demand that is profitable is possible, but a large number of those who had not been in agreement beforehand will not reach a common opinion on the narration of a report that is false. This is because it would not be profitable but injurious. For it is most unusual for many people to be in agreement on a demand that is not profitable. Thus it is that the agreement of people on the truth is regarded as lawful, by reason of the unanimity of their demand. For when they are in accord with truth and falsehood makes a demand, they instinctively mention the things they know to the contrary.

" As to the nature of this demand of the truth, assuredly part of it is due to reason, because falsehood requires disapproval. It has no characteristic to make it attractive, for it neither brings what is profitable nor drives away what is harmful, whereas reason demands in an action that which may be approved and forbids undertaking that which is disapproved."

The rather rambling way in which al-Máwardí argues here for the necessary acceptance of the truth, on the basis of its approval by mankind in general, is not wholly convincing in these modern times, when highly developed agencies for disseminating falsehood have shown how easily vast multitudes of people may be misled. However, we may see in al-Máwardí's point of view a laudable conviction that truth must ultimately prevail, and a faith in the capacity of mankind to recognize and appreciate the value of truth when through experience they learn to distinguish it from falsehood. He has a wholesome regard for the authority of human reason, as it follows the trial-and-error method in making laws or in otherwise meeting the vicissitudes of life.

But what did al-Máwardí and others of the writers of the *adab* literature mean by reason? We find the declaration of Gustave E. von Grunebaum (*Medieval Islam*, p. 252), in accord with a statement in the *Irshád* (I. 19), that "elegance, as the criterion of formal perfection, is supported by taste. And the reason, *'aql*, of the *adíb* is not the earnestly searching and argumentative tool of the philosopher; it is rather a compound of good sense and insight into the nature of people and the ways of the world. Therefore it could be said that there is no religious ethics, *dín*, without discretion, *ḥayá'*, and no discretion without prudence, *'aql*. Nor can there be discretion, prudence, and ethos without *adab*."

One of the most famous books of this character, a splendid compendium of political philosophy, of ingeniously constructed verses, and of ethical instruction, is the *'Uyún al-Akhbár*, which was written by Ibn Qutaiba (d. A.D. 889). The author explains that he wrote this book from the point of view of the *kátib*, or court writer, who would be expected to be master of facetious remarks and apt literary references on a wide range of subjects. The book is divided into five parts of two chapters each. The part on Political Science treats of Government and War, the part on Ethical Qualities explains Nobility and Natural Disposition; the part on Scholars and Saints tells of Learning and Asceticism; the part on Social Obligations is devoted to Brethren and Needs; and the part on Domestic Life gives details about Food and Women. The moral philosophy of this book, as well as of other books of similar character, such as the *'Iqd al-Faríd*, by Ibn 'Abd Rabbihi (d. A.D. 940), and the *Kitáb al-Hayawán*, by al-Jáhiz (d. A.D. 869), is much the same as that which we find in the Ḥadíth. This fact is clearly indicated in the following typical illustrations, which show that public taste or sentiment required a writer or a speaker to take his text from the Qur'án or the Ḥadíth first, and that afterwards he could proceed to develop his subject according to his literary erudition.

In his chapter on Nobility (*al-su'dud*), which is perhaps best translated as "the authority of a chief", Ibn Qutaiba has begun the section on *modesty* (*al-ḥayá'*) by citing two brief sayings of the Apostle of Allah: "Modesty is a portion of faith", and "Rarity of modesty is unbelief." Also, when he introduced what he had to write on *tranquillity and anger* (*al-ḥilm wa'l-ghaḍab*), he quoted several traditions from the Apostle:

1. "Surely one of you will find that he should be like Abi Ḍamḍam, for when he went out from his house he was accustomed

to say, 'O Allah, I have given alms to thy servants for mine own honour.'"

2. "Anger is a coal that burns in the belly of the son of Adam, though his eyes do not see its red colour yet his jugular veins are inflated."

3. "When a man made the request, 'O Apostle of Allah, give me advice', the answer was, 'Do not get angry.' Then the Apostle came back to him and said, 'Do not get angry', and a third time he said, 'Do not get angry.'"

In his chapter on "Natures and Reprehensible Dispositions" Ibn Qutaiba began the section on *envy* (*al-ḥasad*) with the tradition that the Apostle said, "There are three things, no one of which is good—quick temper (*al-ṭayaratu*), suspicion (*al-ẓannu*), and envy (*al-ḥasad*)." When someone asked, "And what is the way of escape from these things?" Muhammad replied, "When you are in temper do not answer, when you only suspect do not be certain, and when you feel envy do not become covetous." Similarly his section on *backbiting and faults* (*al-ghaibat wa'l-'ayúb*) is opened with the tradition that the Apostle once asked a group of his followers, "Shall I tell you who are the worst of you?" When they assented he said, "The worst of you are those who divulge slanderous news, who destroy friendship, and who overcome those who are innocent of crime." The section on *falsehood* (*al-kidhb*) begins with the well-known tradition that the Apostle said, "Falsehood is permitted only on three occasions—war, which is itself deceit (*khud'at*), or when a man brings about reconciliation between two persons, or when a man seeks to please his woman." And in the section on *bad disposition* we find that it is first mentioned that the Apostle of Allah said, "There are two bad habits (*khaṣlatán*, which is a word that also means *branches*) that do not mature among the faithful, (1) bad disposition and (2) miserliness (*bukhl*)."

Ibn Qutaiba's section on "Human Natures" (*ṭabá'iu'l-insán*) begins with an interesting and curious tradition that is suggestive of the early Pythagorean influence in Arabian thought. This tradition, however, is not attributed to Muhammad, but it is something rather that Wahab b. Munabbih is said to "have found in the Tawrát", and it proceeds as though Allah himself were speaking: "Verily when I created Adam I gave him a body with four qualities. Then I made these qualities hereditary in his offspring, to increase in their bodies, which will grow by virtue of them until the Day of Judgement. These four qualities are moist (*raṭb*), dry (*yábis*), hot (*sukn*), and cold (*baríd*). And so it was that I made him of dust (*taráb*) and water (*má'*), and placed in him soul (*nafs*) and spirit (*ruḥ*). The dryness of every body was by influence of the dust, its moisture was due to the water, its heat to the soul, and its coolness to the spirit. Then after this first creation I gave the body four other created things.

They are the supports of the body, for its separate recognition and continuance. For the body will not continue except by them and its individual existence will not remain except by them. They are the measure of bile (*al-ṣufrá'*), the measure of spleen (*al-sawdá'*), the measure of blood (*al-dam*), and the measure of phlegm (*al-balgham*). Then I caused some of these things created to have their place in others. I made the place of dryness in the measure of spleen, the place of moisture in the blood, the place of coolness in the phlegm, and the place of heat in the bile. Whatever the body, these four created things were in due proportion in it. Each one of these things in a fourth part, no more and no less, perfected the health of the body and kept its structure in proportion. If one of them should be excessive, it would constrain and overwhelm the others. Disease would then come upon its sisters from the side from which there was excess. Likewise if there would be deficiency in any one of these things, the others would prevail against it and disease would come because of the deficiency, until the component elements would be weakened in their strength and endurance."

After Allah had given this explanation Wahab went on to say: "And He placed his reason (*'aql*) in his brain (*damágh*) and in his heart (*sirr*—cf. also 'Iqd-i-Faríd) and in his whole body; and his anger in his liver (*kabd*); and his sternness or severity (*ṣaráma*) in his heart; his terror (*ru'b*) in his lung (*ri't*); his laugh in his spleen (*ṭiḥál*); and his sorrow and joy in his face. And He placed in him three hundred and sixty joints."[40]

At an early period in Islamic literature it may be seen that history was regarded as a useful adjunct to moral instruction. The point of view was that "history perpetuates the record of virtuous and evil actions and offers them as examples for the edification of future generations". As may be easily imagined, "such a plea was highly acceptable to the host of moralists and *dilettanti*; for if history were merely a branch of ethics, not a science, they need not scruple to adapt their so-called historical examples to their own ends".[41] There was accordingly no close examination of sayings that were attributed to Muhammad or to 'Ali, and no effort to establish their genuineness, if they were convenient for the treatment of the subject at hand.

Ibn Qutaiba affords examples of this attitude, at times, in his "Choice Histories" (*'Uyún al-Akhbár*). In the chapter on "Friends" (*ikhwán*) he attributes to 'Ali a paragraph of practical advice on the necessity of avoiding evil companions:[42]

40. Ibn Qutaiba, *'Uyún al-Akhbár*, ii, p. 62.
41. H. A. R. Gibb, *Encyclopædia of Islam*, art. "Ta'rikh".
42. *'Uyún al-Akhbár* ("Choice Histories"), by Abu Muhammad 'Abdulla ibn Muslim ibn Qutaiba al-Dinawárí, 4 vols., published Cairo, 1343/1925. Cf. vol. iii, pp. 69, 84, 89, 133, 139.

> Do not associate with an immoral person, for he will certainly influence you by his conduct. He will be pleased to have you like him and will clothe you with the worst of his vices. Base and shameful as it may be, he will simply find profit in you and get you to pay his expenses.
>
> Do not associate with a fool, for though he will exert himself on your behalf he will not assist you. Frequently when he wishes to help you he will cause you loss. His silence is preferable to his speech, you would rather have him far away than nearby, in fact his death is better than his life.
>
> Do not associate with a liar, for his companionship will bring you no advantage. He will tell others your affairs, and will relate the affairs of others to you, and that to such an extent that if he were to tell the truth he would not be believed.

A few pages further on (p. 84), the Prophet is credited with several statements in general appreciation of the importance of family ties:

> Recognize your relations, hold fast your family ties, for there is no nearness of relationship when it is cut off, even though it be nearby; as there is no distance about it when it is maintained, though it be far away.
>
> It is right that a man should cleave to those who have been his father's friends.
>
> The sister's son is to be considered as one of the family, and likewise the freed slave and the ally.
>
> Blood relationship is a root from the Merciful, who said, "Whoever stands by you, then I stand by him, and whoever forsakes you, then I forsake him."
>
> Whoever wishes to have his life prolonged and his resources increased, let him cherish the friendship of his blood relations.

On the question of the extent of paternal authority it is related that a man came to the Prophet and said, "My father is about to take from me something that is mine." The Prophet replied, "Have you not learned that you yourself and whatever is yours belongs to your father?" (p. 86).

The Prophet is also quoted in support of the eldest brother's special rights: "The right of the oldest of a group of brothers over those who are younger is like the right of the father over children" (p. 89).

From the chapter of "Necessities" (*ḥawā'ij*), we may quote from a section that is devoted to the problems of those who have to solicit financial help. A celebrated instance is mentioned (p. 126) of a philosopher who showed his ability to use his rare knowledge of proverbs to advantage. He had waited a long time at the gate of the palace of one of the kings of Persia, when at last he persuaded the guard to take a note from him to the king. It was but a bit of paper on which there were four lines written:

Hope and necessity have brought me to you.
Destitution cannot wait to make a seasonable request.
Returning unrewarded would give enemies cause for laughter.
Either "Yes" will be a ripe fruit, or "No" a green persimmon.

We are told that when the King read this he was so agreeably impressed with each separate line that he gladly decreed that the suppliant should be rewarded with 16,000 *mithqáls* of silver.

It may sometimes serve to mollify the aggravation that is usually felt when one is besieged by suppliants to recall that the Prophet is reported to have made the remark (p. 133): "Present your needs to good-looking people." On another occasion this statement was slightly expanded: "Trust those who are handsome for your needs, because a comely face is one of the greatest human blessings you may encounter."

Again we are told (p. 139) that it was Muhammad's habit not to refuse anyone who came with a need. Either he would provide it or he would dismiss the suppliant with some encouraging remark. When he was asked for what he did not have, he would sometimes answer, "God will do it!" But there is a saying given in this same connexion, from 'Umar ibn al-Khattab, that shows that the disposition to try to get things merely by asking soon had to be restrained: "Understand that coveting means poverty, and that giving up hope means becoming rich, for whoever gives up hope of a thing becomes independent of it."

As Professor Brockelmann has mentioned,[43] "the proverb is from its nature anonymous", but in Islamic literature the great majority of their proverbs have come to be attributed either to their Prophet himself, to one or other of his Companions or, in the case of the Shi'ite sect, to one of their designated "Imáms". Practically all of the books of religious instruction that are circulated throughout the Muslim world make use of these Arabic proverbs as moral maxims. As texts for discourses they are second only to citations from the Qur'án, and their range of subjects is surprisingly wide.

The way in which such short sayings were employed in some of the earliest compendiums of moral instruction may be seen in the *Káfí fí 'Ilm al-Dín*, by al-Kulaini (d. A.D. 941). In contrast to other traditionists al-Kulaini expanded his treatment of "Faith and Unbelief" (*al-Imán wa'l-Kufr*) to include such subjects as tenacity (*ṣabr*), gratitude (*shukr*), modesty (*ḥayá'*), gentleness (*ḥilm*), affability (*mudárá*), economy (*qaná'a*), and independence (*istighná*). And among the recognized evils he describes are hypocrisy (*riyá*), seeking authority (*ṭalab al-riyása*), anger (*ghaḍab*), envy (*ḥasad*), partisanship (*aṣabiya*), oppression (*ẓulm*), and falsehood (*kidhb*).

43. Brockelmann, *Encyclopædia of Islam*, art. "Mathal".

To show the use that is made of moral aphorisms in the development of these separate themes, the following sayings may be quoted from al-Kulaini's discussion of envy (*ḥasad*):

"'Envy will eat the faith as fire eats wood' is a saying that is ascribed to the Prophet. 'Fear Allah, and let not some of you be always envying others' is a saying that is attributed to Jesus.[44] 'Poverty is apt to lead to unbelief, and envy seeks to overcome Fate' is said to have been announced by Muhammad. The Imám Ja'far Ṣádiq is said to have declared: 'The plague of religion consists of envy, vanity, and pride.' On the authority of Muhammad, Moses is believed to have said: 'O Ibn 'Amrán, let not men envy one another what I give them of my bounty.' And the Imám Ja'far Ṣádiq declared: 'The believer is the one who wishes for the happiness of the other man, and who does not annoy him, whereas the hypocrite is the man who envies and who does not wish anyone else happiness.'"[45]

After it had become the accepted custom to collect worthwhile proverbs and to attribute them to Muhammad, to 'Ali, or to one or the other of the Companions or the Imáms, it was only a step further to credit them also with eloquent and appropriate speeches on significant occasions.

However, the early historian, Ibn al-Wádíḥ al-Ya'qúbí (d. A.D. 897), has devoted only twenty pages in his *History*[46] to "the addresses of the Apostle of Allah and his sermons and admonitions in regard to noble qualities (*al-akhláq al-sharífa*)", the nature of which may be seen in the following examples:

"O ye people, truly ye have indications (*ma'álim*), so follow after

44. This saying of Jesus is found in a tradition which Kulaini relates, and which we also find mentioned by Tha'álabí (d. A.D. 1035) in the *Qiṣás al-Anbíya* (ed. Bombay, 1878, pp. 541–2). As translated from the latter by the Rev. James Robinson in his *Christ in Islam*, p. 37 (Wisdom of the East Series), it is as follows: "It is related that he went out one day in his wandering, accompanied by one of his companions, who was a short man who attached himself greatly to Jesus. Then when Jesus came to the sea, he said, 'In the name of Allah, with health and certainty'; and he walked on the surface of the water. Then the short man said, 'In the name of Allah, with health and certainty'; and he also walked on the surface of the water. But wonder then entered into him and he said, 'This is Jesus, the Spirit of Allah, walking on the water, and I am walking on the water!' The narrator said: Then he sank in the water and appealed to Jesus, so Jesus reached out to him from the water and took him out and said to him, 'What did you say, O short one?' He told him what had pervaded his mind, and Jesus said to him, 'You have put yourself in a place other than that in which Allah put you and Allah abhorred you on account of what you said.' The man repented and returned to the rank in which Allah had placed him, so Jesus said, 'Fear Allah and do not envy one another.'"

45. Kulaini, *Káfí fí 'Ilm al-Dín*, lithographed Teheran, 2 vols., 1889. Cf. vol. i, *Usúl al-Kafí*, p. 344.

46. Ibn Waḍíḥ al-Ya'qúbí, *Historiae*, ed. Houtsma, 1883, vol. ii, pp. 98–121.

them; and truly ye have an end in view (*nihâya*), so seek to achieve it. The believer is indeed between two fears, one in regard to time that has passed, when he cannot know what Allah has been doing, and the other in regard to time that remains, when he cannot know what Allah will decree. Surely the true servant will seize from himself for himself, i.e. from *this*, his world now, and for *that*, his world hereafter —in youth before age, and in life before death. Such is the life of Muhammad also in Allah's hand! Death will not ignore even the favoured one, and the world affords no refuge save Paradise or the Fire!"

"Happiness comes to a man when his gain is lawful, when his natural disposition is good, and when his hidden thought is right. He sells quickly the remainder of his property and gives up excess of speech. He avoids people who corrupt him and is just towards those who benefit him. Surely he who knows Allah is one who fears Allah, and he who fears Allah keeps himself free from the world."

"Whoever observes in this world the one who is above him and emulates him, and observes the one who is below him and praises Allah for that in which he is able to excel him, Allah will surely put him on record as one who is thankful and steadfast. On the other hand, whoever observes in this world one who is beneath him and also one who is above him, and grieves over that in which the one has excelled him, surely Allah will not put him on record as thankful and steadfast."

"The man who is favoured with a thankful heart, a considerate tongue, a strong constitution and a healthy wife—he it is who is blessed with this world and the next."

"Happiness depends on two things, obedience and piety."

The several examples that al-Ya'qúbí gives of the speeches of 'Ali have to do solely with political events and are addressed to the people of Kufa.[47] Also those of 'Ali's letters that he mentions are only such as 'Ali would normally have sent as Caliph to his various lieutenant governors,[48] which is certainly a point in favour of this historian. But the meagre material that was furnished by al-Ya'qúbí failed to satisfy the desire of the Shi'ite community, in their more prosperous period, for a book that would exalt 'Ali far above the other Companions. A complete epitome of their own presentation of the history of Islam was needed. It is true that much had been accomplished by Kulaini and Ibn Babawaihi in compiling collections of traditions after the manner of the legists and theologians. But it remained for Saiyid Raḍí (d. A.D. 1015), who was highly esteemed for his Arabic scholarship and his knowledge of the poets, to produce a popular work that would set forth the whole Shi'ite history, faith, and culture

47. Ibn Wadíḥ al-Ya'qúbí, *Historiae*, ed. Houtsma, 1883, vol. ii, pp. 222, 225, and 229.

48. Ibid., op. cit., pp. 235–42.

in an orderly and graphic form, as though it had actually come from the tongue or the pen of 'Ali himself.[49]

This work was the *Nahj al-Balágha* ("The Open Road of Eloquence"), which Shi'ite Muhammadans ordinarily esteem as second only to the Qur'án, for it has come to be generally regarded as the book of the *Amír al-Mu'minín*, because it purports to give not only the several hundred short sayings of 'Ali, but also numerous examples of his letters and speeches. It was compiled fully three hundred and forty years after the death of 'Ali; and as much time had elapsed, it was easy to compensate for imperfections that had been observed in the records by adding such supplementary material as would foster the Shi'ite interpretation of events. While it was doubtless gratifying to the followers of the Imáms to have their partisan point of view thus dramatically presented—in the very words of 'Ali—yet there is every reason to believe that this book is not what it pretends to be. Bearing in mind the comparatively late date at which it was written, it seems rather remarkable that we should find as many as 240 of 'Ali's speeches preserved in such complete form. In connexion with every significant happening in his life he is here represented as having made an appropriate speech—at the time of the death of the Prophet, on the return from the Battle of Ṣiffín, in regard to the defection of Zubair and Ṭalha, in admonition of his son by the Hanifite woman, after the victory of the Battle of the Camel, in condemnation of the people of Basra, at the time homage was paid to 'Uthman, etc.

Of these 240 speeches, however, approximately one-half are neither political nor biographical, but have to do with general subjects of the Tradition books—such as the creation of the heavens and the earth and the angels, reproof of the followers of Shaitán, those who are unworthy to be judges, differences in human dispositions, death and the fear of death, Heaven and Hell, and the guidance of mankind. In fact, the contents of the *Nahj al-Balágha* definitely suggest that by the time of Saiyid Radí considerable progress had been made in both the compilation and the production of Shi'ite traditions, so that the literary undertaking of arranging them in a series of 240 complete speeches, 80 finished letters, and several hundred sententious short sayings was altogether feasible.

But from the point of view of ethics, even pious fictions may serve to reveal the contemporary moral consciousness. In general the Shi'ite tradition literature expresses the opinions and judgements of the opposition party, and it is clear that this opposition was fre-

49. MS. no. 291 in the *Catalogue of the Shrine Library*, Meshed, 3 vols., 1927, chapter "Akhbár". This manuscript, dated A.H. 701, is the oldest of the twelve manuscripts of the *Nahj al-Balágha* that are available in the library. The biographical sketch that is given in the Catalogue describes the author, Saiyid Radí (d. 406/1015), as outstanding in his knowledge of Arabic literature. The text of the *Nahj al-Balágha* that is most esteemed was lithographed in Meshed in 1892.

quently on moral grounds. In agreement with what would naturally be expected, the books of moral and religious instruction, whether for children or for adults, make wide use of such traditional sayings as can be easily related to questions of conduct. And furthermore, the incorporation of many essentially anonymous proverbs into the Ḥadíth literature, whether Shi'ite or Sunnite, was a natural consequence, for in all matters of conduct the recognized authority or standard in interpreting the Qur'án was always the example of the Prophet, or of 'Ali, or of one of the Companions.

4

PHILOSOPHICAL ETHICS IN ISLAM

FOR MUSLIMS the term *philosophy* (*falsafa*) came into use soon after their military occupation of Syria, Egypt, and Persia, when they recognized and appreciated the prevailing Greek culture. But in Islam, philosophy found its first field of development in speculative theology, the obvious aim of which was to state the accepted dogmas of their religion so as "to bring them into agreement with the demands of contemporary knowledge".[1]

While the influence of Greek thought in the East must be regarded as an ancient phenomenon, which was particularly evident when Palestine and Arabia were buffer states between the Ptolemies and the Seleucidae, and which had penetrated far into the ancient Persian Empire and on into India, nevertheless, in relation to subsequent Islamic culture, great importance is attached to the activity of the Christian scholars who first translated outstanding texts of Greek philosophers into the Syriac language. They had begun this work in A.D. 300, and they carried it on progressively—primarily from the centres of Edessa, Jundai-Sábúr, and al-Ḥíra—until approximately A.D. 700. This means that for 270 years before the birth of Muhammad the philosophic and scientific speculations of the Greeks were being translated gradually into the Syriac language. This translation work was going on throughout the 62 years of Muhammad's lifetime, and it continued for 68 years of early Muslim expansion and imperial organization. This latter period included the 38 years of the first four Caliphs—Abu Bakr, 'Umar, 'Uthman, and 'Ali—and the first 30 years of the Umayyad caliphate.

When we are told that Christian scholars and scribes, who worked under Arab patrons, began translating these existing Syriac translations of the Greek philosophers into the Arabic language in the period from A.D. 700 to 900, we should bear in mind that this Arab quest of further knowledge from the Greeks was being made at the same time that the traditional sayings of the prophet Muhammad were being compiled. Ibn Isḥáq, whose records survive only as they are quoted by Ibn Hishám and al-Ṭabarí, died in A.D. 768. Málik

1. Horten, *Encyclopædia of Islam*, art. "Falsafa".

ibn Anas, who compiled the *Muwatta*, which has been called "the first real appearance of the Ḥadíth in literature",[2] died in A.D. 795; Ibn Hishám in A.D. 833, Ibn Sa'd in A.D. 845, Ahmad ibn Hanbal in A.D. 855, al-Bukharí in A.D. 870, and Muslim in A.D. 874. These dates have been cited in order to emphasize the fact that the writings of several of the Greek philosophers were being translated from the Syriac into the Arabic language in the same general period in which the traditional sayings of Muhammad found their way into written Arabic. This fact may be found to be of importance in the study of the later developments in Muslim ethical literature as well as in law and theology. For not only were the above-named traditionists contemporary with the translators of Greek learning, but the early writers of the *adab* literature, the "humanities" or cultural writings, men such as al-Jáhiz (d. A.D. 868) and Ibn Qutaiba (d. A.D. 889), also belonged to this period. Others who related the sayings of Muhammad, but more from the viewpoint of historians than legists, were Abu Hanifa al-Dinawárí (d. A.D. 895), Ibn Wadíh al-Ya'qúbí (d. A.D. 897), and al-Tabarí (d. A.D. 922). It will give occasion to no surprise if we find sayings of Muhammad and of his Companions that have become somewhat "hellenized", particularly in chapters on *'ilm* (scientific knowledge), *'aql* (reason), and *akhláq* (ethics).

The earliest problems that faced Muslim philosophers had to do with the metaphysical foundation for the science of ethics. As they were likewise theological questions they have most generally been so considered, but the reader will recognize at once their striking importance for the Muslim system of ethics, which is admittedly on a theistic basis:

1. Is it necessary to postulate divine righteousness, and if so, then how can it be appreciated and stated without imposing a limitation of divine greatness?
2. To what extent must man have freedom in order that he may be responsible for his actions?
3. Is the Qur'án, as the *word* of Allah, to be considered as *eternal* in Allah's own being, or does it belong to the class of "things created"?
4. How is the *unity* of Allah to be stated in relation to His attributes?
5. What relations does Allah have with mankind and with the material universe?

EARLY RATIONALISTIC DISCUSSIONS

It has been said that "debates on predestination inaugurated rationalism in Islam".[3] The word *qadar* signifies the eternal "decree"

2. D. B. Macdonald, *Muslim Theology, Jurisprudence and Constitutional Theory*, p. 78.
3. Wensinck, *The Muslim Creed*, p. 53.

of Allah. "Everyone is guided to that for which he was created."[4] "Allah wrote down the decrees regarding the created world fifty thousand years before He created the heavens and the earth, while His throne was on the water."[5] Such were the traditional sayings of the Prophet, in accord with the declarations attributed to Allah in the Qur'án:

liv. 49 "Verily, everything have we created by decree (*qadar*)."

iii. 139 "It is not for any soul to die save by Allah's permission, written down for an appointed time."

ix. 51 "Say, 'Nought shall befall us save what Allah has written down for us.'"

For "the prevailing feature of Allah in the Qur'án is his *absoluteness*, His doing what He pleases without being bound by human rules. He extends His bounty (ii. 84), His mercy (ii. 99; iii. 67; xii. 56), and His wisdom (xxvii. 2) to whomsoever He pleaseth; He guideth in the right way (ii. 136, 209, 274; vi. 88; x. 26; xiv. 4) and He leaveth to go astray (xxiv. 34 ff.) whom He pleaseth; if He had so pleased He would have guided all men in the right way (xiii. 50); He createth what He pleaseth (v. 20) and formeth man in the womb as He pleaseth (iii. 4); He forgiveth unto whom He pleaseth (ii. 284; iii. 124; iv. 51 ff.); in short, He doeth what He pleaseth (iii. 35)."[6]

Before the end of the first century of Islam "Mu'bad al-Juhaní (d. A.D. 699) was the first who instituted discussions on the *qadar* at Basra",[7] and he and his followers rejected this conception. Strangely enough, they came to be known by the name of the very doctrine they opposed, which need not suggest more than that they kept bringing it forth for discussion. They were called the *Qadaríya*,[8] while those who supported absolute determinism were known as the *Jabríya*, a name which is derived from the verb *jabara*, which means "he compelled". Incidentally it meant also "to set a bone", which affords in the East an even more graphic illustration of compulsion than that of the potter and his vessel.

The man who soon came to be recognized as the leader of the Qadaríya was Ḥasan al-Baṣrí (d. A.D. 728), whom we must regard as having made a valuable contribution to the Muslim ethical consciousness, for he was inspired with the conviction that man's moral action requires at least some degree of freedom.

4. al-Bukhárí, *Ṣaḥíḥ*, bk. "janá'iz", p. 2.

5. Muslim, *Ṣaḥíḥ*, bk. "qadr", 17. The Qur'án states that before Allah created the heavens and the earth, his throne floated above the primeval waters (xi. 9). For a brief summary of the Qur'án's cosmogony, cf. Levy, *Sociology of Islam*, vol. ii, pp. 4–6.

6. Wensinck, *The Muslim Creed*, p. 84.

7. Muslim, *Ṣaḥíḥ*, bk. "qadr", 1; Wensinck, op. cit., p. 13.

8. *Encyclopædia of Islam*, arts. "Ḳadar" and "Ḳadaríya" and "Djabaríya".

While the Umayyads were in authority they had welcomed the doctrine of fatalism, for they were eager to claim that it indicated divine approbation of the *status quo* politically. After the devastating war that had occurred over the question of the succession in the Caliphate, the Umayyads were the first dynasty of rulers, and their poets praised them as those "whose rule was foreshadowed by the eternal decree of Allah". As represented in the *Aghaní*, the submissive subjects were expected to look upon even the oppressive acts of their rulers "in the light of Fate, whose acts no one should criticize". And when this principle was challenged by the Qadaríya it caused grave concern, so much so indeed that the Caliph 'Abd al-Malik and his general, al-Hajjáj, wrote to Ḥasan al-Baṣrí to call him to account for his revolutionary idea about men having a degree of freedom of will in their actions.

In the course of the epistle that he wrote on this subject Ḥasan al-Baṣrí argued that "in the Qur'án *qadar* is postulated as complete and absolute determinism, not only physical but ethical and spiritual as well. It deprives man of any initiative, any choice, any voluntary share in his conduct. Man's destiny can only be what Allah knew that, by His all-embracing *qadar*, it would be. Any endeavour on man's own behalf is doomed to fail, his fate having been determined beforehand by Allah's knowledge and volition. From the very womb of his mother man has been decreed to be 'blessed or afflicted'. Without any merit acquired, or any iniquity committed, his 'breast' is made wide and easy or strait and narrow. He is created for hell-fire or Paradise, just as he is formed tall or short, black or white. Accordingly he is rewarded for deeds he could not help performing and made to answer for others he had no way of preventing; as when the adulterer is punished for having begotten a child whose birth was, in truth, decreed by the will of Allah (xxii. 2). Man triumphs or suffers for works done, not by him, but in him, through him, despite of him."

In reply to this position of his opponents, which he has thus stated in a way to reduce it almost to absurdity, Ḥasan al-Baṣrí insisted that his predecessors, the Companions of the Prophet "never predicated of Allah anything except what Allah predicates of himself". He insisted that passages in the Qur'án on which such inferences might be based must be weighed against other passages that point to man's religious obligations in commands and prohibitions. "In these obligations Allah clearly and manifestly reveals what He pleases and desires of man, and what in man is obnoxious and offensive to Him. That man is nevertheless capable of doing what is *wrong in the eyes of Allah* shows that here, in the sphere of man's moral conduct, Allah's decree, His will, His knowledge, do not mean the same as in the sphere of man's physical existence. In teaching man to do what is good, in commanding man to refrain from what is evil, Allah reveals that here, in the realm of good and evil, predestination consists in the guidance of His teachings, that *qadar* here is defined by His command. Allah does not forbid man to be tall or punish him for being black. Therefore the only determinant of his physical existence is, of necessity, the *qadar* of Allah, man having therein no share of will, no power of change. But to apply this to man's moral destiny is to maintain that Allah openly, in His revealed teachings, desires of man one thing, but secretly, by His *qadar*, desires of him the opposite; or that He commands man to see and hear, yet predestinates him to be blind and deaf; it means, quite apart from gross blasphemy, to ascribe to Allah the contrary of what he ascribes to Himself."

This conviction that "*what Allah forbids is not from Him*" is an idea that Ḥasan al-Baṣrí frequently stressed. Bold in his accusations against the governors and their officials who sought to justify their acts of tyranny by pointing to the doctrine of absolute determinism, Ḥasan exclaimed: "Violence and tyranny are not of Allah! He does not order abominations! Guidance comes from Allah, but *error* is of man's own doing!"[9]

The most famous group of rationalists, into which the Qadaríya appear to have merged, and which began probably as a political party, was that of the Muʿtazila. The period of the activity of their earliest representatives, Wáṣil ibn 'Atá' (d. A.D. 748) and 'Amr ibn 'Ubaid (d. A.D. 762), both of whom were from Basra and had associated themselves for a time with Ḥasan al-Baṣrí, "covers practically the reign of the caliph Hishám and his 'Umayyad successors", i.e. the years A.D. 723–48.

The Muʿtazila maintained a middle position in regard to the status of a believer who committed a sin that was so grave as to make him an *infidel*. The Khárijís, who were most rigorous literalists, declared that he should be considered to be an infidel, while the Murji'ís claimed that as a matter of fact he continued to be a believer. Ḥasan al-Baṣrí was content to call him a *hypocrite*, but Wáṣil ibn 'Atá' and his associates in the Muʿtazila insisted that he should be regarded rather as holding a midway position (*manzila baina'l-manzilatain*). In other words it was the fixed principle of the Muʿtazila to seek a rational compromise. They were willing, as a rule, to leave the question of war-guilt, as between the parties of 'Ali, Talha, al-Zubair, and 'A'isha, to Allah to determine; though there was at times an inclination to condemn them all by refusing to accept the deposition of any member of these parties against any member of the Muslim community.

But in the study of the development of ethical thought in Islam, the most significant fact in the teaching of the Muʿtazila is that "they

9. This letter from Ḥasan al-Baṣrí has been published by Hellmut Ritter in *Der Islam*, vol. 21, pp. 67–82, and has been analysed with partial translation by Julian Obermann, *Journal A.O.S.*, vol. 55, pp. 138–62.

start from the principle that reason (*al-'aql*) is sound, and that even the will of Allah and His decisions are subordinate to it".[10] This important conception, that was basic in the thought of the Mu'tazila, is brought out clearly by al-Shahrastání,[11] who says: "The Mu'tazila unanimously declare that the Wise (i.e. Allah) can only do what is salutary (*al-ṣaláh*) and good, and that His wisdom keeps in view what is salutary to His servants." According to them things are not to be esteemed as *good* or *evil* because Allah has arbitrarily declared them to be so. We are to consider rather that in His declarations Allah has made the distinction between things that are good and things that are evil because they are intrinsically good or evil. They held that a degree of individual free-will is necessary to man's action if he is to be held morally responsible. It is only thus that "he who is saved deserves reward on account of his own acts, and whoso is damned has caused his punishment by his own acts".[12]

When the 'Abbasids came into power (A.H. 132/A.D. 750), the Mu'tazila gained influence rapidly, and reached the height of their power in the caliphate of al-Ma'mun (A.D. 813–33). In the last year of his reign, al-Ma'mun, who was their avowed patron and protector, used the force of State authority to compel outstanding teachers and theologians to accept the Mu'tazilite contention that the Qur'án must be something *created*, and that it is not to be looked upon as though it were something that was uncreated, that had existed with Allah from all eternity. His official decree required all recognized teachers and judges to adhere to this opinion.

It was on account of his persistent refusal to obey this order that Aḥmad ibn Ḥanbal (d. A.D. 855), the compiler of the *Musnad*, which contains more than 28,000 traditions, suffered repeated persecution and imprisonment. When in the course of his war against Byzantium al-Ma'mun was in camp near Tarsus, he commanded that Aḥmad ibn Ḥanbal should be brought to him in chains all the way from Baghdad. But before Aḥmad ibn Ḥanbal reached Tarsus he found that al-Ma'mun had died. However, the succeeding Caliph, al-Mu'tasim, continued to coerce him by threats of capital punishment and imprisonment, all of which were of no avail, and his faithful resistance gained for him the reputation of heroism and saintliness.

Reliance upon the authority of the State, however, proved to be the undoing of the Mu'tazila. For within nine years after al-Ma'mun died the tide had completely turned, for the Caliph al-Wáthik declared himself against them, and five years later the reactionary Caliph al-Muttawakkil (A.D. 847–61) pronounced their distinctive doctrines to be heretical.

10. Wensinck, *The Muslim Creed*, p. 261.
11. Shahrastání, *Kitáb Malal wa'l-Naḥal*, i. 30.
12. Ibid., op. cit., i. 31.

But it would be a mistake to infer that a dictum from the State had been all that was ultimately necessary to give Muslim orthodoxy this victory. For a man had appeared from among the Mu'tazila, a man who had withdrawn from them, and who had stated a midway position that came to be regarded as rational and yet at the same time as loyal to the faith. This man was al-Ash'arí (A.D. 873–935). In his earnest effort to reconcile antagonistic views he had changed his mind on several points. He then set forth his belief that Allah is indeed exalted above all that is bodily and human, nevertheless he "left to the deity His omnipotence and His universal agency".

On the question of the freedom of the will al-Ash'arí yielded to the doctrine of determinism, but with the qualification that for mankind there is an ability *to give assent* to the works that are *accomplished in them by Allah's agency*, and it is thus that they may be claimed as their own. As for the difficulty about the creation of the Qur'án, he maintained that in the sense in which it is to be regarded as the eternal *word* of Allah it must be considered uncreated, while in the sense that it is a book in the possession of men it has obviously been revealed in time. As Dr. D. B. Macdonald has pointed out in his article on *kalám* in the *Encyclopædia of Islam*, "there is only one certain use of *kalám* for the actual speech of Allah (vii. 141), but Allah is represented again and again by means of verbs as 'speaking', and al-Ash'arí quotes over ten passages (*al-Ibána*, pp. 23 ff.), using different expressions, as bases for the doctrine that both the Speech of Allah, as a quality inherent in him, and the Qur'án as a manifestation of that quality, are uncreated." These conclusions al-Ash'arí stated, moreover, with such force and clearness that they became the accepted standards of belief in Muslim theology.

A modern Muslim writer, Dr. S. M. Nadví, in his *Muslim Thought and Its Source* (pp. 4 ff.), gives this statement of the difference between the Mu'tazilites and the Ash'arites on the question whether God "cannot issue certain commands even should He wish to do so":

"The Mu'tazilites hold that all actions of God must necessarily be bound by aims and objects, whereas the Ash'arites believe that no such compulsion can be imposed on the Deity. In practice all actions of God are based on some object and purpose, but in theory He can act aimlessly if He ever so desires. The Ash'arite view is deduced from those verses which assert that God is an absolute monarch and does whatever He wishes without any restriction. Now if we believe that God's actions must be bound by considerations or conditioned by circumstances, we tend to encroach on His divine powers. He ceases to be absolute or independent if compulsion is imposed upon Him, forcing Him to act in a particular way. The Supreme Being is independent of all considerations or limitations, but He always acts in a way that is calculated to further the interests of the universe.

"The Mu'tazilites believe that it is obligatory on God to reward the virtuous and punish the vicious, and that He cannot do otherwise. Contrary to this, the Ash'arites hold that reward and punishment are entirely in His gift. He can reward whom He will and punish whom He will. Of course, it is certain that He will favour the righteous and punish the wicked, because He has promised to do so; but no consideration can bind His discretion or compel Him to do this or that. To impose a compulsion is really to reduce Him to a dependency, or even a machinery, which must move and act without any initiative of its own. What will be the difference between God, if He is compelled to reward the virtuous and punish the guilty, and a magistrate or a judge whose decisions are guided by the Penal Code? To place the Creator above the creation we must place His judgement above our own. The verses of the Qur'án are clear on the point, e.g. 'He forgiveth whom he will and punisheth whom He will'" (ii. 284).

The Highest Type of Humanity. As early as the ninth century of the Christian era it was a basic conviction in Muslim thought that the highest type of humanity is reached when man attains essential oneness with Allah. A translation of Porphyry's commentary on the *Enneads* (iv–vi) of Plotinus appeared in Arabic as early as A.D. 840 as the *Theology* of Aristotle. This book had profound influence on the Arab philosopher al-Kindī (d. A.D. 873) in his explanation of the emanations from the Godhead, first as Universal Mind (*al-'aql al-kullí*), then as Universal Soul (*al-nafs al-kulliyya*), from which the human soul emanated. Al-Qushairi cites Abu Yazíd al-Bisṭámí (d. A.D. 874) as an early authority for the belief that "after having been invested with certain divine names, the mystic passes away (*faniya*) from them and becomes 'the perfect and complete' (*al-kámil al-tamm*)." Such a person was described as "the perfect man" (*al-insán al-kámil*), an expression that is frequently employed in later books by Ṣúfí writers.[13]

The Brethren of Sincerity (al-Ikhwán al-Ṣafá'). In the tenth century an association, which was known as the Brethren of Sincerity (*al-Ikhwán al-Ṣafá'*), sprang up in Basra under the freer atmosphere of the period of the Buwaihid (Buyid) supremacy. They held meetings at which they read treatises on subjects that were scientific, philosophical, and religious. The preceding hundred years had been years of persecution for all the groups in the area of the Eastern Caliphate that had shown any tendency to diverge from the set form of Sunnite orthodoxy. Not only the Mu'tazilites and Shi'ites and Ṣúfís, but Jews and Christians also, suffered from this long period of the rigorous repression of any degree of free thought. This period of systematic repression had its beginning at the time of the orthodox

13. *Encyclopædia of Islam,* art. "al-Insán al-Kámil", by Professor R. F. Nicholson.

reaction under the Caliph Muttawakkil (d. A.D. 847), and extreme measures were frequently taken. Even the historian al-Ṭabarí had been denied the Muslim rites of burial when he died in A.D. 923.

Nevertheless there are records of the findings of the *Ikhwán al-Ṣafá'* which date from the same period, and which came as a result of free discussion on many subjects by men of varied opinions, and which are still extant in the *Rasá'il Ikhwán al-Ṣafá'* ("Treatises of the Brethren of Sincerity"), a book of an encyclopædic character.[14] This work affords many instances that show clearly that these brethren were not afraid to diverge at times from the accepted point of view of the Qur'án and the Ḥadíth, and also that they had access to sources of information that had not been utilized directly by Muhammad or his Companions.

There was a general conception that prevailed among them that science, philosophy, and religion must in the end be compatible with one another. Thus they dared to give free rein to their intellectual curiosity and deliberately to cultivate a breadth of vision. We may say that the *Rasá'il* affords internal evidence that the writers of these fifty-two chapters were honest in their eclecticism, and that they were therefore receptive to the ideas they derived from surveys of Greek (especially Pythagorean) philosophy, from Indian and Persian wisdom literature, and from Jewish and Christian books of religion. No better evidence of this fact can be given than the sixth section of the forty-fourth treatise, which Stanley Lane Poole has described as containing "the worthiest record of the life of Jesus that can be met with in Arabic literature".[15]

In reviewing their brief résumé of the branches of philosophy we may here pass over the chapters on mathematics, metaphysics, logic, chemistry, and astrology,[16] but we must not fail to point out that their devotion to the acquisition of knowledge, unlimited by authoritarian boundary lines, was inspired primarily by an ethical, and at the same time a religious, ideal.

In their exaltation of the spiritual they may at times have unduly depreciated the body, and they appear to us to have been in danger of falling into something like the popular dualism that prevailed in Irán in Zoroastrian times. But their reiterated faith in the superiority of the spiritual in man's nature is of primary importance in their ethical theory. "Our true essence", they said, "is the soul, and the

14. *Encyclopædia of Islam*, art. "Ikhwán al-Ṣafá", by T. J. de Boer.

15. Stanley Lane Poole, *Studies in a Mosque*, p. 95. It appears in the *Rasá'il*, xliv, section 6; Cairo text, 1347/1928, vol. iv, pp. 94–7, and is translated in the *Bulletin of the Henry Martyn School of Islamic Studies*, Aligarh, India, 1941, by D. M. Donaldson; also in *The Moslem World*, January 1945, by Professor L. Levonian, as "The Ikhwán al-Ṣafá' and Christ"; and a condensation is given by Rev. J. Windrow Sweetman in his *Islam and Christian Theology*, Part I, vol. i, pp. 37–9.

16. Cf. *Rasá'il Ikhwán al-Ṣafá*, 4 vols., ed. Cairo 1928/1347.

highest aim of our existence should be to live, with Socrates, *devoted to the intellect*, and with Christ, *devoted to the law of love*."

After they had stated their belief that Allah had created man with a body (*tan*) and with life (*ján*), and that the body was made up of component parts to which at death it would return, they said that "the *life* is the essence that is spiritual, that comes from Allah, and that while it is here associated with the body, yet it is to return to Allah. In fact, every single thing is to reunite with its own kind (*jins*). While this body and life are opposed to each other in their qualities and in their states, yet they are associated in their activities. As a consequence the situation amounts to this: that since man's life comes from elsewhere its concern is mostly for the hereafter, and since the body will die, its interest is all for adorning itself and seeking pleasure." Accordingly, habits or states that are commendable—such as knowledge, reason, continence, and bravery—are attributed to the spirit; and states that are reprehensible—like ignorance, folly, lewdness, and cowardice—are ascribed to the body. "Nevertheless," they observe, "the body must be properly treated and looked after, in order that the soul may have time to attain its full development."

One of the observations that these men made nearly a thousand years ago sounds like some of the consciously apologetic explanations we occasionally run across to-day in articles and books by modern Muslim writers. "Our Prophet", they said, "was sent to an uncivilized people, composed of dwellers in the desert, who neither possessed a proper conception of the beauty of this world, nor of the spiritual character of the world beyond." From this they concluded that "the crude expressions of the Qur'án, which are adapted to the understanding of that people, must be understood in a spiritual sense by those who are more cultured".[17]

They too had a conception of the "ideal and morally perfect man" (*al-insán al-kámil*), and their specified requirements for this man are interesting. He should be "of East-Persian derivation, Arabic in faith, Babylonian in education, a Hebrew in astuteness, a disciple of Christ in conduct, as pious as a Syrian monk, a Greek in individual sciences, an Indian in the interpretation of mysteries, but lastly, and especially, a Ṣúfí (or mystic) in his whole spiritual life". For it was their final conviction that "obedience to the Divine World Law is worthy of the reward of being raised to the celestial world of spheres. But this requires longing for what is above; and therefore the highest virtue is Love, which strives after union with Allah, the first loved one, and which is evinced even in this life in the form of religious patience and forbearance with all created things."

17. For this and the following translated statements, cf. T. J. de Boer's *History of Philosophy in Islam*, English trans., pp. 94–5.

CONTRIBUTIONS OF AL-FÁRÁBÍ AND IBN SINÁ

Foremost among the Muslim scholars who profited by the new learning from the Greek philosophers were al-Fárábí (d. A.D. 950) and Ibn Siná (d. A.D. 980). With similar background for their studies, it may be said that these two intellectual giants laid the foundations for the structure of Muslim philosophy.

"Al-Fárábí distinguishes between that which has a *possible* and that which has a *necessary* existence (just as Plato and Aristotle distinguished between the changeable and the eternal). If the possible is to exist in reality, a cause is necessary thereto. The world is composite, hence it had a beginning, or was caused. But the series of causes and effects can neither recede *in infinitum*, nor return like a circle into itself; it must, therefore, depend upon some necessary link, and this link is the first being (*ens primum*). The first being exists necessarily; the supposition of its non-existence involved a contradiction. It is uncaused, and needs in order to its existence no cause external to itself. It is the cause of all that exists. Its eternity implies its perfection. It is free of all accidents. It is simple and unchangeable. As the absolutely good it is at once absolute thought, absolute object of thought, and absolute thinking being (*intelligentia, intelligibile, intelligens*). It has wisdom, life, insight, might, and will, beauty, excellence, brightness; it enjoys the highest happiness, is the first willing being and the first object of all will (desire). In the knowledge of this being al-Fárábí sees the end of philosophy, and he defines the practical duty of men as consisting in rising, so far as human force permits it, into likeness with Allah."[18]

In addition to this brief summary, as given by Ueberweg, of al-Fárábí's basic principles, it is essential to point out that it was his firm belief that rules of conduct are taught by reason. It is reason that decides, most fittingly, whether a thing is good or evil, for the highest virtue consists in knowledge.[19]

That al-Fárábí derived this conception of reason from his study of the works of Aristotle is plainly suggested in his definition of the term:[20]

"The noun reason (*al-'aql*) is used with many significations. The first is that which the general public says in regard to man, that he is intelligent (*'áqil*). The second is that which the Mutakallimín repeat according to their custom, when they speak of what reason requires and of what reason opposes. The third use of *'aql* is that which Aristotle mentions in the *Kitáb al-Burhán* (*Organon: the Apodeictic*); the

18. Ueberweg, *A History of Philosophy*, vol. i, p. 412.
19. T. J. de Boer, op. cit., p. 121.
20. Fárábí, *Maqálat fí ma'ání al-'aql*. This text is in Dietireci's *Fárábí's Philosophische Abhandlungen*, Leiden, 1890.

fourth is that which he mentions in the sixth book of the *Kitáb al-Akhláq* (*Nicomachean Ethics*); the fifth is that which he mentions in the *Kitáb al-Nafs* (*De Anima*); and the sixth is that which he mentions in the *Kitáb má ba'da 'l-ṭabí'a* (*Metaphysics*)."

The use that is made by Aristotle of the term "Reason" (*nous*=*ratio*='*aql*) in the *Nicomachean Ethics* (Bk. vi), to which al-Fárábí referred, is clearly shown in his analysis of the intellectual virtues. Reason is the *intellect*, the function of which is to attain truth, by the use of deliberation, intelligence, judgement, and prudence.[21]

The freedom of choice that man has, in distinction from the lower animals, depends upon rational consideration. Thought, or the activity of the intellect, is the true sphere of freedom, "a freedom which is at the same time necessity, inasmuch as in the last resort it is determined by the rational nature of Allah".[22]

It is significant that we find that al-Nazzám (d. A.D. 845) taught "that Allah could do nothing to a creature, either in this world or in the next, that was not for the creature's good and in accordance with strict justice. It was not only that Allah would not do it. He had not the power to do anything evil."[23] Orthodox Islam, however, was not destined to accept this conception of Allah's necessary moral integrity. This was because it was not thought to be in accord with declarations in the Qur'án,[24] for the Qur'án teaches rather that the being of Allah is not to be thought of as restricted in power in any way, or as being limited in His freedom of willing, by any essentially continuous quality, such as justice, love, or truth.

If al-Fárábí could but have developed al-Nazzám's conception of Allah's necessary moral integrity, in connexion with his own teaching that the rules of conduct are taught by reason and that men's highest duty lies in rising into likeness with Allah, he would have pointed out to the Muslim world an ethical system that might well have withstood the tendencies that soon developed towards legalistic subserviency on the one hand and mystical vagueness and antinomianism on the other.

But the wide scope of Greek philosophical writings, with their multifarious distinctions, proved to be overwhelming. Even these two master minds among Muslim thinkers were occupied and baffled by endless analysis and definition.

In illustration of the way in which finely drawn verbal distinctions came to be regarded as the philosopher's stock in trade, examples may be found in Ibn Siná's *Rasá'il fí Ḥikmat wa Ṭabiyát* ("Essays on Wisdom and Natural Dispositions"), though with Ibn Siná there is

21. Aristotle, *Nicomachean Ethics*, bk. vi, English trans. by F. H. Peters, 10th edition, 1906.
22. T. J. de Boer, op. cit., p. 122.
23. D. B. Macdonald, op. cit., pp. 140–1.
24. Qur'án, xiv. 4; vii. 178; xci. 8; xiii. 30; xvi. 9.

the redeeming feature that he is not verbose. In fact his very brevity and conciseness become something of a difficulty for the reader who may wish to ascertain the exact meaning of particular Arabic words which he uses as approximate equivalents for Syriac expressions, which had previously been employed in translation of finely discriminated philosophical terms in Greek, which themselves required interpretation according to Platonic, Aristotelian, or Neo-Platonic points of view. It is not surprising that philosophers became philologists and that surveys of the sciences were the order of the day.

In his short essay on *'Ilm al-akhláq* ("Science of the Dispositions"), from the above-mentioned work,[25] Ibn Siná begins by acknowledging that Allah is "the one who enriches the soul (*nafs*) of the man who is devoted to His virtues (*faḍá'il*) and the means whereby he may acquire them for himself".

"It is a requisite in human life", he continues, "that he who would attain perfection must seek for happiness in this world and in the next. It is incumbent upon him, moreover, to perfect his power of discernment by means of many sciences, each of which is explained fully in books that enumerate the sciences. He must perfect his power of action also in accord with the virtues, whose fundamental qualities are purity (*'iffa*), courage (*shajá'a*), wisdom (*ḥikma*), and righteousness (*'idála*). Furthermore, he must avoid the vices which are directly opposed to these virtues." But when he undertakes to give the opposite of righteousness (*'idála*), he first enumerates the many virtuous qualities that are included in the comprehensive term *righteousness*, such as generosity (*sakhá*), frugality (*qaná'a*), nobility (*karam*), tranquillity (*ḥilm*), steadfastness (*ṣabr*), etc. Each of these then needs to be defined and distinguished from other qualities, some of which are similar and some opposite.

This method of close definition is distinctly Aristotelian and it has had a necessary task to perform. For, once the Muslims were able to have access to Greek scientific literature the need was felt for a systematic analysis of their whole field of general knowledge. In the works of Aristotle the Muslim thinkers appreciated especially his precision of concepts, but they also saw, as Professor Horten has indicated,[26] that Aristotle "did not succeed in giving a comprehensive view of the whole universe under some monistic concept. The universe is not traced to a single origin. Matter is eternal and opposed to God in a dualistic system." It is obvious that for Muslim thought this was wholly unsatisfactory. True wisdom, as well as the teaching of the Qur'án, demanded some philosophical explanation that would relate the universe, and mankind within it, to the sovereign power of Allah.

25. Ibn Siná, *Rasá'il fí Ḥikmat wa Ṭabiyát*, Bombay, A.H. 1318, pp. 98–101.

26. M. Horten, *Encyclopædia of Islam*, ii. 48, art. "Falsafa".

"It is here", Professor Horten observes, "that Muslim philosophy begins, following the Neo-Platonic model. The great notion of contingency brings into a unity the total of the actual. It is the light that explains the individual problems and allows them to be examined under the widest points of view. In the things of the world *being* and *existence* are quite different. The two are not internally and necessarily connected. Existence must thus be imparted to things by a self-existent Being and must be permanently maintained in them. The universe is a stream of being which, emanating from an inexhaustible source, extends to all that is not Allah. This idea, which runs through the whole of Muslim philosophy down to modern times, is again and again formulated anew and developed."

The Neo-Platonic model in Muslim ethical literature was the theory of emanations from God which had been infused into Islamic thought from the *Enneads* of Plotinus. In a universe that has essential unity, there is a movement from God towards man and also an upward movement from man towards God. In its desire to ascend again to the Universal Soul, and thence to the Universal Mind, the human soul engages in processes of purification, to free itself from the vices that would hold it back, and to practise those virtues that would foster its return.

The primary subjects that are included in Muslim ethics, therefore, are the following: the three faculties of the soul; the four cardinal virtues, with an enumeration of vices with which they are contrasted; and the theory of moral progress through discipline, obedience, and knowledge, until the soul is restored to unity with the Universal Soul.

The means or methods for this ascent, however, do not point to a doctrine of humanism among Muslim thinkers. Neither can humanism, in any strict sense, be ascribed to Plotinus. For man's knowledge is regarded as a gift from above, and not merely something which he may learn to acquire by his own efforts. Both al-Fárábí and Ibn Siná maintained that the soul has a longing or love for what is above and yearns thus for its own final absorption into the One. Ibn Siná pictured the moment when the veil would be raised and the soul of man would look once more upon the Invisible, the triumphant moment when "it is filled with joy, and having become purified from the stain of all flesh, and more aware of the inner meaning of all things, it returns whence it came. . . . Through the exercise of reason what is potential within the soul reaches actuality, through the enlightening influence of the Universal Soul, in accordance with the degree of receptivity within the soul and its state of preparedness, which is the result of virtues."[27]

It will be observed that from the very beginning of philosophical speculation Muslim ethics has been an ethics of mysticism. The *insán*

27. Margaret Smith, *al-Risálat al-Laduniyya*, *R.A.S.J.*, 1938, p. 185.

al-kámil must have attained to *baqá'* (duration in reality) through *faná'* (the passing away of the unreal). There have been codes of moral instruction, and manuals to set forth the requirements of the religious and civil law, but when the principles and purposes of conduct are taken into consideration the fundamentally mystical character of Muslim ethical thinking is soon evident. This is why any comprehensive study of Muslim ethics requires a survey of the contributions that have been made by the early Muslim ascetics, and by outstanding poets, saints, and philosophers who were Ṣúfís.

In an article on "The Nature of the Summum Bonum in Islam" (*Islamic Culture*, Oct. 1947), the writer, Abdu al-Ṣubḥán, has observed that "all the Muslim scholastic philosophers, both the Mu'tazilites and the orthodox, have held that the Beatific Vision (*ru'yat al-Bár'í*) is the summum bonum of life under the Islamic dispensation—a conclusion to which the Holy Qur'án undoubtedly refers when it says (x. 26): 'For those who do good is the best (reward) and more (thereto).' " He has undertaken to show, moreover, that "the orthodox have virtually accepted the Mu'tazilite viewpoint on the subject, namely, that God can be seen only spiritually and not with the bodily eyes", all of which points to the necessity of including in any comprehensive survey of the ethics of Islam a consideration of the stages of the moral progress by which the Ṣúfís have claimed to attain knowledge of God.

THE REQUIREMENTS OF THE FAITH

Emphasis on the definite and external nature of the requirements of Islam is evidenced in traditions that show the discussions that arose as to the distinctive meanings of *imán* (faith) and *islám* (submission) and *iḥsán* (righteousness). One tradition declares that the Prophet said, "*Islám* is external, faith belongs to the heart", and that he pointed three times to his heart, and then declared, "The fear of Allah is here."[28]

Another tradition, that attracted more general attention, bears an interesting relation to the subsequent description of the "five pillars" of Islam. "One day the Apostle of Allah gave audience. There came to him a man who asked him: 'O Apostle of Allah, what is *faith*?' He answered: '*Faith* is believing in Allah, His angels, His book, His meeting, His apostles, and the final resurrection.' The man said: 'O Apostle of Allah, what is *Islám*?' He replied: '*Islám* is serving Allah without associating anything with Him, performing the ordered ritual prayer, paying over the obligatory alms-tax, and fasting during the month of Ramaḍán.' The man then asked: 'O Apostle of Allah, what is *righteousness*?' To this Muhammad answered: '*Righteousness* is

28. Aḥmad ibn Ḥanbal, *Musnad*, iii. 134 ff.; cf. Wensinck, *The Muslim Creed*, p. 23.

serving Allah as if He were before thine eyes. For if thou seest Him not, He seeth thee.' "[29]

As given by al-Bukhárí,[30] the tradition of the "five pillars" of Islam is as follows. "Islam is built upon five pillars: witnessing (*shaháda*) that there is no god but Allah and that Muhammad is the Apostle of Allah; the performance of ritual prayer (*ṣalát*); the payment of the alms-tax (*zakát*); the pilgrimage to Mecca (*ḥajj*); and the fasting in the month of Ramaḍán (*sawm Ramaḍán*)." It will be observed that *islám* thus becomes the inclusive term; that faith (*imán*), in so far as it is fundamental, is reduced to the formula of the witnessing (*shaháda*), and the ethically significant righteousness (*iḥsán*) is omitted, except in so far as it is expressed in the meritorious act of the pilgrimage (*ḥajj*).

This precise statement of the concrete and easily recognizable requirements of Islam was a natural development in the discussions that took place, and it was exceedingly convenient in the period of the early conquests. As a matter of statecraft it was undoubtedly of advantage to have the fundamentals of the politico-religious programme so perspicuous. They could thus be made clear to the common people in a form that they could readily remember. Nevertheless, as a consequence of Muhammad's very success in thus giving concrete and external reality to these "pillars" of Islam, we find that faith, in its spiritual aspects, and righteousness, in its ethical character, were obscured and weakened. For officially the conformity of "the faithful" came to be regarded as something that consisted largely in externals. Even during the period of the conquests 'Umar is represented as having declared: "Nowadays we judge people entirely by their outward actions; we protect him who appears to do right, for we know nothing of what is within—Allah is the judge thereof!—and we do not protect him who appears to do wrong, nor do we find faith in him even if he asserts that his motives are pure."[31]

This emphasis on the externals of the faith was not anything new in the history of religions. It occurred repeatedly in Judaism and it has happened conspicuously in Christianity. For apparently the masses of all nations are materially inclined, and when undue concessions are made to their demands for the concrete—by laying stress on forms and rituals, fasts and vigils, sacrifices and pilgrimages—it is not unlikely that a dimming of the visions of faith will be brought about and that there will be failure to attain to standards of conduct that are truly ethical.

Although this criticism on the part of those who make more

29. Wensinck, op. cit., citing Muslim, I. i. 5, 7.

30. Bukhárí, *Sahíh*, ii. 2. Cf. Muslim, i. 19–22; Tirmídhí, 38. 3; Nas. 47, 13; and Ahmad ibn Hanbal, ii. 26, 92.

31. T. J. De Boer, *Encyclopædia of Religion and Ethics*, v. 502, citing Bukhárí, ed. Houdas and Marcais, ii. 209.

exacting ethical demands of Islam must be considered, it should at the same time be mentioned that there is much that is attractive and impressive in the faithfulness of those devout Muhammadans who adhere to the pillars of their religion. With their belief in one God they link their loyalty to Muhammad as His apostle, and in their contacts with animistic and idolatrous peoples there has been continued power in this slogan of their faith. Western travellers frequently mention the ritual prayers of the Muslims, which are so imperative for the individual believers wherever they may be, and which appear to be so reverently expressive of devotion, especially when hundreds of men are seen bowing together in the great mosques of Lahore or Delhi, Cairo or Damascus. Foreigners who reside in Muslim countries know of beautiful mosques, of endowed schools or hospitals, of public fountains, of orphanages, and of houses for the poor that are maintained by the payment of the required alms-tax. Until comparatively recent years the month of Ramaḍán was so generally observed as a month of fasting that ordinary business would be almost at a standstill—whether from the strain of abnormal days or the fatigue of festive nights. And whoever has seen the friends and neighbours of pilgrims who are starting out on their journey to Mecca, to fulfil expectations that they and their families have cherished for years, is sure to feel admiration for a people who are ready to endure such hardship and privation for what they believe to be the will of God.

It is probably in these externals of the religion that Islam has best preserved its unity. The "pillars" have a solid place in traditional belief. Extraordinary events have come like earthquakes at times and the structure of Islam has fallen at places, necessitating modern reconstruction, but the pillars have remained much the same.

But notwithstanding the early simplification of the requirements of Islam to the five pillars, there was still a consciousness in the community that faith (*imán*) was in need of further explication. While it may be seen that "the Qur'án did not proclaim a compendium of faith that could serve as a characteristic description of Islam",[32] yet verses were recalled to indicate that it was necessary to understand and to accept more than the five pillars, as for example the declaration of the Islamic attitude towards previous revelations (ii. 130): "Say ye, 'We believe in Allah, and what has been revealed to us, and what has been revealed to Abraham, and Ishmael, and Isaac, and Jacob, and the Tribes, and what was brought to Moses and Jesus, and what was brought unto the prophets from their Lord; we will not distinguish between any one of them and unto Him we are resigned.'"

Efforts were made very early to derive from the Qur'án, and to incorporate in the Traditions, articles of faith that could be explained

32. Wensinck, *The Muslim Creed*, p. 3.

so as to be intelligible for ordinary believers. In the discussions between conflicting factions, particularly in the rationalizing tendencies of theologians and jurists in the eighth and ninth centuries, there was a marked disposition to require of believers their intellectual assent to a more elaborate statement of Islamic doctrine.

In their doctrines in regard to the true nature of faith, the Kharijites repudiated absolutely the idea of justification by faith without works, and they went so far as to maintain that acts of worship were invalid, in spite of scrupulous attention to required ceremonial ablutions, if the conscience of the worshipper was not clear. And in so far as they were themselves concerned, their own consciences could not be clear unless they were carrying on active and persistent opposition to the evil-workers who had forcibly preempted authority in the Muslim state.

Another heterodox group, the Murji'ites were radically different from the Kharijites, for not only did they deliberately maintain the attitude of quietism in politics, but they announced it as their opinion that a Muslim does not lose his faith through sin. They were content to stand behind and follow a prayer-leader who was known to have committed grievous sin. In their opinion the Caliphs, likewise, could be grotesquely delinquent morally and still be entitled to command the obedience of the faithful. A second of their beliefs was that where there is faith sins will do no harm. This promise, assuring professing Muslims of security in the life hereafter, caused the Murji'ites to be called the "People of the Promise" (*ahl al-wa'd*).

In the course of the controversies over such questions, one of the earliest theologians to undertake to enumerate beliefs that he thought should be included in the faith was Jahm ibn Ṣufyán (d. A.D. 745). He lived in the far north-eastern corner of the empire, at a town called Tirmídh, which was close to Balkh. He insisted that a believer should understand that faith includes "that knowledge of Allah which is gained by reason (*'aql*), and that acceptance of the messages of the prophets that had come by revelation". Like the Kharijites he could not recognize as believers those whose works were obviously not in accord with the knowledge and fear of Allah, and he therefore joined those in Khurasan who rallied in rebellion against the 'Umayyads, and forfeited his life in this effort to break their supremacy.

A friend and contemporary of Jahm ibn Ṣufyán was Wáṣil ibn 'Aṭá' (d. A.D. 748), who was one of the theological school of Mu'tazila, the most famous group of thinkers of the period. They took the name of a the well-known neutral party at the time of the accession of 'Ali (A.H. 35). This party, according to al-Nawbakhtí,[33] "separated (*i'tazalú*) from 'Ali and refused either to fight against him or to take his side, although they had paid homage to him and had received him favourably; they were called Mu'tazilites and are

33. Nawbakhti, *Kitáb Firáq al-Shí'a*, ed. Ritter, p. 5.

the ancestors of all the later Mu'tazilites". When Wáṣil ibn 'Aṭá' and his brother-in-law, 'Amr ibn 'Ubaid, left the ascetic school of Ḥasan al-Baṣrí because of their difference of opinion as to the status of a believing Muslim who has fallen into sin, they and their future associates became the "great theological school which created the speculative dogmatics of Islam".[34] The discussions that they carried on yielded many valuable contributions to the analysis and explanation of the Muslim faith. They held that moral wrong can be recognized among believers without it being necessary or right to condemn them as infidels. Likewise they held that a Muslim who commits a mortal sin can be thought of as entering a state that is intermediate between that of a believing Muslim and that of an infidel (*káfir*). On the question as to the extent of man's free agency they liked to call themselves "the People of Justice" (*ahl al-'adl*), on the ethical thesis that Allah's justice requires that man must in some way be free if he is to be rewarded or punished. Also the Mu'tazilites attempted to make philosophical statements on the question of the nature of Allah's qualities (*sifát*), and this led ultimately to their famous contention that the Qur'án itself should be regarded as "created" and not as "eternal".

To the jurist Abu Ḥanífa (d. A.D. 767) are attributed several small works on Muslim dogmatics.[35] It is said, however, that he did not write them himself, but that they were composed by his disciples and "more especially by his grandson Ismá'il ibn Ḥammád". The earliest, the *Fiqh Akbar I*, is thought to represent statements that had been made by Abu Ḥanífa. There are but ten articles, and it will be observed how they are directed to points of discussion at that time:[36]

1. We do not consider anyone to be an infidel on account of sin; nor do we deny his faith.
2. We enjoin what is just and prohibit what is evil.
3. What reaches you could not possibly have missed you; and what misses you could not possibly have reached you.
4. We disavow none of the Companions of the Apostle of Allah; nor do we adhere to any of them exclusively.
5. We leave the question of 'Uthman and 'Ali to Allah, who knoweth the secret and hidden things.
6. Insight in matters of religion is better than insight in matters of knowledge and law.
7. Difference of opinion in a community is a token of divine mercy.
8. Whoso believeth all that he is bound to believe, except that he says, "I do not know whether Moses and Jesus (peace be upon them) do or do not belong to the Apostles", is an infidel.

34. H. S. Nyberg, *Encyclopædia of Islam*, art. "Mu'tazila".
35. Th. W. Juynboll, *Encyclopædia of Islam*, art. "Ibn Ḥanífa".
36. Wensinck, *The Muslim Creed*, pp. 103–4, and 123.

9. Whoso sayeth, "I do not know whether Allah is in Heaven or on Earth", is an infidel.

10. Whoso sayeth, "I do not know the punishment in the tomb", belongeth to the sect of the Jahmites, which goeth to perdition.

The second of these statements of beliefs, which is called the Waṣíya, "seems to have originated", as Professor Wensinck believes, "in a period between Abu Ḥanífa and Aḥmad ibn Ḥanbal, and probably belongs to the latter part of that period".[37] Two of its twenty-seven articles may be quoted as representative of the further elaboration of theological thinking:

Art. 8. We confess that Allah has seated Himself on His throne, without any necessity or permanence. He occupies the throne and what is outside it, without necessity. If there were any necessity on His part, He would not have been able to create the world and to govern it in the way of created beings; and if he should feel any necessity to sit down and remain sitting, where then was He before the creation? He is elevated above such a supposition.

Art. 9. We confess that the Qur'án is the speech of Allah, uncreated, His inspiration and revelation, not He, nor yet other than He, but His real quality, written in the copies, recited by the tongues, preserved in the breasts, yet not residing there. The ink, the paper, the writing are created, for they are the work of men. The speech of Allah on the other hand is uncreated, for the writing and the letters and the words and the verses are manifestations of the Qur'án for the sake of human needs. The speech of Allah on the other hand is self-existing, and its meaning is understood by means of these things. Whoso sayeth that the speech of Allah is created, he is an infidel regarding Allah, the Exalted, whom men serve, who is eternally the same, His speech being recited or written and retained in the heart, yet never dissociated with Him.

The third of the doctrinal statements that are ascribed to Abu Ḥanífa, the *Fiqh Akbar II*, bears internal evidence that it is of later origin, though probably not later than the tenth century,[38] and yet late enough in that century to allow for the influence of al-Ash'ari (A.D. 935). It will be observed from a few of the twenty-nine articles it contains that the problem of understanding the faith had become more difficult.

Art. 1. The heart of the confession of the unity of Allah and the true foundation of faith consists in this obligatory creed: I believe in Allah, His angels, His books, His apostles, the resurrection after death, the decree of Allah—the good and evil thereof, computation of sins, the balance, Paradise, and Hell; and that all these are real.

37. Wensinck, *The Muslim Creed*, pp. 187 and 127.
38. Ibid., pp. 246 and 188 ff.

Art. 4. Allah is a thing, not as other things but in the sense of positive existence; without body, without substance, without *accidens*. He has no limit, neither has He a counterpart, nor a partner, nor an equal. He has hand, face, and soul, this belongs to His qualities, without how (*bila kaifa*). It must not be said that His hand is His power or His bounty, for this would lead to the annihilation of the quality. This is the view of the Qadarites and the Mu'tazilites. No, His hand is His quality, without how. Likewise His wrath and His good pleasure are two of His qualities, without how.

Art. 22. Allah guideth whomsoever He pleaseth, by grace, and He leadeth astray whomsoever He pleaseth, by justice. His leading astray means His abandoning, and the explanation of "abandoning" is that He does not help a man by guiding him towards deeds that please him. This is justice on His part, and so is His punishment of those who are abandoned on account of sin. We are not allowed to say that Satan deprives the Faithful of his faith by constraint and compulsion. But we say that man gives up his faith, whereupon Satan deprives him of it.

Art. 28. When a man is uncertain about any of the subtleties of theology, it is his duty to cling for the time being to the orthodox faith. When he finds a scholar, he must consult him; he is not allowed to postpone inquiry, and there is no excuse for him if he should persevere in his attitude of hesitation, nay, he would incur the blame of unbelief thereby.

Among the learned these continued discussions on particular requirements of the faith led to a kind of depreciation of the unlearned as a class. Muhammad had referred to "unbelievers" as "those who care not", and had said, "they are like cattle, nay, they go more astray!" (vii. 178). From this verse is derived an unflattering declaration in regard to the common people, whose faith has not been intellectually confirmed, namely, that the unlearned are like cattle (*al-'awwám ka'l-an'ám*).

As Greek culture and philosophy began to be appreciated in the ninth and tenth centuries Muslim theologians continued their efforts to state their faith more explicitly. In the *Fiqh Akbar III*, a catechism of the eleventh century, which, as Wensinck says, has been incorrectly ascribed to al-Sháfi'í, who died in A.D. 820, there are thirty-three articles, the first five of which are devoted to a definition of knowledge. In these statements Greek influence is beginning to be evident.[39]

Art. 1. Everyone who is under the obligation of the law is bound to acquire knowledge of Allah. Knowledge means to know its object, so that none of its qualities remain unknown. Knowledge cannot be acquired through opinion or by taking it on the authority of others.

Art. 2. Knowledge is of two kinds, primary and secondary. The

39. Wensinck, *The Muslim Creed*, pp. 263.

former is independent of the special faculty of the knowing subject. The latter is dependent upon the judgements, opinion, etc.

Art. 3. A definition of obligation (*taqlif*) and of the five categories of legal acts.

Art. 4. Obligation to know Allah applies only to him who possesses full mental capacities, has attained his majority, and has been reached, directly or indirectly, by the preaching of a Prophet. Cf. Sura xvii. 16.

Art. 5. The definition of judgement or reflexion (*naẓar*) is "thought of the heart". This is superior to primary knowledge.

In his *Niháya*,[40] al-Shahrastání (d. A.D. 1153) has summarized the teaching of the philosophers of his time on the relation between good and evil:

"The world order moves towards good, because it proceeds from the origin of good, and the *good* is what everything desires. . . . When the first being knew the perfect good *in potentia* . . . it emanated from him . . . and that is the eternal providence and will. Thus good came within the divine decree essentially, not accidentally, while evil came accidentally. . . . Evil may be said to be deficiency, like ignorance and impotence, or like pain and sickness, or like fornication and theft. In fine, evil *per se* is privation, i.e. the loss of a thing's true and perfect nature. Evil absolutely does not exist, except in speech and thought. Accidental evil exists *in potentia*, because of matter. It begins through a certain disposition (*hai'a*) which prevents its proper receptiveness of the perfection towards which it moves. The pernicious result is due, not to a privative act of the agent, but to the unreceptiveness of the object; thus arise bad morals, the dominion of the bestial over the human mind, giving rise to evil practices and corrupt beliefs; or the evil influence may come from without, as from parents or teachers. Evil, coming in thus accidentally, is rightly rewarded with destruction because of the existence of the opposing cause. . . . When evil is mixed with good it is most proper that it should be brought into existence . . . otherwise a universal good would be lost in the interest of a particular evil. . . . A good example is fire. . . . Any other interpretation involves the error of the Dualists."

In the statement of his own opinion, al-Shahrastání says: "We see the corporeal world full of trials, famine, pestilence, and wars . . . persisting in ignorance and corrupt beliefs, the majority living evil lives, lust and anger prevailing over the mind and intellect, so that you can hardly find one in any country holding the divine wisdom which you regard as the *imitatio dei*, or a remnant obeying the church's laws (*shar'iyya*) which we regard as a copy of the divine commands. Most of them, as it is written, are 'deaf, dumb, and blind

40. Shahrastání, *Kitáb Niháyatu'l-Iqdám fí 'Ilmi'l-Kalám*, edit. and trans. by Alfred Guillaume, Oxford, 1934, pp. 90–1.

and do not understand' (vii. 100). How, then, can your philosophers maintain that the evil that is in the world does not exist, when the facts contradict you?

"Wherever we find nature and the divine determination prevailing over human choice and acquisition, happiness prevails; but wherever human choice and acquisition prevail, evil prevails, so that we return to the position that there is no evil in God's works; and if evil is to be found therein it is relative to one thing and not to another. Evil only enters into men's voluntary acts, and they, in so far as they are linked to the will of God, are good; but if linked to man's acquisition they acquire the name of evil. [Professor Guillaume remarks that this would seem to mean that man's will, if surrendered to God, will produce good; but if his free-will is exercised apart from God's will evil must result. Shahrastání has not stated this explicitly, perhaps because it conflicts with the orthodox doctrine.] Nevertheless the existence of devils and their leader Satan, as revealed by the Scriptures, cannot be denied. . . . The early doctors asserted that every singular in this world existed as a universal in the next . . . so singular evil in this world has its universal counterpart. Thus the Magi postulated two principles, the source of good and evil respectively. See further my *Milal.*"

It is not difficult to see how these discussions of the requirements of the faith, which were so largely influenced by the form and content of scholastic theology, would open the way for the study of ethics. The ethical teachings of Greek philosophers were becoming available to Muslim scholars, and they were to make their own efforts to describe and to rationalize those forms of human conduct that were to be considered praiseworthy and in harmony with the will of Allah.

A very notable contribution, however, was made at this same period by a Syrian Christian translator and author, Yaḥyá ibn 'Adí (d. A.D. 974),[41] who wrote a book with the title, *Tahdhíb al-Akhláq* ("Correction of Dispositions"). This work, which is mentioned in the *Fihrist* by al-Nadím (i. 252), gives an epitome of the Greek ethical thought that was made available in Arabic by Syrian Christian translators. Because of its striking similarity to a book with the same name (*Tahdhíb al-Akhláq*) that was written very soon afterwards by the Muslim scholar Ibn Maskawaihi (d. A.D. 1030), the following summary of its contents is of special interest:

41. G. Graf has published a detailed study of this author, with an estimate of his philosophical and theological writings, in the symposium *Beiträge zur Geschichte der Philosophie des Mittelalters*, Munster, 1909. The learned Syrian Christian, Abu Zakaríya Yaḥyá ibn 'Adí (d. 364/974), was a Jacobite, and he is mentioned by Abu'l-Faraj ibn 'Abrún (Bar Hebraeus) in the *Mukhtasar al-Duwal*, pp 296, 297, and 93.

BRIEF SYNOPSIS OF YAḤYÁ IBN 'ADÍ'S *TAHDHÍB AL-AKHLÁQ*

I. Mention of the Dispositions.

II. The Necessity for Difference of Dispositions.

III. Virtues in Good and Praiseworthy Dispositions:

continence (*al-'iffa*)
self-control (*al-tasawwun*)
dignity (*al-waqára*)
mercy (*al-raḥma*)
trustworthiness (*idá' al-imána*)
humility (*al-tawaḍu'*)
truth of speech (*al-sidq al-lahja*)
generosity (*al-sakhá*)
aspiration (*al-munáfasa*)
steadfastness in adversities (*al-ṣabr 'ind al-shadá'id*)
frugality (*al-qiná'a*)
tranquillity (*al-ḥilm*)
love (*al-wadd*); cf. *al-muwadda*
fulfilment of a promise (*al-wafá'*)
keeping a secret (*kitman al-sirr*)
cheerfulness (*al-bishr*)
good intention (*salamat al-niyá*)
courage (*al-shajá'a*)
great ambition ('*azm al-himma*)

IV. Vices in Corrupt Dispositions:

dissoluteness (*al-fujúr*)
greediness (*al-sharah*)
shabbiness (*al-tabadhdhul*)
levity (*al-safah*)
awkwardness (*al-khurq*)
excessive love (*al-'ishq*)
pitilessness (*al-qasáwa*)
treachery (*al-ghadr*)
perfidy (*al-khiyána*)
divulging a secret (*arsha al-sirr*)
sternness (*al-'ubús*)
falsehood (*al-kidhb*)
deceit (*al-khubth*)
secret hate (*al-ḥiqd*)
avarice (*al-bukhl*)
cowardice (*al-jubn*)
envy (*al-hasad*)
impatience in misfortune (*al-jaz'u 'ind al-shadda*)
smallness of ambition (*al-ṣighar al-himma*)
injustice (*al-jawr*)

V. Dispositions that are Virtues among Some People and Vices among Others:

love of regard (*ḥubb al-karáma*)
love of adornment (*ḥubb al-sina*)
requiting commendation (*al-mujázát 'ala'l-madḥ*)
asceticism (*al-zuhd*)

Comments. Up to this point 37 pages of the book are devoted to analysis and definition. The remaining 23 pages have to do with hortatory admonitions in regard to acquiring mastery over the three selves (irascible, concupiscent, and rational), so as to acquire the virtues and avoid the vices. There is to be a conscious struggle towards the perfecting of the human personality.

On page 48 there is an enumeration of the necessary qualities of the man who is complete or perfect. But first all that has been mentioned in the way of "being broken in" (*al-irtiyáḍ*) to the excellencies of dispositions (*makarim al-akhláq*) is required; and there must be a choice of the road that leads gradually to their laudable qualities. For when man has subjected himself to training, for the most part by guarding and diligently looking after his soul, virtues will become customary for him and laudable actions (*maḥásin*) will be but characteristic and natural.

This having been said, the author proceeds to mention the qualities (*'awsáf*) of the man who is complete (*al-tám*) in all the laudable acts of the dispositions, and to indicate the way by which he arrives at perfection. "We would say, therefore, that the man who is complete (*al-insán al-tám*) is he whom no one of the virtues has weakened and whom no one of the vices has injured. This is the limit of the arrow, so to speak, the distance which mankind may reach. And if we may suppose that a man reaches it, then he would be like the angels in his relation to other men.

"But the way for him to arrive at perfection and completeness is for him to take great pains in the consideration of the true sciences. He must aim to comprehend the intrinsic values of existing things, to have an explanation of their causes and reasons, and to maintain a diligent search for their ends and final purposes.

"For him who would seek perfection there is no way to attain his object as long as pleasure and concupiscence occupy his mind. He must observe moderation in eating and drinking and must remember that wealth does not minister to the needs of his real self. He should observe that one who is angry resembles the beasts and acts without knowledge or reflexion. He needs also to recognize that he himself is under obligation to all mankind, and that in as much as all men have the distinguishing reasoning self in common, they should therefore be loving and friendly to one another. The man who would be perfect should make it his ambition, therefore, to accomplish that which will be good for all mankind. But he must be aware that none of his faults or base qualities can remain concealed from men, and for this reason he should cheerfully welcome the friend who points out to him anything in which he is deficient."

5

THE MANUAL OF ETHICS BY IBN MASKAWAIHI

THE SCIENCE of ethics in Islam is set forth at its best in Arabic by writers of the eleventh and twelfth centuries, and it is significant to observe that their books were written in periods of political upheaval, when there was greater freedom for philosophical discussion and speculation than was possible under more firmly established Islamic authority.

IBN MASKAWAIHI (d. A.D. 1030)

Abu 'Ali Aḥmad ibn Muḥammad ibn Maskawaihi lived in the turbulent period of the Buwaihid (Buyid) military dictators, who had taken the 'Abbasid Caliphs under their enforced protection and authority. The Buwaihids were a family of princes of Iranian origin, and of the Shi'ite sect, who had captured Baghdad in A.D. 945, and as they succeeded in maintaining their supremacy for 110 years they may be considered as the actual rulers during the third century of the Eastern Caliphate. It was by their favour that the Shi'ites were no longer forced to resort to dissimulation in following their distinctive faith and practice, and were therefore free to compile and to circulate their own books of Traditions.[1] To commemorate the tragedy that had taken place at Kerbela, when the Imám Ḥusain had been killed, it was at this period that the Shi'ites instituted a public mourning procession on the tenth day of the month of Muḥarram, when they beat their breasts, cut their heads with swords, and lacerated their bodies with chain-lashes, thus giving witness to a fanatical sectarian loyalty and at the same time invoking the intercession of the Imám Ḥusain, their martyr and their hero.

The Buwaihid prince who had captured Baghdad was known as the Mu'izz al-Dawla, the "Strengthener of the Dynasty". It was his vizier, al-Muhallabi, who had negotiated with the Caliph for the surrender of Baghdad; and it was al-Muhallabi's young secretary, Ibn Maskawaihi, who included in the scholarly studies to which he gave attention the preparation in Arabic of an outline of the science of ethics, as he had come to appreciate it through what the Syrian

1. For the earliest collection of the Shi'ite traditions, cf. *The Shi'ite Religion*, by D. M. Donaldson, Luzac, 1933, ch. xxvii.

Christian translators were making available from the writings of the Greek philosophers. To this book he gave the name, *Tahdhíb al-Akhláq wa Taṭhír al-A'ráq*, "The Correction of Dispositions and the Cleansing of Veins".[2]

This is the most important book on philosophical ethics in Muslim literature. Professor Carra de Veaux has said of it in his article on "Ethics" in the *Encyclopædia of Religion and Ethics* that "its underlying psychology, and, indeed, the structure of the system as a whole, is Platonic, though in matters of detail the author quotes frequently from Aristotle, as well as from Socrates, Hippocrates, Galen, and al-Kindi". Mention is made by Yá'qút (*Irshád*, ii. 89) that a certain Abú Ḥaiyán had given Ibn Maskawaihi a commentary on the *Isagoge* of Porphyry and on the *Categories* of Aristotle. Yá'qút further observes that he was in association with Abu'l-Khayr al-Khammar, a Christian author and philosopher, and that he was interested in the works of Yaḥyá ibn 'Adí (d. A.D. 974). It is most likely, therefore, as mentioned in the previous chapter, that he had the use of the *Tahdhíb al-Akhláq* that had been written in Arabic by this Syrian Christian scholar.

Ibn Maskawaihi[3] served as a librarian at Shiráz and at Ray, and in both of these places he worked assiduously as a writer. Notwithstanding the political disturbances of the times in which he lived, he showed a scholar's interest in medicine, chemistry, history, theology, and ethics. In writing history, as Leone Caetani has remarked, "He is not satisfied merely to collect materials to set forth in chronological order, for he holds that all these events of the past were bound together by a web of human interest."

An attractive introduction to Ibn Maskawaihi's formal treatise on ethics is found in his personal programme for moral conduct, which he formulated to assist him in the struggle he found that he had to carry on against himself. It required that he should exercise restraint, show courage, and be judicious. Restraint he would exercise in regard to the desires of his body—so that it would not overcome him with its evil, or do him physical injury, or bring him into disgrace. Courage he would show in fighting battles with his reprehensible self so as not to allow base desire or untimely anger to conquer him. To be judicious he would seek wisdom through study and reflexion about his beliefs, trying always, as far as he could, to avoid letting

2. Of Ibn Maskawaihi's *Fí Tahdhíb al-Akhláq* two clear texts may be mentioned: that of Cairo, A.H. 1322, which has al-Ghazálí's *Kitáb al-Adab fí Dín* on the margin, and that of Cairo, A.H. 1305, which is printed on the margin of al-Ṭabarsí's *Mukaram al-Akhláq*.

3. For biographical details consult the *Encyclopædia of Islam*; the Introduction to Leone Caetani's edition of the *KitábTa járib al-Umam*; Yáqút's *Dictionary of Learned Men*, ii, p. 95; T. J. de Boer's *The History of Philosophy in Islam*, English trans., pp. 128–31; and Muḥammad Luṭfi's *Taríkhi Falasafat al-Islam fí al-Mashriq wa al-Maghrib*, Cairo, 1928, pp. 305–20.

any useful knowledge escape him, that he might discipline his soul to bring forth the fruit of righteousness.

To this end he set before himself the following fifteen points:[4]

1. He had striven to maintain what we would call personal integrity. This he defined as the preference (*ithár*) for what is worthy (*al-ḥaqq*) over what is futile in beliefs; for what is true (*al-ṣidq*) over what is false in statements; and for what is good (*al-khair*) over what is evil (*al-sharr*) in actions.
2. He had emphasized the continuous struggle that he needed to keep up between his essential manhood (*al-mar*) and his animal nature.
3. He had felt the importance of adhering to the Law (*al-sharí'a*) and of recognizing the necessity of its functions.
4. He had endeavoured to remember agreements and to fulfil them, particularly any agreements that he had made with Allah.
5. He had shown little confidence in men, and this he accomplished by avoiding familiarity with them.
6. He had cultivated the love of the beautiful for its own sake and for no other reason.
7. He had appreciated the value of silence in times of agitation, until reason would direct him.
8. He had striven to continue any state of mind that was beneficial until it would become a habit.
9. He had approved taking the initiative in things that were creditable.
10. He had found that whole-hearted sympathy was necessary in order to work on any important undertaking without distraction.
11. He had felt that the fear of death and of poverty could be counteracted by doing what was still possible and by not being indolent.
12. He had shut out from his mind such anxieties as were aroused by sayings of the base, and he had tried to suppress his desire at night to plan something against them.
13. He had come to realize that he must be inured to wealth or to poverty, and to liberality or to contempt.
14. He had tried to remember times of sickness when he was in health, and occasions of joy and pleasure when anger was apt to arise, so that there might be less injustice and transgression.
15. He had rejoiced in times of trust, appreciating the goodness of hope and confidence in Allah, turning his whole heart to Him.

As an example of the discursive and didactic style that Ibn Maskawaihi employed in his *Tahdhíb al-Akhláq*,[5] the following selection is given in translation.

4. Yáqút, *Dictionary of Learned Men*, ii, p. 95.
5. *Fí Tahdhíb al-Akhláq*, Cairo, A.H. 1305, pp. 6 ff. Of this book there is a lithographed text of a Persian translation, Teheran, A.H. 1315, which has been given the name *Kímiyá-i-Sa'ádat* ("Alchemy of Happiness"), which is the name of al-Ghazálí's Persian version of the *Iḥyá'*.

HAPPINESS AND THE VIRTUES

"It has now been made clear to you that the happiness (*sa'áda*) of any being (*mowjúd*) is dependent upon the highest aspects of the distinctive acts of that being, when these are considered from the point of view of its completion or perfection. The happiness of man will depend therefore upon the highest aspects of his actions, i.e. the humanity (*insániya*) that he manifests with discrimination (*tamyíz*) and consideration (*rawíya*). Accordingly, with reference to degrees of consideration, and works that require it, happiness has many stages; for as has been said, the best of consideration is that which is given to things that are most excellent. It descends then stage by stage until it comes to be merely consideration of matters in the world of sense perception (*al-'álam al-ḥissí*). The individual who gives much consideration to these things will be degraded thereby, for he employs his thinking, which is his most particular function—on which all his happiness is conditioned and by which he could have exercised continuous sovereignty—in making it subject to baser works, worldly things that have no permanency, of which it might indeed be said that they have no true existence.

"There is now set before you, in a kind of summary, the various kinds of happiness and their opposites the kinds of misery (*shaqáwa*). Each is given with its respective varieties. The things that are good (*khairát*) and the things that are evil (*al-sharúr*) are matters of choice (*al-af'ál al-irádíya*), i.e. by choice of the highest (*al-afḍal*) and by doing it, or by choice of the lowest (*al-adwan*) and desiring it. Since the types of human good, and the qualities of the soul that pertain to them, are exceedingly numerous, so much so indeed that no one person could possibly acquire them all, it follows that they could only be attained by a group of a number of men of different capacities who would act together. This is why individual types of men are so numerous. And if they should agree at one time to work together in the quest of these many kinds of happiness, on the basis of mutual assistance (*mu'áwina*), then there would be many kinds of good attained in common (*al-khairát mushtaraka*), and happiness would be something allotted or shared among them. They would rival one another for it, so that each one would get part of it. In this way the perfection of mankind would be accomplished for all, by the help of all.

"It would be needful, therefore, that some of mankind should have loving care and regard for others, so that each would kindle his perfection in another. Otherwise there would be no completion to this corporate happiness. Each individual may be considered as one of the members of the body, and thus the very constitution of society (*qawám al-insán*) depends upon all the members of the general body of mankind.

"Those who have directed their attention to the subject of the soul and its faculties say that they are three:

1. The faculty by which the soul may exercise thought (*al-fikr*) and discrimination (*al-tamyíz*) and observation (*naẓar*) in determining the nature of things.
2. The faculty by which the soul exercises anger (*al-ghaḍab*) and vigour (*al-najda*) and initiative (*al-iqdám*) in meeting dangers, or in combating desire for dominion, or promotion, or varieties of honours.
3. The faculty by which the soul exercises passionate desire (*al-shahwa*) in the quest of food and in its eagerness for the pleasures there are in eating and drinking, and in marriages, and in varieties of sensual enjoyment.

"These are the three faculties that may be distinguished. Evidently if any one of them is too strong it will be injurious to the others. Very often one does interfere with the activity of another. Thus it was indeed that the soul (*nafs*) was supposed to be plural, and was not regarded as something single with separate faculties. But further consideration of this matter is not fitting at this point.

"In the study of dispositions (*akhláq*) it will be sufficient for you to know that there are distinct faculties, and that each one of them is strengthened or weakened according to the individual's constitution (*mizáj*) or habit (*'ádat*) or training (*ta'díb*):

1. The faculty of rational discrimination (*quwwat al-nátiqa*) is that which is also called the angelic faculty (*quwwat al-malakíya*); and the instrument (*álat*) which it employs from the body is the brain (*al-damágh*).
2. The faculty of passionate desire (*quwwat al-shawíya*) is that which is called bestiality (*al-bahímíya*), and the instrument which it employs from the body is the liver (*al-kibd*).
3. The faculty of anger (*quwwat al-g̱haḍabíya*) is that which is called ferocity (*al-sabu'iya*), and the instrument which it employs from the body is the heart (*al-qalb*).

"To correspond with these faculties there should be a number of virtues (*faḍá'il*), and their opposites will be vices (*radhá'il*). For whenever there is a movement of the rational soul which is moderate, in that it does not go beyond the demands of the essence of the soul, and that has its desire fixed on understanding true sciences—not imaginary—for they are a cause of ignorance, then the virtue of knowledge (*faḍl al-'ilm*) is found, and following after it come wisdom (*ḥikma*). In the same way, whenever there is a movement of 'the bestial soul' (*al-nafs al-bahímíya*) that is moderate and in obedience to the rational soul (*al-nafs al-áqila*) in what it determines justly for it, and is not refractory (*muta'bbíya*), and is not engrossed in following its craving, then the virtue of purity (*'iffa*) occurs, and following after it comes generosity (*al-sakhá*). Likewise when there is a movement of the soul of anger (*al-nafs al-ghaḍabíya*) that is moderate and in obedience to the rational soul in what it determines justly for it, and is not aroused out of season, and that does not get hotter than is fitting, then occurs the virtue of tranquillity or forbearance (*al-ḥilm*), and following after it comes the virtue of courage (*al-shajá'a*).

"We observe that from these virtues, i.e. knowledge, purity, and courage, according to moderation (*i'tidál*) and the correct proportion they bear to one another, there occurs yet another virtue which is but their perfection and completion. It is the virtue of righteousness (*'adála*). Accordingly, the philosophers are agreed that the primary kinds of the virtues are four: wisdom (*al-ḥikma*), purity (*al-'iffa*), courage (*al-shajá'a*), and righteousness (*al-'adála*). No one glories or vies with others except in these virtues. Whoever takes pride in his fathers or predecessors, surely it is because they excelled in some of these virtues, or perhaps because they had them all.

"Now in the case of each one of these primary virtues, we observe that if its possessor exercises it for the benefit of others than himself he will be noted and commended for that virtue. But if it is confined to himself, then he will not be designated by the name of that virtue but will be given another name. For example, take the virtue of generosity (*al-júd*), if its possessor does not benefit others by it he will not be called a generous man but a spendthrift (*minfáq*). In respect to courage also, if it is not employed for others its possessor will be called a vehement man (*al-anif*). With regard to wisdom or learning, likewise, if it is not for others, then its possessor will be called no more than a man who is a good observer (*al-mustabṣir*). But if the possessor of generosity and of bravery makes common cause with others in the employment of these his two outstanding virtues he will derive hope (*rajá*) from one of them and reverence (*intishám*) and honour (*haib*) from the other. This applies in this world only, however, for after all these two are but animal virtues. But as for the virtue of knowledge (*al-'ilm*), if its possessor extends it to others, he will surely have hope and reverence both in this world and the next, for this is distinctively a human virtue with a spiritual nature (*malakíya*).

"Remember that for these four virtues there are also four opposites (*aḍdád*); ignorance (*al-jahl*), greed (*al-sharh*), cowardice (*al-jubn*), and violence (*al-jawr*). And under each one of these there are many varieties, which we will try to mention as far as possible in general, though the varieties that occur in the cases of individuals are innumerable.

"Personal afflictions give rise to many diseases (*amráḍ*), such as fear (*al-khawf*), sorrow (*al-huzn*), anger (*al-ghaḍab*), various kinds of lustful desire (*al-'ishq al-shahwání*), and forms of evil nature (*su' al-khulq*). We will mention these further later on, along with their cures, if Allah the Most High so wills, but that which falls to us now is something which has to do with these things, namely, the description of the four primary kinds of virtues that include all the other virtues.

"*Wisdom* is that distinguishing virtue of the human soul that understands existing things (*mawjúdát*), and that accurately perceives each of them in its particular existence. If you wish you may say that it understands both the works of Allah and the works of mankind, with the advantage that thereby it is able to know intelligible things (*ma'qulát*) and thus to determine those which should be acted upon and those which should be ignored.

"*Purity* (or self-control) is a virtue of the sensual feeling (*al-ḥiss al-shahwáni*). It is shown in man when he employs his desire thoughtfully (*bi hasab al-ra'y*), to determine whether it agrees with sound judgement, so that he may remain free (*ḥurr*), and may not allow himself to be led by it and then to be enslaved to some object of his desire.

"*Courage* is a virtue of the passionate self (*nafs al-ghaḍabíya*), and it is shown in man when the passionate self is kept in subjection to the rational and discriminating self. It is ready to do what the will requires in circumstances that are frightful (*al-umúr al-há'ila*), so that he will not be afraid of things that are terrifying, when doing them is worthy and enduring them is commendable. This virtue is righteousness or justice (*'adála*), and it is required of a person through the combination of the three virtues which we have mentioned. It occurs on the right adjustment of these powers, one to another, and the surrendering of them to the faculty of discrimination, so that they will not be in opposition, and will not break away for the objectives of their respective natures. In relation to excess and deficiency, a man chooses by this virtue of justice (*'adála*) a position in which he is fair to himself in the first place, and also one in which equity is observed between himself and others."

Ibn Maskawaihi's *Tahdhíb al-Akhláq* has been accepted as the authoritative text in Muslim ethical philosophy. It is not a large book, and, as has been mentioned, it follows very closely the *Tahdhíb al-Akhláq* that was written by the Syrian Christian Yaḥyá ibn 'Adí. As it drew thus freely on Greek philosophy it was used as an indispensable source by al-Ghazálí when he wrote the *Iḥyá'* and the *Mizán al-'Amal*. It was Ibn Maskawaihi's Arabic text that was edited and elaborated by subsequent writers on ethics in both Arabic and Persian. In view of its recognized importance the following brief synopsis is given to show its general character.

BRIEF ANALYSIS OF IBN MASKAWAIHI'S *TAHDHÍB AL-AKHLÁQ*

In Chapter I, which treats of the faculties of the soul and explains virtues and vices, Ibn Maskawaihi argues that in so much as the soul is neither a body nor an accident, since it imagines bodies without assuming their qualities, and can have unlimited mental perceptions, it must be a form of existence that is essentially different from bodies. It has, moreover, the power of correcting sense illusions, "after examining them and drawing conclusions as to their causes". And more significant still, the soul is self-conscious and feels a sense of independence of anything outside itself.

The superiority of an individual soul is to be estimated by its pursuit of knowledge, that its discernment may be truer, its reflexion sounder, and its choice wiser. The cardinal virtues are then enumerated—wisdom, continence, courage, and justice. Each virtue is shown as the happy mean between deficiency and excess,[6] so that every virtue must have at least two opposing vices.

Attention is called also to the necessary exercise of an individual's virtues in relation to other individuals, in so much as man's nature and environment makes association with other men necessary. This is why the quest of virtue through the practice of asceticism and by withdrawal into oneself is a manifest error.

In Chapter II there is discussion of the individual character (lit. "state of the soul", *hál-i-nafs*). It is defined as that which causes the soul to perform its action spontaneously, whether from natural inclination or by acquired habit. This involves belief in a natural disposition, capacity, or aptitude for the development of character, and the goal is perfection.

The purpose of ethics is to set forth a method of self-discipline that may be rationally approved. To begin with, desires must be regulated —first the desire for food, then the desire for the expression of the irascible self in anger, then the desire to receive honour or advancement, and finally the desire to obtain knowledge. Character training, therefore, is a course of action that involves necessary processes, in fact it is an art, an art that is far nobler but similar in a way to the art of tanning, which has to do only with the improvement of the hides of dead animals.

Extreme difference among men must of course be frankly recognized. In this connexion the Prophet is said to have remarked, "Men are like camels: out of a hundred thou canst pick a single one that is fit to be ridden." Indeed he felt himself to be vastly different from other men, for he said, "I was weighed against all my people and I outweighed them."

The best of men may be described as the man who performs persistently his own distinctive function, making use of his intellectual faculty as a means, and exercising his practical faculty so as to attain the end in view. The end is to reach an existence that will be complete in itself, and therefore eternal, and worthy to receive the "over-

6. It is claimed that the doctrine of the "happy mean" can be found in the teaching of the Qur'án (ii. 137; xvi. 92; xli. 3; lxxii. 4; and cxviii. 4). Ghazálí identified it with the *sirát al-mustaqím* (*Iḥyá'*, iii. 55).

flowing of the divine grace", with only a veil separating him from Allah.

Plato's illustration of the hunter, who rides a horse and is accompanied by a hunting dog, is used to make clear the necessity of the rational self retaining full authority over the other selves in the struggle for moral perfection; and the man who fails to appreciate his power of reason is compared to a foolish person who cast a precious ruby into the fire.

For a more detailed statement of the kinds of discipline that are necessary in the process of moral development, a section is quoted from the Arabic translation of the "Economics" of "Bryson",[7] which gives very explicit instructions for the education of a boy. Bashfulness (*hayá'*) on a boy's part must be recognized as a symptom that he is using his reason to choose the good (*al-jamál*) and to reject the evil (*al-qabíh*). But his initial rational judgements must have sensible confirmation and encouragement, especially by the praise of worthy deeds and motives.

He must learn, however, that he has desires that need to be restrained. His food, for example, he must come to regard as a medicine that his body requires, in duly regulated quantities. His sleep also is to meet a bodily need, but it should not be made too comfortable on a soft bed. He should have his main meal at night, so as not to be dull or drowsy in the daytime. For acts of meanness or disobedience he should be rebuked or punished by whipping, but not before others, for such unnecessary humiliation would tend only to make him impudent and resentful.

What is spoken of as the evolutionary philosophy of nature in Islam, which amounts to a recognition of different stages of development—from the stage of minerals to that of plants, from the stage of plants to that of animals, and from the stage of animals to that of man—is used as a background for the presentation of the struggle that man must make for moral progress. Only by proving himself in some way superior to the stage of the animals can man attain to that high type of existence for which he has potential capacity or aptitude.[8]

In Chapter III, where Ibn Maskawaihi distinguishes between the different kinds of *good* (*al-khair*), there is an avowedly *verbatim* quotation from a book ascribed to Aristotle, the *Faḍá'il al-Nafs*, which is said to have been translated by Abu 'Uthman al-Dimishqí, who was one of the pupils of the celebrated translator, Ḥunain ibn Isḥáq (A.D. 809–77). In A.D. 915 Dimishqí is known to have been an

7. Martin Plessner, *Der Oikonomiko wortlich des Neupythagoreers* '*Bryson*', Heidelberg, 1928, pp. 49 ff.

8. Dieterici, *Die Philosophie der Araber*, ch. ix, "Der Darwinismus im zehnten und neunzehnten Jahrhundert", Berlin, 1878. Cf. *Rasá'il Ikhwán al-Ṣafá'*, ii. 141 ff.; iii. 221 ff.; and iv. 314 ff.; as also Sir Muhammad Iqbál, *Reconstruction of Religious Thought in Islam*, Introduction.

inspector of hospitals in Baghdad, Mecca, and Medina; and in addition to works that he translated from Aristotle, Euclid, and Porphyry, he translated and commented upon books of Galen.[9]

Chapter IV, which is on Justice (*'adála*), describes the distinguishing divine essence that characterizes the human soul, and which by its likeness to God may be regarded as capable of union with Him, when it is set free from the impurities that come from contact with the material things of nature. Aristotle's *Nicomachean Ethics* is used frequently to set forth the idea that by obeying his intellect and reason man is to rise above the level of other creatures, and the restrictions that come from their needs, in order to realize his own participation in absolute good.[10] That exalted experience will bring him a pleasure that is not to be compared with any other pleasures.

Chapter V, on the "Kinds of Love" (*anwá' maḥabbati*), begins with the statement that that kind of love for which pleasure (*ladhdhat*) is the reason is quickly confirmed and quickly exhausted, because pleasure is quick to change; whereas love that has its cause in the good (*al-khair*) is confirmed quickly and exhausted slowly. Furthermore, love that finds its reason in the useful is slowly confirmed and slowly exhausted. These forms of love occur particularly among mankind, for they depend on volition (*iráda*) and reflexion (*rawíya*). They also involve punishments (*mujázát*) and rewards (*mukáfát*).

The obligation of men towards their Creator is to meditate on things divine, seeking to add all that is possible to their knowledge of Allah, that His unity may be fully appreciated. They must fulfil their duties to Allah and direct their efforts towards Him, as Aristotle said, "in accord with the differences that occur among people in their attainments in knowledge".

Later philosophers said that there are three high ranks that men may attain in their relation to Allah: (1) the rank of learned men, such as philosophers and scientists; (2) the rank of those benevolent people who act according to what they know; (3) the rank of those who are especially virtuous, who are sent as representatives of Allah for the welfare of the people; and (4) the rank of those who have thoroughly overcome themselves and who are sincere in their love for their Creator, a love that leads to union with Him.

In their associations with one another also, men should be bound by ties of love, united in true friendship, so that each will wish for his friend what he wants for himself.

Chapter VI is devoted to the treatment of the diseases that afflict the human soul. Since the soul and the body are mutually dependent, there is need to determine first whether an unhealthy condition is in the mind or in the body. Much indeed that contributes to unhappiness is in the mind. For this reason association with those of high

9. *Isis*, viii (1926), p. 710.
10. Aristotle, *Nichomachean Ethics*, 1155, and 1177–9.

moral purpose is most important, and this means that one should be careful to avoid association with acquaintances who indulge in debasing conversations and vulgar stories or poems. All inclination to be covetous must also be suppressed. Among other people one should seek to be agreeable in ways that are interesting, without condescending to that which would be unworthy.

Mental disquietude and dissatisfaction can be overcome frequently by the persistent and diligent pursuit of knowledge, by keeping the mind at hard work, and by continuing to appreciate the treasures it may lay up in store.

The author has observed men of wealth and position, whose responsibilities and cares were tremendous, men who were ever anxious on account of those about them, some of whom were envious of them and scheming against them. He recalls how Abu Bakr said, "Kings are the most unhappy of men, both in this world and the next."

He admonishes all to regard the taking of food as merely one of the bodily requirements. It should not be a luxurious indulgence. Similarly, the concupiscent faculties should not be stimulated by continued re-thinking and imagination, but be restrained within reason so that they will not militate against one's higher powers and discernment. Habits of good judgement and self-control should be deliberately cultivated, and that with foresight, so that when occasions of testing come they may be in readiness.

Galen's advice, that a man should find a friend to tell him frankly about his faults, is mentioned—advice which he gives in his book on "A Man's Knowledge of the Defects of His Soul",[11] Attention is called also to the teaching of al-Kindi, that a man should not be like a mere book, which tells others of wisdom which it does not have itself, nor like a whetstone which sharpens many knives but which is itself too dull to cut anything.

In Chapter VII, the concluding chapter on the cure of the diseases of the soul, the author makes many apt observations which serve to show how he diagnosed various human frailties. *Anger* is a disease of the irascible soul, when a man becomes like a cave full of flames, from which the "voice of fire" (*waḥi al-nár*) comes forth. A vessel tossed at sea may be saved by the diligence and skill of the sailors that man it, but those who seek to assist a man in anger, whether by remonstrating with him or giving him counsel, only intensify his rage. But the causes of anger may be dealt with somewhat as follows:

Conceit, which is essentially a false belief about one's own importance, must be spurned by any man who really knows the nature of his soul, which cannot attain perfection except through the virtue of other souls. So why should he be puffed-up over virtues that are not found in himself?

11. al-Nadím, *Fihrist*, i. 271.

Vanity. A slave is said to have reproached a proud horseman: "If thou lookest down upon me because of your horse, forget not that his beauty and alertness are his and not yours!" And in like manner, when a philosopher called upon a merchant who was vain and rich, he observed tapestries on the walls and costly oriental rugs on the floors. For some reason he wanted to spit, and after gazing around a moment with his mouth all set, he finally spat right into the face of his host. When he was asked why he had done such a thing he replied, "I could find no other suitable place".

Jesting, which is another cause of anger, may be said to be profitable only so long as it is in moderation, and he who does not know the right limit should beware of it.

Boastfulness adds to conceit a certain disdain of others, both of which are despised by men of wisdom.

Perfidy (*ghadr*) assumes many forms but it is rebuked by every tongue.

Unfairness (*ḍaym*) shows itself especially in acts of retaliation.

Laying-up Treasures. How often the distress and rancour of kings is due to the loss of some mere ornament! Men of common rank also have suffered dire misfortune for becoming too much attached to high-priced things of beauty.

In addition to these several causes of anger, it is well to keep in mind its consequences, namely, that the man who is overcome with anger wrongs himself, his friends, and all who come in contact with him. To the slaves and women in his harem he becomes "a whip for torture". In his mad rage he may mutilate his donkey, or seize upon a bird, or bite a lock. And it is noticeable how often the vice of anger goes with that of gluttony, for when the glutton does not find what he wants to eat he vents his feelings upon women, children, and servants.

Fear (*khawf*) may be mentioned as another disease of the irascible faculty of the soul. It is a vice from the side of deficiency, which in this case is like a fire which is dying out, but which can be revived by fanning or blowing. It is caused by anticipating evils,[12] things that are admittedly contingent and that may not take place at all.

As for the fear of old age, a man should have recognized previously that it necessarily involves a diminution of bodily powers, and to this lessening of his strength he must become accustomed.

Perhaps the most intense fear is that of death, which is shown by those who are ignorant of immortality, or by those who think that death will bring with it great pain, or by those who dread punishment after death, or by those who hate to think of having to give up their money and property. But when it is rightly understood that death means only the soul's giving up the use of its tools, its bodily organs, and that the soul is itself an *essence* and not an *accident*, then there is hope that at death it will be but purified and perfected, and

12. Aristotle, *Nichomachean Ethics*, 1115.

that it will live on in eternal existence, perfectly happy. Why should a man be afraid of attaining his own perfection?

If a man fears that after death he will be punished for his misconduct, the reasonable course of action would be for him to guard against his faults, in ways such as have been indicated, in order to avoid vices and to cultivate virtues. It is knowledge that he needs, so that he may follow a straight path to a worthy goal. For true knowledge enables a man to overcome fear and grief, since grief comes because of his losing something in this world of generation and corruption, when he forgets that only those things endure which belong to the world of intellect. This is in keeping with the declaration in the Qur'án (x. 63): "Verily, the friends of Allah shall have no fear, nor shall they be put to grief."

6

THE ETHICAL TEACHINGS OF AL-GHAZÁLÍ

THE BEST-KNOWN Muslim writer on ethical subjects is Abú Ḥámid al-Ghazálí.[1] He lived and wrote in another period of political upheaval, when the Buwaihid princes had been forced to give way before the powerful advance of the Seljuqs from Turkestan.

When the Seljuqs captured Baghdad in A.D. 1055,[2] they not only took the 'Abbasid Caliph under their protection and custody, but they constituted themselves the defenders of orthodoxy. With the help of able viziers, to mention the outstanding Nizám al-Mulk in particular, they were successful in restricting the activities of the several Shi'ite sects, and they took the lead in defending the newly united Muhammadan Empire against the Christian crusaders.

In al-Ghazálí's comprehensive manual of Muslim faith and practice, the massive "Revivification of the Ṛeligious Sciences" (*Iḥyá' al-'Ulúm al-Dín*), which he wrote also in Persian as the "Alchemy of Happiness",[3] many ethical questions are dealt with from a practical and religious point of view. The chapters that treat of "Intention", of "Marriage", and of "Earning a Living" have been translated into German by Professor Hans Bauer. They have been published as *Islamische Ethik*,[4] but they have very much more to do with accepted legal practice than with scientific or philosophical ethics.

A small book was published in the "Wisdom of the East Series" in 1910, which is entitled *The Alchemy of Happiness*. It consists of translations in English by Claud Field of a few passages from an Urdu translation of the original Persian *Kímiyá*.

In the selection on the treatment of wives (pp. 95–8) it is pointed out that it is written in the Qur'án, "Men should have the upper hand over women", and that al-Ghazálí observes that the Prophet said, "Woe to the man who is the servant of his wife", for she should be his servant.

1. Cf. article by D. B. Macdonald, *Encyclopædia of Islam*, vol. iii, pp. 146–9.
2. Cf. Huart, art. "Seldjuks", *Encyclopædia of Islam*, vol. iv, pp. 208–13.
3. Ch. 10, Part ii of the *Iḥyá'* is omitted from the *Kímiyá*, and a chapter on "Taking Care of Subjects" is substituted. Ch. 1, Part iii of the *Iḥyá*,' appears in the *Kímiyá* in the Introduction; and a chapter on the "Cure of the Love of Position" is inserted in Part iii after the chapter on the "Blameworthiness of Greed and the Love of Wealth".
4. Hans Bauer, *Islamische Ethik*, Halle, 1916, 1917, 1922.

"Wise men have said," he remarks, "'Consult women and act contrary to what they advise.' In truth there is something perverse in women, and if they are allowed even a little licence, they get out of control altogether, and it is difficult to reduce them to order again. In dealing with them one should endeavour to use a mixture of severity and tenderness, with a greater proportion of the latter. The Prophet said, 'Woman was formed of a crooked rib; if you try to bend her you will break her; if you leave her alone she will grow more and more crooked; therefore treat her tenderly.'

"As regards propriety, one cannot be too careful not to let one's wife look at or be looked at by a stranger, for the beginning of all mischief is in the eye. As far as possible she should not be allowed out of the house, nor to go on the roof, nor to stand at the door. Care should be taken, however, not to be unreasonably jealous and strict. . . .

"If a man's wife be rebellious and disobedient, he should at first admonish her gently; if this is not sufficient he should sleep in a separate chamber for three nights. Should this also fail he may strike her, but not on the mouth, nor with such force as to wound her. Should she be remiss in her religious duties he should manifest his displeasure to her for an entire month, as the Prophet did on one occasion to all his wives. . . .

"The Prophet said, 'If it were right to worship anyone except God, it would be right for wives to worship their husbands.'"

It was in the course of his high moral and religious aspiration that al-Ghazálí carried on his studies beyond the analysis of Muslim law and practice, beyond the realm of systematic theology and philosophy, into the region of the mystic's heart-felt certainty of the divine presence. Like Ibn Maskawaihi, he too had rules for his spiritual self-discipline. They are observations from his experience, which he explains in his *al-Risálat al-Laduniyya* ("The Inspired Treatise"), and from which the following brief statements are derived:[5]

1. His intention must be good, and lasting without change.
2. Unity of purpose must be maintained in serving Allah alone.
3. He must conform throughout to truth, with self-discipline.
4. Against procrastination there must be steadfast zeal and determination.
5. It is necessary to conform in life to established practice and to avoid innovations.
6. With a sense of dependence on Allah, humility should be cultivated towards men.
7. While salvation is by faith, yet this includes true fear and hope.
8. A life of devotion and prayer is to be recommended.

5. *Risálat al-Laduniyya*, trans. by Margaret Smith, *J.R.A.S.*, 1936; and the citation in *The Arab Heritage*, Symposium, Princeton, 1944, pp. 149 ff.

9. One must watch continuously over his own heart, to banish from it everything but Allah.

10. He sought consecration to that knowledge wherein one could see Allah.

In the *Iḥyá'* al-Ghazálí gives a remarkably lucid and comprehensive account of what we might call the popular moral philosophy of Islam in connexion with his explanation of the ethics of mysticism. The authority of the Qur'án and the Traditions for all the orthodox beliefs and practices is set forth with such thoroughness in the *Iḥyá'* that it could scarcely be suggested that the author had failed to do justice to any one of them. But as Dr. Margaret Smith has recently pointed out (*Al-Ghazálí: The Mystic*, pp. 202 ff.), Ibn Tufayl (d. A.D. 1185) observed at the close of his philosophical romance *Ḥayy ibn Yaqzán* that "the mysteries which we have confided to these pages we have concealed with a light veil, easily withdrawn by those fitted to do so, but impenetrable by those who are unworthy of what lies beyond it", so al-Ghazálí may be considered to have included in the *Iḥyá'* his three kinds of opinions, to which he has himself referred in the *Mizán al-'Amal*, p. 162: "(1) that which is shared with the vulgar and is in accordance with their view; (2) the opinion given to anyone who comes asking for guidance; and (3) the opinion which a man keeps to himself, which is not disclosed except to one who himself holds it." Dr. A. J. Wensinck has also remarked on the comprehensive character of the *Iḥyá'*, for in indicating its many similarities to the *Ethikon* of Bar Hebraeus (d. A.D. 1286), "who may perhaps be called the best known of Syriac authors in Europe", he mentions that they both "treat of the whole domain of human life; it is not only prayer and love which are described in their forms and religious depth, but also commerce and marriage, the daily meals and the education of children".

In the third book of the *Iḥyá'*, which we consider to be the most important for our study from the ethical standpoint, al-Ghazálí has presented the system of ethics that was adopted into Islam from the Greeks, as has been shown—by way of the Christian Syriac scholar Yaḥyá ibn 'Adí and the Muslim historian and philosopher Ibn Maskawaihi. This debt to Christian Syriac influence was soon repaid, however, for in A.D. 1278, 167 years after the death of al-Ghazálí, the Christian Syriac author Bar Hebraeus followed the *Iḥyá'* closely when he wrote the *Ethikon*. General parallelism appears, as Dr. Wensinck has shown conclusively,[6] between the *Ethikon* and the *Iḥyá'*. This is clearly recognized in the third book of the *Ethikon*, on "The Purifying of the Soul from Vices", where the ten chapter headings in the *Iḥyá'* may be readily compared with eleven chapters of the *Ethikon*:

6. *Bar Hebraeus's Book of the Dove* (together with some chapters from the *Ethikon*), trans. by A. J. Wensinck, Leyden, 1919, xvii ff.

Ihyá'	*Ethikon*
On the heart.	On the soul.
On the training of the soul.	On the training of the soul.
On lasciviousness and sensuality.	On wantonness.
	On lasciviousness.
On the tongue.	On the tongue.
On anger, rancour, and envy.	On anger, rancour, and envy.
On the world.	On worldly desires.
On avarice.	On covetousness.
On bluffing and false appearance.	On hyprocrisy.
On pride.	On pride.
On self-deception.	On boasting.

Moreover we find that in both works each separate chapter in this third book is prefaced by a series of citations, in the one case from the Qur'án and the Ḥadíth and in the other case from the Bible and Christian traditions. Then comes the definition of the subject, which al-Ghazálí designates as the *ḥadd* or *ḥaqíqat*. Al-Ghazálí's division of moral works into three states—knowledge (*'ilm*), action (*'amal*), and disposition (*ḥál*)—as shown in the *Iḥyá'* (iv, p. 208), is followed also by Bar Hebraeus, and they both make use of the distinction in spiritual knowledge between that which is practical (*'ilm al-ma'ámala*) and that which is contemplative (*'ilm al-makáshafa*).

On first thought one would be inclined to think that this distinction was but analagous to that distinction which had long been employed between speculative and practical knowledge (*'ilm naẓarí wa 'ilm 'amalí*). Only in the ethics of mysticism the spiritual knowledge that is practical comes first and contributes to the second form, the contemplative spiritual knowledge which culminates in revelation. "By contemplative knowledge", al-Ghazálí has written, "we mean that the veil is raised and that the Divine Glory is revealed so clearly that it cannot be doubted. . . . In proportion as the heart is polished and turned Godwards, is the Divine Reality manifested therein. There is no way to attain this except by self-discipline and knowledge and study."[7]

In this division of spiritual knowledge into the practical and the contemplative it has been suggested that al-Ghazálí may have been at least indirectly influenced by Christian writers, for the Christian monk John Cassian (d. A.D. 432) taught that the contemplative (θεωρητιή) "can be revealed only by acquiring the practical (πρακτική), for the stains of sin must first be eradicated before the vision of God can be attained".[8]

7. *Iḥyá'*, I, pp. 18–19. Cf. Margaret Smith, *al-Ghazálí: the Mystic*, pp. 120–1.

8. Margaret Smith, op. cit., p. 120.

Almost the same ethical teaching that is contained in the third book of the *Iḥyá'* is given also in al-Ghazálí's much smaller book, *al-Mizán al-'Amal*, which, "since his ethical teaching was of a standard and type which closely resembled that of Judaism", was translated in the thirteenth century into Hebrew by Abraham ibn Ḥasdai of Barcelona.[9] In the *Iḥyá'*, however, there is a fuller and more satisfactory discussion of such problems of moral philosophy as the freedom of the will, the functions of reason, and the attainment of moral integrity.

We may note first that in both of these books, in his consideration as to whether it is possible for anyone to bring about a moral change in his dispositions (*Iḥyá'*, III, pp. 48–50, and *Mizán al-'Amal*, pp. 67 ff.), al-Ghazálí takes the position that an effective kind of freedom of the will is appreciated as a fact in human experience.

THE POSSIBILITY OF CHANGING DISPOSITIONS

"There are those who are somewhat inclined to be careless who have expressed the opinion that the disposition (*al-khulq*) is like the created nature (*al-khalq*), and that it is therefore incapable of change (*al-taghyír*). They have referred to the saying, 'Allah ceased from creation' (*faragha Allahu min al-khalqi*). Consequently they say that the desire for a change in disposition is equivalent to the desire for a change in what Allah, the Great and Glorious, has created.

"Observe, however, that they have forgotten the text, 'Refine your dispositions.' Now if this were not possible, surely it would not have been commanded. For if it were indeed impossible, then commandments (*waṣaya*) and admonitions (*muwa'iz*), encouragement (*targhíb*), and threatening (*tarhíb*) would be useless. For if actions are but the results of dispositions, just as a material object falls in consequence of its gravity (*thiql al-tabí'i*), then is reproach to be attached to action from a disposition and to to the falling of an object?

"And aside from this, how could anyone deny the correction of man, with his predominance of Reason, and yet admit a change of disposition among animals—as when a beast of prey is changed from its wildness to domesticity (*ta'annus*), or a dog is changed from a devourer to a being of good manners (*ta'addub*), or a horse is changed from refractoriness (*jinah*) to gentleness (*salasa*), for assuredly each one of these is a change of disposition.

"We should make a clear statement about this matter, for what Allah created is of two kinds. The first kind includes that which has a created nature that requires no action on our part; as for example the heavens, the stars, the members of our bodies and their separate parts, and also many things that take place around us. The second kind includes what Allah has created with a capacity to take on perfection when ever it finds the proper condition for development

9. Margaret Smith, op. cit., p. 218.

(*tarbiya*). But in the process of this development there is an act of choice (*ikhtiyár*). In the case of the date stone, it is neither an apple nor a date, but it does have the capacity to become a date by development, whereas it lacks the capacity to become an apple. As a matter of experience, however, it becomes a date only when human choice is exercised.

"In a way that is similar to this, if we desire completely to uproot anger (*al-ghaḍab*) and bodily desire from our souls, we do not have the capacity to do so in this world (for they belong to our nature). If, however, we desire rather the subjection (*kahr*) and taming of these passions by discipline (*riyaḍa*) and earnest effort (*mujáhida*), this we are able to accomplish. It is to this task that we are commanded, and this it is that has come to be a condition of our happiness (*sa'áda*) and indeed of our salvation (*naját*).

"Yes, natural dispositions are admitted to be different, as in acquiring knowledge there are some who are rapid and some who are slow; and for these differences of natural dispositions there are two reasons. The first is priority in existence. In the case of the three special powers of man—the power of bodily desire, the power of anger, and the power of thinking—the most difficult of these for man to change, and the most obstinate, is the power of bodily desire. This power has had priority over the other powers and this is why it is the strongest in its persistence (*tashabbuth*) and tenacity (*iltisáq*). It has been with mankind from the beginning and it is found in animals that are the same genus as man. Afterwards comes the power of indignation (*ḥamiya*) and anger (*ghaḍab*). Note that the power of thinking (*tafakkur*) comes last of all. This is because the disposition (*al-khulq*), as distinguished from the nature, has a tendency to be confirmed by occurrences of actions that are in agreement with it, and by its acceptance of these occurrences as good and pleasant.

"In this particular we may group mankind in four stages. The first are those who are heedless, who do not distinguish truth (*al-ḥaqq*) from folly (*al-bátil*), or the beautiful (*al-jamíl*) from the base (*al-qabíḥ*). They lack conviction (*i'tiqád*), and in the pursuit of pleasures they are unable to control their desires. They are the easiest, however, of the several kinds of men, to cure, for they need only the instruction of a teacher (*murshid*) and a sufficient motive to direct them. Thus the disposition of anyone of this kind of men may become good in but a short time.

"The men who are at the second stage are those who know well enough the baseness of what is base, but they do not become habituated to good conduct because they consider that their evil conduct is something enjoyable. As a consequence they engage in it submissively, in accord with their desires, but contrary to their own better judgement. As a result the situation of those in this stage is much more difficult than that of those in the first stage, for they are more at fault. They can, however, resort to one of two expedients. Either they may root out their established habits that make for corruption, or they may direct their desire towards something else that is not corrupt, relying on 'the expulsive power of a new affection'. On the whole they may be said to be capable of exercising this discipline, but it will require strenuous effort.

"Those in the third stage actually approve of base dispositions, maintaining that they are necessary, right, and beautiful. So they pursue them wholeheartedly. It is almost impossible for men in this third stage to be cured. In fact there is no hope for them, except in the rarest instances, for their opportunities for error (*asbáb al-ḍalál*) are being constantly increased.

"The fourth kind are those who, along with what accompanies corrupt belief and practice, see also a sort of virtue in their very excess of evil and in the destruction of lives. In this they vie with one another, and they think they gain fame by the amount of evil they accomplish. It will be seen that they are the most difficult of the four stages, and it is of them that it has been said, 'It is a real torture for anyone to have to train a wolf to be well-bred, or to wash black hair-cloth to make it white.'

"In summarizing the men of these four stages, we observe that the first are those who may be called ignorant (*jáhil*); the second are those who are also in error (*ḍallun*); the third are ignorant, in error, and dissolute (*fásiq*); and the fourth are ignorant, in error, dissolute, and wicked (*sharír*).

AN EXCELLENT WAY TO CHANGE DISPOSITIONS

"Understand that the purpose of putting forth effort and of exercising discipline in commendable actions is the perfection of the soul (*takmíl al-nafs*), to sanctify it and to purify it by the correction of its dispositions. Between the soul and these physical powers there is a kind of narrow connexion. It is beyond our ability to describe exactly how this connexion is made, somewhere in the storehouse of memory (*khazánat al-takhayyul*), but we venture to assert that it is not a sensation (*maḥsúsa*) but a concept (*ma'qúla*). The explanation of this connexion, however, is not our immediate object, though everyone is undoubtedly influenced by this inter-relation of his mind and his body. For assuredly, if the mind is perfected and purified it will improve the deeds of the body, so that they too will become commendable. And conversely, if the impressions that are given to the mind by the body are wholesome they will put the mind in a favourable state, and the dispositions will tend to become agreeable. Therefore the way to purify the mind is to make habitual those actions which are completely pure, having in view that when this has become a custom by means of frequent repetition, then the state that has been produced on the mind will become constant. Thus the desired actions will have become necessary, for the new state of mind will demand them. They will have become a natural habit, and the good deed that was difficult at first will prove to be a lightsome task.

"For example, if anyone wishes to acquire for his mind the virtue of generosity (*al-júd*), he should take pains to engage in some action that is generous, such as giving away some particular thing that he possesses. And he should not cease to be interested in this giving until he has fully entered into the spirit of it and has actually become generous. Likewise if anyone wishes to acquire for his mind the virtue of humility (*tawáḍu'*), when perhaps at present pride has been getting the better of him, he should pay especial attention to occupying himself with actions that are deferential and humble. This attention he should also definitely direct against pride, and he should make this conscious effort at frequent intervals.

"The peculiar thing about this relation between the mind and the body is that it is like a circle, for by the actions of the body there is produced on the mind some particular quality (*ṣifa*), and this quality in turn purifies the body. It demands the recurrence of those acts which the body has become accustomed to accomplish altogether naturally, after having engaged in them for some time before as a matter of obligation.

"This question of moral progress is precisely like progress in the arts, for if anyone wishes to acquire skill in calligraphy, for instance, he must exercise the necessary mental perseverance. He must engage in what the skilful writer gives him to do, which is the reproduction of a well-written line. At first this will be a matter of requirement and of imitation. And afterwards he must not cease to give his attention to making this well-written line until his aptitude (*malaka*) in doing so is established, and until his skill becomes actually a mental quality. In the end he will do naturally and easily what was at first an arduous effort. The line, however, will be good which he has made good, first with conscious effort but in the end quite naturally. This is all because of the mind's capacity to receive an impression.

"It is the same way in the case of anyone who wishes to develop the legal mind. There is no possibility of his doing this except through diligent application to the law, by committing it to memory and by frequently reviewing it. At first it will be a real task, until gradually the legal aspect of things comes to make an impression on his mind more readily. It is in this way that the legal mind is acquired. So it is that a lawyer comes to have a mind that is ready to bring out the law, and this becomes easy for him whenever he wishes to do it. And it is the same way in the case of all other qualities of the mind.

"Moreover, we should observe that when anyone seeks a particular attainment in the science of law he does not forfeit it by one night's rest, and neither does he procure it by a little more than one night's work. So it is with anyone who seeks the perfection of the soul (*kamál al-nafs*). He does not attain it by the worship of a day and he does not forfeit it by the omission of a day. Nevertheless it is to be conceded that omitting it for one day may call for its omission another time, and by degrees the soul will develop a tendency towards laziness (*kasal*), and gradually give up study and actually lose the knowledge it had.

"We find that this is the case also in regard to the *lesser sins* (*saghá'ir al-ma'así*). Some of them demand others. Though the repetition of one of these lesser sins may be scarcely perceptible in the impression it makes on the mind, for this becomes evident very gradually, as in the growth of the body or in the increase of stature, yet it is fitting that we should not make light of one act of disobedience, for a large number of such acts certainly do have an influence. And as this number will be made up of single units, it is obvious that to each act we must attribute some particular effect (*ta'thír*). In a similar way it can be shown that there is no act of obedience for which there is not some real value, even though it should not be apparent. . . .

"It is for this reason that the *Amír al-mu'minín*, the Prince of the Faithful (*'Ali ibn Abu Ṭálib*) declared:

> *Faith* appears in the heart like a white spot,
> as it increases so this white increases,
> and when the servant is perfect in faith his heart
> is entirely white; and in the same way
> *Hypocrisy* (*nifáq*) appears in the heart like a black spot,
> as it increases the blackness increases.
> and when the servant is perfect in his hypocrisy
> his heart is entirely black."

Another selection from this third book of the *Iḥyá'* that is of interest is the following.

THAT WHICH IS PERMISSIBLE OF FALSEHOOD

(*Iḥyá'* III, p. 104 ff.)

"Understand that falsehood in speech (*al-kidhb*) is not forbidden (*harám*) in itself, but because of such injury as there may be in it to the speaker, or to others. Its lesser degree is when the one informed believes something to be different from what it actually is. He would then be ignorant, and in such a case the injury would fall upon another than the speaker. It often occurs, however, that in ignorance there is some profit or advantage, and if falsehood is the cause of such ignorance, then it has in it that which is permissible. In fact it is not only permissible but is frequently required (*wájib*).

"Maimun ibn al-Mahr said that falsehood is at some times better than truth (*al-ṣidq*). For example, if you see that a man is trying to fall upon another man with a sword in order to kill him, that he has entered the gate and has come to you and has said, 'Have you seen such a person?' You will not say, 'I have seen him', but you will say, 'I have not seen him.' This type of falsehood is required, for we say that speech is but a means to an end. Nevertheless, when a good end may be assisted by means of either truth or falsehood, then the use of falsehood is forbidden. But if the attainment of the end can be more readily achieved by falsehood than by truth, then it must be regarded as permissible when the end is permissible, and as necessary when the end is necessary.

"If the purpose of the falsehood is to prevent the shedding of the blood of a Muslim, then it is necessary. When it is truly a case that involves the shedding of blood, then it is incumbent upon a Muslim to save himself from the oppressor, and falsehood is necessary. Also, when there is no way to bring about a purpose in war, or to effect concord among people, or to make a heart that is set against you become favourably inclined, except by the use of falsehood, then falsehood is permissible (*mubáḥ*). It is of course desirable that a man should avoid falsehood as far as possible, for when he has once opened the door of falsehood to his heart, he has reason to fear lest he should employ it when it is not needed. In any such instances, when a man is not content to limit its use to sheer necessity, it must be considered that falsehood is forbidden *per se*.

"In consideration of the necessity of falsehood at particular times and in exceptional circumstances, there is the tradition that has been related by Umm Kulthum (who was one of the Prophet's wives). She said, 'I did not hear the Apostle of Allah grant any concession in regard to the use of falsehood except in the three following circumstances: (1) when a man says something by which he desires to bring about a reconciliation; (2) when a man speaks about something in time of war; and (3) when a man relates something to his wife, or when a wife relates something to her husband.' She also said that the Prophet declared, 'That is not to be reckoned as falsehood which is said to reconcile two individuals, something which is good or productive of good.' It is related that 'Uṣma, the daughter of Yazíd, said that the Prophet declared, 'Every falsehood is written down against the son of Adam except when he speaks falsely with Muslims in order to bring about reconciliation between them.' Also it is related from Abí Káhil, that he said that a discussion had arisen between two of the Prophet's companions, which reached a point at which they were about to break off their association. But he met one of them and said, 'What is the trouble between you and such and such a person, for I have heard him speak well of you?' Then he went to the other and said the same thing to him, so that they were reconciled. But he fell to thinking whether he was destroying his soul in order to effect reconciliation between these two, and he told the Prophet about it. The Prophet replied, 'O Abí Káhil, bring about reconciliation, even though it must be by falsehood.'

"'Atá ibn Yasír has related that a man reported to the Prophet that he had spoken falsely to his wife, and that the Prophet had replied that there was no good in falsehood. The man then explained that he had recounted something to her, and had accused her of saying what she had not said. Then the Prophet answered, 'You have no sin.'"

In another instance 'Umar is said to have laid down a principle for Muslim women as follows: "If one of you wives does not love one of us husbands she is not to tell him that she does not love him. There are few houses that are built upon love, but people are mated rather because of their common faith in Islam and their nobility of family."

Likewise, on another occasion the Prophet is said to have remarked that if a man brings about a reconciliation between women in their conflicting needs by saying to each one that she is the one that he loves the most; or that if a woman will not comply with a man's wishes unless he promises her something which he is not able to give her, then he should give her the promise by way of "treating her heart", or in propitiation. And if there is no way to treat her heart except by a denial of his fault and an excess of affection, then there is no harm in his so doing. Nevertheless there is the limitation that comes from remembering that a lie is something to be avoided.

Elsewhere al-Ghazálí teaches clearly that men at their best must aspire to imitate divine qualities, qualities for which their natures have a God-given capacity. In his suggestive book on the names of Allah, *Al-maqsad al-Asná fí Sharh Asmá al-Husná* ("The Highest Aim in Explanation of the Excellent Names of Allah"), he declares that "the perfection of the worshipper, as well as his happiness, lies in imitating (*takhalluq*) the qualities (*akhláq*) of Allah the Most High, and in adorning himself with the meanings of His attributes and of His names—in that measure of course that may be considered within his right."[10]

In further explanation of this relationship that man has potentially between himself and Allah, al-Ghazálí comments on the meanings of the ninety-nine names of Allah, and in connexion with each one of these names he gives special admonitions that are to be observed by worshippers. In other words, the ways of legitimate imitation are plainly suggested.

The worshipper has a duty for himself in the name *al-Raḥmán*, which is "that he should be merciful towards the worshippers of Allah the Most High, and especially towards those among them that are careless. . . . It is his part to look upon the disobedient with the eyes

10. al-Ghazálí, *al-Maqsad al-Asná fí Sharh Asmá' al-Ḥusná*, Cairo, A.H. 1322, pp. 23 ff.

of mercy and not with the eyes of censure." And in the name *al-Malik* (the King), the worshipper also has his part, for "the kingdom that is peculiarly his own is his heart, which he examines and inspects. The troops are made up of his desire, his anger, and his passion. His subjects are his tongue, his eyes, his hands, and all the members of his body. When he governs his kingdom, then manifestly it does not govern him." The name *al-Quddus* (the Holy) makes a demand on the worshipper also, for "any man whose ambition does not extend to the correction of his secret life is not worth his price, but he whose sole ambition is for Allah, who has caused his knowledge to ascend beyond the attainment of sense impressions and imaginations, and has caused his will to become *holy* from the influence of passions, surely he will dwell in the midst of Paradise!"

There are some of the names for Allah, like the Creator (*al-Kháliq*), the Artificer (*al-Bárí*), and the Fashioner (*al-Musawwir*), of which al-Ghazálí makes exception, saying that "there is no entrance for the worshipper into these names except by a kind of remote figure of speech"; and he adds also that "there are a few other names that have their actual application to the worshippers, and that are only used figuratively with respect to Allah the Most High. These are names like the Persevering (*al-Ṣabúr*) and the Thankful (*al-Shakúr*)". And he adds that "it is of course inappropriate that a sharing in a name should be assumed by neglecting the distinctions we have mentioned".

The conception remained with al-Ghazálí, however, that there were many of the divine attributes, as expressed in the names of Allah, in which the worshippers should seek to share, and that Allah desires that men should live up to their highest human potentialities by aspiring to these divine qualities, by imitating them, and by attaining their share of them.[11]

Shahrastání (d. A.D. 1153) asks the question, "What is the intelligible difference between the relation of father and son and the relation of cause and effect?" He goes on to observe, "I have often thought that what the Nazarenes believe of the Father and the Son is really the same as the philosophers' supposition of the Necessitative and the Necessitated and the (first) cause and the (first) effect."[12]

If we take another group of al-Ghazálí's examples of the excellent names, we read that "from among the worshippers he is *the Secure*

11. Attention is called to a similar conception in New Testament references to those who are "born again", those who are "led by the Spirit of God", and those who are spoken of as "heirs of God and joint heirs with Jesus Christ". Cf. John iii. 3–7; and Romans viii. 14, 17. There is a familiar Persian proverb: *pisar gar nadárad az pidar, tó bigánah khánish, nakhánish pisar* (If a son has no likeness to his father, then you do not call him his father's own son).

12. Shahrastání, *Kitáb Niháyat al-Iqdám fi 'Ilm al-Kalám*, edit. and trans. by Alfred Guillaume, London, 1934, pp. 178–9.

(*al-Salám*) who is the nearest in his likeness to the one who is absolutely and truly *Secure*, the one who has no two-fold nature in His character." Also he says that "the truest of the worshippers in the name of *al-Mu'min* (the Protector) is the one who is himself reason for the security of the people from the punishment of Allah by virtue of the guidance he gives in the way of Allah and in following the path of salvation". So also "the *Mighty* (*al-'Aziz*) from among the worshippers is the one for whom the worshippers of Allah the Most High have great need in their more important affairs, such as the future life, everlasting happiness, and all those things which concern him whose unique existence is undoubted and whom it is difficult to comprehend".

Those qualities which man is admitted to have potentially (*bi 'l-quwwa*) he seeks by his moral and religious efforts to acquire actually (*bi 'l-fi'l*),[13] and it appeared to al-Ghazálí to be fully in accord with the divine economy that in so doing men should be thought of as imitating the divine attributes, as expressed in many of the excellent names of Allah, in order to obtain their share in these qualities.

Not only did al-Ghazálí hold this conception of self-realization through the imitation of divine qualities, but he included in the *Iḥyá'* (IV. vi) a significant explanation of the love of Allah, i.e. of the love of the creature for Allah. Of this statement Dr. D. B. Macdonald has written an authoritative abstract in the *Encyclopædia of Religion and Ethics* (ii. pp. 677–80), a part of which may be quoted:

"In the human heart there is a property of apprehension, named variously 'the Divine light', 'reason', 'the inner light', 'the light of faith'. Its nature impels it to apprehend the essences of all things; and in that is its delight, even as the other human apprehensions have their delight in exercising their functions. But as the things apprehended rise in the scale—the external senses, the inner apprehension, etc.—so does the delight in them. Of necessity, then, the knowledge of Allah is the greatest delight of all.

"But what is the essence of love, and what are its causes and conditions? Especially, what is the meaning of the love of the creature for Allah? Love is a natural turning to an object which gives pleasure. It springs from perceptions and varies with them, being either from sense perception, or, in man alone, from that spiritual perception

13. Cf. T. J. de Boer's article on *Quwwa* (*Kuwwa*) in the supplement of the *Encyclopædia of Islam*: "The whole theory is closely connected with the dynamic view of the existence of the world. Thus as in Aristotle, in the Muslim philosophers, physics and psychology are developed into an hierarchical system of natural forces and faculties of the soul. . . . Galen's influence may be traced, especially in the doctrine of the faculties of the soul and their localization. Ibn Sina enumerates some 25 *kuwwa* from the highest faculty of the reasoning soul to the powers of the simplest bodies."

whose seat is in the heart. The pleasure through it is the most complete and absolute.

"Some have held that it is unthinkable that any man should love another than himself for the sake of that other, and without any happiness accruing to the lover apart from the perception of the beloved. That, however, is an error; it is both thinkable and takes place. A man loves by nature, first, himself, for the continuance and perfection of his self; then he loves another than himself, because that other serves the same purpose and benefits him. Thirdly, he loves a thing for its own sake, not for any happiness that it brings, but the thing itself is his happiness, like the love of beauty, simply for itself. So, if it stands fast that Allah is beautiful, He must certainly be loved by him to whom His beauty is revealed. Beauty is of different kinds, and is not sensuous only: beauty of mental and moral qualities can be loved. But, lastly, there is often a secret relationship of souls between the lover and the beloved, and it suffices. It follows, then, that the Being worthy of love, in the absolute sense, is Allah only."

Al-Ghazálí maintained that when he considered all that is marvellous and incomprehensible in his own creation, the wonderful adaptation to their purposes of the several parts of the body, and with what forethought his various wants for food, lodging, etc., are met, then he was able to gain some conception of the wisdom, the power, and the mercy of the Creator. In illustration he liked to refer to the hand, "with its five fingers of unequal lengths, four of them with three joints and the thumb with only two, and the way in which it can be used for grasping, or for carrying, or for smiting".

"Thus from his own creation man comes to know God's existence, from the wonders of his bodily frame God's power and wisdom, and from the ample provisions made for his various needs God's love. In this way the knowledge of oneself becomes a key to the knowledge of God.

"Not only are man's attributes a reflexion of God's attributes, but the mode of existence of man's soul affords some insight into God's mode of existence. That is to say, both God and the soul are invisible, indivisible, unconfined by space and time, and outside the categories of quantity and quality; nor can the ideas of shape, colour, or size attach to them. People find it hard to form a conception of such realities as are devoid of quality and quantity, etc., but a similar difficulty attaches to the conception of our everyday feelings, such as anger, pain, pleasure, or love. They are thought-concepts and cannot be cognized by the senses; whereas quality, quantity, etc., are sense concepts. Just as the ear cannot take cognizance of colour, nor the eye of sound, so, in conceiving of the ultimate realities, God and the soul, we find ourselves in a region in which sense-concepts can bear no part. So much, however, we can see, that, as God is Ruler of the universe, and, being Himself beyond space and time, quantity and quality, governs things that are so conditioned, so the soul rules the body and its members, being itself invisible, indivisible, and unlocated in any special part. For how can the indivisible be located in that which is divisible? From all this we see how true is the saying of the Prophet, 'God created man in His own likeness.' "[14]

In a previous chapter we noted that al-Farábí discerned six different ways in which Aristotle employed the Greek term *νοῦς* (reason). But the usages that were generally recognized by later Muslim philosophers for the Arabic term *'aql* (reason) were four:[15]

1. The *'aql hayúlání* (*ὑλικός*, *materialis*), or the *'aql bi'l-qúwa* (*ἐν δυνάμει*, *potentia*).
2. The *'aql bi'l-malaka* (*ὁ καθ' ἕξιν*, *habitu*).
3. The *'aql bi'l-fi'l* (*ὁ κατ' ἐνέργειαν*, *actu*).
4. The *'aql mustafád* (*ἐπίκτητος*, *adeptus sive adquisitus*).

The first is the capacity for understanding the nature of material things, whether by abstract thinking or by receiving this understanding from above. The second comprehends the intellect as it is trained in the principles of knowledge. The third is the human intellect when it is *active*. The fourth refers to man's intellect as a perfect gift from the superhuman *'aql fa'ál*, the "Dispenser of Forms", in the universe. With some writers the fourth use of *'aql* is as a faculty of appropriation (*'aql mukhtasab*).

The term *'aql* (reason), as employed by al-Ghazálí in the *Iḥyá'*, is in agreement with these accepted distinctions, except that he shows an inclination to identify the third and fourth, contending that there is no separate faculty for apprehending spiritual truths, but that this knowledge is an intellectual experience of which the fully developed *'aql* becomes capable. The soul, or self, under the guidance of reason, learns to control anger (*al-ghaḍab*), the tendency to self-assertion, and desire (*al-shahawat*), the appetitive tendency, and in this process of self-discipline it may receive divine assistance, but at the same time there is a Satanic force that is believed to weaken the self in its efforts to regulate and keep within bounds these animal propensities.

The expression employed in the Qur'án, *al-nafs al-muṭma'inna* (the tranquil soul) (xxxix. 27), is explained by al-Ghazálí as indicating the state of the soul when reason succeeds in resisting and controlling the evil passions, when it has subdued and harmonized the animal forces, and has learned to make use of them as sources of constructive energy. "Thus if the soul seeks to help the intellect and establishes anger and indignation over desire, at the same time not

14. *The Alchemy of Happiness*, trans. C. Field, pp. 33–4.
15. Cf. art. "'aql", by T. J. de Boer, in the *Encyclopædia of Islam*.

permitting anger and indignation to become headstrong, and even making use of desire to keep them under due restraint, thus making use of one against the other as the occasion demands, then its powers will remain justly balanced and its qualities become virtuous."[16]

This rational self, which is designated in the Qur'án as *al-nafs al-muṭma'inna*, is able to experience a range of freedom, for it comes to appreciate that in attaining to this stage, and in managing to continue in it, reason has been frequently called upon to exercise the power of choice, and to this extent al-Ghazálí believed that experience suggests that man is free. This freedom of rational choice, it will be observed, approximates what was meant by some writers as the function of the faculty of appropriation (*al-'aql mukhtasab*). In this way the soul would attain a unity and mastery within itself, which might be described as a harmony of the inner self, or as individual moral integrity.[17]

It is equally possible, however, and indeed more frequent in occurrence, for anger and desire to be so instigated by the Satanic force, *al-shaiṭániya*, that they gain ascendancy over the soul. Reason then loses its proper mastery and becomes a slave. The soul, overwhelmed by evil and making that which the passions suggest look pleasing (Qur'án xvi. 63), will then act as the instigating soul (*al-nafs al-'amárat*). Nevertheless al-Ghazálí insists that, even when evil comes to be most frequently suggested, there is in conformity with the Qur'án (lxxv. 2) a divine element that keeps struggling against the evil tendencies and that is seldom completely subdued. This divine element expresses itself through the upbraiding soul (*al-nafs al-lawwáma*), which appears to function in much the same way as a "conscience".

After he has set forth a general analysis of the conflicting forces in the human soul, al-Ghazálí enumerates the qualities of character that result when desire and anger are allowed to exercise predominating influence. Desire (*shahawat*) induces shamelessness (*waqáḥat*), wickedness (*khubth*), extravagance (*tabdhír*), stinginess (*taqtír*), hypocrisy (*riyá'*), defamation (*hutkat*), impudence (*mujánat*), folly (*'abath*), greed (*ḥirṣ*), cupidity (*jasha'*), flattery (*malaq*), envy (*ḥasad*), rancour (*ḥiqd*), rejoicing at another's misfortunes (*shamátat*), gluttony (*sharah*), and lewdness (*shabiq*). Anger likewise induces rashness (*tahawwur*), excessive spending (*bidhálat*), haughtiness (*badhakh*), boasting (*ṣalaf*), arrogance (*takabbur*), self-admiration (*'ujb*), derision (*istihzá*), making light of others (*istikhfáf*), disdain (*taḥqír*), mischief-making (*irádat al-shar*), love of aggrandisement (*shahawat al-ẓulm*),

16. *Iḥyá'* vol. III, p. 6, trans. M. Umaruddin, *Some Fundamental Aspects of Imam Ghazáli's Thought*, Aligarh, 1946, p. 37.

17. This important conception of moral unity within the self needs to be developed further in Muslim thinking. Perhaps it must be accepted first as a necessary quality in the self of the Creator before it can find its full meaning as an ideal for the self of the creature.

enmity (*'idáwat*), hatred (*baghzá'*), and rushing at people with violence and abuse.

A further group of objectionable qualities is described by al-Ghazálí as the result of the predominance of the Satanic influence through its accentuation of both desire and anger. These qualities are deceit (*makr*), cunning (*ḥila*), subtlety (*daká'*), boldness (*jará'at*), dissembling (*talbís*), exciting enmity (*taḍríb*), fraud (*ghishsh*), wickedness (*khubth*), and obscene talk (*khaná*).

This influence of devilry (*shaitániya*), or diabolical malice, includes in Islamic thought the seductiveness of Shaitán. "In religious thought Shaitán is the power that opposes God in the hearts of men. He whispers his insidious suggestions in their ears and makes his proposals seductive to them. The Qur'án ascribes this activity now to one *shaitán* now to several. Later it is said that one *shaitán* is attached to each man so that it is possible for everyone to speak of 'my *shaitán*'. . . . The popular view is that every man is attended by an angel and a *shaitán*, who urge him to good and evil deeds respectively. Ḥasan al-Baṣrí is reported to have said: '*They are two thoughts that rush into the minds of men.*' He thus reduced these spirit forces to mental states."[18] This is not the opinion, however, of al-Ghazálí, who supplements his classification of the vices that come from the predominance of desire and anger with a section on the further evils that are due to the accentuation of desire and anger by *shaitániya* (devilry).

In a passage in the *Iḥyá'* (III, pp. 23–7 and 35–8) al-Ghazálí undertakes to explain by an illustration the "Entrances of Shaitán to the Heart". "Understand that the heart is compared to a fortress. Shaitán is the enemy who is eager to enter. His object is to conquer it and to exercise dominion over it. But there is no way to protect this fortress from the enemy except by guarding its entrances, and any breaches there may be in the walls. Obviously anyone who does not know the gates of the fortress will not be able to protect them.

"First it must be realized that defence of the heart from the suggestions of Shaitán is an absolute obligation for every responsible servant of God . . . and that the entrances are the servant's qualities of character, which are many. We will point out the great gates, the open water-ways, and the mountain paths that are not narrow enough to exclude the hosts of troops of Shaitán.

"Among the great gates are anger and desire. For anger is a calamity that befalls reason. It is when the forces of reason are weak that the forces of Shaitán make their attack, and we should remember that whatever angers a man gives sport to Shaitán, as when a boy plays with a ball." Then follows a conversation that tradition relates that Shaitán had with Moses, to show how dependable he found his approach to the human heart through desire, anger, and greed. Also

18. Cf. *Encyclopædia of Islam*, art. "Shaitán", by A. S. Tritton.

"it is related that a learned man asked Shaitán, 'Which of the dispositions of the sons of Adam is the most helpful to you?' He replied, 'Passionate desire (*al-ḥiddat*), for when the servant is dominated by desire we manipulate him as freely as a boy does a ball.'

"Also among the great gates are envy and greed, which make the servant blind and deaf, for as the Prophet has said, 'It is your love for things that makes you blind and deaf.' The light of insight recognizes the entrances of which Shaitán may take advantage, but when envy and greed blot out this light one fails to see, and Shaitán finds his opportunity. For in the opinion of the man of greed, whatever fosters his desire seems good, and if he is denied he becomes unreasonable.

"It is related that when Noah boarded the ark, after having taken into it two pairs of everything that God had commanded him, he saw there an old man whom he did not know. Noah said to him, 'How did you get entrance here?' He replied, 'I entered through the tendencies of the hearts of your companions, for their hearts are with me and their bodies with you.'"

In *The Foreign Vocabulary of the Qur'án* Dr. Jeffery has pointed out that the word *shaitán* was used by the old Arab poets with the meaning of a snake, that the serpent was an old Semitic totem, and that the Arabs believed that serpents had some connexion with supernatural powers, "so that the use of the name Shaitán for the Evil One could be taken as a development from this . . . but the theological connotation of Shaitán as leader of the hosts of evil is obviously derived from Muhammad's Jewish or Christian environment . . . the word was in use long before Muhammad's day, and he in his use of it was undoubtedly influenced by Christian, probably Abyssinian Christian, usage."[19]

From the ethical point of view a more surprising supplementary section in al-Ghazálí's classification of evil qualities is that in which he ascribes those evil qualities that come from unrestrained ambition to the divine element in the soul, when it transcends its bounds. The love of overlordship (*ḥubb al-istílá'*), the love of supremacy (*ḥubb al-ista'lá'*), the appropriation of special privileges (*takhṣíṣ*), and the usurpation of absolute authority (*istibdád*)—are these qualities really due to the divine element in the human soul, feeling itself to be godlike in contrast to other men? Is it because of the divine element within him that such a man "rejoices when knowledge is ascribed to him and grieves when ignorance is imputed to him"? With the Muslim conception of God as being primarily power and authority, it is possible to see how al-Ghazálí was led to such a notion as that when a man lets his divine element gain too much supremacy he is disposed to vaunt himself over other men. Or this section may be due

19. Professor Arthur Jeffery, *The Foreign Vocabulary of the Qur'án*, Gaekwad's Oriental Series, vol. lxxix, pp. 189–90.

in part to an artificial balance in the classification of the influence of lordship (*rabubbíya*) against devilry (*shaitáníya*).

In his classification of the virtues that result from reason's controlling desire and anger, al-Ghazálí enumerates qualities that are conducive to the realization of the ideal in human character. The control of desire leads to chastity (*iffat*), contentment (*qaná'at*), quiet (*hudú'*), abstinence (*zuhd*), the fear of God (*wara'*), piety (*taqwá*), cheerfulness (*imbisát*), a comely appearance (*husn al-hai'at*), modesty (*hayá'*), ingenuity (*ẓarf*), and helpfulness (*masá'adat*). Similarly the control of anger is said to make for courage (*shajá'at*), generosity (*karam*), boldness (*najdat*), self-control (*ḍabt al-nafs*), fortitude (*ṣabr*), clemency (*ḥilm*), endurance (*iḥtimál*), forgiveness (*'afw*), stability (*thabát*), genius (*nubl*), bravery (*shahámat*), and gravity (*waqár*).

According to the usual explanations of these virtues it is reason that enables man to bring under control the forces of desire and anger. This is al-Ghazálí's general position also, except that he adds a special list of outstanding qualities which he says are the result of the authority exercised by the divine element in the soul over these same two forces, desire and anger. These special qualities are knowledge (*'ilm*), wisdom (*ḥikmat*), and conviction (*yaqín*), qualities that make for the supremacy of reason over everything through knowledge and insight. Here again we see that al-Ghazálí's primary thought in connexion with the divine element in the human soul is the idea of supremacy and dominating authority.

It is, however, a dominating authority that is attained by knowledge, wisdom, and conviction that he exalts, it is not an authority or power that results from the use of force, or from the amassing of wealth. "If the objection is made", he wrote in the *Kímiyá*,[20] "that it is man's nature to seek the perfection of the divine element (*kamál i-rubúbíyat*) in the soul,[21] and that this may be attained only by the acquisition of knowledge and power, on the basis that the quest of knowledge is commendable in so much as it makes for perfection, then on the same grounds the seeking of wealth and position must also be commendable for it likewise leads to power, which is part of perfection and one of the attributes of God just as truly as knowledge, know that the answer is that *knowledge* and *power* are two perfections, and they are both among the qualities of the divine element (*rubúbíyat*), but for man there is an approach to true knowledge, whereas man has no approach to true power. His knowledge is perfect in so far as it enables him to draw near to God, and moreover it remains with him. But power is not so obtained, for though he

20. *Kímiyá-yi-Sa'ádat*, p. 344.

21. From the use of the word *rabb* in pre-Islamic poetry and in inscriptions, we know that it was employed with reference to human chieftains as well as for the deity. "The special development of its use with God was in the Syriac and Christian communities" (Jeffery, *The Foreign Vocabulary of the Qur'án*, p. 137).

imagines that he has it he soon finds that it does not remain with him. Power is associated with wealth and with the creature, but by death it is cut off. Surely anything that is made futile by death has no part in the things that abide, and for one to determine the manner of his life by seeking for any such thing would be to live in ignorance. Only so much power is needed as may be instrumental in attaining knowledge. Knowledge that remains is in the heart and not in the body, and the heart (here used for the soul) continues to survive forever.

"When a learned man passes from this world his knowledge remains with him. It serves as a light whereby he will be able to see God, and this will be the highest of all pleasures in Paradise. There is nothing connected with knowledge which is cast off at death, for it is not attached to wealth and a heart of flesh but to the very essence of the Most High God and His qualities."

In his meditation on man's relation to God and to the world about him, al-Ghazálí outlined what we might describe as a moral cosmology. First there is the physical world that is manifest to the senses, a material visible world, the *'álam al-mulk wa'l-shaháda*. It is pointed out that in relation to the Originator (*al-Mudhith*), this material world may not be regarded as having positive or independent existence, for it is composed solely of originated qualities (*ḥawádith*)—substances (*a'yán*) and accidents (*'arád*). Man, however, has a God-given capacity to attain unto true existence, but he will not attain to this existence in the world that is manifest to the senses. It is not in his adaptation to this world that he can reach his true destiny and realize his extra-mundane being.

For the perception of the second sphere, the mental world, the eyes of the soul are turned within. It is the *'álam al-jabarút* (Heb. *geburah*, power), and is described as "the world of celestial power", or "the sphere of divine omnipotence". This is the world that al-Ghazálí treats primarily as the world of the human mind (reason, will, and power), which is also one of the spheres of the Creator's power.[22] In this sphere the reflective soul discovers the limits of human freedom and appreciates the realm of determinism. By processes of reflexion the rational faculty (*al-'aql*) exercises the function of "the good will" in its regulative aspects, and also the function of cognition, in seeking to understand the true nature of things, in both their theoretical and practical aspects.

The third sphere of the Creator's power in the world as a spiritual reality is the world invisible, which is manifest only to the spirit. It is spoken of as a region above that of earthly things, and also above that of real individual things. It has been compared with the Platonic

22. T. J. de Boer, art. "'álam", in the *Encyclopædia of Islam*, with reference to A. J. Wensinck, "On the Relation between Ghazálí's Cosmology and his Mysticism", in *Verl. Ak. Amst.*, vol. lxxv, ser. A., No. 6, 1933.

world of ideas, in that the things in this visible world are "only a type or symbol, or imperfect copy, of the archetype, the reality 'laid up in heaven'".[23]

"In this (invisible) world", al-Ghazálí has written, "there are wonders, in relation to which this visible world is seen to be of no account. He who does not ascend to that world . . . is but a brute beast, indeed he is more in error than any brute beast, since the brutes are not given the wings wherewith to take flight to that world. Know that the visible world is to the world invisible as the husk to the kernel, as the form and body to the spirit, as darkness to light, and as the ignoble to the sublime. Therefore the Invisible World is called the World Supernal, and the Spiritual World, and the World of Light. . . . He who is in that world above is with God and has the keys of the Unseen."[24]

It is rational reflexion in the second world, however, the *'álam al-jabarút*, which is considered by al-Ghazálí to be the means unto the end, or the bridge between the first and the third worlds. This second world is a world of conscious struggle, in his description of which al-Ghazálí endeavours to distinguish a sufficient degree of human freedom of choice to justify his belief in the individual's moral responsibility.[25] Very early the Mu'tazilites, who represented themselves as the "partisans of justice and unity" (*ahl al-'adl wa'l-tawḥíd*), had insisted on the necessary ethical character of God, and had contended, therefore, that man is the author of his acts. But the Ash'arites, who championed the orthodox reaction, maintained that "man cannot create anything: God is the only creator. Nor does man's power produce any effect on his action at all. God creates in his creature power (*qudra*) and choice (*ikhtiyár*). He then creates in him his action corresponding to the power and choice thus created. So the action of the creature is created by God as to initiative and as to production; but it is *acquired* by the creature. By acquisition (*kasb*) is meant that it corresponds to the creature's power and choice, previously created in him, without his having had the slightest effect on the action. He was only the *locus* or subject of the action."[26]

John of Damascus had observed that in the eighth century of the Christian era the difference regarding predestination and free-will was "one of the chief points of divergence between Christianity and Islam".[27] The Qur'án could be quoted to support each side, but it is

23. Margaret Smith, *al-Ghazálí: the Mystic*, p. 111.

24. *Mishkát al-Anwar*, pp. 108–9. Reference from Margaret Smith, op. cit., pp. 174 ff.

25. The most important passages in the *Iḥyá'* in this connection are: III. 23–7; 35–8; and IV. 218–20.

26. D. B. Macdonald, *Development of Muslim Theology, Jurisprudence and Constitutional Theory*, p. 192.

27. A. J. Wensinck, *The Muslim Creed*, p. 51, with reference to John of Damascus, *Opera*, ed. Migne, vol. xciv, col. 1589 sqq.

most interesting to observe that, according to Wensinck,[28] "Tradition has not preserved a single *ḥadíth* in which *liberum arbitrium* is advocated." But in the creed that was compiled and edited by Muhammad al-Faḍáli (d. A.D. 1821), which represents the orthodox Muslim position, we read: (1) that "the connexion of Power and Will is common to every possible thing to the extent that the affections of the mind (*khatarát*) which arise in the mind of an individual are specified by the will of God and created by His power"; and (2) that "Knowledge and Will and Power are called qualities of impression (*sifat al-ta'thír*), for making an impression depends on them. Because he who wills a thing must have knowledge of it before he aims at it; then, after he has aimed at it, he busies himself with doing it. For example, when there is something in your house and you wish to take it, and after you wish to take it, you take it actually. The connexion of these qualities, then, is in a certain order, in the case of an originated being; first comes the knowledge of the thing, then the aiming at it, then the doing."[29]

In al-Ghazálí's explanation of the extent of man's consciousness of a degree of freedom of choice, on which moral responsibility may be based, special attention is directed to these psychological determinations that are accomplished in the *'álam al-jabarút*, the world of the human mind. This is the sphere of operation for reason, will, and power, which are evident in the processes of the mind, and which lead to actions. The *khawátir* (affections of the mind) are all those impressions that reach the heart (or soul). They are ideas, whether thoughts that come from immediate sensations, or recollections that come through memory. It is in these ideas that al-Ghazálí sees what he calls the springs of human actions.

These ideas are capable of exciting strong desire or inclination (*raghba*). This inclination must then be followed by *i'tiqád*, which is defined as intellectual conviction, i.e. the decision or permission of reason. This decision of reason is in turn confirmed or accepted by will (*iráda*), and the result is directed power, or action (*'amal*). The psychological determination of action may be expressed, therefore, as an equation:

khawátir + *raghba* + *i'tiqád* + *iráda* = *'amal*.

In the decision of reason, in acceptance or rejection by the will, and in the direction of power in action, a man is conscious of a sense of freedom, and it is in the exercise of this freedom that he becomes a responsible agent. "Now this will which is produced after deliberation, when translated into acceptance or rejection, constitutes *ikhtiyár*, literally choice, i.e. freedom. The word *al-ikhtiyár* is derived from *khair*, which means *good*. So *al-ikhtiyár* means the choice of an

28. A. J. Wensinck, op. cit., p. 51.
29. D. B. Macdonald, op. cit., pp. 331–3.

idea or an object. When the decision of the intellect is accepted as good, one is impelled to act accordingly."

But the first two elements of the equation, ideas (*khawâtir*) and inclination (*raghba*), are recognized as being beyond man's own complete control, so that the conclusion would be that while the occurrence of a strong desire or inclination may come without man's responsibility, yet his reason is free to make a decision, and his will is free to accept the decision of reason as *good* and to implement the corresponding action. In such a case man would be free to do what he desires, but the complete control of his desires would lie beyond his power.[30]

When we approach the other side of al-Ghazálí's moral philosophy, we observe that the case he makes for determinism in the universe is not based on man's inability completely to control his ideas and inclinations. After conceding that to a limited extent human experience is conscious of psychological determinations in the sphere of the mind, which is sufficient to establish moral responsibility, he then proceeds to take a wider outlook, and to consider the whole problem of causation in accord with eternal power (*al-qudrat al-azaliya*) and divine wisdom (*al-ḥikmat al-azaliya*).

In the first place he quotes a few passages from the Qur'án as declarations that point to God as the one whose will is supreme:

vi. 125 Whomsoever God wishes to guide, He expands his breast to Islam; but whomsoever he wishes to lead astray, He makes his breast tight and straight.

lxxxii. 13, 14 As for the Righteous, they will be in Bliss;
And the Wicked, they will be in Fire.

xxi. 23 He cannot be questioned for His acts, but they will be questioned (for theirs).

lxxvi. 29–31 This is an admonition: whomsoever will,
Let him take a (straight) path to his Lord.
But ye will not except God wills.
For God is full of knowledge and wisdom.
He will admit to His mercy whom He will,
But the wrong-doers—
For them has He prepared a grievous penalty.

He then proceeds to make clear the common error of misjudging an observed uniformity in the succession of events. To associate events in the relation of cause and effect is, in al-Ghazálí's opinion, unjustified. One event may appear necessarily to precede or condition another, but "Allah alone is the efficient cause". This is a point of view with which we are familiar in the Jewish and Christian scriptures, where so-called secondary causes are frequently overlooked, in praise of divine sovereignty.

30. M. Umaruddin, *Some Fundamental Aspects of al-Ghazálí's Thought*, pp. 57–63.

In the *Kitáb al-Tawḥíd* ("The Book of Unity"), *Iḥyá'*, iv. 220 sqq., there is a discussion of the relationship between divine sovereignty, with its determinism, and man's limited free-will. Dr. Wensinck has described this treatment of the question of man's free-will as "unrivalled in Muslim literature".[31]

"The sense in which the word *tawḥíd* is employed must first be distinguished from the several meanings that the term includes, for 'unity' is far from being a simple idea; it may be internal or external, it may mean that there is no other god except Allah, who has no partner (*sharík*); it may mean that Allah is a Oneness in himself; it may mean that He is the only being with real or absolute existence; it may even be developed into a pantheistic assertion that Allah is All." [32] The meaning that is most consistent with al-Ghazálí's subject matter in this section is that Allah is the only being with real or absolute existence.

In man's limited individual cosmos there is what experience teaches him to recognize as *power*, but this power in him cannot have real or absolute existence—it must rather be dependent on the Supreme Power. God, therefore, must be the real *cause* of man's actions, for His is the only truly creative power. When the word "cause" has the connotation of creative power it must be applied to God alone. In a secondary sense, however, man's power may be considered as the image, or the gift, of God's power.

Tawḥíd, consequently, here signifies unity of existence. "He alone is self-existing. The existence of all other things depends on Him. Everything is in His grip. He is the eternal and the everlasting. He is the manifest and the hidden. He is the first and the last."[33]

Accordingly, when the seeker after truth sees a piece of paper with a spot of ink upon it, and asks the paper why it had blackened its face, and then successively inquires of the ink, of the pen, of the hand, and hears the excuses also of power, will, reason, and knowledge, he comes at last to appreciate that God is the only real cause (*fá'il*).

Thus it was from his belief in God as the sole cause and the moving force in the universe that al-Ghazálí derived his sequence theory of causation, which provided for a consciousness of limited free-will in human experience.

We are told that al-Ghazálí's writings were read by Jewish scholars, "not only those writings dealing with philosophy, which aroused widespread interest and discussion in Jewish circles, being studied by Maimonides among others, but his mystical works also, and within a century of his death, Hebrew and Latin translations of his works appeared, e.g. his philosophical works were translated into Latin by Avendeath (Ibn Da'úd, *c.* 1090 to *c.* 1165) of Toledo,

31. A. J. Wensinck, *The Muslim Creed*, p. 157.
32. D. B. Macdonald, art. "Tawḥíd", in the *Encyclopædia of Islam*.
33. M. Umaruddin, op. cit., p. 71.

a converted Jew working in conjunction with Dominic Gundisalvus, Archdeacon of Segovia; and his *Mizán al-'Amal* was translated in the thirteenth century by Abraham ibn Ḥasdai of Barcelona, who did much work in translating from Arabic into Hebrew. The *Mishkát al-Anwár* also aroused great interest among Jewish thinkers. It was translated by Isaac Alfásí, and quoted by the sixteenth-century writer Moses ibn Habíb, a native of Lisbon, who was himself a poet, translator, and philosopher."[34]

The influence of al-Ghazálí's writings on medieval Jewish and Christian thought is not surprising when we bear in mind the general cultural outlook of such centres as Palermo in Sicily and Toledo in Spain. When the Normans conquered Sicily in the eleventh century they ruled until the thirteenth, and at the court of King Roger II there were "both Christians and Muslims, who were equally versed in Arabic literature and Greek science. . . . The King himself spoke and read Arabic." And in the first half of the thirteenth century, Frederick, King of Sicily and Emperor of Germany, who is described as "philosopher, free-thinker, and polyglot", surrounded himself with Muslims, and kept his harems and his libraries both in Sicily and in Italy. In Naples he gathered a collection of Arabic manuscripts, and had translators who busied themselves with the works of Aristotle and Averroës.

Of Toledo we know from Miguel Asin that it "had throughout the twelfth century been an important centre for the dissemination of Arabic science and *belles-lettres* in Christian Europe. In the first half of that century, shortly after that city had been captured from the Moors, Archbishop Raymond began the translation of some of the more celebrated works of Arabic learning. Thus, the whole encyclopædia of Aristotle was translated from the Arabic, with the commentaries of Alkindius, Alfarabius, Avicenna, Algazel, and Averroës; as also the master works of Euclid, Ptolemy, Galen, and Hippocrates, with the comments upon them of learned Muslims, such as Albatenius, Avicenna, Averroës, Rhazes, and Alpetragius."

And furthermore, "Alphonso the Wise, who had been educated in this environment of Semitic culture, on ascending the throne personally directed the work of translation, and gathered to his court as collaborators wise men of the three religions, an instance demonstrative of the tolerance of his time. . . . From Arabic sources he wrote his *Grande General Estoria*, and he ordered the translation of Talmudic and cabbalistic works, and, lastly, of the Qur'án."[35]

We are reminded that "the grouping of the *Sefírót*", the ten spiritual agencies of the cabbalistic doctrine, of which the three highest represent the intelligible world of creative ideas, the second the moral world of creative formation, and the third the material

34. Margaret Smith, *al-Ghazálí: the Mystic*, pp. 217–18.
35. Miguel Asin, *Islam and the Divine Comedy*, pp. 239–45.

world of creative matter, correspond, in some measure, to al-Ghazálí's '*álam al-malakút*, '*álam al-jabarút*, and '*álam al-mulk wa'l-shahada*" (as explained above).[36]

To the court of Alphonso the Wise came Brunetto Latini in A.D. 1260, as the Ambassador of Florence. It was after his sojourn there in Toledo with the School of Translators that he wrote his two encyclopædias, one small and one large, which set forth a compendium of medieval learning. It was also in the period that followed the years that he spent in Toledo that he became the teacher and friend of Dante Alighieri, and he "may well have been the medium through which some at least of the Islamic features apparent in the *Divine Comedy* were transmitted to the disciple".[37]

This was the belief of the late Professor Miguel Asin of Madrid University, which he has fully set forth in his *Islam and the Divine Comedy*. Professor Asin has also made a careful study of al-Ghazálí's *Iḥyá'*, with a useful comparison of Christian doctrines, in his *La Espiritualidad de al-Gazel*, and has shown Ibn Arabi's relation to Christian asceticism in his *el-Islam Christianizado*. From another of his books, the *Logia et Agrapha Domini Jesu apud Moslemicos Scriptores, asceticos preasertim, usitata*,[38] the author of *Christ in Islam*,[39] a convenient little book that appeared in the Wisdom of the East Series, has given a large number of passages that are cited from the *Iḥyá'* of al-Ghazálí.

The general and comprehensive character of the *Iḥyá'* appears in the following brief analysis, in which the chapters that set forth al-Ghazálí's ethics are given in more detail.

ANALYSIS OF AL-GHAZÁLÍ'S *IḤYÁ' AL-ULÚM AL-DÍN*

PART ONE

FIRST QUARTER (*rub' al-'ibádat*), or the Acts of a Creature towards his Lord.

Book I. Knowledge (*al-'ilm*). [vol. i, p. 4.

Its excellence. When commendable and when reprehensible. Errors of the vulgar (*al-'ámma*). Contradiction and disputation. Deportment of the student and the teacher. Evils of knowledge. Concerning reason.

Book II. Articles of Faith (*qawá'id al-aqá'id*). [vol. i, p. 73.

The confession of faith (*kalimát al-shaháda*). Progress towards showing the right way (*al-tadríj ila'l-irshád*). Rays of proofs for the belief. Faith (*al-ímán*) and Islam (*al-islám*).

36. Margaret Smith, op. cit., p. 218.
37. Miguel Asin, op. cit., p. 254.
38. *Patrologia Orientalis*, vols. xiii and xix.
39. *Christ in Islam*, by Rev. James A Robson, M.A., London, 1929.

Book III. The Secrets of Purity (*asrár al-ṭahára*). [vol. i, p. 102.

Cleansing the impure (*ṭahárat al-khubuth*). Cleansing pollutions of the body: the ablution (*al-wuḍú'*); the bath (*al-ghusl*); cleansing with sand (*al-tayammum*); and cleansing of the private parts (*al-istanjí*). Cleanness and purifying (*naẓafat wa'l-tanzíf*). Things that are filthy (*al-awsákh*). Things that are moist (*al-ruṭubát*). Things that happen to the body from its various members.

Book IV. The Secrets of the Performance of Worship. [vol. i, p. 117.

The excellence of the performance of worship (*al-ṣalá*). Particulars of external acts. Particulars of inward acts. The leadership. The Friday worship and its regulations. Problems that give trouble. Voluntary performances.

Book V. The Secrets of the Stipulated Alms (*asrár al-zakát*). [vol. i, p. 163.

The different kinds of alms. Payment. The one receiving. Alms given in supererogation.

Book VI. The Secrets of Fasting (*asrár al-ṣawm*). [vol. i, p. 181.

Requirements (*al-wájibát*). Inner requisites. Supererogation in abstaining from food.

Book VII. The Secrets of the Pilgrimage (*al-ḥajj*). [vol. i, p. 187.

Its excellencies and required conditions. The order of external acts: setting out; on donning the garb of the pilgrim; on entering Mecca; the circumambulation of the Ka'aba; expressing a purpose (*al-sa'y*); standing (*al-wuqúf*) on Mt. Arafat; remaining acts; the "Lesser Pilgrimage" (*al-'umra*); the farewell; the visit to al-Medina; and the return journey. Admonition for the observance of the inner acts.

Book VIII. Instructions for Reading the Qur'án. [vol. i, p. 211.

The excellence of the Qur'án. Correct ways of reading. The inner acts necessary. The understanding of the Qur'án.

Book IX. Prayers and Petitions (*al-da'wát*). [vol. i, p. 228.

The excellence of praise. Instruction in prayer. Examples of prayers: by 'Á'isha, Fátima, Abu Bakr, Barída, Qabíṣa, Abu Dardá', Ibrahím, Isá', Khiḍr, al-Karkhí, 'Utbá, Adam, 'Ali ibn Abu Ṭálib, Sulaimán, and Ibrahím ibn Adham. Examples of the prayers of the Prophet. Other memorable examples.

Book X. On the Order of the Daily Rehearsals. [vol. i, p. 249.

Their excellence and importance. How to facilitate rising at night for prayer.

SECOND QUARTER (*rub' al-'ádát*), or Usages of Life.

Book I. Usages in Eating (*al-akl*). [vol. ii, p. 3.
Before eating, at the time of eating, and afterwards. Eating in company with others. Giving food to brethren and visitors. Being a guest.

Book II. Usages in Regard to Marriage (*al-nikáḥ*). [vol. ii, p. 15.
The allurement in marriage (*al-targhíb fi'l-nikáḥ*). Its evils and its advantages. The '*aqd*, or contract. The rights of the husband.

Book III. Trade and Making a Living (*al-kisb wa'l-ma'ásh*). [vol. ii, p. 42.
The excellence of trade. Knowledge of trade. Giving the token payment (*al-bai*). Profit on goods (*al-ribá*). Money paid in advance (*al-salam*). Rental (*al-ijára*). Debts (*al-qiráḍ*). Justice and abstaining from violence in transactions. Courtesy in doing business. A merchant should be mindful of his religion, and of the hereafter.

Book IV. The Permitted and the Forbidden. [vol. ii, p. 63.
The value of the one and the reproach of the other. Their various kinds and degrees. Scruples about them. Differences of opinion about justice. Disputing and questioning. The escape of the penitent from the oppressions of opulence. The pensions of kings. What is permitted in the society of kings. Various related topics.

Book V. Friendship and Brotherhood. [vol. ii, p. 118.
The value of friendship and brotherhood. The rights of brotherhood. The right of the Muslim.

Book VI. Self-seclusion (*al-'uzla*). [vol. ii, p. 162.
Its several advantages. The revelation of truth. Leisure for worship and meditation.

Book VII. Usages of the Journey. [vol. ii, p. 181.
The advantages of travel. Usages on the journey. Determining the *qibla* and the times of prayer.

Book VIII. Manners of Song and Ecstasy. [vol. ii, p. 199.
(Trans. by Dr. D. B. Macdonald, *J.R.A.S.*, 1901–2.)

Book IX. The Command to What is Right and the Prohibition of What is Wrong. [vol. ii, p. 230.

Book X. Concerning the Customs and the Conduct of the Prophet. [vol. ii, p. 271.
His showing forgiveness when he was in power. His humility.

Third Quarter (*rub' al-muhlikát*), or Destructive Matters of Life.

Book I. The Marvels of the Heart (*'ájá'ib al-qalb*). [vol. iii, p. 1.

Al-qalb, distinguished from *al-nafs*, *al-ruḥ*, and *al-'aql*. The troops of the heart. The distinguishing characteristic of the human heart. A summary of the qualities of the heart. The figure of the heart in relation to the special sciences, and to other branches of knowledge—philosophical and religious, terrestrial and celestial. Divine inspiration (*al-ilhám*), as distinguished from *al-ta'allum* (learning). Difference in stations (*al-maqámín*) explained. Evidences of the faith (*shawáhin al-shar'*) according to the Ṣúfís, by the acquisition of knowledge (*iktisáb al-ma'rifa*)—not by learning and not by habit (*mu'tád*). Shaitán, and his dominion over the heart by temptation (*waswás*). The entrances to the heart. How the servant of God is seized by temptations—imaginings, notions, and projects. Invoking (*al-dhikr*) the name of God against temptations. Change of heart (*taqallub al-qalb*), as distinguished from the division of the heart in alteration and determination.

Book II. Self-discipline (*riyaḍatu'l-nafs*). [vol. iii, p. 39.

The correction of dispositions and the cure of diseases of the heart. Good disposition (*ḥusn al-khulq*) and bad disposition (*sú' al-khulq*). May dispositions be changed by discipline? The method for correcting dispositions. Symptoms of mental diseases. How man may come to know his personal faults. The training of boys. Conditions of the will (*al-iráda*). Prerequisites for conflict and progress. The advance of the disciple is by degrees. The path of discipline.

Book III. Breaking the Two Appetites. [vol. iii, p. 64.

The value of hunger. The reproach of satiety. Discipline in breaking the bodily appetite. The desire for honour. Why a disciple should refrain from joining in marriage (*al-tazwíj*). The excellence of the one who abandons the lust for honour.

Book IV. The Evils of the Tongue (*áfát al-lisán*). [vol. iii, p. 85.

The excellence of silence. The utterance which does not express the meaning. The use of extravagance in speech. Futile discussion. Disputation and altercation. Animosity. Speaking gutturally with a drawl. Talking obscenely and reviling. Cursing. Song and poetry. Jesting. Ridicule. Betraying secrets. False agreement. Falsehood in a statement or in an oath. An explanation of the extent to which falsehood (*al-kidhb*) is permitted. Caution about giving false impressions in illustrations or parables. Speaking evil of an absent person (*al-ghaiba*). Its specified punishments. Causes that give occasion for slander. How prevented from the tongue. Prohibiting slander in the heart. An explanation of excuses that are permissible. Atonement for slander. Calumny or detraction (*al-manima*). The definition of calumny and what is needed to resist it. The word of the person who has two tongues. The evil there is in encomium. The things that are to be praised. Carelessness in correcting mistakes. The questions of the ignorant about the attributes of God.

Book V. The Reproach of Anger, Rancour, and Envy (*dham al-ghaḍab wa'l-ḥiqd wa'l-ḥasad*). [vol. iii, p. 123.

The true nature of anger. Whether the removal of its true cause is possible. Reasons for the excitation of anger. How it may be cured after being excited. The value of restraining rage (*kaẓm al-ghaiẓ*).

Self-preservation (*al-intiṣár*) and calmness (*al-tashaffá*). The meaning of rancour. The advantage and value of forgiving (*al-afw*). Showing courtesy (*al-rifq*). The reproach of envy. Its true nature and causes. The tendency to compete with others. The reason for an excess of envy among those of a similar status—readers of the Qur'án, brethren, cousins, and neighbours. The medicine that will drive away the sickness of envy. The power needed to banish it from the heart.

Book VI. The Reproach of the World. [vol. iii, p. 151.

An explanation of sermons on the subject. A description of the world by an example. The true nature of the world and its character. The relation of the servant to God. The occupations in the world.

Book VII. The Reproach of Stinginess and the Love of Wealth. [vol. iii, p. 184.

In commendation of wealth. Its evils and its advantages. The reproach of avarice (*al-ḥirs*). Covetousness (*al-ṭama'*). The cure for them both. An explanation of the value of generosity. Stories of generous men. Stories of misers. Definitions of generosity (*al-sakhá'*) and of stinginess. The cure for stinginess. An explanation of the obligations on the servant of God in regard to his property. The reproach of opulence (*al-ghaní*), praise for poverty (*al-faqr*).

Book VIII. The Reproach of Position and Hypocrisy (*al-dham al-já' wa'l-riyá'*). [vol. iii, p. 206.

The love of position (*ḥub al-já'*). The blame that goes with notoriety. The value of obscurity. The meaning of position and its true character. Why position is coveted. Aspects that are futile. Reasons for the love of praise and congratulation. The cure for the love of position. The cure for the dislike of blame or criticism. The variety of circumstances in regard to praise and blame.

The blame of hypocrisy. Its essential nature and its stages. Hypocrisy that is concealed. Works that are done in vain because of hidden hypocrisy. When the manifestation of acts of devotion is permissible. When the concealing of sins is permitted. Giving up acts of devotion because of fear of hypocrisy. How much of satisfaction is there to the worshipper in being seen of men? The extent to which a disciple should examine himself.

Book IX. The Reproach of Pride and Vanity (*al-dham al-kibr wa'l-'ujb*). [vol. iii, p. 255.

Strutting and showing pride in walking and dragging garments. The nature of humility (*al-tawáḍu'*). The nature of pride. The title for Allah (*al-Mutakabbir*). Dispositions of those who are humble. A cure for pride and a means for acquiring humility.

That which is blameworthy in haughtiness, or vanity (*al-'ujb*). The true nature of haughtiness. Circumstances in which it is shown.

Book X. The Reproach of Deception (*al-dham al-ghurúr*). [vol. iii, p. 288.

Varieties of those who are deceived—the learned, leaders in worship, followers of the Ṣúfís' teaching (*al-mutasawfat*), and men of wealth (*'arbáb al-aḥwál*).

FOURTH QUARTER (*rub' al-munjiyát*), or Saving Matters.

Book I. Repentance (*al-tawba*). [vol. iv, p. 2.

Essential nature and requirements. Those things from which repentance is necessary. The completion of repentance. Concerning prayer in repentance.

Book II. Steadfastness (*al-ṣabr*) and Thankfulness (*al-shukr*). [vol. iv, p. 48.

The value and character of each. The nature and varieties of wealth. How to unite steadfastness with thankfulness.

Book III. Fear (*al-khawf*) and Hope (*al-rajá'*). [vol. iv, p. 112.
The nature of hope. The nature of fear. The states (*al-ahwál*) of the prophets, the angels, and of various saints.

Book IV. Poverty (*al-faqr*) and Devotion (*al-zuhd*). [vol. iv, p. 148.
The nature and varieties of poverty. The true character and excellence of devotion.

Book V. Belief in Allah's Unity (*al-tawhíd*), and the Cultivation of Trust (*al-tawakkul*). [vol. iv, p. 187.

Book VI. Love (*al-muḥabba*), Desire (*al-shawq*), Affection (*al-uns*), and Readiness to Please (*al-riḍá*). [vol. iv, p. 227.

Book VII. Intention (*al-niya*), Sincerity (*al-ikhlás*), and Truth (*al-ṣidq*). [vol. iv, p. 282.
Concerning intention. Concerning sincerity. Concerning truth, its value and its nature.

Book VIII. Contemplation (*al-muráqaba*) and Concentration (*al-muhásaba*). [vol. iv, p. 306.
Requisite restraint. The nature and the stages of contemplation. The self, its nature and its faults. Putting forth special effort (*al-mujáhida*). Concerning self-reproach.

Book IX. The Act of Thinking (*al-tafakkur*). [vol. iv, p. 331.
Its value and nature. Channels of thought. How to think about God's creation.

Book X. Death and What Follows. [vol. iv, p. 352.
Consideration of death. The prolongation of life and the value of diminishing hope. The agony of death (*saharat al-mawt*). The decease of the Apostle, and of several of the Caliphs. Dying words of Caliphs, amirs, and saints. Sayings of Ṣúfí saints (*al-'arifín*) in regard to biers and graveyards, and the command about visiting tombs. What the dead encounters in the grave until the trumpet blast (for resurrection). What is known of the states of the dead from the trumpet blast until settling (*istiqrár*) in Paradise or in the Fire. A description of the trumpet blast. The place of assembly (*'arḍ al-muḥásharí*). The sweat. The length of the Day of Resurrection. The questioning. The balance. The antagonist (*al-khuṣamá'*). The bridge (*al-ṣirát*). Intercession (*shifa'a*). The reservoir (*al-ḥawḍ*) in Paradise. A description of Hell (*al-Jahanam*). A description of Paradise (*al-Jannat*). The mercy of Allah the Most High.

7

PRINCIPAL PERSIAN WRITERS ON ETHICS

AGAIN WE observe that in Islamic literature books of outstanding ethical value appeared during periods of grave political disturbance, for ethical judgements are apt to carry implications which smug authority resents. When in Persia the Shi'ite elements of the population were thrown out of power by the rise of the Seljuqs, who took over from the Buwaihids the protection or custody of the 'Abbasid Caliphs, books on ethics began to appear.

At the same time the Fatimid Caliphs, who owed their origin to the Shi'ite Ismá'ílís, were exercising sovereignty over Syria, North Africa, and Egypt. In Egypt they had established their rule in A.D. 969, and they succeeded in maintaining themselves there for about two centuries. Thus the Fatimids in Egypt were almost contemporary with the successive periods of the Buwaihids and the Seljuqs in Persia, and it is well known that they encouraged malcontents from Persia to go to Egypt and study their teachings and their methods, so that they might return as propagandists for Ismá'ílí doctrines and political theories.

One of these men was the poet Náṣir-i-Khusraw (d. A.D. 1061). In his diary, the *Safar Náma,* he gives a brief account of the conditions that prevailed at the time when the Seljuqs were fighting their way gradually from Bukhara to Baghdad. When he had set out from his home in Merw to make the pilgrimage to Mecca, he observed that "the country was being laid waste by the continued wars between the various princes". This general devastation he saw particularly in Irán and 'Iráq, whereas there was as yet prosperity and security in Egypt, which was under the authority of the Fatimid Caliph al-Mustansir (A.D. 1036–94). When he returned to Khorasan it was as a partisan of this Fatimid Caliph, in whose interest he was to spend the rest of his life as an Ismá'ílí agent—first in Balkh, then in Mazandaran, and finally "among the inaccessible mountains of Badakhshán" near Bukhara. There he lived and wrote important books.

He had gone to that segregated mountain district for his personal safety. At the time it was known mainly because they had there found rubies and lapis lazuli. There in Badakhshán he died in A.D. 1061, and to this day there is a sect of Ismá'ílís in that town who revere his grave, and who are known as the Náṣiríya.

His two books on ethics are the *Rawshaná'i Náma* ("Book of Light") and the *Sa'ádat Náma* ("Book of Felicity").[1] They each treat of ethical subjects in verse, and are distinctly from the Ṣúfí point of view.

But the most influential of the Shi'ites who returned from Egypt to Persia was Ḥasan ibn al-Ṣabbáḥ,[2] who secured the fortress of Alamut; and from this remote village, not far from the modern town of Qazvín, soon a whole series of mountain fortresses were occupied by his Ismá'ílí organization, which came to be known as the Háshíshiyán ("Assassins"), which was because its members were addicted to the use of the herb *háshísh* (*Cannibus indica*) in order to induce the ecstatic state or to promote reckless courage.

There in Alamut, within Persia itself, Ḥasan ibn Ṣabbáḥ and his associates set up an Ismá'ílí sphere of influence which continued for 165 years (A.D. 1090–1255); and it is interesting to note that a number of men of learning who found themselves out of favour with the Seljuqs went to live in his fortified Ismá'ílí villages. For there they could be safe from State interference on the ground of their unorthodoxy—whether it were theological, social, or political.

At the same time this Ismá'ílí organization was in active opposition to the rule of the Seljuqs, and they took measures against those prominent Persians who were giving them support. In asserting their influence they employed at times the extreme methods of intimidation and assassination. We are told that "the fact that they availed themselves of murder to get rid of their foes was no new phenomenon in Islam. Abú Manṣúr al-Ijlí and Mughaira ibn Sa'd, whose followers were called "Stranglers" (*khannáq*), had previously resorted to it and had magnified assassination for political ends as a religious and meritorious act."[3] For this opinion precedents could be cited readily from early Muslim history, as for example the expeditions that were sent against the personal opponents of the Prophet, the killing of 'Uthmán and of 'Ali, and the murder of Abu Muslim by the Caliph Mansur in the palace at Baghdad.[4]

1. Náṣir-i-Khusraw's three books were printed together by the Kaviáni Press, Berlin, A.H. 1341. The *Sháh-náma* has been edited and translated by Schefer, Paris, 1881; and the two latter appeared in the *Z.D.M.G.*, vol. xxxiii, pp. 645–65; vol. xxxiv, pp. 428–68, 617–42, and 643–74.

2. Mention is made of books that were written by Ḥasan ibn Ṣabbáḥ, but as the Mongols ultimately destroyed most of the Ismá'ílí strongholds there are none of his writings that remain. A record of his teachings that was written about eighty years after he died, the *Haft Báb-i-Bábá Sayyid-i-ná* ("Seven Chapters of the Old Man Our Leader"), is considered to be "the earliest known genuine work belonging to the Alamuti school of Ismá'ílí literature in Persia". Cf. W. Ivanow, *Two Early Ismá'ílí Treatises*, Intro., p. 1, published by the Islamic Research Association, No. 2, 1933.

3. C. H. Becker, art. "Assassins", in the *Encyclopædia of Islam*.

4. Al-Dinawárí, edit. Kratchkovsky and Guirgass, p. 377.

Malik Sháh, who was the Seljuq sovereign at the beginning of the period of the opposition of the Assassins, had been willing to accept tribute from them. But this greatly displeased his powerful vizier, the Nizám al-Mulk, who was al-Ghazálí's friend and patron. He warned Malik Sháh that "if any calamitous event should befall this victorious dynasty, or if any reverse should happen, these dogs would emerge from their hiding places, and rise against the Empire to carry out their Shi'ite propaganda".[5]

A few years later on, when the Nizám al-Mulk had been dismissed from his office as vizier, he himself met his death from one of these very "dogs". At a place called Nahawand, where he had stopped for the night, a youth who was dressed as a beggar, but who is generally believed to have been an agent of the dreaded Hasan ibn Ṣabbáḥ, approached him and stabbed him. That was on the 14th October, A.D. 1042, in the first decade of the period of the Assassins.

A hundred years later the Assassins were still in power and they continued to pursue the same policy. One of the writers who then came in conflict with them was Fakhr al-Dín al-Rází (A.D. 1149–1209), who wrote among other books a massive commentary on the Qur'án and a brief encyclopædia on the sciences. When he was a young man he too had been disposed to speak bitterly against the Ismá'ílís, until on the occasion when a bag of gold and a dagger were laid before him, and he was informed that he might take his choice. If he kept on in his attitude of opposition and criticism he could expect the assassin's dagger, but if he were willing to hold his tongue he could take the gold. Afterwards he is said to have remarked that the chief of the Assassins had converted him "by weighty and trenchant arguments".

That there were real differences of opinion and serious discussions among the learned men of this period is evidenced by Fakhr al-Dín al-Rází's "Ten Rules for Polite Disputation":[6]

1. Brevity should not be stressed to the point of leaving a statement incomplete.
2. Elaboration should not be allowed to become tiresome.
3. Caution should be observed in the use of words that are strange and uncommon.
4. In answering the speech of an antagonist, his statement should be repeated with the omission of whatever is unimportant.
5. In questions and answers words with two meanings should be avoided.
6. There should be no contention in matters that are outside the point of discussion, as the talking would get out of control and one meeting would not suffice for the debate.
7. Until the statement of an antagonist is fully understood one should not plunge into the answer.

5. Professor E. G. Browne, *A Literary History of Persia*, vol. iii, pp. 215–16.
6. Fakhr al-Dín al-Rází, *Jama'al-'Ulúm*, p. 11.

8. In discussion a man should be affable and sensible. From any effort to prevail by an excess of zeal, from getting angry, from laughing, and from giving offence to the antagonist he should by all means be on his guard.

9. It is well to be cautious of an antagonist who is highly honoured and well liked, for when fear is felt the power of attention and the sharpness of memory are apt to be inhibited.

10. No antagonist is to be despised or lightly esteemed, for thus a weak argument may be used, and even a weak antagonist may thereby prevail.

AKHLÁQ-I-NÁSIRÍ

In the study of Persian books of ethics we are especially concerned with the last years of the period of the Assassins, and are interested particularly in the brilliant Shi'ite scholar who had been constrained to go and live in one of their fortresses. Whether his going there was through deception or by force is not altogether certain. This man was Naṣír al-Dín al-Ṭúsí (A.D. 1201–74). Born ninety years after the death of al-Ghazálí, in his study of philosophy he "was six teachers removed" in the succession from Abu 'Ali ibn Siná (Avicenna); and in reading the Law (*Fiqh*), he was three teachers removed from the 'Alam al-Hudá, who was the chief of the Shi'ite doctors of the sect of the Twelvers in the Buwaihid period. The young Ṭúsí was exceedingly eager to propagate the Shi'ite faith, not that of the Ismá'ílí branch however, but the faith of those who believe in the Twelve Imams. As far as we can learn he had not gone to Egypt and had no leanings towards the Fatimid Caliphs.

But when he heard that the 'Abbasid Caliph al-Mustasim had appointed a prominent Shi'ite from Qumm as his vizier, al-Ṭúsí conceived the idea that if he could go himself to Baghdad he might have opportunity to help this vizier convert the Caliph al-Mustasim to the Shi'ite doctrines. In following out this purpose he wrote a letter to the vizier, enclosing some of his Arabic verses to be presented to the Caliph. Although the vizier appreciated al-Ṭúsí's learning and accomplishments, he did not fall in with his idea that he should come to Baghdad to convert the Caliph.

When he was disappointed over this matter, he came to realize that it was perilous for him to remain longer among the fanatical Sunnites who were then dominant in Ṭus. He was growing apprehensive also about reports that he had heard in regard to ruthless ravages by advancing hordes of Mongols. Then while he was uncertain as to what he ought to do, the governor of one of the Ismá'ílí fortresses, Násir al-Dín Mutasham, induced him "by tricks of diplomacy" (*laṭá'if al-ḥiyál*) to go and serve him in his fortress in the double capacity of tutor and astrologer.

This governor showed him every favour and took keen interest in his studies. And one evening al-Ṭúsí called his attention to a book that had been written in Arabic many years before, a book that undertook to give a philosophic statement of what is right in human conduct. Perhaps we can picture him as he sat along with this governor, in some pleasant spot in a garden in the mountain village, when they first examined that book. A score or more of armed retainers would be standing about at a respectful distance. The book in question was Ibn Maskawaihi's *Tahdhíb al-Akhláq* ("Correction of Dispositions"), and it was determined that al-Ṭúsí should prepare a work of that kind in the Persian language, only his book should be somewhat more comprehensive, in that it was to include more than a statement of philosophical ethics. It was to carry the discussion of the principles of right and wrong into two other fields, that of domestic life and that of political affairs. When after great labour he completed this task, he named the book in honour of his governor and patron, the *Ethics of Násir* (*Akhláq-i-Násirí*).

This governor of the fortress at Sartakht was subject to the supreme ruler of the Assassins at that time, who was the famous 'Alá al-Dín, whose methods for training young men to render absolute obedience to him have been celebrated by Marco Polo's classic description. Marco Polo's right to apply the term "the Old Man of the Mountain" (*shaikh al-jabal*) to the Persian Grand Master of the Assassins has been challenged, in so much as we know that this term was used by the Crusaders to designate the chief of the Syrian Assassins, with whom they had repeated encounters;[7] but at any rate we have Marco Polo's statement that it was the Persian Grand Master who had made his mountain valley into a veritable Paradise —as Paradise is portrayed in the Qur'án. For as Marco Polo said, "the Old Man desired to make his people believe that this was actually Paradise. So he fashioned it after the description that Muhammad gave of his Paradise—to wit, that it should be a beautiful garden, running with conduits of wine and milk and honey and water, and full of lovely women for the delectation of the inmates. And sure enough, the Saracens of those parts believed that it was Paradise!"

No one was to enter except those who were to be the Grand Master's *háshíshiyán* ("Assassins"). When promising young men had been drugged with *háshísh* until they were in a deep sleep they would be carried into this garden Paradise. Afterwards, when they awoke in a place so charming, and according to all their hopes and desires, they would never be willing to leave. But the Old Man could have them drugged again and taken out to his palace, and when they would awake and find themselves no longer in the Garden, they would readily consent to carry out his orders and to go on dangerous missions, to put to death this prince or that merchant, on the

7. C. H. Becker, art. "Assassins" in the *Encyclopædia of Islam.*

assurance that whether they lived or died the angels would bear them again into Paradise.

It was this same Persian Grand Master whom Marco Polo named, 'Alá al-Dín Muhammad (A.D. 1220–55), who had ordered his subordinate, the Governor of Sartakht, to send his friend Naṣír al-Dín al-Ṭúsí to him. He went, therefore, to associate with the Grand Master himself at 'Alamut. And from there he was not allowed to take his departure, but he was treated with honour nevertheless and was given all needed facilities for carrying on his studies.

If we keep in mind 'Alá al-Dín's personal character and Marco Polo's description of the way in which he was accustomed to train his devotees, we can imagine that al-Ṭúsí's discourses on moral standards there in Alamut must have seemed rather pointed when he would come to a passage like this.[8]

WHAT MEN HAVE IN COMMON WITH ANIMALS

"It may be said in regard to what man has in common with animals and other forms of life, that if his animal nature prevails over him and his inclination is in that direction, he will be degraded from his proper rank to that of the order of beasts, or even lower. For the Qur'án says, 'They are like the brutes. Yea, they go more astray' (vii. 178). He reaches the place, for example, where he longs to gain the pleasures and the desires of the body, those for which the bodily senses and powers are eager and have a craving—such as things to eat, things to drink, things to wear, and marriages. The result is that the power of lust soon gets the upper hand. Or his development is similarly curtailed if he takes to violence and assault and vengeance, which are the fruits of anger having sway.

"If anyone stops to think, however, he will surely realize that failure of ambition in this matter of seeking human perfection amounts simply to worthlessness and deficiency. In seeking to gratify their appetites most animals are more proficient than man. This is made clear by the greed of a dog in eating, the wantonness of a pig in lascivious debauchery, and the ferocity of the lion in overcoming and breaking his prey. So it is with other kinds of wild beasts, and brutes, and birds, and water animals.

"Consider, therefore, how is it that the reason of a man can be satisfied with effort that is put forth in such a direction that, even with the utmost exertion, he will not equal a dog? And on what grounds will a man of ambition consider that it is permissible for him to seek something which is of such a nature that, though he spend his whole life in its quest, he will not be able to surpass a pig? And it is the same way in regard to the power of anger, for if men will

8. Nasír al-Dín Al-Ṭúsí, in the *Akhláq-i-Náṣirí*, I, i, 5. Cf. al-Ghazálí in the *Kímiya-yi-Sa'ádat*, p. 12.

compare themselves with the least of the wild beasts, it will be seen that the beast will excel them."

Along such lines al-Ṭúsí would discourse with groups of the Assassins who would gather around him, and it appears that they took a kind of academic interest in the subject of ethics. He would proceed to show:

HOW HUMAN LIFE IS DISTINGUISHED FROM ANIMAL LIFE

"Human life is distinguished from the types of animal life by one single power which is called the power of reason, *nutq*. In this power there is perception without an instrument, *idrák-i-bí-álat*, and distinction between things perceived, *tamyíz miyán-i-mudrakát*. In so much as it gives attention to knowledge of truths (*haqá'iq*) about existing things, and to the comprehension of kinds of probabilities, it is by virtue of this belief that they call that power speculative reason (*'aql-i-naẓarí*). But since it also gives attention to the occupation of places, to distinction between advantages and evils, and to evaluating the arts in estimating and arranging the affairs of living, this power is also called practical reason (*'aql-i-amalí*). It is because this power has these two functions (*shu'ba*) that the science of philosophy (*'ilm-i-ḥikmat*) is divided into two branches, the one speculative and the other practical."[9]

A good example of the character of al-Ṭúsí's teaching may be found in his explanation of the perfection of the human soul, in which he makes a special effort to show the loss that comes to those who act contrary to the truth in this respect.[10]

EXPLAINING THE PERFECTION OF THE HUMAN SOUL

"As it has been shown in the previous chapter that the human soul is capable of perfection and of deficiency, and summary mention has been made of that perfection, still some further comment is necessary by way of explanation, so that when the readers become acquainted with the true nature of this perfection they may not withhold even the greatest expenditure of effort in seeking it.

"In the case of any existing thing that is a compound (*murakkab*), we maintain that its perfection as a whole is different from the perfection of its component elements. For example, the perfection of the sherbet (*sakangabín*) is different from the perfection of the vinegar (*sirka*) and the honey (*angabín*) of which it is made. Likewise the perfection of a house is different from the perfection of the wood and the stone. And in so much as man is himself a compound, his perfection is also different from the perfection of his component elements. He has a perfection of his own which no existing thing shares with him.

9. Al-Ṭúsí, op. cit., I. i. 2.

10. Id., op. cit., I. ii. 6.

The most perfect of mankind, therefore, would be the one that showed the greatest capacity in the manifestation (*iẓhár*) of that particular characteristic (*khásiyat*); and that man would rank highest whose conduct in this particular would show no negligence (*taháwun*) or variableness (*talawwun*).

"And now that the state of virtue is known, the state of worthlessness, and the deficiency that characterizes it, will be evident.

"Human perfection is of two kinds, for the human soul (*nafs-i-nátiqa*) has two powers: the power of knowledge (*quwwat-i-'ilmí*) and the power of action (*quwwat-i-'amalí*). The perfection of the authority and power of knowledge lies in a man's desire to understand what is known, and to acquire a mastery of the sciences, until, by the compelling necessity of that desire, and according to his ability, he gains a comprehension of the stages of existing things, and information in regard to their realities. It is after this that he is honoured with a knowledge of ultimate truth and general purpose; when he comprehends that the final cause of all created things is with Him (i.e. Allah), and he reaches a conception of the realm of Unity (*tawḥíd*) and the very point of Union (*ittiḥád*). Then his mind becomes at rest and assured, and the dust of consternation and the rust of doubt are wiped away from the face of his conscience and from the mirror of his memory. Speculative philosophy has to do with the analysis of this kind of perfection.

"As to the power of action, it may be said that it is that which causes the powers and the particular activities of the self to be orderly (*murratab*) and restrained *manẓúm*), so that they correspond and harmonize with one another and do not overcome one another. It is by their being reconciled (*tasálum*) that a man's conduct becomes acceptable (*marḍí*). After that comes other perfection that has to do with the orderly arrangement of the affairs of households and of cities, so that his very circumstances of living may be made to contribute to his assurance (*i'tibár*). As a consequence, a number of men may work along this line together until they reach a true happiness in which they all will share. It is this kind of perfection that constitutes the subject matter of Practical Philosophy."

Another interesting example of al-Ṭúsí's explanations is found in his statement of the inter-related powers of the human soul.[11]

ANALYSIS OF THE POWERS OF THE HUMAN SOUL

"As we have mentioned, mankind has three powers; the lower (*adwán*), which is the bestial self (*nafs-i-bahímí*); the intermediate (*awsaṭ*), which is the ferocious self (*nafs-i-sabu'í*); and the superior

11. Ibid., I. i. 6 (end). Cf. E. E. Calverley, art. "Nafs" in the *Encyclopædia of Islam*; and also "Doctrines of the Soul (Nafs and Ruḥ) in Islam" in *The Moslem World*, vol. xxxiii, p. 4.

(*ashraf*), which is the angelic self (*nafs-i-malakí*). What he has in common with the beasts belongs to the lower as distinguished from the superior. What he has in common with wild animals belongs to the intermediate as distinguished from the superior. It is what he has in common with the angels (*malá'ika*) that belongs essentially to the superior, and those who depart from this their proper status belong to a stage which is lower.

"Remember that the reins of choice (*'anán-i-ikhtiyár*) and the halter of preference (*simán-i-ithár*) are in man's own hand. If he so wishes he can descend to the status of beasts, till he is one of them. Also, if he so wishes, he can live on a level with the wild animals, till he becomes one of them.

"An explanation of these three selves is given in the glorious Qur'án, with the following terminology: the soul that is wont to command to evil (*nafs-i-ammára*), xii. 53; the reproaching soul (*nafs-i-lawwáma*) that restrains, lxxv. 2 and ix. 119; and the tranquil soul (*nafs-i-muṭma'inna*), lxxxix. 27. The *nafs-i-ammára* urges and insists on the indulgence of sensual appetites. The *nafs-i-lawwáma* recognizes inwardly what causes deficiency and seeks to make any effort (*iqdám*) in that direction seem despicable to the eye of understanding (*chasm-i-baṣírat*) by expressing regret and criticism. The *nafs-i-muṭma'inna* can be satisfied only with the good deed (*fi'l-i-jamál*) and the acceptable consequence (*athár-i-marḍí*).

"Philosophers have said that of these three selves there is but one that is truly and essentially cultured and honourable, and that is the *nafs-i-malakí* (the angelic self). As for the second, the *nafs-i-sabu'í* (the ferocious self), while it is not cultured (*adíb*), it is capable of culture and complies with a teacher at the time of instruction. But the third, which is utterly destitute of culture (*árí az adab*) and lacks any capacity for it, is the *nafs-i-bahímí* (the bestial self). They say that the only reason for its existence is to provide for the duration of the body, which is the site or vehicle of the angelic self, for the period of time that it requires to attain its perfection and to arrive at its purpose. Likewise the reason for the existence of the vindictive self (*nafs-i-ghaḍabí*) is the restriction and subjection of the bestial self, so that the corruption that comes from its ascendancy may be expelled, for the beast is incapable of culture. This conception (of the philosophers) comes very close to an explanation (*ta'wíl*) of that which has been related by way of revelation (*tanzíl*).

"Plato (*Aflátun*) has said in describing the ferocious self and the bestial self: 'But this is like gold in its softness (*lín*) and pliability (*in'itáf*), whereas that is like iron (*ḥadíd*) in its hardness (*ṣalábat*) and inhibition (*intiná'*).' Similarly, in another place, he said, 'It is not difficult to bear with passions in order to attain to superiority.'

"Accordingly, whoever chooses to do a good deed, if he finds that his sensual self does not assist him, must seek aid against it through anger (*ghaḍabi*), which is the exciting force to prohibit (*mahaiyij-i-ḥimyat*), so as to subdue and restrain it. Also, if in spite of such help and assistance the power of lust should prevail, and if after complying with its demand the individual concerned should feel regret and shame, he would still be in line for improvement and there would be hope for his recovery. But to accomplish the purpose of rooting out and suppressing lust it is needful that use should be made of the assistance of some such state as anger. Otherwise the result would be as Aristotle has said: 'I see that for the most part men lay claim to the love of good deeds, but they seek to avoid the hardship that is involved in maintaining this good conduct, or in acquiring knowledge of its excellence, and so it is that weakness and futility prevail among them. Soon there is no difference between them and the one who is not marked with the love of the good deed and its excellence. For if the one who sees and the one who does not see both fall into a well, both are companions in destruction, though the one seeing would alone be deserving of blame and criticism.'

"Teachers in olden times compare these three selves to three different animals in one courtyard—an angel, a dog, and a pig, so that whichever one would get the best of the others would have the authority. Others said that the situation of mankind with reference to these selves is more like that of a man mounted on a powerful horse, when with a dog he goes out to hunt. If the authority is with the man he will employ his riding animal and his hunting animal with discretion. He will be attentive to what is necessary for the well-being of all of them in time of danger, and he will make arrangement for what food is needed for them all in just measure. Thus as companions in eating and drinking, and in other matters of subsistence, they will be maintained according to the needs of their respective natures.

"But if the riding beast has his own way and does not recognize the authority of the rider, then he will start to run wherever he sees the best grass. In roughness of gait, in straying from the road, and in making speed at the wrong place, he will give great annoyance to himself and to his companions. Finally, when he arrives at the good grass, without any solicitude for the others, he will leave them to famish from hunger until they are at the point of destruction. At times in the midst of his running he will encounter a tree or a thorn-patch or a deep river or some dangerous water, and then by injury or stumbling or some other mishap, he will destroy himself and the others too.

"Also if the hunting animal has its own way, at the time when it sees the prey it will lead the riding animal and its rider in that direction as fast as it can, with resultant hardship and fear of destruction, as has been mentioned. It is even probable that in the course of the encounter, when fighting with the animal that is hunted, it will itself be so wounded and worn out that it will perish.

But if the two beasts are subject to the rider, who knows what is best and who has the right to command, they will be saved from these misfortunes and accidents.

"It is to be noted, however, that the state of these several powers, in being reconciled (*tasálum*) and in mingling (*imtizáj*), is different from any state of separate bodies. For in the union of the three, the two other selves are dependent upon the prudence of the angelic self, so that you may then say that all three are in reality but one. With these separate powers and effects, which each self is expected to exercise at its own time, there is then no conflict or opposition, so that you think when you consider them separately that they are the same as they were at first, and yet by their obedience and harmony with one another you can regard them as one power only. It is for this reason that a difference of opinion has arisen among scholars as to whether they are three powers of one self or whether they are three selves. But if it is any arrangement that is not fully committed to the angelic self, then conflict and difference will occur, and every hour this will increase, until it becomes the cause of the loosening of the instruments (*álat*) and the destruction of all three powers.

"There is no state more ruinous than that which means the abandonment of the divine administration (*siyásat-i-rabbání*) and the wasting of His favours (*taḍí-yi-na'im-i-ou*). That is the very essence of unrighteousness (*fisq*). For it is ingratitude for His benefits (*kufrán-i-ayádí*) and a denial of His rights (*inkár-haqúq-i-ou*), which is the equivalent of unbelief (*kufr*). For the true content of oppression (*ẓulm*) is the placing of things in wrong places. Thus the manager becomes the managed, the King becomes the subject, and the lord becomes the slave—which shows creation turned upside-down (*intikás-i-khalq*). Such a notion or consequence would be the demand of devils, and would be following in the custom (*sunnat*) of *Iblís* (the Devil) and his army. We take refuge with Allah from that and seek from Him sinlessness (*iṣmat*) and protection (*tawfíq*)."

In his discussion of "Opposites that make up the Varieties of Vices",[12] al-Ṭúsí has emphasized the practical importance that is attached to moderation in Muslim ethics.

OVERDOING (AL-IFRÁT) AND NEGLECTING (AL-TAFRÍT)

"Departures from the accepted standards are of two kinds: one comes by way of overdoing and the other by way of neglecting. In relation to every virtue, therefore, there are two sorts of vices. The virtue itself is midway and the vices lie to either side. But since it has been stated that virtues are of four kinds, then there must be eight sorts of vices: two in relation to wisdom, which are to be absent-minded (*safah*) and to be ignorant (*bulh*); two also in relation to

12. Al-Túsí, op. cit., II. ii. 5.

bravery, which are rashness (*tahawwur*) and cowardice (*jubn*); two in relation to purity, which are the excess of cupidity (*shirra búr*) and the abating of passion (*khumud-i-shahawat*); and two in relation to righteousness, which are oppression (*ẓulm*) and being oppressed (*inẓilám*).

"To be absent-minded is on the side of excess, for it is the employing of powers of thought on what is not necessary, or to a greater extent than is fitting. Some call this self-deception (*gurbuzí*), or being like a large over-ripe cucumber (*kurbuzí*). To be ignorant or stupid (*bulh*) is to err on the side of carelessness or neglect, in voluntarily failing to make use of the power of thought, not because of any physical limitation.

"Rashness, which is from excess, is always ready to start something which it is not seemly to start; whereas cowardice, which is on the side of insufficiency, is avoiding things which it is not commendable to avoid.

"Cupidity, which is on the side of excess, is greed for sexual pleasures beyond the measure that is proper; whereas the abating of passion, which is on the side of deficiency, is lack of initiative in seeking necessary pleasures, or such as reason and the law permit—when this indifference is voluntary and is not due to physical limitation.

"Oppression, which is on the side of excess, is the acquirement of the means of living by methods that are reprehensible; whereas being oppressed, which is on the side of deficiency, consists in affording opportunity to anyone who is seeking the means of living by methods of violence and plunder, i.e. in submitting to their being taken without justification and merely because they are themselves abject.

"Since there are many ways of acquiring properties, powers, etc., the man who is an oppressor and a deceiver is apt to always have much money, whereas the one who suffers oppression has little with which to get along. The righteous man is in a state that lies midway.

"While we are treating this topic of the varieties that come under the different kinds of virtues, sufficient explanation should be given to show that for each variety of virtues there will be two sorts of vices, one on the side of excess and the other on the side of deficiency. It is altogether possible that there may not be a particular name for each one of these types and varieties, but conceptions of them will be sufficient, for philosophic explanation has to do rather with essential meanings than with names."

For al-Ṭúsí there was an underlying religious ideal in all his ethical studies. This is clearly shown in his remarks in regard to *good* (*khair*) and *happiness* (*sa'ádat*), for he maintained that they are sought in the course of the effort that is put forth in order to arrive at the perfection of the human soul.[13]

13. Al-Túsí, op. cit., I. i. 7.

CAN MANKIND HAVE SPIRITUAL PERFECTION?

"As every act has an end (*ghâyat*) and a purpose (*gharaḍ*), so the perfecting of the soul (*takmíl-i-nafs*) must also be for a purpose. Its purpose, as has been explained, is its happiness, in the increase of which we may say that its good consists.

"Reference will be made in the first place, therefore, to our apprehension of the nature (*máhíyat*) of *good* and *happiness*. It is by appreciating the good in its imperfection that desire is awakened for it in its perfection. In the seeker this new desire will prevail, so that anyone who is attaining perfection will experience greater gladness and joy in accomplishing things.

"Aristotle has expressed this thought in the beginning of his book on ethics, and we think that his opinion is correct: 'For the beginning of the idea is the end (or purpose) of the action, as appears in all trades. Until a carpenter first sees what a board is good for, he does not consider any mode of action; and until he has thought out a mode of action he does not start to do anything with the board. Furthermore, until the action is complete, the use of the board that occurred to him at first does not fully appear. So it is indeed with the reasoning individual ('*áqil*). Until he considers *good* and *happiness* as results of the perfecting of the soul, anxiety to acquire perfection does not find a place in his mind; and it is noteworthy that until this act of acquiring perfection begins to take place he will make no progress towards *good* and *happiness*.'

"Abu 'Ali Ibn Siná has remarked that Aristotle says also in his book on ethics that the youth, or those that have the nature of youth, 'will not derive much advantage from this book'. He observes further that he does not mean *youth* to apply merely in the matter of age, 'for age is not what counts in this connexion, but by the youth is meant those whose characters are confused by the lusts of sense so that sensual desire controls their moods'.[14]

"So it is that I also say that the object of this section, which includes a discussion of *happiness* and *good* in the book of ethics, has not been written with the understanding that youth could reach this standard, but it is with the hope that the idea may come within their ken and that they may know that for some men there is such attainment. They may indeed realize that they themselves have the capacity ultimately to attain it too, so that something of that same desire (to acquire perfection) may be found in them, and afterwards, if divine assistance is vouchsafed to them, they can reach that stage. . . .

"There are some who have used the word *happiness* to apply also to animals, but that application of the word is but a figure of speech (*mujáz*), for when animals reach their perfection it is not by reason

14. Aristotle, *Nicomachean Ethics*, I, 3, par. 7.

of will or contemplation on their part, but it is by virtue of such aptitude as they have by nature. It is not therefore real happiness that is attributed to them, for all the things that are procurable for animals—such as delicacy of food and drink, covering, rest, and ease—do not have to do with happiness, but they are like things that are connected with fortune or chance, as they are in fact in the case of mankind. However, on account of what we said, that the *absolute good* (*khair al-muṭlaq*) has one signification in which all individuals share, that is, that every movement is to arrive at an objective and every act is to attain an end, this would have to apply to animals also if they were to attain happiness. Reason does not permit us to think that anyone would put forth continued motion and extreme effort without some consciousness of an objective. Whatever the end in view may be in any action, the actor must have some conception of it. Otherwise it is in vain and reason counts it base. Accordingly, if the end or purpose in the individual soul is good, it may be called absolute good, but if it is something relative, then it is only relative good: and since the arts and meditations of all reasoning people have such good in view, then absolute good has one signification in which they all share."

After he had studied human nature at close quarters in the fortresses of the Assassins, al-Ṭúsí had interesting remarks to make about the amazing variety of individuals in the human race, and in regard to those of mankind who may attain the highest happiness.

DIFFERENTIATION OF INDIVIDUAL TYPES[15]

"It is important to observe that as every variety of animals, vegetables, and minerals is essentially different from other varieties, so among mankind there must be differentiation of individual types. You cannot consider the Arab racehorse the same as the sluggish pack-pony, or regard an Indian razor that is well furbished as the same as a rusty blade of soft iron. Observe then that in the case of mankind the difference between individuals is still greater. In fact, among all kinds of existing things there is no such differentiation and distinction of individual types as in the human race . . . for among mankind it is possible that one man may be the lowest of beings, whereas another may be the noblest.

"It is by means of the art for the correction of dispositions (*tahdhíb al-akhláq*) that the lowest ranks of mankind are brought to the highest stages. Assuredly this will be in accord with each individual's capacity (*isti'dád*) and the measure of his aptitude (*qadr-i-ṣalaḥiyat*), for not all individuals are capable of the same kind of perfection. If we have here, therefore, an art which can make the lowest of beings become the noblest, what a remarkable art it must be!"

15. Al-Ṭúsí, op. cit., I. ii. 2.

CAN THE HIGHEST HAPPINESS BE ATTAINED IN THIS LIFE?[16]

"There is a difference of opinion among the philosophers whether the greatest happiness for mankind can be attained in this present life or only after death. The first group are ancient philosophers who maintained that the body has no part in happiness. They said that while the human soul is connected with the body, handicapped and defiled by the foulness of nature and of physical corruption, and occupied by the needs of the body for many things, it cannot be absolutely happy. Nevertheless, since by the mystical revelation of the real nature of things (*kashf a-haqá'iq*) ideas reach a stage that transcends the darkness of matter, and material faults and defects are hidden (*maḥjub*), so when the soul escapes from this foulness of the body it becomes free and clean (*pák*) from ignorance (*jahl*). With purity (*ṣafá'*) and sincerity (*khulus*) it takes on a nature or substance (*jawhar*), with the name of Perfect Reason (*'aql-i-tám*), that has a capacity for illumination (*anwár-i-iláhi*). Consequently, with these thinkers true happiness was thought to be possible only after death.

"But Aristotle, and a number of his followers, declared that it is odious (*shaní'*) and abominable (*qabíḥ*) for us to say that anyone in this world should be obedient to the behests of truth, and careful to maintain good conduct, and desirous of all sorts of virtues, become perfect in nature (*kámil bi dhát*) and praiseworthy in general, be called indeed to the vicegerency of the Lord of the Throne and be occupied in the improvement of all sorts of beings, and yet, notwithstanding this nobility of talent (*manqabat*), that he must remain miserable (*shakí*) and deficient (*náqis*), and that only when he would die, and these influences and achievements would come to nothing, then he would become perfectly happy. Their opinion was that happiness has degrees and stages (*madárij wa marátib*), that it is in fact a gradua l attainment in proportion to effort, and that when it arrives at its final stage it then becomes perfect happiness, even though the individual be still in the bondage of life (*qaid-i-hayát*). They mention, moreover, that when perfect happiness is acquired it will not be injured by the dissolution of the body (*bi i-hilál-i-badan*). These are the statements of the Ancients (*mutaqaddamán*) on this subject.

"When the modern philosophers (*muta'ákhirán*) considered these two points of view, and compared them with the foundations of wisdom (*qawá'id-i-ḥikmat*) and the rules of reason (*qawáin-i-'aqlí*), they declared that man can have spiritual perfection or excellence (*faḍilat-i-rúháni*), and that in this regard he is like the exalted angels, but that he has also bodily vileness (*radhilat-i-jismání*) in partnership with animals and four-footed beasts. For the sake of acquiring that which makes for the perfection of the spiritual part (*jazw-i-ruháni*)

16. Al-Ṭúsí, op. cit., I. i. 7.

he abides a few days in this world that is inferior (*'álam-i-suflí*) in the bodily part (*jazw-i-jismání*) in order to build up and discipline and fully acquire his virtues for the spiritual part. Then finally, in his spiritual part, he will be transported to the higher world (*'álam-i-'ulwiya*) to be in fellowship with the court of heaven (*malá'-i-a'lá*) for ever. Observe that their object in the use of the terms *higher* and *lower* is not with reference to place, but according to their idea that whatsoever is perceived by the physical senses is lower, however lofty its position may be, and that whatsoever is perceived by reason is higher, however lowly its place.

"While men are in the world happiness will be conditioned for them on the attainment of both of these perfections; *first*, so that they may acquire what will afford them advantage in eternal happiness, and *second*, so that they may enjoy happiness in the midst of complications with material affairs. In contemplation of that noble and sublime nature (which is their goal), men must have for it desire, curiosity, and eagerness. This is the first of the stages of happiness.

"When man passes to the world beyond this he will not be in need of happiness of the body. His happiness will be confined to witnessing the holy beauty (*jamál-i-muqaddas*) of things sublime (*'ulwiyat*), i.e. true wisdom, until he becomes immersed in the Lord of Glory and adorned with the majestic qualities of truth. Then he will have arrived at the second of the stages of happiness. . . . [The discussion of degrees of happiness is omitted.]

"For the mass of mankind Allah has opened the way to perfection. By many an inducement (*targhib*) and many an admonition (*tarkib*) He has called them. He has provided means for facilitating their advancement and for removing their defects, but they have neglected to put forth the necessary effort and exertion. With an habitual preference for the opposite course, they have employed the life that should have been used with noble powers in the acquisition of things that are base.

"Cattle are of course to be excused for having no hope of association with holy spirits or of reaching the most noble degree of happiness. But in the case of this crowd of mankind we recognize that for them there is the right of blame, of criticism, and of regret—yes, and also the right of repentance. For as has been remarked about one man who could see and another man who was blind, when they both went off the road and fell into a well, although they were partners in destruction, the one who could see should be an object of censure (*malum*), whereas the blind man should be an object of mercy (*marhum*).

"For human beings, therefore, happiness must be in two stages. Those in the first stage, i.e. those who are animated by a desire for a nobler existence, would not be liberated from a mixture of pains and regrets. This would be from disappointment at not reaching a higher degree, or it would follow as the result of occupation with the delusions of nature (*khadá'i-yi-ṭabí'i*) and the vanities of sense perception (*zakhárif al-hissí*). Such happiness is in reality defective.

"Those in the second stage, however, are free from these things. They are engaged in seeking the illumination of divine lights and the abundance of their unlimited influences (*athár-i-námutanahí*). Whoever reaches that point has attained the utmost happiness. He is not concerned at separation from a friend, or annoyed at the passing of a pleasure, or disturbed at the loss of a delicacy. All the wealth and all the glories and all the good things of the world, even his own body, which is the nearest thing to him, are for him but a heavy load. If he acquires a little something in the way of temporary property, this is merely in accord with the necessity of his nature, from which it is impossible for him to be freed, but it is not because of his own desire. His conduct, therefore, will not be found to be contrary to what is in agreement with the will of Allah. The deception of nature and the opposition of passion and lust will make no impression upon him. Hence it is that he does not become distraught (*anduhqín*) over the loss of a friend, and he does not make complaint and lamentation over the passing away of something that is desirable. Neither does he exult (*ihtizáz kunad*) over accomplishing any particular object, and neither does he become proud (*mumbasit*) on attaining culture."

AKHLÁQ-I-JALÁLÍ

Late in the fourteenth century there occurred another widespread devastation of the lands of the Eastern Caliphate. In the extreme heat of summer, in the year A.D. 1393, Timur came to Baghdad with his onrushing hordes of Turkomans. Once more the glamorous city of the Arabian Nights was looted. This time its buildings were burned, its inhabitants were almost entirely annihilated, and Timur sought deliberately to make Samarqand the centre of Muslim civilization.

It was in agreement with this purpose that a few years later, in A.D. 1407, Shah Rukh appointed his son, Ulugh Beg, to rule in Samarqand, for he was a man of letters, an artist, a learned mathematician, and an astronomer. To him may be attributed the glory of having erected many illustrious buildings in Samarqand. But when on the death of Shah Rukh, Ulugh Beg became head of the Timuríd empire, in the series of ineffective struggles that he made to suppress rival princes, struggles that lasted for two years and ten months, he was worn down and overcome and slain.

Nearly twenty years later one of his successors in the Timuríd line of sovereigns, Abu Saíd, who ruled from A.D. 1459–69, manifested the military and political genius that Ulugh Beg had lacked, and acquired the whole region of Transoxiana, Badakhshán, and

Qandahár, with the border districts of India, Persian 'Iráq, and Khurasan. In undertaking to extend his conquests to the west, however, he came into conflict with the leader of another branch of Turkomans, one Uzun Ḥasan, "The Long Ḥasan", who had maintained himself as governor of the district of Diyár Bakr from the year A.D. 1458. At that time also, it may be noted, the last Armenian emperor of Trebizond, David by name, had given his niece Catherine to Uzun Ḥasan in marriage. Then in the course of about twelve years' time he had pressed forward into Persia, had overcome Abu Sa'íd, and had reduced his Timuríd rivals to subjection.

It was at the court of this Uzun Ḥasan, whose political relations were with Venice and Constantinople to the west and with Samarqand and Hèrát to the east, that a great book of ethics, the *Akhláq-i-Jalálí*, had its origin. At a time of grave political turmoil and uncertainty and of poorly established authority, men were asked in this book to consider again what was morally right.

The author was a man of whom not much is known, Muhammad ibn As'ad Jalál al-Dín al-Dawwání,[17] (A.D. 1427–1501). He was born at Dawwán in Qazarún; he wrote a book called *Nisba al-Ṣiddiqí*, in which he claimed to be a descendant of the Caliph Abu Bakr, who was designated "*al-Ṣiddiqí*" (the truthful); he served as *qaḍí* of the province of Fars; and he taught for some time in a school in Shiráz, in the *Madrasa al-'Aitám*. His writings in Arabic cover a wide range of philosophical and mystical subjects, but the best known of his works in Persian is the *Lawámi' al-Ishráq fí Makárim al-Akhláq* ("Flashes of Splendour concerning Excellencies of Dispositions"). This book has been frequently printed, for it is widely read in Irán and in India, not only for its value as a book of moral instruction, but because of its literary interest. The author has made skilful use of his knowledge of Persian and Arabian poets, and has quoted them aptly and frequently throughout the entire book. The most convenient Persian text for Western readers is the one that was edited by Muhammad Kazim Shirazi, under the supervision of Major W. G. Grey, I.A., in Calcutta, 1911. The English translation of the *Akhláq-i-Jalálí* by W. F. Thompson appeared under the title *Practical Philosophy of the Muhammadan People*, London, 1839, and has long been out of print.

Comparison shows that Jalál al-Dín al-Dawwáni made little use of the Arabic text of the *Tahdhib al-Akhláq* of Ibn Maskawaihi, and he selected his basic material *ad lib.* from al-Ṭúsí's *Akhláq-i-Násirí*. But he freely abbreviated and simplified many of al-Ṭúsí's philosophic statements and added much by way of literary adornment.

The three main parts of the book, as it follows al-Ṭúsí, are: The Individual State, The Domestic State, and The Political State. The contents of the first part, which is ethics as limited to the individual

17. Cf. Brockelmann, art. "al-Dawwání" in the *Encyclopædia of Islam*.

state, may be represented in its relation to the *Akhláq-i-Násirí* and to the *Tahdhíb al-Akhláq* of Ibn Maskawaihi by the following table of the chapter headings that are given in Mr. Thompson's translation, with references that are added to show the similar passages in the two earlier works:

1. Statement of the Commendable in Morals (*makárim al-akhláq*).
   Persian texts, *lam'ah* i.
   Thompson's English translation, pp. 52–64.
   Akhláq-i-Násirí, I, ii, 3.
   Ibn Maskawaihi, *Tahdhíb al-Akhláq*, ch. 3.
2. Statement of the Laws and the Varieties of the Virtues.
   Persian texts, *lam'ah* ii and iii.
   Thompson's English translation, pp. 65–87.
   Ibn Maskawaihi, *Tahdhíb al-Akhláq*, ch. 4.
3. Distinction between Virtues and Their Counterfeits.
   Persian texts, *lam'ah* iv.
   Thompson's English translation, pp. 88–98.
   Akhláq-i-Násirí, I, ii, 6.
   Ibn Maskawaihi, *Tahdhíb*, ch. 4.
4. On the Vices.
   Persian texts, *lam'ah* v.
   Thompson's English translation, pp. 99–111.
   Akhláq-i-Násirí, I, ii, 5.
   Ibn Maskawaihi, *Tahdhíb*, ch. 1 (end).
5. On the Eminence of Equity (*'idálat*).
   Persian texts, *lam'ah* vi and vii.
   Thompson's English translation, pp. 112–45.
   Akhláq-i-Násirí, I, ii, 7.
   Ibn Maskawaihi, *Tahdhíb*, ch. 4.
6. On the Order to be observed in Acquiring the Virtues.
   Persian texts, *lam'ah* viii.
   Thompson's English translation, pp. 146–54.
   Akhláq-i-Násirí, I, ii, 8.
   Ibn Maskawaihi, *Tahdhíb*, ch. 5.
7. On the Maintenance of Mental Health.
   Persian texts, *lam'ah* ix.
   Thompson's English translation, pp. 155–68.
   Akhláq-i-Násirí, I, ii, 9.
   Ibn Maskawaihi, *Tahdhíb*, ch. 7.
8. On the Cure of Mental Diseases.
   Persian texts, *lam'ah* x.
   Thompson's English translation, pp. 169–244.
   Akhláq-i-Násirí, I, ii, 10.
   Ibn Maskawaihi, *Tahdhíb*, ch. 6.

AKHLÁQ-I-MUḤSINÍ

Note should be made also of a work of a more popular character that has been widely used in the moral instruction of Muslim youth. It is a book of stories, with their morals clearly indicated, called the

"Morals of the Beneficent" (*Akhláq-i-Muḥsini*); it was written by Ḥuṣain Wá'iẓ Káshifí (d. A.D. 1504), and has been frequently lithographed. A printed text of the first twenty lessons appeared in 1850, which had been prepared for the use of Indian students who were studying Persian in the Calcutta University. Fifteen of these twenty lessons were translated into English by Rev. H. G. Keene in 1867, and this translation was published in convenient form for the use of students.[18]

The subjects of each of these twenty lessons, accompanied in each case by one of the author's most pertinent statements or illustrations, are presented as follows:

Worship ('ibádat). When Sháh Sanján was asked by a sovereign of Herát for advice, he replied, "If you wish for safety here, and glory hereafter, pour forth continually the complaint of your misery by night, in the presence of Allah; and turn constantly by day, in your palace, to the cries of the wretched."

And the author observes that 'Ali is supposed to have declared, "If I should rest by day, public business would go to ruin; and if I should take repose at night, my own state will be wretched in the Day of Judgement: and therefore I attend to public concerns by day, and devote myself to the service of Allah by night."

Sincerity (ikhlás). It is related that when a man who had been condemned to death began to abuse the Caliph personally, this Caliph ordered him to be set free, and then declared: "I did not wish to let my own passions interfere in what is the work of the Almighty, for such a case would be far from the spirit of Sincerity."

> The proceeding which is not replete with sincerity,
> Is one which it would be better to abandon.

Prayer (du'á). Prayer is either for gaining some advantage or for getting rid of some evil, and princes have no exemption from either of these two reasons for prayer.

> That man may sit on the throne of pleasure according to his desire,
> Who hath opened for his heart a path of supplication.

Thanksgiving (shukr). Thanksgiving, then, does not consist in letting the melodious nightingale of the tongue warble for a moment on the rose-bush of praise to Allah. It is said that he who is grateful is deserving of further blessings, but for a Prince gratitude for sovereignty consists in justice towards all creatures, and beneficence to the whole of mankind.

Steadfastness (ṣabr). The merit and value of a man are not

18. *Akhláq-i-Muḥsiní*, by Ḥuṣain Wá'iẓ Káshifí (d. A.D. 1504), Persian text (20 chapters), ed. Ousely, publ. Calcutta, 1850; English trans. (15 chapters), by Rev. H. G. Keene, London, 1867.

according to his pretensions: his worth should be determined by his steadfastness.

While an officer was standing before a King a scorpion got into his shirt and kept pricking him every moment. But during the interview the officer gave no sign of disturbance. On the following day, when the King heard what had happened, he asked the officer why he had not removed the scorpion. His reply was: "If to-day, in the banquet room, I cannot endure the sting of a scorpion, how shall I to-morrow bear the envenomed sword of the enemy in the battle-field?" He was of course promoted and rewarded for his steadfastness.

Contentment (raḍá). This is being pleased with all that may happen to a man from Allah, for there is a tradition that Allah said to one of His prophets, "My delight in thee depends upon thy showing pleasure in my decrees: when thou art satisfied with what I ordain, I also am pleased with thee."[19]

Resignation (tawakkul). This is withdrawing the mind from secondary causes and turning attention to the Great First Cause; and looking to the accomplishment of our undertakings from the Lord. For whoever commits his ways unto the Lord, and trusts in everything that occurs to the divine mercy, all his affairs are carried on and fulfilled according to the wishes of his heart.

The Sense of Shame (ḥayá'). As a branch of the faith, the sense of shame is essential to the good order of society, that men may not just do as they please, but that there may be a veil of chastity, that the generous may not turn the petitioner from his dwelling. For it was the Caliph Ma'mún who said, when he sent the Arab who had brought him ill-tasting water back to his own country with a rich reward, "In comparison with the water with which the Arab has been brought up, it seemed to him the water of Paradise. If I had not sent him back, he would perhaps have gone on and seen the water of the Tigris, and he would have been struck with shame at what he had done. We felt embarrassed that anyone should expect our generosity and then turn back with the dust of mortification on the page of his fortune."

> The liberal man feels ashamed that the beggar should
> return abashed from his court.

Purity ('iffat). This is abstaining from committing any of the things which are forbidden by the Law: especially from unlawful lust; and it is one of the most virtuous points in morals. The wise have said

19. Cf. Th. W. Juynboll, art. "Ḥadíth" in the *Encyclopædia of Islam*: "In some cases it is even believed that the actual 'word of Allah' is to be found in the Ḥadíth as well as in the Qur'án. Such traditions, usually beginning with the words 'Allah said', are designated *ḥadíth qudsí* (or also *iláhí*, i.e. 'holy' or 'divine' *ḥadíth*) by Muslim scholars in opposition to the ordinary *ḥadíth nabawí* (ḥadíth of the Prophet)."

that man has a two-fold affinity: one with the angels, by which he is endowed with wisdom and good conduct; the other with brutes, by which relationship he is greedy of eating and drinking and sensuality.

> Thou hast a portion with the angels, and likewise with the brutes: pass on from the pleasure of animals, that thou mayest excel the angels.

Decorum (adab). This is restraining the mind from improper words and reprehensible actions; keeping ourselves and all men in the due degree of honour; and not throwing away our own character and that of others. The true nature of decorum (*adab*) is, that in all circumstances a man should imitate the Prophet Muhammad, for he it is who is perfect in decorum. He it was who prayed, "Teach me, O Lord, and I shall be perfect in my teaching."

When one day the Prince of Egypt wrote to the Byzantine Emperor that he had collected for his son many stores and valuable things, with garments and horses and utensils and furniture, the Byzantine Emperor replied, "Wealth is a faithless friend and an inconstant mistress. I have adorned my son with the ornament of decorum, and I have laid up in store for him the treasures of what is most noble in morals."

A Lofty Spirit ('ulúw-i-himat). When the bird of ambition expands her wings, honour and success are her nest. But it is well to remember that the highest aspirations are not satisfied in this world, and it is advisable to heed the words of Aristotle to Alexander:

> Seek the kingdom of futurity, for it is joyful;
> An atom from that kingdom would be a hundred worlds;
> Strive, that, in the midst of this abode,
> The expanse of that world may come into thy hand.

Resolution ('azm). It is the forerunner of our desires and the finisher of our enterprises.

> Without firm resolution and complete exertion,
> To no man do his wishes become accomplished.

Labour and Perseverance (jidd wa jahd). Labour is exertion in obtaining the objects of pursuit, and perseverance is bearing trouble in the attainment of our wishes and wants.

A bird saw an ant carrying a grain of sand from a hill with great exertion. When asked about what he was doing the ant replied, "I have affection for one of my race, and when I sought a union with her, she proposed the condition that I carry off this hillock of sand." When the bird declared that this task was beyond the strength of an ant, the little ant replied, "I am resolved on pursuing this service with labour and perseverance; if it goes forward, that is my aim; and if not, they will hold me excused."

Firmness and Constancy (thabát wa istiqámat). This is steadfastness in the accomplishment of our objects, and persistence in the repulse of evils and misfortunes. The Byzantine Emperor asked the Persian Emperor in what the stability of empire consisted. He answered, "I never command any useless undertaking; and every affair for which I give orders, I bring to a completion."

But sometimes kings have felt that they should abide by rather thoughtless commands, as when Sultan Mahmud had taken pity on a porter who was carrying a tremendously heavy stone across the public square. He ordered him to drop it on the spot, and it proved to be most inconvenient afterwards to those who would pass. However, when the Sultan was asked to have the porter remove it, he replied: "It hath passed from our tongue thus, 'Lay it down'; if we should say, 'Take it up', men would ascribe this to our inconstancy, so let that stone remain in that very spot."

Justice ('adl). There is a declaration in the Qur'án, "Truly Allah gives a command for justice and liberality." One moment of justice in a king is more preponderating, in the scale of the balance of obedience, than sixty years of formal worship (*ibádat*). This is illustrated by the story of a prince who sought to pay a dervish to be his proxy in making the pilgrimage to Mecca. The dervish said that he was willing to sell him the merit of all his sixty pilgrimages, but only on the condition that the prince would administer justice on the suit of one that is oppressed, and then bestow upon him the merit that he had gained for this one act of justice.

Pardon ('afw). This is refraining from the punishment of the wrongdoer when one has power over him. The example of Muhammad in forgiving the Quraish at the time of his victory over Mecca is recalled, and also how Alexander asked Aristotle what he should do in regard to a certain wrongdoer. The reply was, "O King, if it were not for sin, then forgiveness, which is the highest virtue, would have no occasion to be known. Sin, therefore, is but the mirror for forgiveness."

Clemency (ḥilm). One of the divine qualities is clemency, for as Allah the Most High hath said, "Surely Allah is gracious and clement" (ii. 225).

Anushirwán asked Abu Dharr al-Ghifárí,[20] "What is *ḥilm* (clemency)?" He said, "It is the very salt of moral qualities, for if you reverse its letters you get *malaḥ* (salt) and as no food without salt has taste, so no creature without *ḥilm* appears to advantage." Anushirwán then asked, "What are the distinguishing signs of a man who has *ḥilm*?" He replied, "They are three: first, if a scowling fellow speaks to him with bitterness, he in turn gives him an answer with sweetness, meeting provocation with a favour; second, when

20. Abu Dharr was one of Muhammad's Companions who came to be considered by the Súfís and the Shi'ites as "a model of a pious Mussulman". Cf. Houtsma, art. "Abu Dharr al-Ghifárí" in the *Encyclopædia of Islam*.

the malediction and awfulness of anger is at its height, then he remains silent; and third, he subdues his anger, even though the person provoking it is worthy of punishment."

Humanity and Benevolence (khulq wa rifq). The philosophers have said that there are ten signs of good disposition:

1. Not hindering men in good work.
2. Exercising justice spontaneously.
3. Not looking for anyone's fault.
4. Returning good for injury.
5. Accepting the wrongdoer's excuse.
6. Meeting the wants of the needy.
7. Sharing in people's suffering.
8. Seeing one's own fault.
9. Keeping a cheerful expression.
10. Speaking pleasantly.

Ardashír Bábak, who adorned the throne of empire with the ornament of wisdom, saw that his son had put on a very costly robe. He told him that the son of an emperor should wear a robe that could not be found in any of the treasure-houses, and that others could not wear. The young man asked where such a robe could be found and of what it was made. The father then explained that its warp was a good disposition and its woof was agreeableness and patience (*burd bárí*)—which meant that it was made of all kinds of good qualities.

Sympathy and Kindness (shafáqat wa marḥamat). The philosophers have declared that one of the marks of a sultan's sympathy is that he should love his subjects as a father loves his son, and not desire any thing for them that he would not desire for himself, so that they would be ready to devote their wealth and their lives and whatever they may have to him and eagerly wish for his long life and extended rule. For the more he shows mercy and sympathy towards his people, the more mercy the Almighty will have towards him.

Charities and Good Works (khairát wa mabarrát). It is revealed in a tradition that when a man goes to his last abode all of his works will be cut off from him except three, alms that are to continue, work that yields a profit, and a good son to pray for his welfare. Under the head of alms that are to continue are included the establishment of a *masjíd*, or a school, or a dormitory, or a bridge, or an inn, or a public cistern, or things of that kind. Another tradition makes a promise, that whoever builds a *masjid* or repairs an old *masjid* will find that Allah has prepared a house for him in Paradise. But after the *masjid* has been built it should be provided with an *imám* and a *muedhdhin*, with their stipends, that its services may be assured. We are told also that one of the Companions of the Prophet said to him, "I want to do some good work for the sake of the spirit of my mother." The Prophet then told him that the best charity was a gift of water, so that Companion bought a well which he then had assigned to public use, and the merit for this charity he gave to the spirit of his mother.

MIR'ÁJ AL-SA'ÁDAT

In the early years of the nineteenth century, when the established moral instruction of Islam in Persia had as yet been but little influenced by modern Western educational methods, Mulla Aḥmad Nuráqí (d. A.D. 1828) wrote a book that he called the *Mir'áj al-Sa'ádat* ("The Ladder of Happiness").[21] It represents the systematic ethical teaching that had come to be general about one thousand years after the first Muslim contacts with Greek philosophy. It is a comprehensive book of well over three hundred pages, and the author's general ethical principles may be gained from a useful condensation of this work that has been published as a text-book for Muslim theological students by the present-day writer, Shaikh 'Abbás al-Qummí. It is called the *Muqámát* ("The Stations") and is divided into only five chapters:[22]

Introduction. The true characteristic of man, which distinguishes him from all the animals, is his soul (*al-nafs*), which is subject to pleasure (*lidhdha*) and to sorrow (*'alam*), to health (*siḥḥa*) and to sickness (*bímárí*).

Chapter I. The reason for a man's departure from the way of rectitude, and for his acquiring dispositions that are reprehensible, appears to lie in the inherent powers of his rational soul (*nafs-i-nátiqa*), powers that serve him as though they were the commanders of an army that looked to him as the King. These commanders are Reason, Imagination, Desire, and Anger. If each one of them is faithful in his duty four fundamental virtues will result—wisdom, justice, courage, and temperance. It will be readily observed that the four virtues have one thing in common, i.e. that each one represents a determined mean between deficiency and excess. Thus there would appear to be at least two kinds of evil qualities (*akhláq-i-radhíla*) for every virtue.

Chapter II. A description of good dispositions and of bad dispositions includes a statement of their respective advantages and evils, and it will show also how those qualities that are good may be acquired and how to deal with those that are reprehensible.

In the first place, justice or righteousness (*'idála*), when it is employed in the universal sense, may be defined as taking the middle course in all things.

The cure for reprehensible dispositions is dependent upon the power of reason, and it may be seen that there are two kinds of vice,

21. *Mir'áj al-Sa'ádat*, by Mulla Aḥmad Nuráqí (d. A.D. 1828), Persian, lith. Teheran, A.H. 1300.

22. *Kitáb-i-Muqámát-i-'Aliyya*, by Shaikh 'Abbas al-Qummí, lith. Najaf, A.H. 1357.

slyness (*jarbaza*) and elementary ignorance (*jahl-i-basit*). From these several reprehensible qualities proceed, each of which may be said to have its possible cure in its opposite. Confirmed error (*jahl-i-murakkab*), doubt (*shak*), and amazement (*ḥaira*) must give way to the virtue of assurance (*yaqín*). *Shirk*, which is the vice of attributing partnership with some other being to Allah must find its cure in the habit of persistently ascribing unity (*tawhíd*) to Allah. Selfish thoughts (*khawátir-i-nafsániya*) and the temptations of the Devil (*wasáwis-i-Shaitániya*) are ever present, and since the mind cannot be kept empty it must be deliberately filled with other things, the remembrance of Allah and praiseworthy ideas. The cure of fraud and cunning (*makr wa ḥíla*), however, comes only from fully realizing that he who digs a well for his brother will fall into it himself.

Chapter III. This chapter is devoted to the presentation of eighteen qualities that are fundamentally dependent upon the power of anger (*quwwat-al-ghaḍabíya*):

1. Fear (*al-khawf*), with an explanation of the kinds of fear that are reprehensible, including the fear of death.
2. Confidence (*'ímaní*), which is the opposite of fear, in relation to the punishments of Allah, or to apprehension of an evil end (*sú'-i-khatima*).
3. Despairing (*ya's*) of the mercy of Allah, with an explanation of hope (*rajá'*) and trust in the Most High Truth (*ḥaq-ta'ála*).
4. Weakness of the self (*ḍaf-i-nafs*), with its opposite, the enlargement of the self, which is assurance.
5. Baseness (*daná'a*) of ambition.
6. A sharpening of zeal (*dharbí-yi-ghairatí*).
7. Haste (*'ajala*), with its opposite, sedateness (*waqár*).
8. Malice (*sú'-i-ẓann*).
9. Anger (*ghaḍab*), which may be cured by the two virtues, tranquillity (*al-ḥilm*) and restraint of rage (*ḥazm-i-ghaiz*).
10. Vengeance (*intiqám*), with the virtue of forgiving (*'afw*).
11. Rudeness (*ghilza*) and roughness (*darushtí*), and their opposite, which is courtesy (*rifq*).
12. Bad temper (*kaj khulqí*), "which does more to separate a man from his Creator and from his fellow creatures than anything else", with its opposite, a friendly disposition (*khush khulqí*).
13. Enmity (*'idáwa*), which leads to beating (*ḍarb*), obscenity (*fuḥsh*), and cursing (*l'an*) and reviling (*ṭa'n*).
14. Haughtiness (*'ujb*) is to be reproved by self-purification (*tazkíya-i-nafs*) and unselfishness (*shakasta nafsí*).
15. Pride (*kibr*) likewise is to be reproved by humility (*tawaḍ'u*).
16. Prejudice (*'aṣabíya*) may be either from ignorance or from patriotic zeal for one's faith or country, in which case it becomes a virtue.
17. Concealing truth (*kitmán-i-ḥaq*) is a vice when it amounts to cowardice or false witness.
18. Hardness of heart (*qasáwat-i-qalb*) manifests itself in oppression or in failure to assist those in need.

Chapter IV. The fourth chapter shows how the vices that are connected with physical appetites may be overcome by the cultivation of particular virtues. Greed (*sharah*) should be met by temperance (*'iffa*), the love of the world (*muḥabbat-i-dunyá*) by devotion (*zuhd*) to religious exercises, wealth (*ghaní*) by poverty (*faqr*), avarice (*ḥirṣ*) by economy (*qiná'a*), covetousness (*ṭama'*) by contentment (*istighná'*), and stinginess (*bukhl*) by liberality (*sakháwa*). This latter virtue may be manifested in giving the stipulated alms, in making special presents, in providing feasts, in readily paying labourers, in lending to friends, in granting extra time to borrowers in adversity, and in giving assistance to Muslims in general.

Chapter V. The fifth and the last chapter has to do with the practical use of the virtues that depend on one or more of the three powers of the soul—reason, anger, and desire. In one brief homily after another the author rebukes envy (*ḥasad*), praises helpful appreciation, and condemns oppression and indifference to Muslims in need. On the authority of the Qur'án and the Traditions, and at times with references to philosophers and poets, he shows the evil character of those who neglect "the command to do what is right" (*amr bi'l-ma'rúf*) and "the prohibition of what is wrong" (*nahy bi'l-munkar*), of those who separate themselves from a brother believer, or who abandon mercy, or who fail to cherish the bonds of kinship, and of those who are disobedient to their parents or disrespectful to their elders. Critical moods of fault-finding, the thoughtless divulging of secrets, detracting remarks, corrupting stories, rejoicing at others' misfortunes, the spirit of contention, the habit of derision and excess of humour—all of these must be eliminated. The inclination to slander, the habit of lying, the love of position or of congratulation, the tendency to affectation and hyprocrisy—these too must be overcome. Flattery, obstinacy, forgetfulness, dislike of people, refusing to accept religious obligations—these also must be definitely given up. Moreover, grief and lack of trust in Allah are classed along with ingratitude, restlessness, and disobedience—to all of which the virtuous man must hold himself superior by the controlling authority of reason.

Text-books on ethics that have appeared in recent years in Irán call special attention to the value of the moral teachings of the Zoroastrians, for the dynasty that has been in power since A.D. 1925 has harped back to pre-Islamic times and has called itself Pahlevi (Parthian). Very early in Muslim history Ibn Muqaffa (d. A.D. 760), who is said to have been a convert from the religion of the Magi, wrote a book for the moral instruction of children, *al-Adab al-Wajíz li'l-Waladi'ṣ-Saghír*. This book is said to have been translated into Persian by Nasír al-Dín al-Ṭúsí, the author of the *Akhláq-i-Násirí*.

While there is some doubt as to whether it is a genuine work of Ibn Muqaffa, it is being used to fill a needed place in the programme for the moral instruction of school children in Irán.[23] Some of the exhortations to children in this little book are:

> Let it be the habit of your tongue to speak the truth.
>
> Cultivate the habit of silence and avoid useless speech.
>
> Be not wanting in the beauty of a good disposition, the finesse of cheerful conversation, the adornment of friendship, and elegance in association with people.
>
> Beware of vexation and sadness, and of a lack of patience amidst your activities, and of other blameworthy dispositions.

Ibn Muqaffa is the translator of one of the best known classics in Arabic and Persian literature, the *Kalíla wa Dimna*,[24] which brought Muslims in touch with the fables and wisdom stories of ancient India. Even to-day one is likely to be assured in Irán that no one could hope to succeed as a barrister without the ability to quote freely from this great work. It is, however, the much modified and elaborated Persian translation of Ḥuṣain Wá'iẓ Káshifí (d. A.D. 1504), the *Anwár-i-Suhailí*, with which Iránians are most familiar.

When in Irán the reforms of the Pahlevi dynasty were at their height in 1937, there appeared in Teheran a book that was entitled the *Akhláq-i-Rúhí*). The author was a member of the Iránian *Majlis* and his book has the endorsement of the Department of Public Instruction. With its comprehensive table of contents it has proved to be an excellent manual for the use of Muslim teachers in their moral instruction in the schools. The special effort that the author has put forth to foster patriotism and a spirit of self-respect, to emphasize the advantages of truthfulness, and to promote loyalty are characteristic of the hopeful period in which the book was written. Like the *Akhláq-i-Muhtashimi*, by Hasan Isfandiyárí, a work that was published but two years earlier, it has made frequent use of quotations from the Qur'án and the Traditions, and has cited many appropriate passages from the Iránian poets. The method that has been pursued in both of these modern text-books on ethics is that of making literature of moral science, which has been characteristic of the Islamic *Adab* writings.

23. This work has been published, Teheran, A.H. 1312, Shamsí, with an illuminating introduction on Ibn Muqaffa and his writings by Dr. 'Abbás Iqbál.

24. *Kalíla wa Dimna*, trans. from Pahlevi into Arabic by Ibn Muqaffa, ed. Beirut, A.D. 1912. See articles in the *Encyclopædia of Islam*, "Ibn Muqaffa" and "Kalíla wa Dimna".

8

ETHICS OF EARLY MUSLIM ASCETICS

MUHAMMAD WAS himself more a mystic than a theologian, more a poet than a philosopher. The Qur'án is rich in instances of his intoxicating God-consciousness and his reverent amazement at the marvellous works of Allah: and the conviction that he was himself in close relation with Allah was the driving force of his life, the source of his fortitude, and the secret of his leadership.

It is altogether natural that this reality of Muhammad's personal religious experience should have been discerned and appreciated by his immediate companions (*ṣahábá*), and that from among them we should find men who sought to attain a similar knowledge of the divine presence, and who are specially mentioned in the Traditions for their piety and their ascetic tendencies.

According to the Muslim historian Ibn Khaldun, "the way of life adopted by the Ṣúfís was in force from the beginnings of Islam and the most eminent of the Companions and their disciples considered it to be the way of Truth and Guidance. It was based upon devotion and separation to God and the renunciation of the pomps and vanities of this world, and the reckoning as nothing pleasures and riches and fame, and (it included) retreat for purposes of devotion. Nothing was more common among the Companions and others of the faithful in the earliest times, and when the love of the world was widespread in the second century (of the Islamic era), and later, and most men allowed themselves to be dragged into the whirlpool of the world, those constituted to piety were called Ṣúfís."[1]

The Companions who most nearly approached the ascetic life were the "People of the Veranda" (*ahl-i-ṣuffá*). "Know that all Muslims are agreed", writes al-Hujwírí (d. A.D. 1072), "that the Apostle had a number of Companions, who abode in his Mosque and engaged in devotion, renouncing the world and refusing to seek a livelihood. God reproached the Apostle on their account and said: '*Do not drive away those who call unto their Lord at morn and eve, desiring His face*' (Qur'án vi. 52). Their merits are proclaimed by the Book of God, and in many traditions of the Apostle which have come down to us.

1. Ibn Khaldun, *Prolegomena*, Arabic text, ed. Quatremere, iii, pp. 59–60; trans. by Dr. Margaret Smith, *Early Mysticism in the Near and Middle East*, p. 158.

It is related by Ibn 'Abbás that the Apostle passed by the People of the Veranda, and saw their poverty and their self-mortification and said: 'Rejoice! for whoever of my community preseveres in the state in which ye are, and is satisfied with his condition, he shall be one of my comrades in Paradise.' . . . Now and then they had recourse to some means of livelihood (*ta'alluq ba-sababí kardandí*), but all of them were in one and the same degree (of dignity). Verily, the generation of the Companions was the best of all generations; and they were the best and most excellent of mankind, since God bestowed on them companionship with the Apostle and preserved their hearts from blemish."[2]

Among the men whom al-Hujwírí mentions by name as belonging to the *ahl-i-ṣuffá* were Salmán-i-Fársí and Abú Dardá. In the differences of opinion that occurred between these two men the Prophet is reported to have usually spoken in support of Salmán, whose general sense of expediency appears to have been more fully developed. For example, when Salmán had interfered with Abú Dardá in his desire to pray and to fast, the latter said to him, "Why do you hinder me in my praying and fasting?" Salmán answered "From your point of view alone you are in the right, but surely your family have their rights from you. You should fast, then eat, then pray, and then sleep." At that moment the Prophet came and said, "Truly Salmán is full of learning."

On another occasion Salmán came to visit Abú Dardá on Friday. He was told that he was sleeping, and so he asked, "What is the matter with him?" The family informed him that it was customary for Abú Dardá to pray on Thursday night and to fast the following day. Salmán, however, commanded them to prepare food, and when it was brought he said to Abú Dardá, "Eat!" He replied, "But I am fasting." Nevertheless Salmán did not let him off until he ate. It was then that the Prophet came, and they told him about the matter, and he said to Abú Dardá, "Salmán has been brought up to know more than you." He struck him on the knee and repeated this three times, and then he said, "Do not think that Thursday night is a special night for praying, or that Friday is itself a particular day for fasting over and above all other days."

At a time when Abú Dardá complained to the Prophet that Salmán had interfered with his piety, the Prophet gave this good advice: "You should not make a resolution and then let it be cut off, nor set yourself to a thing and then let it be interrupted. Make up your mind to arrive at the end of the journey in spite of fevers on the way and nodding at night."[3]

Abu Dharr al-Ghifárí (d. A.D. 653) frequently spoke of the Apostle,

2. *Kashf al-Maḥjúb*, trans. Nicholson, pp. 81–2.
3. Ibn Sa'd, *Ṭabaqát*, IV, i, pp. 53 ff. Cf. art., "Salmán the Persian", by the present writer in *The Moslem World*, vol. xix, pp. 338–52.

as "my friend". When he was asked why it was that he had told his female slave to sell a household article that might be of use to him, or that might meet the need of a guest, he answered, "My friend (*khalili*) promised me that whatsoever of gold or silver I would commit to him he would keep for its owner until the time when he would be released 'in the way of Allah'." Again he said, "My friend has left me seven rules: (1) to love the poor and the ignoble; (2) to have regard for the man who is beneath me and not for the one who is above me; (3) that I should not ask anyone for anything; (4) that I should consider the rights of blood-kindred even though I have been provoked to anger; (5) that I should speak the truth even though it should be unpleasant (bitter); (6) that in Allah's protection I should not fear the reproach of the base; and (7) that I should progress in the knowledge that there is no strength and no power except in Allah. 'These,' he told me, 'are among the jewels at the foot of the Throne.'"

When he was unwell his friend had advised him, "Do not undertake an affair on Monday, and do not take upon yourself the care of the property of orphans." And once when he had asked the Apostle for a house he was admonished, "Consider that you are now weak in body and this house is something that you would hold in trust. On the Day of Resurrection it would be a cause of shame and regret, unless you had acquired it rightfully and had paid for it what was due."[4] It is interesting to note, however, that he survived his "friend" about twenty years, when in 'Uthmán's caliphate he died in al-Rabadha in the neighbourhood of Medina, after a period of exile in Syria. His offence had been that he "preached the equality of all believers and denounced the growing luxury".[5]

It would be incorrect to leave the impression that the poverty of many of the Prophet's Companions was long continued. As Professor Margoliouth has indicated, "the Companions of the Prophet, then, for the most part amassed wealth, and the transformation of Meccah and Medinah from obscure settlements into the religious and political capitals of a mighty empire was sufficient of itself to enrich those who possessed land or houses in either, owing to what is now called unearned increment. A Meccan house which had been purchased in pagan days for a skin of wine was afterwards sold for 60,000 dirhems—and this was far below its value. The value of the estates possessed by the Prophet's cousin Zubair was found to be 50,200,000 dirhems, and fabulous figures are quoted for other Companions of the Prophet."[6]

4. Ibn Sa'd, op. cit., IV, i, pp. 168–70.

5. E. G. Browne, *Literary History of Persia*, i, p. 217; with reference to Mas'udi's *Murúj al-Dhahab*, iv, pp. 268–74. Cf. also *Encyclopædia of Islam*, art. "Abu Dharr al-Ghifárí".

6. Margoliouth, *Early Development of Muhammadanism*, p. 136, with references to Bukharí, ed. Krehl, ii, 281; Jaḥiẓ, *Bayán*, ii. 108; and to the *Jamharát al-Amthál*, 58.

Hudhaifa ibn Yimán Abu 'Abdulla al-'Aisa (d. A.D. 656) is said to have been one of the Companions who enjoyed the Apostle's very special confidence. In the early battles he had served as a scout, and it was he who had brought the news of the enemy's dispersal after the Battle of 'Uhud. Afterwards, under the Prophet's instruction, he learned to watch carefully for any of those who seemed to waver from the faith, so as to distinguish those who were hypocrites. According to the Ḥadíth he expressed the opinion that "the most learned of the Companions of Muhammad were (at first) among the *Munáfiqún* (Hypocrites)"—as distinguished from the *Muhájirún* (Emigrants) and the *Ansár* (Helpers). But in the time of 'Uthmán, when Islam had been established firmly by State authority as the religion for all Arabs, we find that he said, "there was no hypocrisy except in the time of the Prophet, for at this time there is nothing but *infidelity* or *belief*".[7]

Hudhaifa is more particularly remembered in Muslim tradition as one of the men who advised the Caliph 'Uthmán to arrange for the recognition of but one authorized version of the Qur'án. "Stop the people," he urged, "before they differ in regard to their Scriptures as did the Jews and Christians." It is known that 'Uthmán accepted his advice and undertook an official recension of the Qur'án, and it is generally said that the text that was followed for the most part had been secured from the treasures of Hafza, who was one of the Prophet's surviving widows.[8]

Hudhaifa was seriously ill at Kufa in A.H. 36, the year in which 'Uthmán was murdered and the people gave their allegiance to 'Ali. He said, "O God, I bear witness that I give my allegiance to 'Ali. Praise be to Allah who has brought me to this day!" According to some authorities he died seven days later, but others say that his death occurred after forty days.[9]

It was those of the Companions who continued to live simply, and who sought to know more about God, who were a positive influence in the development of Ṣúfísm. Those early devotees of a life of devotion and meditation frequently wore rough woollen garments, and it is generally considered that the word Ṣúfí is derived from *ṣúf*, the word for wool. With perhaps an exaggerated consciousness of sin and an overwhelming dread of divine retribution they soon discovered that the teaching of the Qur'án about God has two apparently conflicting aspects. On the one hand they found that God is represented as working his arbitrary will in unapproachable supremacy, while on the other hand there were verses that showed His all-pervading presence and intimate relations to His creatures.

7. Ibn Sa'd, *Ṭabaqát*, II, ii, p. 106; and *Mishkátu'l-Masábih*, trans. Matthews, i, p. 21. Cf. also Muir, *Life of Mahomet*, iii, p. 328.
8. Muir, op. cit., i, xiii; and Grimme, *Mohamed*, iii, p. 328.
9. Mas'udí, *Murúj al-Dhahab*, iv, pp. 363–4.

For example, there was the verse, "Wherever ye turn there is the face of Allah" (ii. 109). And another well-known verse about God's relation to man declares, "We are nearer to him than his neck-vein" (l. 15).[10]

Towards the end of the first century of Islam there were pious Muslims whose hearts craved a closer and more intimate consciousness of God's presence. Such a man was Ḥasan al-Baṣrí (d. A.D. 728), whose appreciation of personal moral responsibility led him openly to oppose the extreme predestinarianism that prevailed in orthodox Islam at that period (cf. above, Ch. 4), and also to seek to discriminate the true values in a religious life from merely perfunctory and legalistic conformity. "A grain of genuine piety", he said, "is better than a thousand-fold weight of fasting and prayer." In urging his hearers to give more attention to meditation and the remembrance of God, his message was, "Cleanse ye these hearts, for they are quick to rust; and restrain ye these souls, for they desire eagerly; and if ye restrain them not they will drag you to an evil end."

Among other outstanding Ṣúfís who earnestly sought a life of quietism and self-abandonment in the eighth century were Ibrahím ibn Adham (d. A.D. 783), who is said to have forfeited royal dignity to meditate upon divine glory; and Fudayl ibn 'Iyáḍ (d. A.D. 801), who was a leader of a band of robbers when he first came under a strong sense of sin; and Rábi'a al-'Adwiyya (d. A.D. 802), the woman Ṣúfí, who is fondly remembered for her unquestioning resignation (*tawakkul*) to the One who is sure to "provide for those who love Him".

In the opinion of Professor Nicholson, these early ascetics "loved God, but they feared Him more, and the end of their love was apathetic submission to His will, not perfect knowledge of His being. They stand midway between asceticism (*zuhd*) and theosophy or gnosis (*ma'rifat*). The word that best describes their attitude is quietism (*riḍá*)."[11]

This early tendency towards asceticism, therefore, is regarded as one stage in the development of that elaborate system of thought and practice that constitutes the religious philosophy of Ṣúfism.[12]

Within the lifetime of Muhammad the Arabs possessed some knowledge of Christians who had chosen to live in monasteries. For there is a declaration in the Qur'án, as it were in the words of Allah, "And we put into the hearts of those who followed him (Jesus) kindness and compassion: but as to the monastic life (*rahbániyat*), they invented it themselves" (lvii. 27). As to whether this was said in

10. *Encyclopædia Britannica*, art. "Sufiism", by R. A. Nicholson.
11. R. A. Nicholson, "Origin and Development of Sufiism", *J.R.A.S.*, 1906, pp. 304–6; and Subhán, *Sufism: Its Saints and Shrines*, Lucknow, 1938, pp. 12–16.
12. *Encyclopædia of Islam*, art. "Tasawwuf", by Louis Massignon.

criticism or in commendation has been a matter of discussion. Under the influence of al-Zamakhshari, the rigidly orthodox Muslims have been disposed to exclude ascetic mystics from the community of the faithful, both on account of this reference to the monastic life in the Qur'án and also on the ground of a familiar tradition: *lá rahbániyata fí 'l-Islám* ("there is no monasticism in Islam"). But we are informed that recent studies of the *Ḥadíth* indicate that this tradition, which dates from the tenth century, was "invented to encourage and strengthen a new, deprecatory, and interdictive interpretation" of the verse quoted from the Qur'án, and that this verse "was unanimously interpreted in a permissive and laudatory sense" by the exegists of the seventh, eighth, and ninth centuries. Those were the centuries when Christian monks and hermits, and especially Christian ascetic writers, made a most favourable impression upon Muslim scholars who came to know them.

Undoubtedly the ascetic teachings of the early Ṣúfís show distinct evidence of such influence. The figure of the "eye of the soul", which by penitence and self-discipline is enabled to see the secret light of God, is traceable to Ephraim the Syrian. The teaching that purification and sanctification are necessary before the soul can be adorned with virtues and come into fellowship with God is in accord with the Book of the Holy Hierotheos. The separate Stages on the Way towards fellowship with God, through purification and illumination, are found in the Mystic Treatises of Isaac of Nineveh.[13]

The important place that was given to the study of medicine by Muslim philosophical writers led directly to the conception of the *healing* of the soul as well as of the body. The vices were diseases of the soul, and reason demanded that a diligent search should be made for expedients by which to eradicate them. The Syrian Christian mystic, Simon of Ṭaibúthah (d. A.D. 680), was a healer of both body and soul,[14] and we find that the principal Muslim writers on ethics, as well as on Ṣúfism, have adopted this medical phraseology, with chapters that appear in their books, "On the Maintenance of Mental Health" and "On the Cure of Mental Diseases".

Nowhere is appreciation of Christian ascetics shown more clearly than in a statement that is to be found in the *Rasá'il Ikhwán al-Ṣafá'* ("Treatises of the Brethren of Sincerity")[15]: "The contempt that these disciples of the Messiah had for their bodies shows that they had discerned and firmly believed in the permanent existence of the soul (*baqá al-nafs*), and in its continued state of happiness after the bodily death. Among the wonderful works of the monks, and they

13. Dr. Margaret Smith, *An Early Mystic of Baghdad*, pp. 84 ff., and *Early Mysticism in the Near and Middle East*, ch. v.
14. Ibid., *An Early Mystic of Baghdad*, ch. vi (end).
15. *Rasá'il al-Ikhwán al-Safá'*, Cairo text, 1928, vol. iv, p. 97.

were the best of his companions and followers, was that one of them confined his body in his cell for many years—denying it food, wine, pleasures, comfortable clothes, and the desires of the world. All such conduct goes to show that they were firmly convinced in regard to the permanent existence of the soul and its continued state of happiness after the bodily death."

This is but one expression of what was a widespread recognition of the moral values of Christian asceticism, and it is asceticism that distinguishes the first period in the development of Muslim mysticism.

An early representative of a school of Arabic poetry that fostered philosophic asceticism in the ninth century was Abu al-'Aṭáhiya (d. A.D. 828). We are told that he was one of those "who neglected the positive precepts of Islam in favour of a moral philosophy that was based on experience and reflexion".[16] He had been a favourite at the court of al-Mahdi, where his poems on love themes had been much appreciated. But when he became enamoured with one of al-Mahdi's slave girls and failed to win her favourable consideration, he adopted the garb of a dervish and gave himself to writing about the vanity of the pleasures of the world and the inevitable approach of death[17]:

> The world is like a viper soft to touch that venom spits.
>
> Strip off the world from thee and naked live,
> for naked thou didst fall into the world.

The promises of rewards for accomplishing good works brought him little personal satisfaction at times, because of the load of sin that he bore upon his neck[18]:

> But those that do good works and labour well
> Hereafter shall receive the promised pay.
> As if no punishment I had to fear,
> A load of sin upon my neck I lay,
> And while the world I love, from Truth, alas,
> Still my besotted senses go astray.
>
> 'Twas my despair of Man that gave me hope
> God's grace would find me soon, I know not how.

His sense of delinquency as a saint may have been due to an ethical consciousness of obligation to his fellow men[19]:

> I keep the bond of love inviolate
> Towards all mankind, for I betray
> Myself, if I am false to any man.

16. Professor R. A. Nicholson, *Literary History of the Arabs*, p. 296.
17. 'Aṭáhiya, *Diwán*, Beyrouth, 1896, pp. 51 and 74, trans. Nicholson, op. cit., pp. 300 and 302.
18. Nicholson, op. cit., pp. 300–1.
19. Nicholson, op. cit., p. 302.

Certainly one of the most ethical of the Ṣúfí ascetics of this period was the assiduous writer Abú 'Abdullah Ḥárith al-Muḥásibí (d. A.D. 857), whose broad education included a discriminating familiarity with the philosophical writings that were available in Baghdad, whether Greek, Muslim, Jewish, or Christian. The outward and inward law of conduct (*al-záhir wa'l-báṭin*) gave him much concern, for he frequently manifested his appreciation of the essential need for moral, rather than external, purification.

Dr. Margaret Smith has made a comprehensive study of the life and teachings of al-Muhásibí,[20] and has shown clearly how his sincere reflexion on the demands of the inner life led him to go beyond the mere letter of the Law to ethical discernment and a high degree of spiritual aspiration.

As to his general religious attitude, we observe that he wrote of his conclusions after studying the various Muslim sects, and note the following statements[21]:

> Then I found that the way of salvation consists in cleaving to the fear of God, and the fulfilment of what He has ordained (*fará'id*), and scrupulous observance (*wará'*) of what He has made lawful and unlawful, and all His canonical sanctions (*ikhláṣ*), and in taking His Apostle as a model.

Here he appears to have aligned himself with the orthodox Sunni faith and practice, and he shows no trace of that antinomian aloofness to the requirements of the Law that has characterized Ṣúfís of later periods.

He too had his code of ten commandments, which are outstanding in their striking emphasis on personal integrity. They suggest that he was well acquainted with Jewish and Christian commandments, and that in these explicit statements he expressed those ethical demands which he had confirmed by experience and reflexion[22]:

> 1. Do not call to witness the name of God in an oath, whether it be true or false, broken or fulfilled.
> 2. Keep yourself from all falsehood.
> 3. Undertake no obligation which you are unable to fulfil.
> 4. Curse no man, even though he do you wrong.
> 5. Wish no evil to any creature, and seek no retribution when injured, for retribution is in the hands of God.
> 6. Never give evidence in regard to any man's acts, whether it be infidelity or polytheism or hypocrisy, for in refraining from this you display compassion towards man, and thus you keep far from presumption in regard to God and keep near to His mercy.
> 7. Do not premeditate any sinful act, whether secret or open,

20. Dr. Margaret Smith, *An Early Mystic of Baghdad*, London, 1935.
21. al-Muḥásibí, *Kitáb al-Waṣáya*, ref. trans. by Dr. Margaret Smith, op. cit., p. 19.
22. Id., op. cit., pp. 24–5.

and preserve your members from all such acts, and you will have your reward in this world and in the next.

8. Do not inflict upon anyone else that which would mean pain to yourself and would be a burden to you, whether it be for something you need or something which you can do without, for if you act thus you will fulfil what is due to others.

9. Withdraw your confidence from creatures, desire not of what they possess, and depend upon God alone, for He can give you all things.

10. Do not consider yourself to be better than your fellow men, but rather as of less value than all others, for it is such who are accounted great in the sight of God.

The asceticism that al-Muḥásibí practised called for the self-mortification of both his body and his spirit, a real renunciation of the world, that he might attain to a direct knowledge of God. Of that state of mystic communion he tells us that "the joy of fellowship with his Lord so takes possession of his heart and mind that he can no longer be concerned with this world and what is therein, or with aught save God alone".[23]

In further explanation of moral qualities he insists that *charity*, which involves service to one's fellow men, must go along with godliness. Taking pleasure in showing disparagement or contempt towards others he heartily condemns, for "the springs of compassion and kindness disappear from the heart and the rivers of hostility and harshness rise up". And in showing *generosity* the gift ought to be concealed. Spiritually, also, a man must be ready to give the best that he has, "when he considers the spiritual sickness of his fellows, whose cure has become difficult, and when he knows what will give them new life and raise them from their prostration and heal the sickness of their hearts". For *justice* is shown when "there are not two rules of life, one for yourself and one for others, but one rule for yourself and others, and impartiality towards others on your part".[24] And as for justice towards God, his rule was that the first thing which is due to God, and which justice requires should be rendered to Him, is *worship*, and then right action in accordance with the observance of His Law. Furthermore, the old Arabic virtue of *patience*, or steadfastness (*ṣabr*), is emphasized as "the essence of reason" and as a sign of strength. For in his view it leads to *gratitude* (*shukr*), which is a highly exalted virtue, because "it represents the vision of the Giver, not the gift". Right discrimination must be used in the appreciation of gifts, for the servant who is well-pleasing to his Lord will be particularly grateful for the gift of faith, the gift of knowledge, and the gift of reason. "I know of no gift", he observes, "after knowledge, of

23. al-Muḥásibí, *Kitáb al-Waṣáya*, ref. trans. by Dr. Margaret Smith, op. cit., p. 26.

24. Id., *Ádáb al-Nufús*, fol. 65b; ref. trans. op. cit., p. 193.

greater worth than the gift of reason and the gift of will, gifts for which he cannot be sufficiently grateful, and the last of God's favours is the gift of a good end."[25]

Mention may be made briefly of other Ṣúfí thinkers of this period, when personal asceticism was diligently practised and strongly recommended, men who gained a high degree of moral discernment through experience and reflexion. There was Abú 'l-Hasan Sárí al-Saqatí (d. A.D. 870), who handed down opinions such as these: "I have seen nothing so liable to make good works of none effect, or so likely to corrupt men's hearts and bring them to speedy destruction, or more productive of lasting sorrow, or more liable to incur the wrath of God and induce the love of hypocrisy and arrogance and self-will, than a man's failure to know himself, while he observes the faults of others." [26] "Ṣúfism", he said, "meant three things for the Ṣúfí: that the light of his gnosis did not extinguish the light of his abstinence (*wara*'), that his inward speculations did not make him opposed to the outward conduct taught by the Qur'án and the Sunna, and that the favours of God bestowed upon him did not lead him to tear aside the veil from what God had made unlawful to him."[27]

Moreover, Abú Ḥamza al-Buzzáz (d. A.D. 883), who is considered to have been the first regular occupant of a "chair" of Ṣúfism in Baghdad, is known to have given discourses on the perfect form of *recollection* (*ṣafá' al-dihkr*), the concentration of *attention* (*jama' al-himma*), *love to God* (*maḥabba*), *yearning* for Him (*shawq*), *drawing near* to Him (*qurb*), and *fellowship* with Him (*uns*).[28]

But one of the best known of the Muslim ascetics was the Sunni theologian and mystic, Sahl ibn 'Abdullah al-Tustarí (d. A.D. 896), who is remembered for his strict moral discipline and for his insistence that repentance (*tawba*) is obligatory (*farḍ*). For himself and his associates he adhered to six principles:

1. To hold fast to the Book of Allah.
2. To model ourselves upon the Apostle.
3. To eat only what is lawful.
4. To refrain from hurting people even though they hurt us.
5. To avoid forbidden things.
6. To fulfil obligations without delay.

It will be observed that "his doctrine inculcates endeavour and self-mortification and ascetic training, and he used to bring his disciples to perfection in self-mortification", which came to be known as "the path" of the Sahlís. His guiding principle was that "resistance to the lower soul is the chief of all acts of devotion, and

25. Id., op. cit., pp. 196–7.
26. al-Hujwirí, *Kashf al-Mahjúb*, p. 110; trans. Nicholson, London, 1911. Ref. op. cit., p. 39.
27. al-Qushayrí, *Risála*, p. 10, ref. Margaret Smith, op. cit., p. 39.
28. al-Khatíb *Ta'ríkh Baghdad*, i, p. 393, ref. op. cit., p. 30.

the crown of all acts of self-mortification and only thereby can man find the way to God, because submission to the lower soul involves his destruction, and resistance to it involves his salvation".[29]

There is also mention made by al-Hujwirí of the important teaching of Abú 'Abdullah Muhammad ibn 'Ali al-Tirmidhí (d. A.D. 898,) who was contemporary with al-Tustarí. As the first step towards understanding his doctrine, "you must know that God has saints (*awliya*), whom He has chosen out of mankind, and whose thoughts He has withdrawn from worldly ties and delivered from sensual temptation; and He has stationed each of them in a particular degree, and has opened unto them the door of these mysteries. . . . You must know that the principle and foundation of Ṣúfism and knowledge of God rests on saintship (*wiláyat*), the reality of which is unanimously affirmed by all the Shaykhs, though every one has expressed himself in different language." Etymologically al-Tirmidhí came to the conclusion that "*walí* may be the form *fa'il* equivalent to *fá'il*, with intensive force, because a man takes care (*tawallí kunad*) to obey God and constantly to fulfil the obligations that he owes to Him. Thus *walí* in the active meaning is 'one who desires' (*muríd*), while in the passive meaning it denotes 'one who is the object of God's desire' (*murád*). All of these meanings, whether they signify the relation of God to Man or of Man to God, are allowable, for God may be the protector of His friends, in as much as he promised His protection to the Companions of the Apostle, and declared that the unbelievers had no protector (*mawlá*) (Qur'án, xlvii. 12). And moreover, He may distinguish them in an exclusive way by His friendship, as He hath said, 'He loves them and they love Him' (Qur'án, v. 59), so that they turn away from the favour of mankind: He is their friend and they are His friends (*awliyá*)."[30]

It has been pointed out by L. Massignon that al-Tirmidhí borrowed from the Shi'ites the term *wiláya*, which he employed in his explanation of the criteria of "sanctity", and that in this statement "he gives a particular role to Jesus", and "insists on the introspection of the heart and professes a very high morality".[31]

Likewise Ahmad al-Baghawí (d. A.D. 907), who was known as al-Núrí, was "an ascetic of the ascetics, rejecting flattery and self-indulgence, and practising mortification to an extreme degree. He held and carried into practice the doctrine of 'preference' (*íthár*), the choice of another's interest rather than his own, and the principle of vicarious suffering." There are several legends as to why he was called "Núrí", which means "a light". Both 'Attár and Hujwirí

29. *Encyclopædia of Islam*, art. "Sahl b. Abdullah al-Tustarí"; also cf. *Kashf al-Maḥjúb*, pp. 195–6.
30. *Kashf al-Maḥjúb*, pp. 210–11.
31. *Encyclopædia of Islam*, art. "al-Tirmidhí, Abu 'Abd Allah", by L. Massignon.

relate "that he had a cell in the desert to which he repaired each night to engage in devotion, and people watching that spot used to see a light shining forth from that cell and streaming up to the heavens". In the *Nafaḥát al-Uns*, al-Jámí mentions this saying of al-Núrí's, "One day I looked upon a Light, and I did not cease to contemplate it until I became that Light."[32]

"The true nature of preference", al-Hujwírí explains, "consists in maintaining the rights of the person with whom one associates, and in subordinating one's own interest to the interest of one's friend, and in taking trouble upon one's self for the sake of promoting his happiness, because preference is the rendering of help to others, and the putting into practice of that which God commanded to His Apostles: '*Use indulgence and command what is just and turn away from the ignorant*' (Qur'án, vii. 198). . . . Now, preference is of two kinds: firstly, in companionship, as has been mentioned; and secondly, in love. In preferring the claim of one's companion there is a sort of trouble and effort, but in preferring the claim of one's beloved there is nothing but pleasure and delight.

"It is well known that when Ghulám al-Khalíl persecuted the Ṣúfís, Núrí and Raqqám and Abú Ḥamza were arrested and conveyed to the Caliph's palace. Ghulám al-Khalíl urged the Caliph to put them to death, saying that they were heretics (*zanádíq*), and the Caliph immediately gave orders for their execution. When the executioner approached Raqqám, Núrí rose and offered himself in Raqqám's place with the utmost cheerfulness and submission. All the spectators were astounded. The executioner said: 'O young man, the sword is not a thing that people desire to meet so eagerly as you have welcomed it; and your turn has not yet arrived.' Núrí answered, 'Yes; my doctrine is founded on preference. Life is the most precious thing in the world: I wish to sacrifice for my brethren's sake the few moments that remain. In my opinion one moment of this world is better than a thousand years of the next world, because this is the place of service (*khidmat*) and that is the place of proximity (*qurbat*), and proximity is gained by service.'"

Among the stories that al-Hujwírí proceeds to relate in illustration of the practice of "preference" is the anecdote that "ten dervishes lost their way in the desert and were overtaken by thirst. They had only one cup of water, and everyone preferred the claim of the others, so that none of them would drink and they all died except one, who then drank and found strength to escape. Some person said to him, 'Had you not drunk it would have been better.' He replied: 'The Law obliged me to drink; if I had not, I should have killed myself and been punished on that account.' The other said, 'Then did your

32. Dr. Margaret Smith, op. cit., p. 32, with reference to Attár, *Tadhkirat al-Awliya*, ii, p. 46; Hujwirí, *Kashf al-Maḥjúb*, pp. 190–4; and al-Jámí, *Nafaḥát al-Uns*, p. 87.

friends kill themselves?' 'No,' said the dervish, 'they refused to drink in order that their companions might drink, but when I alone survived I was legally obliged to drink.'" [33]

Junaid al-Baghdádí (d. A.D. 910), who was called the "Peacock of the Learned" (*ṭá'ús al-'ulamá*), was said to have made the pilgrimage to Mecca thirty times, travelling by himself and on foot. He employed a rosary for his prayers, as he devoutly repeated the ninety-nine names of Allah. But notwithstanding this apparent striving for merit as an ascetic, he continued to believe that knowledge of Allah could be attained by demonstrative reasoning, and like the Apostle Paul, he is said to have "preferred sobriety to mystic intoxication of the soul". His definition of Ṣúfism is frequently quoted, "that Allah should make thee die to thyself and should make thee live in Him". As a contemplative Muslim theologian, in distinction from those conformists who were able to assent without contemplation, he faced the problem of reconciling the prescribed Law (*sharí'a*) with essential truth (*ḥaqíqa*).[34] Another definition of Ṣúfism (*al-tasawwuf*)[35] was that of al-Junaid's contemporary, al-Núrí, who said that it was "hatred of the world and love of the Lord". Such was the basic religious feeling of this early Muslim asceticism, a pious devotion to the will of Allah, that was still subject to the outward requirements of the Law, but sought earnestly for confirmation in the inner life through experience, with the controlling belief that by worshipful contemplation and grateful reflexion, with an ever more exacting self-discipline, a kind of intuitive knowledge of Allah could be attained.

The "seventh discourse" of the *Fihrist*, which is a classified list of authors and their books prepared by the book-dealer Muhammad ibn Isháq al-Nadím (d. A.D. 995), is conclusive evidence on the question of the availability in the ninth and tenth centuries of Arabic accounts of the different Greek philosophers, with the names of those of their books that were known to the Muslims.[36] Also the "Book of Religions and Sects" (*Kitáb al-Milal wa 'l-Niḥal*), though written considerably later by al-Shahrastání (d. A.D. 1153), throws light on the books that were accessible to Muslim scholars in the period before the great libraries of Baghdad were destroyed by the Mongols. The opinions of a large number of the Greek philosophers are reviewed by al-Shahrastání, with lists of translations from Aristotle and Porphyry in particular (pp. 311–48), and of some of the works of "scholars of India" (pp. 444–55).

The general doctrines of the Ṣúfís gained widespread popularity in the tenth century, but with syncretism from both East and West,

33. *Kashf al-Maḥjúb*, pp. 190–2.
34. *Encyclopædia of Islam*, art. "Junayd al-Baghdadí", and cf. Nicholson, *L.H.A.*, p. 392.
35. *Encyclopædia of Islam*, art. "Tasawwuf".
36. Nicholson, op. cit., p. 363, and Browne, *L.H.P.*, vol. i, pp. 384 ff.

so that there came to be a considerable variety in their teachings. The pantheistic extremist Huṣain ibn Mansur al-Ḥalláj carried the doctrine of unification with Allah to the point where his claims were regarded as blasphemous. The declaration that he frequently repeated, "I am the Truth (God)", was similar in purport to sayings of Yazíd al-Bisṭámí (Báyazíd), who had said, for example: "Beneath this cloak of mine there is nothing but God", and "Verily I am God; there is no God beside me!"[37] But on account of the vehemence with which he kept insisting on his claim al-Ḥalláj encountered increasing opposition and persecution until in the end he was put to death. "On the 26th of March, A.D. 922, on the esplanade of the new prison of Baghdád (on the right bank of the river) opposite the Báb al-Ṭáq, al-Ḥalláj was flogged, mutilated, exposed on a gibbet (*maṣlúb*), and finally decapitated and burned."[38] Ibn Khallikán observes that he was a disciple of al-Junayd and that "people are still at variance respecting his true character; some extolling him to the utmost while others treat him as an infidel". Attention is also called by Ibn Khallikán to the way in which al-Ghazálí, some one hundred and fifty years later, "places all these expressions in a good light, and gives them an interpretation (by which their impiety is removed)".[39]

Several notable efforts were made in the tenth century to set forth the Ṣúfí teachings in comprehensive books. The most valuable of these *compendia* that are still extant are the *Risála* of al-Qushayri (d. A.D. 998), the *Qut al-Qulúb* of al-Makkí (d. A.D. 996), the *Kitáb al-Luma'* of al-Sarráj (d. A.D. 998), and the *Kitáb al-Ta'arruf* of al-Kalábádhí (d. A.D. 995). Of these, the *Ta'arruf* has been translated into English by Arthur J. Arberry, and has been published as a most convenient manual for reference. The author's aim was to relate the main Ṣúfí doctrines to accepted teachings of the Qur'án and the *Ḥadíth*, and the student who is interested primarily in appraising Ṣúfí teachings from the viewpoint of ethics will value it especially as a brief presentation of fundamental Ṣúfí conceptions prior to the influence of the exaggerated pantheism of the Persian Ṣúfí poets. On the one hand, they laid the foundations on which al-Ghazálí, in the following century, could build his masterly vindications of Ṣúfism, and on the other hand, they provided the outline for symbolical representations by Muslim poets and saints for the succeeding thousand years.

A few examples of those teachings in which the Ṣúfís of the tenth century are said to have been in agreement may be mentioned.[40]

Their Doctrine of Vision. "They are agreed that God will be seen

37. *Tadhkiratu'l-Awliya*, ch. xiv, "Báyazíd Bistamí".
38. L. Massignon, art. "al-Ḥalláj", in the *Encyclopædia of Islam.*
39. Ibn Khallikán, *Biographical Dictionary*, trans. de Slane, vol. i, p. 423.
40. Abu Bakr al-Kalabádhí, *Kitáb al-ta'arruf li madhhab ahl al-tasawwuf*, trans. by Arthur J. Arberry, *The Doctrine of the Súfís*, Cambridge, 1935. Selections from chs. xi–xxii.

with the eyes in the next world, and that the believers will see him but not the unbelievers, because this is a grace from God: for God says, 'To those who do what is good goodness and an increase' (Qur'án, ii. 27). They hold that vision is possible through the intellect, and obligatory through the hearing. As for its being intellectually possible, this is because God exists, and everything which exists may (logically speaking) be seen. For God has implanted in us vision: and if the vision of God had not been possible, then the petition of Moses, 'O Lord, show thyself to me, that I may look upon Thee' (Qur'án, vii. 139) would have been (evidence of) ignorance and unbelief." . . . "They are agreed that God is not seen in this world", however, "either with the eyes of the heart, save from the point of view of faith: for this (vision) is the limit of grace and the noblest of blessings, and therefore cannot occur save in the noblest place (i.e. in Paradise)."

Their Doctrine of Predestination and the Creation of Acts. "They agreed that God is the Creator of all the acts of His servants, even as He is the Creator of their essences: that all that they do, be it good or evil, is in accordance with God's decree, predestination, desire, and will; otherwise, they would not have been servants, subject to a Lord, and created. God says, 'Say, God is the Creator of everything'; and again: 'Verily, everything have we created by decree . . . and everything they do is in the books.' Now since acts are things, it necessarily follows that God is the Creator of them: for if acts had not been created, God would have been the Creator of certain things but not of all, and then His words, 'Creator of everything', would be a lie—far exalted is God above that! Moreover, it is certain that acts are more numerous than essences: therefore, if God had been the Creator of the essences, and the servants the creators of the acts, created being would have been worthier the ascription of praise for the act of creation, and the creation of the servants would have been greater than the creation of God: consequently, they would have been more perfect in power and more fruitful in creation than God. But God says: 'Or have they made associates with God who can create as he creates, so that the creation seems familiar to them? Say, God is the Creator of everything, and He is the One, the Dominant.' " . . .

"Since it is possible, then, for God to create an essence which is evil, it is also possible for Him to create an action which is evil. Now it is generally conceded that the action of a man trembling is a creation of God (as an involuntary act): it follows therefore that all other motions are the same, except that in the one case God has created both motion and freewill, and in the other motion without freewill."

Their Doctrine of Capacity. "They are agreed that every breath they draw, every glance they make, and every motion they perform, is by virtue of a faculty which God originates in them, and a capacity which He creates for them at the same time as their actions, neither before them nor after them, and that no action can be performed without these: for otherwise they would have the attribute of God, doing whatever they wished and decreeing whatever they desired, and God would no longer be the Strong, the Powerful—in His words, 'And God does what He wishes' (Qur'án, iii. 35)—any more than any poor, weak, contemptible slave." . . .

"They are agreed that they are accredited with acts and merit in a true sense, for which they are rewarded and punished, and on account of which God issued command and prohibition, and announced promises and threats: the meaning of the term 'merit' being that a man acts through a faculty (divinely) originated." . . .

"They are further agreed that they exercise freewill and desire with respect to their 'merit', and that they are not constrained or forced into it against their will. We mean by 'freewill' that God has created in us freewill, and therefore there is no question of compulsion in these matters or of renunciation."

Their Doctrine of Compulsion. "The believer chooses belief, likes it, approves it, desires it, and prefers it to its opposite; while he dislikes unbelief, hates it, disapproves it, does not desire it, and prefers its opposite to it. God has created for him the choice, approval, and desire for faith, and the hatred, dislike, and disapproval for disbeliefs: for God says, 'God has made faith beloved by you, and has made it seemly in your hearts, and has made misbelief and iniquity and rebellion hateful to you' (Qur'án, xlix. 7). The unbeliever, on the other hand, chooses unbelief, approves it, likes it, desires it, and prefers it to its opposite; while he dislikes belief, hates it, disapproves of it, does not desire it, and prefers its opposite to it. God has created all this: for He says, 'So do we make seemly to every nation their work' (Qur'án, vi. 107); and again, 'But whomsoever he wishes to lead astray, He makes his breast tight and straight' (Qur'án, vi. 125). Neither of them was prevented from (following) the opposite of what he chose, or forced into that which he acquired: therefore they are all bound by God's proof and subject to His pronouncement. The resort of unbelievers is hell for what they have earned (Qur'án, ix. 96), and 'We have not wronged them, but it was themselves they wronged' (Qur'án, xliii. 76). God does what He wills (Qur'án, ii. 254), 'He shall not be questioned concerning what He does, but they shall be questioned' (Qur'án, xxi. 23)."

Their Doctrine of Advantageousness. "They are agreed that God does with His servants whatever He wishes, and decrees for them however He desires, whether that be to their advantage or not: for the Creation is His Creation, and the command is His command (cf. Qur'án, vii. 52 ff.).

"They are agreed that all God's dealings with His servants—kindness, health, security, faith, guidance, favour—are only a condescension on His part: if He had not acted thus, it would still have been quite feasible. This is in no way incumbent upon God: for if God had been obliged to follow any such course of action, He would not have been deserving of praise and gratitude.

"They are agreed that reward and punishment are not a question of merit, but of God's will, generosity, and justice: men do not deserve eternal punishment on account of sins from which they have afterwards desisted, neither do they deserve an eternal and unlimited reward because of a limited number of (good) deeds.

"They are agreed that God does not do things for any cause: for if they had a cause, then that cause would have a cause, and so *ad infinitum*; and that is false."

Their Doctrine of Intercession. "They are agreed upon confirming all that God has mentioned in His Book about intercession, and all that has come down in the stories told of the Prophet. God says, 'And in the end thy Lord will give thee, and thou shalt be well pleased' (Qur'án, xciii. 5); 'It may be that thy Lord will raise thee to a laudable station' (Qur'án, xvii. 81); 'And they shall not intercede except for him with whom He is pleased' (Qur'án, xxi. 28–9); and the infidels say, 'But we have no intercessors' (Qur'án, xxvi. 100). The Prophet said: 'My intercession is over those of my community who have committed major sins.' He also said, 'My prayer conceals intercession for my community.'"

Their Doctrine of Duties imposed by God on Adults. "They are agreed that all the ordinances imposed by God on (His) servants in His Book, and all the duties laid down by the Prophet (in the Traditions), are a necessary obligation and a binding imposition for adults of mature intelligence; and that they may not be abandoned or forsaken in any way by any man, whether he be a veracious believer (*ṣiddíq*), or a saint, or a gnostic, even though he may have attained the furthest rank, the highest degree, the noblest station, or the most exalted stage. They hold that there is no station in which a man may dispense with the prescriptions (*ádáb*) of the religious law, by holding permissible what God has prohibited, or making illegal what God has declared legal, or legal what God has pronounced illegal, or omitting to perform any religious duty without excuse or reason, which excuse and reason are defined by the agreed judgement of all Muslims and approved by the prescriptions of the religious law. The more inwardly pure a man is, the higher his rank and the nobler his station, so much the more arduously he labours, with sincerer performance and a greater fear of God.

"They are agreed that acts are not a cause of happiness or unhappiness, but that happiness and unhappiness are predestined and prescribed by the will of God. . . . They are agreed that the bliss of Paradise belongs to those for whom happiness has been foreordained by God, without any cause, and that the punishment of hell belongs to those to whom unhappiness has been foreordained by God, without any cause. . . . Nevertheless, they are agreed that God rewards and punishes for the acts: for He promised on account of righteous deeds, and threatened in connexion with evil deeds; and He fulfils His promise and realizes His threat, for He is true, and what He says is the truth. They say that it is the duty of every man to strive his utmost to perform what has been prescribed for him to do, and to discharge what he has been called upon to do subsequent to that prescription: and when he has fully discharged his duty, then follow the revelations, in accordance with the Tradition: 'If a man acts in accordance with what he knows, God will bequeath him the knowledge of what he does not know.' "

Their Doctrine of the Gnosis of God. "Al-Junayd said: 'Gnosis is of two sorts: gnosis of Self-revelation (*ta'arruf*), and gnosis of instruction (*ta'ríf*).' The meaning of 'Self-revelation' is, that He causes them to know Him, and to know things through Him, or, in the words of Abraham, 'I love not gods that set' (Qur'án, vi. 76); the meaning of 'instruction' is, that He shows them the effects of His power in the heavens and in the souls, and then implants in them a special grace (*luṭf*), so that the (material) things indicate that there is a Maker. This is the gnosis of the main body of the believers, while the former is the gnosis of the elect: and no man has known God in reality, save through God."

The task of relating the teachings of the Ṣúfís to the Qur'án and the Traditions, and of gaining for them a recognized place in Muslim theology, was continued effectively and with eminent success by al-Ghazálí. One of his most significant achievements was that he gained a place of honour for the Ṣúfí *gnosis*. In the sense that this gnosis is "the life of the heart in God",[41] he writes that "the purpose of the gnostics is only to attain to this knowledge and to possess it, for it is a consolation unknown to the souls from which it is hidden, and when it is attained, it destroys all anxieties and sensual desires and the heart becomes filled with its grace."[42]

He had learned that by speculative philosophy "the ultimate and unconditioned could not be reached",[43] and after a few months protracted illness, with the conviction that he should turn away the eye of the soul from all save God, he gave up his position as an esteemed professor in the Nizámiya College of Baghdad. For a while he travelled, visiting pilgrimage places in Arabia, Syria, Palestine, and Egypt. Afterwards he retired to his early home at Ṭús, in Khorasan, where he devoted the last years of his life to the completion of numerous books on jurisprudence and theology, at the same time exalting the way of the mystic. According to Ibn Khallikán he

41. Margaret Smith, *Studies in Early Mysticism*, p. 210.
42. al-Ghazálí, *Iḥyá'*, IV, 267, trans. by Margaret Smith, op. cit., p. 210.
43. *Encyclopædia of Islam*, art. "al-Ghazáli", by D. B. Macdonald.

erected a convent for Ṣúfís near his own house,[44] and by his personal piety and his prestige as a scholar, as well as by his writings, he led the orthodox Muslim community to appreciate the mystics and to value their ethical and spiritual attainments.

In reviewing the experiences that led him to become a Ṣúfí al-Ghazálí wrote that in his quest for truth he had soon learned to distrust mere sense impressions, as they were frequently misleading and needed to be corrected by reason. Later he had come to be sceptical also about some of the intellectual notions that he had based on the evidence of reason. The thought came finally that perhaps there was another judge above reason that would convict reason of falsehood.

He relates, however, that at last God healed him of this mental malady, not by proofs and arguments, but by a light which God caused to penetrate his heart. From that time on he considered that "to suppose that certitude can be only based upon formal arguments is to limit the boundless mercy of God".

He expresses the opinion also that the professors of moral philosophy "occupy themselves with defining the attributes and qualities of the soul, grouping them according to genus and species, and pointing out the way to moderate them and to control them". "They have borrowed this system", he goes on to say, "from the Ṣúfís", who, while in a state of ecstasy, "have received revelations regarding the qualities of the soul, its defects and its evil inclinations. These revelations they have published, and the philosophers, making use of them, have introduced them into their own systems." Accordingly, he explains how he gave himself to the study of the writings of the Ṣúfís, whose aim he found was "to free the soul from the tyrannical yoke of the passions, to deliver it from its wrong inclinations and evil instincts, in order that in the purified heart there should only remain room for God and for the invocation of His holy name".[45]

44. Ibn Khallikán, *Biographical Dictionary*, trans. de Slane, vol. ii, p. 622.
45. Cf. *The Confessions of al-Ghazáli*, trans. Claud Field, in the Wisdom of the East Series, pp. 11–34.

9

ETHICS OF THE PERSIAN ṢÚFÍ POETS

ABU SA'ÍD IBN ABI'L-KHAYR

THE POEMS that are ascribed to Abu Sa'íd ibn Abi'l-Khayr (d. A.D. 1049) are said to "form a miscellaneous anthology, drawn from a great number of poets who flourished at different periods, and consequently they reflect the typical ideas of Persian mysticism as a whole".[1] Outstanding in his personality and sagacity, it was Abu Sa'íd's lot "to give the presentations and forms of the Ṣúfí doctrine", as H. Ethé observed, "those fantastic and gorgeous hues which thenceforth remained typical of this kind of poetry".[2]

More than a century after his death an unnamed cousin of his great-great-grandson wrote a short treatise on his life, the *Ḥálát ú Sukhanán-i-Shaykh Abu Sa'íd ibn Abi'l-Khayr*, which the great-great-grandson subsequently expanded into the large biography, *Asrárú'l-Tawḥíd fí Maqámáti 'l-Shaykh Abi Sa'íd*. In this work, which is a compilation of autobiographical passages that were handed down by oral tradition, we find that "the portrait of Abu Sa'íd, amidst the circle of Ṣúfís and dervishes in which he lived, is drawn with extraordinary richness of detail, and gains in vividness as well as in value from the fact that the great part of the story is told by himself".[3]

Much of his preaching was in Nishapur, where he came to be the most revered "saint" in the Ṣúfí fraternity, and where the brother of the great Maḥmud of Ghazna was serving as Governor. At one time a complaint that had been brought against him by the Sunnites, Shi'ites, and Mu'tazilites of Nishapur was sent to the religious authorities at Ghazna. It was charged that in his sermons he recited poetry without quoting from the Qur'án or the Traditions, and further, that "he holds sumptuous feasts and music is played by his orders, whilst the young men dance and eat sweetmeats and roasted fowls and all kinds of fruits. He declares that he is an ascetic, but this is neither asceticism nor Ṣúfism. Multitudes have joined him and are being led astray."[4] While the authorities in Nishapur received

1. R. A. Nicholson, *Studies in Islamic Mysticism*, p. 48.
2. Professor E. G. Browne, *Literary History of Persia*, vol. ii, p. 261, citing Ethé's description of Abu Sa'íd in the *Sitzungsb. d. bayr. Akad., philos.-philolog. Klasse*, 1875, pp. 145–68, and 1878, pp. 38–70.
3. R. A. Nicholson, op. cit., p. 2.
4. Id., pp. 29 ff.

instructions from Ghazna to deal with the case locally, they showed themselves susceptible to Abu Sa'íd's courteous attentions and tactfully given presents, so much so indeed that they withdrew their charges and quoted Muhammad's uncompromising declaration in the Qur'án (cix. 6), "To you be your religion: to me my religion", as though it were a counsel for religious toleration.

It is not that his extreme pantheistic ideas were new, for they were much the same as those that had been introduced by Bayazíd (d. A.D. 874), but he gave them much greater popularity. Moreover, he was outspoken in his contempt of every kind of positive religion,[5] for by following his own inner light, as though it were infallible, he arrived at a kind of exalted antinomianism, in which he is represented by his biographers as vindicating himself from time to time by his use of what appeared to be an unusual power of telepathy. The stories that are related by his followers about encounters that he had with his great Ṣúfí contemporary, al-Qushayrí (d. A.D. 998), who was deeply concerned to confine Ṣúfí teachings within the bounds of Muhammadan religious law, always give Abu Sa'íd the advantage.

In the quatrains that have been compiled in his name by his successors there is a broad tolerance of other religions that sprang from the conviction that there was something essentially universal in the mystical approach to knowledge of God.

> By whatsoever path, blessed the feet
> Which seek Thee; blessed he who strives to meet
> Thy Beauty; blessed they who on it gaze,
> And blessed every tongue which Thee doth greet!
> The Gnostic, who hath known the Mystery,
> Is one with God, and from his Self-hood free:
> Affirm God's being, and deny thine own;
> This is the meaning of "*no god but He*".

"The veil between God and His servant", as his biographers say he explained succinctly, "is neither earth, nor heaven, nor the Throne, nor the Footstool: thy self-hood and illusion are the veil, and when thou removest these thou hast attained unto God." But when they told him of a man who could walk on water, about another who could fly in the air, and about a third man who could instantly move from one city to another, he commented: "The frog can swim and the swallow skim the water, the crow and the fly can traverse the air, and the Devil can pass in a moment from east to west. These things are of no great account: he is a man who dwells amongst mankind, buys and sells, marries and associates with his fellow creatures, yet is never for a single moment forgetful of God."[6]

This conception of man's reaching his highest capacity in the

5. *Encyclopædia of Islam*, art. "Abu Sa'íd", by R. A. Nicholson.
6. Professor E. G. Browne, op. cit., Nos. 38 and 54, trans. from Ethé's German verse-translation of ninety-two of Abu Sa'íd's *rubá'ís*.

discipline of normal adjustment to the life he must live among his fellow men is frequently lost by Ṣúfís in their elaboration of the way of Negation. It may well represent one of those sayings of Abu Sa'íd's which are described as "experimental, not doctrinal or philosophical",[7] or as belonging to those principles that "bear directly on the religious life and are the fruit of dearly bought experience".[8]

Another of his declarations has become one of the maxims in Ṣúfism: "So long as anyone regards his purity and devotion, he says, 'Thou and I', but when he considers exclusively the bounty and mercy of God, he says, 'Thou! Thou! and then his worship becomes a reality."[9]

In his effort to distinguish the divine command (*amr*) from the divine will (*iráda*), suggesting that although sin is an act of disobedience to the one while it is nevertheless determined by the other, he employed the following illustration:[10]

"On the Day of Resurrection Iblís (Satan) will be brought to judgement with all the devils, and he will be charged with having led multitudes of people astray. He will confess that he called on them to follow him, but will plead that they need not have done so. Then God will say, 'Let that pass! Now worship Adam, in order that thou mayest be saved.' The devils will implore him to obey and thereby deliver himself and them from torment, but Iblís will answer, weeping, 'Had it depended on my will, I would have worshipped Adam at the time when I was first bidden. God commands me to worship him, but does not will it. Had He willed it, I should have worshipped him then.' "

Abu Sa'íd maintained that God's object in his relations to man is the manifestation of His own mercy. "Had there been no sinners God's mercy would have been wasted." "Adam would not have been visited with the tribulation of sin unless forgiveness were the dearest of all things to God."[11]

"The *inward striving* after selflessness is identical with the state which Abu Sa'íd calls 'want' (*niyáz*). There is no way nearer to God than this. It is described as living and luminous fire placed by God in the breasts of His servants in order that their 'self' (*nafs*) may be burned; and when it has been burned, the fire of 'want' becomes the fire of 'longing' (*shawq*) which never dies, neither in this world nor in the next, and is only increased by vision."[12]

The meaning of *samá'* in Ṣúfism is "the listening to music, singing, chanting, and measured recitation in order to produce religious

7. Professor E. G. Browne, op. cit., pp. 268–9.
8. R. A. Nicholson, *Studies in Islamic Mysticism*, p. 48.
9. Ibid., p. 53, citing in translation *Asrár*, 410, 16.
10. Ibid., p. 54, citing in translation *Asrár*, 332, 14.
11. Ibid., p. 54, citing in translation *Asrár*, 401, 17.
12. Ibid., p. 55, citing in translation *Asrár*, 328, 10, and *Asrár*, 388, 10.

emotion and ecstasy (*wadjd*) and also such performances by voice or instrument".[13] In connexion with the *samá*ʿ the young men would frequently engage in dancing, and this brought about criticism which Abu Saʿíd undertook to answer rationally on the basis of physiological considerations: "Then, as to the young men's dancing in the *samá*ʿ, the souls of young men are not yet purged of lust: indeed it may be the prevailing element; and lust takes possession of all the limbs. Now if a young dervish claps his hands the lust of his hands will be dissipated, and if he tosses his feet the lust of his feet will be lessened. When by this means the lust fails in their limbs they can preserve themselves from great sins, but when all lusts are united (which God forfend), they will sin mortally. It is better that the fire of their lust should be dissipated in the *samá*ʿ than in something else."

A natural objection to some of the Ṣúfí doctrines was that they were not to be found in the Qur'án. This objection Abu Sa'íd met by the declaration that there is an "eighth seventh" of the Qur'án, so to speak: "Ye imagine that the Word of God is of fixed quantity and extent, Nay, the infinite Word of God that was sent down to Muhammad is the whole seven sevenths of the Qur'án; but that which He causes to come into the hearts of His servants does not admit of being numbered and limited, nor does it ever cease. Every moment there comes a message from Him to the hearts of His servants, as the Prophet declared, saying, 'Beware of the clairvoyance (*firása*) of the true believer, for verily he sees by the light of God.' "

He also made use of the Tradition "that the Guarded Tablet (*lawḥ-i-maḥfuẓ*) is so broad that a fleet Arab horse would not be able to cross it in four years, and the writing thereon is finer than a hair. Of all the writing which covers it only a single line has been communicated to God's creatures. That little keeps them in perplexity until the Resurrection. As for the rest, no one knows anything about it" (*Hayát ú Sukhanán*, 49, 22; and *Asrár*, 132, 3).

In this connexion Dr. Nicholson comments: "Here Abu Sa'íd sets aside the partial, finite, and temporal revelation on which Islam is built, and appeals to the universal, infinite, and everlasting revelation which the Ṣúfís find in their hearts. . . . Abu Sa'íd does not say that the partial and the universal revelations are in conflict with each other: he does not repudiate the Qur'án, but he denies that it is the final and absolute standard of divine truth. He often quotes Qur'ánic verses in support of his theosophical views. Only when the book fails him need he confound his critics by alleging a secret communication which he has received from the Author."[14]

When he was asked why it was that he had never made the pilgrimage to Mecca, his reply was this: "It is no great matter that thou

13. *Encyclopædia of Islam*, art. "samá", by D. B. Macdonald.
14. R. A. Nicholson, op. cit., pp. 60–1.

shouldst tread under thy feet a thousand miles of ground in order to visit a stone house (i.e. the Ka'ba). The true man of God sits where he is, and the *Bayt al-Ma'múr* (the celestial archetype of the Ka'ba) comes several times in a day and night to visit him and perform the circumambulation above his head."[15] It would appear also from remarks that he made to his disciples that he had strong objection to the pilgrimage being made by any of them, for he insisted that the pilgrimage of the true mystic must be made within himself. "If God sets the way to Mecca before anyone," he said, "that person has been cast out of the way to the Truth" (*Asrár*, 374, 15). And as in later times Sháh 'Abbás, the great Safáwíd, took special pains to encourage pilgrimages to those shrines that lay within Persian territory, in order that less money might be carried out of the country,[16] so Abu Sa'íd was accustomed to send those of his disciples who thought of making the *ḥajj* to visit the tomb of Abu'l-Faḍl Hasan, the *shaykh* who had been his own instructor in Ṣúfism, who was buried at Sarrakhs. They were to circumambulate his tomb seven times and to consider that they had accomplished their purpose of going on the pilgrimage to Mecca.[17]

There were also requirements of those who would follow in the Ṣúfí path, with its rigid asceticism, that could be superseded, as being of merely temporary value, when a mystic reaches the final stage. For "when the unveiling is completed, he has no further use for ascetic practices and religious forms, for he lives in permanent communion with God Himself." For example, he explained[18]: "When a man seeks to win the favour of a king and to become his companion and intimate friend, before attaining to that rank he must suffer all sorts of tribulation and patiently endure injuries and insults from high and low, and submit with cheerfulness to maltreatment and abuse, giving fair words in return for foul; and when he has been honoured with the king's approval and has been admitted to his presence, he may serve him assiduously and hazard his life in order that the king may place confidence in him. But after he has gained the king's confidence and intimacy, all this hard and perilous service belongs to the past. Now all is grace and bounty and favour; everywhere he meets with new pleasures and delights; and he has no duty but to wait upon the king always, from whose palace he cannot be absent a single moment day or night, in order that he may be at hand whenever the king desires to tell him a secret or to honour him with a place by his side" (*Asrár*, 42, 1).

That Abu Sa'íd did not hesitate to capitalize on his reputed nearness to "the King" is clearly shown in the claims he made to the

15. R. A. Nicholson, p. 62, with reference to E. J. W. Gibb, *History of Ottoman Poetry*, vol. i, p. 37.
16. D. M. Donaldson, *The Shi'ite Religion*, p. 259.
17. R. A. Nicholson, op. cit., p. 62.
18. Id., op. cit., p. 63.

right and power of intercession with God on behalf of his adherents[19]:

> Whoever has seen me and has done good work for my family and disciples will be under the shadow of my intercession hereafter (*Asrár*, 418, 4).
>
> I have prayed God to forgive my neighbours on the left, on the right, in front, and behind, and He has forgiven them for my sake. My neighbours are Balkh and Merv and Nishapur and Herat. I am not speaking of those who live here (in Mayhana) (*Asrár*, 418, 6).
>
> I need not say a word on behalf of those around me. If anyone has mounted an ass and passed by the end of this street, or has passed my house or will pass it, or if the light of my candle falls on him, the least thing that God will do with him is that he will have mercy upon him (*Asrár*, 418, 9).

Thus it is that the great Muhammadan mystics came to be regarded as saints and as intercessors. They "are the object of endless worship and adoration, their tombs are holy shrines whither men and women come as pilgrims to beseech their all-powerful aid, and their relics bring a blessing that only the rich can buy. . . . Their title to saintship depends upon a peculiarly intimate relation to God, which is attested by fits of ecstasy and, above all, by thaumaturgic gifts (*karámát*)."[20] It is only natural, therefore, that the bulk of what is recorded about Abu Sa'íd should be devoted to stories about his *karámát*. The narrators claim to have received their information ultimately from former members of the Ṣúfí fraternity who had been in personal association with him. Their authority is the same in kind as that of those who related traditions orally, passing them on from one generation to another, about the sayings and the conduct of the Prophet.

It is significant to observe that Abu Sa'íd was himself deeply impressed by the number of people who visited him: "Filled with burning love they come from the ends of the world to seek God from me. What miracle is greater than this?" And then he added in comment, "When God makes a man pure and separates him from his self-hood, all that he does or abstains from doing, all that he says and all that he feels becomes a wondrous gift" (*Asrár*, 369, 5).[21]

ABÚ'L-MAJD MAJDUD B. ÁDAM SANÁ'Í

Towards the end of his life (he died about A.D. 1150) al-Saná'í wrote in Persian verse a comprehensive work on Muslim mysticism which he named the *Ḥadíqatu'l-Ḥaqíqat* ("The Enclosed Garden of Truth"). The entire work is in ten chapters: (1) Praise to God, His Unity; (2) Praise of Muhammad; (3) The Understanding; (4) Knowledge; (5) Love, the Lover and the Beloved; (6) Heedlessness;

19. R. A. Nicholson, op. cit., pp. 64–5.
20. Id., op. cit., p. 65.
21. Id., op. cit., pp. 66–7.

(7) Friends and Enemies; (8) Revolution of the Heavens; (9) Praise of the Emperor Sháh Jahán; (10) Qualities of the Whole Work.

Of the *Ḥadíqat* Major J. Stephenson has edited and translated the first chapter.[22] From this translation, which was published in Calcutta, 1910, a *résumé* of the translator's brief analysis is given, along with several aspects of al-Saná'í's Ṣúfí teaching:

(*a*) *Analysis*. The impotence of reason for attaining a knowledge of God, in His Unity, and as a First Cause and Creator. Rejection of anthropomorphic conceptions of God. The first steps of the ascent towards God include worldly wisdom, work, and serenity.

As a Provider God can be depended upon to care for man throughout his life, his earthly possessions are relatively useless, but the self must first be abandoned (pp. 11–16). After he has overcome self-hood, then God's special favour is granted to the traveller on the Path. He has ordered all things well, and what seems evil is so only in appearance (pp. 18–25).

The life and experiences of the Ṣúfí, with his thanksgiving and his continued trust in God (pp. 25–51).

The interpretation of dreams, the abandonment of earth and self, and the attainment of the utmost degree of annihilation (pp. 51–8). Discipline needed on the Ṣúfí Path, charity and gifts as forms of renunciation, and how prosperity injures the soul.

Preparation for prayer consists in purity of heart, humility, and dependence on God. God's kindness in drawing men towards Himself, and His majesty and omnipotence (pp. 67–86).

The excellence and sweetness of the Qur'án, though the letter is not the essential, and its true meaning is not to be discovered by reason alone. The Godlessness of the world before the advent of Muhammad, and the constant need of humility and self-effacement (pp. 87–100).

(*b*) *God's incomprehensibility*. "In every dwelling is God adored; but the Adored cannot be circumscribed by any dwelling. The earthly man, accompanied by unbelief and anthropomorphism, wanders from the road; on the road of truth must thou abandon thy passions; rise, and forsake this vile sensual nature; when thou hast come forth from Abode and Life, then, through God, thou wilt see God.

"How shall this sluggish body worship Him, or how can Life and Soul know Him? A ruby of the mine is but a pebble there. Speechlessness is praise—enough of thy speech; babbling will be but sorrow and harm to thee. Have done!

22. *The First Book of the Ḥadíqatu'l-Ḥaqíqat*, edit. and trans. by Major J. Stephenson, Calcutta, 1910. The Arabic text of this first book has 100 pages, and the translation 166. The pages indicated in the brief analysis and in the several selections are those of the Arabic text.

"His nature, to one who knows Him and is truly learned, is above '*How*' and '*What*' and '*Is it not*' and '*Why*'. . . . Reason in her uncleanness, wishing to see Him, says, like Moses, 'Show me'; when the messenger comes forth from that glory, she says in its ear, 'I turn repentant unto thee'" (pp. 16–17).

(*c*) "*All are seekers*". "What matters at His door, a Muslim or a fire-worshipper? What, before Him, a fire-temple or a monk's cell? Fire-worshipper and Christian, virtuous and guilty, all are seekers, and He the sought" (p. 28, end).

(*d*) *God must be free from blameworthy qualities.* "Malice and rancour are far removed from His attributes; for hate belongs to him who is under command. It is not permissible to speak of anger in respect of God, for God has no quality of anger; anger and hatred are both due to constraint by superior force, and both qualities are far distant from God" (p. 80).

(*e*) "*Of Him Who feeds me and gives me drink.*" "When they capture the hawk in the wilds, they secure its neck and feet; they quickly cover up both its eyes and proceed to teach it to hunt. The hawk becomes accustomed and habituated to the strangers, and shuts its eyes upon its old associates; it is content with little food and thinks no more of what it used to eat. The falconer then becomes its attendant, and allows it to look out of one corner of an eye, so that it may only see himself, and come to prefer him before all others. From him it takes all its food and drink, and sleeps not for a moment apart from him. Then he opens one of its eyes completely, and it looks contentedly, not angrily, upon him; it abandons its former habits and disposition, and cares not to associate with any other" (p. 81).

(*f*) *The Dervish's sighing rebuked.* "Thy sighing is mere self-adornment, thy proper path is to observe God's law; thy path is a polished mirror, but thy sighs veil it over" (p. 97).

In the translations that are given by Professor Browne from al-Saná'í's works,[23] there is first of all the widely related narrative from the *Ḥadíqat* that portrays the varying impressions of the visiting Sultan's elephant that were received by the dwellers in the city of the blind. These impressions are used to set forth men's partial and distorted conceptions of God[24]:

Blind delegates by blind electorate
Were therefore chosen to investigate
The beast, and each, by feeling trunk or limb,
Strove to acquire an image clear of Him.
Thus each conceived a visionary whole,
And to the phantom clung with heart and soul.

23. Professor E. G. Browne, *Literary History of Persia*, vol. ii, pp. 317–22.
24. *Ḥadíqatu'l-Ḥaqíqat*, Bombay lith. edit., A.H. 1275, A.D. 1859, pp. 9–10.

A few selections are also given by Professor Browne from al-Saná'í's *Diwán*, which he considers to be of a higher order of poetry. The following *ghazal*, or ode, is a good example, and its theme is one that we find is reiterated by many subsequent Ṣúfí poets[25]:

That heart which stands aloof from pain and woe
No seal or signature of Love can show:
Thy Love, thy Love I chose, and as for wealth,
If wealth be not my portion, be it so!
For wealth, I ween, pertaineth to the World;
Ne'er can the World and Love together go!
So long as Thou dost dwell within my heart
Ne'er can my heart become the thrall of Woe.

In addition to the extended *Ḥadíqat* there are six other *mathnawís* of al-Saná'í, but these have been available only in rare manuscripts,[26] until recently one of them, the *Sayru'l-'ibád ila'l-Ma'ád* ("Pilgrimage of Servants to the Hereafter"), appeared as published in Teheran (A.D. 1938), with an introduction and annotations by Ágá Sa'íd Nafísí.

This verse is well adapted both in form and in content for the measured recitation that was customary in connexion with the *samá'*, with the object of stimulating or fostering the ecstatic state. Without attempting to reproduce the Persian metre and rhyme, the following examples are given in translation:

Those Asserting the Unity[27]

The first order are the curtain of the Essence,
In the Tavern (the world), but two bows' length removed.
In reason's quest they put forth effort,
In the assembly they give their witness.
Whether in drunkenness or when the mind is clear,
Whether in assertion or in self-effacement,
All are both the intoxicating and the intoxicated,
All are both non-existent and existent;
In their essence have they done a thousand works,
These skilled painters in the eternal workshop.

May you too go beyond the threshold,
And lower your head to take their bonds.
Rise and place your foot on created things,
Face towards the entrance of sincere friendship,
Leave the plain of foolish questioning,
Escape from the net of the captive breast.

25. *Ḥadíqatu'l-Ḥaqíqat*, op. cit., p. 168.
26. Professor Browne has indicated (op. cit., p. 318) that "they are all contained in No. 3346 of the India Office Persian MSS. (Ethé, No. 914), and other copies of all save the *Gharíb-náma* exist in the same collection".
27. From al-Saná'í's *Sayru'l-'ibád ila'l-Ma'ád*, Teheran, A.D. 1938, pp.66–8.

What have I striven by command to attain!
Beyond that now, He Himself is my purpose.
An enemy now the first stage repels me,
No longer am I in *my* time, He has become me!
When from that first substance I found I had changed,
As when a child has become a man,
For my very fabric is something new,
And my face have I turned to the Road again.

A Description of the Travellers on the Road

For years I journeyed amid the dangers
That lurked in these wide-spread curtains;
Whether to Baghdad or to the desert,
Whether to Paradise or to the depths of Hell.
My heart was a candle in the way of zeal,
My life was drowned in the sea of passion,
Or poverty sprang upon me like a lion,
While in safety I was curtained like an onion.
Once by sudden wound was I laid low,
Then by open bounty was I made drunk,
But having passed through all the curtains,
I encountered Him whom they revealed.

When about a hundred years ago Sprenger edited Abdu'l-Raẓẓák's *Dictionary of Ṣúfí Terms*, he took occasion in the preface to express his personal opinion of their claims: "The mysticism of the Ṣúfís is a hypertrophy of the religious feeling, and a monomania in which man blasphemously attempts to fathom the depths of the essence of God. The mystics give up worldly affairs; devote themselves to austerity and are a nuisance to the world. This disease attacks every nation after it has passed the meridian of its grandeur."[28]

In a popular Persian manual of moral instruction, the *Akhláq-i-Ḍiyá'í* (lith. Bombay, 1867), there is a statement that shows that Muslims also have not been entirely uncritical, but that they have been disposed to question the genuineness of some of those who have claimed to have given up the world: "Whoever withdraws his heart from whatever is other than God, he is the true devotee (*záhid*). Whoever withdraws his hand from some of the pleasures of the world, but still seeks position and honour, or whoever gets along with a mere minimum of food but still adorns himself in expensive clothing (in spite of his claims), such a man must be numbered among the seekers after the world, and he has no portion with the true devotees. Or if someone gives up his worldly ambition simply because he cannot attain it, or that otherwise he may acquire a good name, or for

28. From Clarke's translation of the *Awarifu'l-Ma'arif*, by Surhawardi, which is published as vol. iii, with his translation of the *Diwán-i-Ḥafiẓ*, Introduction, p. 2, and *J.R.A.S.*, vol. xxv (1856), p. 145.

the sake of popularity with the people, or to make a display of courage, or for the sake of marvellous works and such like, a man of this sort is a hypocritical devotee. It is plain that the true way lies in this, that each one of you should put the world and the sorrows of the world out of his heart, that he should not take any great delight in anything that occurs to him in this world, nor be too greatly distressed over anything in this world that fails to come to him. Obviously it is the opposite to love of the world that is called devotion (*zuhd*), which is truly withdrawing the heart from the world and getting along with only what is necessary for the maintenance of bodily health."

The section of al-Saná'í's *Ḥadíqatu'l-Ḥaqíqat* that treats of "Old Age and Weakness" shows clearly how easy it was for the Ṣúfí to exalt death as a deliverance from life that was not worth while. There was no lament over tasks unfulfilled, no thought of trials that would fall on a widowed wife or fatherless children, and no grief over ties that would be broken with friends or loved ones. Death afforded rather an individual escape that was to be welcomed eagerly, an escape from the suffering, the insecurity, the pain, and the responsibility of human life. A few verses are translated to show the theme[29]:

Old Age and Weakness

In the world of Reason and of Faith
The body's death is the birth of the soul.
Be it forfeit, that in the world of speech,
The soul may live when the body dies.

Destroyed because it opposed the truth,
Whose object is the heart to cleanse;
Corruption comes always from the clay,
And adornment only from the faith.

Pursue the Way ere Death arrives,
Disdain to beg, it profits not,
Accept the gift when it may come,
The giver the uninvited guest.

In faith esteem it a gift of God,
That the unsummoned guest has come.
When Death will make its sudden call,
Rejoice o'er the gift with heart and soul.

Cry not when you see the face of death,
But meet it with a soul that is free;
Take with you the bread you have at hand,
With Reason and Soul your two young guards.

. . . .

29. *Ḥadíqatu'l-Ḥaqíqat*, p. 210, Bombay text.

You bring not the soul to its abode
Till from the body you walk away.
The soul that advanced from animal life
Before it reached the stage of man,
Goes on beyond the "rational self"
Till crowned with the spirit of holiness,
It transcends indeed the "human self",
Attaining at last angelic life.

The familiar proverb that was used by Jesus (Matt. 6. 21), "For where thy treasure is there will thy heart be also", is expanded into a mildly satirical rebuke of those who are disposed to be too fond of their food in this earthly existence:

Give your gold for food if it is permitted (*ḥalál*),
But the heart goes wherever the treasure is:
And if you spend your treasure for food,
You commit yourself to the quest of food.

A verse in the Qur'án that depreciates this life in order to exalt the next life[30] was very probably in al-Saná'í's mind when he wrote:

Seek then for death, as in this habitation
Death is true and life is futile.

FARÍD AL-DÍN ABÚ MUHAMMAD IBN IBRAHÍM AL-'ATTÁR

Present-day Ṣúfís in Iran have unreserved admiration for Faríd al-Dín al-'Attár (d. circ. A.D. 1230). Though he was born in Nishapur, some thirteen years of his youth were spent in Meshed. Then much of his life he gave to travel, staying for long periods in Ray, Kufa, Damascus, and Mecca; and also sojourning in Egypt, India, and Turkestan. During those years of travel he collected many of the sayings and the poems of the Ṣúfís, and hundreds of these are preserved in his *Tadhkirat al-Awliyá* '("Memoirs of the Saints").[31]

Finally al-'Attár came to be esteemed as a saint and a poet himself, and he settled down in Nishapur, where he wrote assiduously. We are told that on one occasion his house in Nishapur was looted because of a Shi'ite poem that he had written in praise of 'Ali ibn Abú Ṭálib, for this poem was resented as heretical by the orthodox party in Samarqand. It is thought that he went to Mecca for a while after this, but that he returned again to Nishapur, where he appears to have lived until about A.D. 1230.

30. Rodwell's translation of the Qur'án (xxix. 64), "This present life is no other than a pastime and a disport: but truly the future mansion is life indeed."

31. Professor E. G. Browne, *L.H.P.*, vol. ii, pp. 506–15. The *Tadhkiratu'l-Awliyá*, edit. by R. A. Nicholson, in the *Persian Historical Texts*, has a preface by Mirza Muhammad Qazwíní, which gives the information in regard to Attár that he was able to gather from his works. The *Tadhkirat* was translated into Urdu in Lahore by the Manzil-i-Nakhshbandiya.

With the conviction that the human soul is of divine origin, the Ṣúfí ethics is founded on the belief that the soul of man is his real self, and that as such it is only the real that can hope to apprehend Reality, i.e. to know God. As summarized briefly by Dr. Margaret Smith, their teaching is that "if the soul is related to God, then is God also related to the soul. But the soul, tied to a material body, dwelling in a material world, has wandered far from its Source, and the way of return, the path of ascent, to its home in God, is long and arduous. Only by purification and self-stripping can the soul hope to tear aside the veils between itself and the All Holy, and to see clearly the Divine Vision. Only that soul which, by ceasing to think of self, has passed beyond itself can enter into that abiding state of Union with the One."[32]

The reply of al-'Attár to Sprenger's above-mentioned criticism of the Ṣúfís would have been to admit that it is indeed little short of blasphemous to consider that the human reason can comprehend the Divine Essence, but also he would have maintained that in addition to reason God had given to men two special gifts, love and ecstasy, and that to those who are receptive to these God-given states or attitudes the very reality of God will be revealed.

In the poem of al-Attár's that is called the *Manṭiq al-Ṭayr* ("The Discourse of the Birds") there are many things said in exceedingly striking ways.[33] The author makes a Ṣúfí shaikh assert that while a dog is unclean externally, yet it has an inner self for which his own inner self need have no repugnance. Another shaikh glories in the poverty which set his power of appreciation free from the desire for material welfare, until he could say: "Those who aspire to spiritual things are willing to stake both body and soul, and they spend their years consumed by their love to God." It is in this sense that the Ṣúfí is regarded as a traveller, to whom a thousand steep valleys will appear, but, "beside himself with love", eventually he "will seek like the moth to fling himself into the flame". He is not so much concerned with conformity to the faith, in fact he may be accused of infidelity because of his irregularity, but "when that door is opened" that leads to God, his anxiety is no longer about either infidelity or faith. One seeking saint is said to have dreamed that an angel came and assured him: "O chosen one, now that thou hast cast away all that thou hadst, remain here where thou art. It needs not that thou shouldst go in search of thy Lord, for He Himself will come to thee." It is at this stage that the Ṣúfí is apt to consider that "good and evil are all one to him as he goes on the Way, for Love has transcended

32. Dr. Margaret Smith, *The Persian Mystics: Attár*, in the Wisdom of the East Series, p. 20.

33. Attár, *Le Manticu'ttair ou le Langage des Oiseaux*, trans., with comments, by Garcin de Tassy, Paris, 1864. Cf. Margaret Smith, op. cit., pp. 38–63.

both". He declares that "reason cannot continue to exist alongside of Love's madness, for Love has nothing to do with human reason". And yet there was the basic principle to be observed, "He who has lived for aught else but the Beloved, were he Adam himself, must be rejected. Those who dwell in Paradise know that the first thing that they must give is their heart, but if they are not worthy to know the divine secrets and to remain in Paradise, they will recoil before the sacrifice of their hearts."

Here also we find that a kind of broad tolerance is expressed as the Ṣúfí attitude towards those of other than the Muslim faith: "Each finds a way of his own, on this road of mystic knowledge, one by means of the *miḥráb* (prayer niche in the *masjid*), and another through the idol. When the Sun of Gnosis shines forth from the heaven above, on to this most blessed road, each one is enlightened according to his capacity, and finds his own place in the knowledge of the Truth."

Asserting it as a maxim that "Whosoever loses himself finds himself", al-'Attár declared: "Therefore lose thyself and say naught of thy loss: surrender thy soul, and seek naught from others. I know of no greater happiness for a man than this, that he lose himself." . . . "He whose heart is lost in that Ocean is lost therein for ever, and is eternally at rest. The heart, in this sea, is filled with tranquillity, for it finds there naught but oblivion. If it is ever granted to a man to return from this oblivion, the whole creation will become clear to him and many mysteries will be revealed to him." . . . "Whoever leaves this world behind him passes away from mortality, and when he has passed away from mortality, he attains to immortality."

At the same time the purified inner self is but a mirror: "Know that thine heart is the mirror in which thou dost behold Him. Take thine heart in thine hand and behold His beauty there; make a mirror of thy soul and contemplate His glory therein." . . . "Dost thou know what thou dost possess as thine heritage? Enter then at last within thyself and meditate. So long as thy soul is not the bond-slave of the Eternal King, how wilt thou find acceptance here with Him? So long as thou wilt not humiliate thyself in annihilation, thou wilt never know the state of immortality."

The first use of the word *faná'* (annihilation) is to express the transitoriness of the created things in this world, which is itself destined to become non-existent.[34] It was then employed by the Ṣúfís in an ethical sense, when they compared the human will with the divine will.[35] Thus for man's will, as in the case of this present world, there is to be annihilation (*al-faná'*); but for God's will, as for the life that is hereafter, there is *baqá'* (subsistence). It was an altogether natural step for the Muslim ascetics, influenced as they were directly by Christian mystics, to arrive at the conception of the

34. Lane, *Arabic-English Lexicon*, p. 2451.
35. *Encyclopædia of Islam*, art. "Faná", by Baron Carra de Vaux.

necessary annihilation of the human will in obedience to the will of God. It was an ethical rather than a metaphysical conception, and in this respect the use of *faná'* among the earlier Ṣúfís differed radically from the *nirvana* of the Hindus. It is easy to see, however, that poetic extravagance of statement would tend to displace what was at first a distinctly ethical ideal with developed pantheistic conceptions that are obviously similar to Hindu beliefs.

The guiding principles that were followed by the Persian Ṣúfí poets, and that were illustrated in their poems, have been well expressed by al-Hujwírí in the *Kashf al-Maḥjúb*: [36]

"Knowledge of annihilation (*al-faná'*) lies in your knowing that this world is perishable, and knowledge of subsistence lies in your knowledge that the next world is everlasting." . . . "A different signification, however, is attached to the terms in question by the elect among the Ṣúfís. They do not refer these expressions to 'knowledge' (*'ilm*) or to 'state' (*ḥál*), but apply them solely to the degree of perfection attained by the saints who have become free from the pains of mortification and have escaped from the prison of 'stations' and the vicissitudes of 'states', and whose search has ended in discovery, so that they have seen all the things visible, and have heard all things audible, and have discovered all the secrets of the heart; and who, recognizing the imperfection of their own discovery, have turned away from all things and have purposefully become annihilated in the object of desire, and in the very essence of desire have lost all desires of their own, for when a man becomes annihilated from his attributes he attains to perfect subsistence, he is neither near nor far, neither stranger nor intimate, neither sober nor intoxicated, neither separated nor united; he has no name, or sign, or brand, or mark.

"In short, real annihilation from anything involves consciousness of its imperfection and absence of desire for it, not merely that a man should say, when he likes a thing, 'I am subsistent therein', or when he dislikes it, that he should say, 'I am annihilated therefrom'; for these qualities are characteristic of one who is still seeking. In annihilation there is no love or hate, and in subsistence there is no consciousness of union or separation. Some wrongly imagine that annihilation signifies loss of essence and destruction of personality, and that subsistence indicates the subsistence of God in Man; both these notions are absurd."

JALÁL AL-DÍN AL-RÚMÍ

Jalál al-Dín al-Rúmí (1207–73), who lived for some forty years as a Ṣúfí lecturer and poet at Qóniya, was the founder of the order of Mawlawís, who are best known as dancing dervishes. In his extensive

36. al-Hujwírí, *Kashf al-Maḥjúb*, trans. by R. A. Nicholson, Gibb Memorial Series, vol. xvii, pp. 242–5.

poem the *Mathnawí* he has gathered a vast collection of fables and anecdotes and symbols to illustrate Ṣúfí teachings.[37]

In the preface to the Fifth Book of this great work he explains that the religious Law is like a candle to show the way: "Unless you gain possession of the candle there is no wayfaring; and when you have come on to the Way, your wayfaring is the Path; and when you have reached the journey's end, that is the Truth. Hence it has been said, 'If the truths (realities) were manifest, the religious laws would be nought.'" This is in accord with a saying that is ascribed to Muhammad, "The Law is my words, the Path is my works, and the Truth is my inward state."[38]

Again he compares the Law to learning the science of medicine, and the Path to regulating the diet, and the Truth to "gaining health everlasting and becoming independent of them both". The Law, which is the teaching of the Qur'án, and the Path, which is conduct in accord with the Sunna, are both temporary expedients. The goal is the Truth, or that inward state of "God's freedmen". "The Law is knowledge, the Path action, the Truth attainment unto God."[39]

By the thirteenth century the distinction between the established Ṣúfí doctrines and the beliefs of the early Muslim ascetics had come to be clearly recognized. This distinction is briefly stated by Jalál al-Dín[40]: "The gnostic (*'árif*) is the soul of religion and the soul of piety: gnosis (*ma'rifat*) is the result of past asceticism. Asceticism is the labour of sowing; gnosis is the growth of the seed. Therefore the ascetic's hard struggle and his firm religious conviction are like the body, while the soul of this sowing is the growth of the seed and its harvesting. He (the gnostic) is both the command to do right and the right itself: he is both the revealer of mysteries and that which is revealed. He is our king to-day and to-morrow: the husk (i.e. the phenomenal world) is forever a slave to his goodly kernel. When the Shaykh (al-Halláj) said, 'I am God', and carried it through to the end, he throttled (vanquished) all the blind sceptics. When a man's 'I' is negated and eliminated from existence, then what remains? Consider, O denier. If you have an eye, open it and look! After 'not', why, what else remains?"

But along with the characteristic pessimism and pantheism of developed Ṣúfism, Jalál al-Dín used the poet's freedom to criticize Muslim practices that he considered to be abuses of familiar sayings in the Qur'án or the *Ḥadith*. For four hundred years Muslim theologians, poets, and mystics had been struggling with the problem of

37. *Encyclopædia of Islam*, art. "Djalál al-Dín al-Rúmí", by Baron Carra de Vaux.

38. "The Mathnawí of Jalálu'd-Dín Rúmí", trans. by R. A. Nicholson, Gibb Memorial Series, 1934, preface to Part V.

39. Id., op. cit., Part V, p. 3.

40. Id., op. cit., Part VI, p. 374.

suffering and the fact of evil in the world that God had created. What was the real meaning of *má shá Alláhu kána* ("whatever Allah willed comes to be")? In language that ordinary men would understand, Jalál al-Dín rebuked the fatalistic indifference with which these words were often quoted, when he declared[41]: "The saying of (God's) servant, 'whatever God wills comes to pass', does not signify 'be lazy (inactive) in that (matter)'; nay, it is an incitement to entire self-devotion and exertion, meaning, 'make yourself exceedingly ready to perform that service'."

Similarly, the tradition, "the Pen has dried", is employed as a text in expounding a verse in the Qur'án (ix. 121), "Verily Allah suffereth not the reward of the righteous to perish": "The Pen has dried (after writing) that if you do wrong (in this world) you will suffer wrong (in the next), and if you act rightly here the result will be your felicity there. If you behave unjustly you are damned: the Pen has dried on that. If you show justice you eat the fruit of blessedness: the Pen has dried on that. When anyone steals, his hand goes: the Pen has dried on that. When he drinks wine, he becomes intoxicated: the Pen has dried on that.

"Do you deem it allowable, can it be allowable, that on account of the eternally prior decree Allah should come, like a person dismissed from office, saying, 'The affair has gone out of My hands, do not approach me so often, do not entreat Me so much'? Nay, the meaning is: 'the Pen has dried' on this, that justice and injustice are not equal in My sight. I have laid down a distinction between good and evil; I have also laid down a distinction between bad and the worse. If there be a single mote of self-discipline in excess of that of your companion, the grace of Allah will know, and will bestow on you that mote's amount of superiority: the mote will step forth as big as a mountain to meet you."[42]

A story is related in the *Mathnawí* of a thief who made the excuse that the act he had done had been decreed by Allah. The magistrate replied, "That which I am doing is also decreed by Allah", and he went on to explain to him that by making such an excuse he forfeited his life, his property, and his wife. For he showed him how anyone who might wish to wrong him could make the very same excuse.[43]

Many a devout and hard-pressed Ṣúfí would find himself pondering over his own restrictions in view of the unlimited power of the god he worshipped. One such man brought his difficulties to the judge (*Qaḍi*)[44]:

The Ṣúfí said, "He (God) whose help is invoked hath the power to make our trading free from loss. He who turns the fire (of Nimrod) into roses and trees is also able to make this (World-fire) harmless. He who brings forth roses from the very midst of thorns is also able

41. Id., op. cit., Part V, p. 187.
42. Id., op. cit., Part V, p. 189.
43. Id., op. cit., Part V, p. 184.
44. Id., op. cit., Part VI, pp. 355 ff.

to turn this winter into spring. He by whom every cypress is made 'free' (evergreen) hath the power if he would to turn sorrow into joy. He by whom every non-existence is made existent—what damage would He suffer if He were to preserve it forever? He who gives the body a soul that it may live—how would He be a loser if He did not cause it to die? What, indeed, would it matter if the Bounteous One should bestow on His servant the desire of his soul without (painful) toil, and keep far off from poor (mortals) the cunning of the flesh and the temptations of the Devil (which lurk) in ambush?"

To these challenging questions the Qaḍi made reply: "Were there no bitter (stern) Commandment (from God), and were there no good and evil and no pebbles and pearls, and were there no flesh and Devil and passions, and were there no blows and battle and war, then by what name and title would the King call his servants, O abandoned man? How could He say, 'O steadfast one' and 'O forbearing one'? How could he say, 'O brave one' and 'O wise one'? How could there be *steadfast and sincere and spending men* without a brigand and accursed Devil? Rustam and Ḥamza and a catamite would be (all) one; knowledge and wisdom would be annulled and utterly demolished. Knowledge and wisdom exist for the purpose of (distinguishing between) the right path and the wrong paths: when all paths are the right path, knowledge and wisdom are void (of meaning). Do you think it allowable that both the worlds should be ruined for the sake of this briny (foul) shop of the (sensual) nature?

"I know that you are pure (enlightened), not raw (foolish), and that these questions of yours are (asked) for the sake of (instructing) the vulgar. The cruelty of Time (Fortune) and every affliction that exists are lighter than farness from God and forgetfulness (of Him), because these afflictions will pass, but that forgetfulness will not. Only he that brings his spirit to God, awake and mindful of Him, is possessed of felicity."

One of Jalál al-Dín's frequent references to the delusion of greatness may also be mentioned[45]:

"Since you are attached to those worldly goods, oh, beware! How often afterwards will you sob piteously in repentance! The names 'princehood', 'vizierate', and 'kingship' are enticing, but hidden beneath them is death and pain and giving up the ghost. Be a slave of God and walk on the earth like a horse under the rider, not like a bier which is carried on the necks of the bearers. The ungrateful worldly man wishes all people to carry him: they bring him, like a dead rider, to the grave. . . . Do not lay your burden on anyone, lay it on yourself: do not seek eminence, 'tis best to be poor."

A stupid lack of prudence, however, was to be condemned, as shown in the story that "a certain man had a ram which he was

45. "The Mathnawí of Jalálu'd-Dín Rúmí", trans. by R. A. Nicholson, Gibb Memorial Series, 1934, Part VI, p. 275.

leading along behind him: a thief carried off the ram, having cut its halter. As soon as the owner noticed, he began to run to left and right, that he might find out where the stolen ram was. Beside a well he saw the thief crying, 'Alas! Woe is me!' 'O master,' said he, 'why are you lamenting?' He replied, 'My purse of gold has fallen into the well. If you can go in and fetch it out, I will give you a fifth with pleasure. You will receive a fifth part of a hundred dinars in your hand.' The owner of the ram said to himself, 'Why this is the price of ten rams. If one door is shut ten doors are opened: if a ram is gone, God gives a camel in compensation.' He took off his clothes and went into the well: at once the thief carried away his clothes too. (Therefore) a prudent man is needed to find the way to the village: if prudence be absent, cupidity brings calamity. The Devil is a mischievous thief: like a phantom he has a shape at every moment. None but God knows his cunning: take refuge with God and escape from that impostor."[46]

But as Dr. Nicholson has indicated in his article on "Ṣúfíism" in the *Encyclopædia Britannica*, the teaching of Jalál al-Dín Rúmí in the *Mathnawí* is presented "in such a discursive and unscientific manner that its leading principles are not easily grasped". As they are set forth, however, in Dr. Nicholson's own brief statement their significance for the student of Muslim ethics is obvious[47]:

1. It is the nature of beauty to desire manifestation: the phenomenal universe is the result of this desire, according to the famous tradition in which God says, "*I was a hidden treasure, and I desired to be known, so I created the creatures in order that I might be known.*" Hence the Ṣúfís, influenced by Neoplatonic theories of emanation, postulate a number of intermediate worlds or descending planes of existence, from the primal intelligence and the primal Soul, through which "the Truth" (*al-Ḥaqq*) diffuses itself.

2. As things can be known only through their opposites, Being can only be known through Not-being, wherein, as in a mirror, Being is reflected; and this reflexion is the phenomenal universe, which accordingly has no more reality than a shadow cast by the Sun.

3. Its central point is man, the microcosm, who reflects in himself all the divine attributes. Blackened on one side with the darkness of Not-being, he bears within him a spark of pure Being.

4. The human soul belongs to the spiritual world and is ever seeking to be re-united to its source. Such union is hindered by the bodily senses, but though not permanently attainable until after death, it can be enjoyed at times in the state called ecstasy (*ḥál*), when the veil of the sensual perception is rent asunder and the soul is merged in God.

5. This cannot be achieved without destroying the illusion of

46. Id., op. cit., Part VI, pp. 283–4.
47. *Encyclopædia Britannica*, 11th edit., art. "Súfiism", by R. A. Nicholson.

self, and self-annihilation is wrought by means of that divine love, to which human love is merely a stepping-stone.

6. The true lover feels himself one with God, the only real being and agent in the universe; he is above all law, just as a flute produces harmonies or discords at the will of the musician; he is indifferent to outward forms and rites, preferring a sincere idolater to an orthodox hypocrite and deeming the ways to God as many in number as the souls of men.

And from these principles of the Ṣúfí theosophy, as it was developed in Persia and set forth in the great masterpiece of Jalál al-Dín Rúmí, the following tendencies are designated by Dr. Nicholson as "perilous consequences":

1. It tends to abolish the distinction between good and evil—the latter is nothing but an aspect of Not-being and has no real existence.

2. It leads to the deification of the hierophant who can say, like Ḥusain b. Manṣur al-Ḥalláj, "I am the Truth".

3. Ṣúfí fraternities, living in a convent under the direction of a sheikh, became widely spread before A.D. 1100 and gave rise to Dervish orders, most of which indulge in the practice of exciting ecstasy by music, dancing, drugs, and various kinds of hypnotic suggestion.

SHAIKH MUṢLIḤ AL-DÍN SA'DÍ

Of Shaikh Sa'dí (A.D. 1184–circ. 1292), unquestionably the most popular of all the Persian poets, it may be said that his chief work, the *Gulistán*, or "The Rose Garden", is cast in the form of an ethical treatise,[48] but there is no effort at consistency in following any particular ethical theory. Very conscious of life's dilemmas, as they face both the rich and the poor, he presented realistic pictures with master strokes, and we find that it is hard to take issue with a wit who does not himself take too seriously the point of his jibe[49]:

When Fortune favours the tyrant vile,
The wise will forgo their desire awhile.

. . . .

Wait rather till Fortune blunts his claws:
Then pluck out his brains amidst friends' applause.

On the question as to whether he should be counted among the Ṣúfí poets, it is interesting to observe the judgement that is expressed in the article about him, in the *Encyclopædia of Islam*, by J. H.

48. In the *Translation of the Gulistán of Sa'di*, 2nd edit., by John T. Platts, the chapter headings are: 1—On the Character of Kings; 2—On the Morals of Dervishes; 3—On the Excellence of Contentment; 4—On the Advantages of Silence; 5—On Love and Youth; 6—On Feebleness and Old Age; 7—On the Effect of Education; 8—On the Duties of Society.

49. Professor E. G. Browne, *Literary History of Persia*, vol. ii, p. 531.

Kramers[50]: "The question whether Sa'dí was himself susceptible of mystical feelings is probably to be answered in the negative, as his practical nature made him more inclined towards a moralizing attitude, in which he made mysticism only serve a higher moral conception of earthly life. In many instances he puts moderate common sense against the exaggerated zeal for the life to come. In his *Bustán* the lofty mystical sentiments of the *Mathnawí* or the *Mantiq al-Ṭair* should not be sought for. Sa'dí often speaks of the Ṣúfís, but his attitude towards them is always that of a moralist rather than of a fellow mystic."

The first chapter of the *Gulistán* treats of the character of kings. One king is made to declare, in conformity with a well-known tradition in regard to the use of *kidhb* (falsehood), that "an expedient falsehood is preferable to a mischievous truth".[51] However, toward the end of the *Gulistán* we read[52]: "It is better to speak the truth and remain in bondage than that your lie should set you free." And following this is an explanation: "Lying is like a hard blow; although the wound heals, the scar remains. . . . When the brothers of Joseph were convicted of lying, their father no longer had any confidence in their speaking the truth."

Another king expressed it as his judgement that "no one whose origin is bad ever catches the reflexion of the good. Education for the base-born, is as a walnut on a dome."[53]

The Persian king, Hurmuz the son of Nushirwán, gives as a reason for his detaining his father's viziers in prison: "I saw that fear of me was boundless in their hearts, and that they had not full confidence in my promise, and so I apprehended that, through dread of injury to themselves, they might form the design of destroying me."[54]

The second chapter of the *Gulistán* is "On the Morals of Dervishes", and about these Ṣúfí dervishes Sa'dí makes some shrewd observations:

Exert thyself in well-doing, and wear what thou pleasest;
Place a crown on thy head, or a banner on thy shoulder.
Renouncing the world and fleshly lusts and appetites constitutes

50. *Encyclopædia of Islam*, art. "Sa'dí", by J. H. Kramers.

51. On the authority of Umm Kulthum, one of the Prophet Muhammad's wives, it is related by several of the traditionalists that Muhammad declared that false statement is allowable in three circumstances: "(1) when a man relates something to his wife in order to please her; (2) falsehood in warfare; and (3) falsehood to effect reconciliation among people" (Bukhárí, 52: 10; Tirmidhí, 33: 3; Aḥmad ibn Ḥanbal, 6: 403, 404, 454; and in the chapter of falsehood (*báb al-kidhb*) in al-Kulainí's *Káfí fí 'Ilm al-Dín*. Cf. *The Moslem World*, art. "Truth and Falsehood in Islam", by D. M. Donaldson, vol. xxxiii, pp. 276–85.

52. *Gulistán*, ch. viii, maxim 87 in Platts' trans., end of stanza.

53. *Gulistán*, Persian text, ch. i, story 4, and in Platts' English trans., p. 11.

54. Ibid., text ch. i, story 8; trans. p. 21.

Holiness; not throwing off the clothes, and nought beside.
(Text, ii: story 5, trans. p. 80)

If the dervish continued in one state,
He would snap his fingers at both worlds.
(Text, ii: story 9, trans. p. 88)

A certain righteous man saw, in a dream, a king in Paradise, and a devotee in hell. He inquired, "What is the reason of the exaltation of the former, and what the cause of the degradation of the latter, for I used to think the opposite of this?" A voice came saying, "This king is in Paradise in consequence of his good feeling for dervishes; and the devotee is in hell because of his attachment to kings."

Of what avail will the mendicant's cloak, and rosary, and ragged garment prove?
Keep thyself from blameworthy acts.
(Text, ii: story 15, trans. p. 93)

He whom I considered all substance, like a pistachio nut,
Was merely coat upon coat, like an onion.
(Text, ii: story 17, trans. p. 95)

One secret of Sa'dí's popularity was that he so frequently expressed the average Muslim's accepted beliefs and prejudices:

When a beggar asks a thing of thee with wailing,
Give it; otherwise the oppressor will take it by force. (Text, ii: story 18, trans. p. 97)

Wert thou to wash a dog in the seven seas,
He would be dirtier when he got wet.
(Text, vii: story 1, trans. p. 255)

A king placed his son in a school,
And put a silver tablet in his lap:
At the top of his tablet there was written in gold:
"The severity of a master is better than a father's tenderness. (Text, vii: story 4, trans. p. 260)

If thou hast nothing coming in, spend the more slowly,
For boatmen sing a song:
"Were it not to rain in the mountains
For a year, the Tigris would become a dry bed."
(Text, vii: story 5, trans. p. 260)

Hard it is, after once having authority, to submit to orders from others.
(Text, vii: story 2, trans. p. 256)

But Sa'dí is especially appreciated in the *Gulistán* because of his sagacity in discerning fraud. From this point of view the moral that he ordinarily attached to the end of a story is charmingly concise, as may be seen in these few examples[55]:

> Oh! the reluctance to bend the neck in God's service,
> If the hand of liberality have to accompany it!
> For one dinar requested of him he will be as immovable
> as an ass in mire;
> But if thou ask of him an expression of praise (to God),
> he will repeat a hundred.

> So long as thou art a worshipper of the world,
> Seek not His regard, for thou art a mass of hypocrisy.
> When a servant calls Him his own God,
> He should know none other but God.

> Void art thou of wisdom, for the reason that
> Thou art stuffed full of food up to the nose.

> They asked one of the Elders of Damascus, "What is the real nature of Ṣúfism?" He replied, "Previous to this they (the Ṣúfís) were a body of men in the world apparently unsettled (in worldly matters) but inwardly calm and collected; but now they are a body apparently calm and composed, but inwardly disturbed (by worldly concerns)."

> When thy heart each moment strays from thee to another place
> Not in solitude wilt thou find pureness of heart:
> Even though thou possess riches, high rank, tilled fields, and
> merchandise,
> Thou art a recluse, if thy heart be with God.

The *Bustán*, or "The Scented Garden", is also arranged as a treatise on morals. There are ten chapters, and the subjects are: 1. Justice, Equity, and Good Government; 2. Doing Good (*dar iḥsán*); 3. Love (*dar ʿIshq*); 4. Humility; 5. Education (*dar tarbiyat*); 8. Gratitude (*dar shawkr*); 9. Repentance (*dar tawba*); 10. Prayers (*munáját*).

The general character of the pithy sayings of the *Bustán* may be readily discerned by English readers from selections that have been translated by Reuben Levy, and which are published as the first half of "Stories from Saʿdí's *Bustán* and *Gulistán*", a volume that is included in "The Treasure House of Eastern Story". From this only a few sentences can be given here as examples:

> The heart is the prison-house of secrets, which, once uttered, never return to their bonds (p. 4).

> Whether a man is a slave bearing a load on his head or whether he holds his head high as zenith, when fortune changes each loses his head in death. Neither grief nor joy lasts, but the reward of one's labour and one's good name continues (p. 14).

55. *Gulistán*, Persian text, ch. vi, story 7; trans. p. 252; ii, 17, trans. p. 96; ii, 21, trans. p. 102; and ii, 24, trans. p. 106.

> O fortunate man of blessed spirit, think not that if you have obeyed God's will you have found a footing at His court. To compose your heart by well-doing were better than a thousand prayers in every stage of your road (p. 18).
>
> Because of the bounty which the raging elephant has received it will not attack its keeper. Therefore, honest man, deal kindly with the wicked, for a dog will keep guard if it has eaten your bread; the panther's teeth are blunted for the man whose cheese its tongue has licked, be it only for two days (p. 24).

The demonstrative host who welcomed with many bows and kisses, but who gave no food, is thus described: "He was a man ready with his polished manners and politeness, but the grate beneath his saucepan was very cold" (p. 24). And in advising contentment, Sa'dí says: "Honey, my soul is not worth a sting; it is better to be content with one's own date-syrup. God is not pleased with His servant who is not content with the divinely allotted portion" (p. 51).

So many of his sayings have direct relation with the daily associations of ordinary men with one another. For example: "Do not destroy your brother's reputation in a single street, lest fortune destroy your fair name throughout the whole city" (p. 58); and also, "If you constantly repeat that some men are asses, do not delude yourself that you will always be reckoned among the other men" (p. 61).

One of the anecdotes that produced an abundant crop of sage admonitions tells of his visit to a Hindu temple when he was in India.[56] It was at Somanát, and there was a beautiful ivory idol there. "From every land there came streams of caravans to see the soulless beauty." To his Hindu friend and companion he expressed his wonder that living beings should worship lifeless things. But what he said was taken as an insult, and when he was about to be mobbed by the enraged Hindus he resorted to dissimulation and appealed to the chief Brahman in cajolery and soft words, admiring the carving of the ivory figure, and beseeching him to tell him of the inner meaning that must lie within its outward form. The Brahman was impressed by his obvious interest, and invited him to remain in the temple for the night, that in the early morning he might see for himself how this idol would raise its hands to God the Law-giver.

About dawn the people of the place came crowding into the temple, and then suddenly, when all were expectant, the image raised its hand. The people went away, after great shouting, and the Brahman assured Sa'dí: "I know that you have no difficulties left; the truth has been revealed and all falsehood banished."

56. *Bustán*, Persian text, ch. viii, Graf's edited text, pp. 388–95; and Levy's trans., pp. 67–72.

But Sa'dí was not so easily convinced, though for a time he stood hypocritically weeping in repentance for what he had said, and then went and kissed the idol's hand. For as soon as he found that he was trusted in the temple, he undertook to get behind the scenes, and there, behind a curtain of gold embroidery, he saw the arch-priest sitting with the end of a cord in his hand. At once the whole matter became clear to him. "It must be", he thought, "that when he pulls the cord the idol raises its hands in supplication."

"The Brahman was ashamed before me," he goes on to relate, "for the covering was stripped from his wickedness. He fled, and I ran after him and flung him headlong into a well, for I knew that if the Brahman remained alive he would exert all his efforts to slay me, and would consider it lawful to destroy me lest I should reveal his secret."

At this point Kipling or Mark Twain would have very likely concluded such a fantastic tale, but with Sa'dí the story serves only as a setting for the admonitions it suggests:

> When you have discovered the doings of a villain, make him powerless if you can; for if you spare the dishonourable man's life, he will not desire to see you alive any longer.
> And even though he lays his head down in obeisance at your door, if he should find power, he will cut off your head.
>
> Do not follow in the footsteps of a treacherous man; but if you go and you see him, give him no respite.

After he had thrown the Brahman into the well, he "slew the vile wretch outright with a stone", and then he left that land and fled. In justifying his flight he adds the observations:

> When you have set fire to a reed-bed, you will beware of the lions in it if you are wise.
>
> Do not kill the young of a man-biting snake, but if you have done so, do not remain in that house.
>
> If you have disturbed a bee-hive, run from that quarter, for you will be hotly overwhelmed.
>
> Shoot no arrow against a man more skilful than yourself; but if (you have done so and) it fails, draw up your skirts to your teeth and flee.
>
> In Sa'dí's book there is nothing beyond this piece of counsel: if you have undermined a wall, do not stand beneath it.

SHAMS AL-DÍN MUHAMMAD AL-ḤÁFIẒ (d. A.D. 1389)

In the latter part of the fourteenth century, when Murad I was reigning for thirty years (1359–89) as the Ottoman Sultan, and Sháh Shujá was ruling in Fars (1359–84), Ḥáfiẓ was writing letter-perfect odes and lyrics in Shiráz. He was by no means a pious ascetic, but as Fitzgerald has observed, he delighted "to float luxuriously between Heaven and Earth, and this World and the Next, on the wings of a poetical expression that might serve indifferently for either".[57] His universal popularity is due in part to the fact that the separate stanzas of his odes are so eminently quotable. Each one is a pearl in meaning and in form. This explains also the wide use of his book by all classes of people in taking omens or in casting lots, since it is employed in Persian-speaking countries for this purpose as much or even more than the Qur'án.

In many of his separate stanzas Ḥáfiẓ evidently regards himself as a Ṣúfí, as when he writes[58]:

> Arise, that we may seek an opening through the door of the tavern,
> That we may sit in the Friend's path and seek a wish.
>
> This borrowed life which the Friend hath entrusted to Ḥáfiẓ—
> One day I shall see His Face and shall yield it up to Him.

But at other times, as in the stanza which he is said to have written for inscription on his tomb, he is animated rather by a dry sense of humour[59]:

> When thou passest by our tomb, seek a blessing, for it shall become
> A place of pilgrimage for the libertines of the world.

Some of Ḥáfiẓ's poems had given offence to the *'ulama* of Shiráz, and when he died they refused at first to offer prayers over his body. As the story goes, the dispute which arose was settled by all agreeing that slips of paper, each bearing a couplet from the poet's odes, should be placed in a vessel, and that a child should draw the verse on which their judgement should be based. The verse that was drawn, as legend says fortuitously, was this[60]:

> From the bier of Ḥáfiẓ thy foot withdraw not,
> For, though immersed in sin, he goeth to Paradise.

To some extent Ḥáfiẓ shared in the general inclination of the Ṣúfí poets to assume a kind of superior aloofness to the ordinary requirements in conduct for good Muslims. But along with this he also had that spirit of broad tolerance of men of other faiths which they

57. Walter Leaf, *Versions from Ḥáfiẓ*, London, 1898, Intro., p. 17, quoting from Fitzgerald's preface to the second edition of the *Rubaiyyat* of Omar Khaiyám.

58. Professor E. G. Browne, *Literary History of Persia*, vol. iii, pp. 311 and 315.

59. Ibid, op. cit., p. 301.

60. *The Díwán-i-Ḥáfiẓ*, trans. into English prose by Lt.-Col. H. Wilberforce Clarke, 2 vols., Calcutta, 1891. Cf. Ode 60, couplet 7.

showed in conformity with the teaching of Ibn al-Arabi (d. A.D. 1240),[61] so that at times he impresses his readers as more of a free-thinker than a mystic, as appears in these stanzas that Dr. Nicholson has translated[62]:

Love is where the glory falls
Of Thy face—on convent walls
Or on tavern floors, the same
Unextinguishable flame.

Where the turbaned anchorite
Chanteth Allah day and night,
Church bells ring the call to prayer
And the cross of Christ is there.

The text of the *Díwán* of Ḥáfiẓ, as edited with German verse-translations by Rosenzweig-Schwannan, contains 693 separate poems. According to Professor Browne's analysis,[63] these include 573 odes (*ghazaliyyát*), 42 fragments (*muqaṭṭa'át*), 69 quatrains (*rubá'iyyát*), 6 narrative poems (*mathnawís*), 2 longer odes (*qaṣídas*), and there is 1 "five-some" (*mukhammas*). In 1891 Colonel Wilberforce Clarke published a translation of the entire *Díwán* in English that has frequent and confusing parenthetical explanations as well as copious notes.[64] While this work is of considerable value to students who read the poems in the Persian text, still it fails to convey to the English reader anything like an adequate appreciation of the real beauty there is in Ḥáfiẓ's poetry. A few years later, in 1898, Walter Leaf published his *Versions from Ḥáfiẓ*,[65] in which he has endeavoured to present 28 of the poems from the *Díwán* in their own Persian metre, and with as close an imitation as possible of their rhymes. And it was about this same time that Miss Gertrude L. Bell published her *Poems from the Díwán*

61. R. A. Nicholson, *The Mystics of Islám*, pp. 87–8: "Those who adore the Sun (says Ibn al-Arabi) behold the Sun, and those who adore Him in living things see a living thing, and those who adore Him as a Being unique and unparalleled see that which has no like. Do not attach yourselves to any particular creed exclusively, so that you disbelieve in all the rest; otherwise, you will lose much good, nay, you will fail to recognize the real truth of the matter. God, the omnipresent and omnipotent, is not limited to any one creed, for He says (Qur'án, ii. 109), 'Wheresoever ye turn, there is the face of Allah'. Everyone praises what he believes; his god is his own creature, and in praising it he praises himself. Consequently he blames the beliefs of others, which he would not do if he were just, but his dislike is based on ignorance. If he knew Junayd's saying, 'The water takes its colour from the vessel containing it', he would not interfere with other men's belief, but would perceive God in every form of belief."

62. Id., op. cit., p. 88.

63. Professor E. G. Browne, op. cit., p. 102.

64. *The Díwán-i-Ḥáfiẓ*, English prose trans. with notes by Lt.-Col. Wilberforce Clarke, 2 vols., Calcutta, 1891, with a companion volume, vol. iii, which is an abridged translation of Suhrawardí's *Awarifu'l-Ma'arif*.

65. *Versions from Ḥáfiẓ*, by Walter Leaf, London, 1898.

of Ḥáfiẓ, in which she has presented 46 artistic translations, with an excellent introduction.[66]

In this introduction to her poems from Ḥáfiẓ Miss Gertrude Bell has shown clearly that "to some at least of the innumerable difficulties which assail every man who turns a thoughtful eye upon life and its conditions, Ḥáfiẓ seems to have accepted the solution presented to him by Ṣúfism. He understood and sympathized with the bold heresy of al-Halláj, 'though fools whom God hath not uplifted know not the meaning of him who said, "I am God"'. Sometimes we find him enumerating one of these abstruser Ṣúfí doctrines: 'How shall I say that existence is mine when I have no knowledge of myself, or how that I exist not when mine eyes are fixed on Him?'—a man, that is, can lay claim to no individual existence; all that he knows is that he is a part of the eternally existing."

It is sometimes difficult to determine, in the case of particular poems, whether Ḥáfiẓ wrote primarily as an ardent lover or as a poet or as a mystic. Number xxviii in Miss Gertrude Bell's collection may be submitted for the reader's judgement:

Hast thou forgotten when thy stolen glance
Was turned to me, when on my happy face
Clearly thy love was writ, which doth enhance
All happiness? or when my sore disgrace
(Hast thou forgot?) drew from thine eyes reproof,
And made thee hold thy sweet red lips aloof,
Dowered, like Jesus's breath, with healing grace?

Hast thou forgotten how the glorious
Swift nights flew past, the cup of dawn brimmed high?
My love and I alone, God favouring us!
And when she like a waning moon did lie,
And Sleep had drawn his coif about her brow,
Hast thou forgot? Heaven's crescent moon would bow
The head, and in her service pace the sky!

Hast thou forgotten when a sojourner
Within the tavern gates and drunk with wine,
I found love's passionate wisdom hidden there,
Which in the mosque none even now divine?
The goblet's carbuncle (has thou forgot?)
Laughed out aloud and speech flew hot
And fast between thy ruby lips and mine!

Hast thou forgotten when thy cheek's dear torch
Lighted the beacon of desire in me,
And when my heart, like foolish moths that scorch
Their wings and yet return, turned all to thee?

66. *Poems from the Díwán-i-Ḥáfiẓ*, by Gertrude L. Bell, London, 1897; 2nd edition, 1928, p. 72.

Within the banquet-hall of Good Repute
(Hast thou forgot?) the wine's selfpressed my suit,
And filled the morn with drunken jollity!

Hast thou forgotten when thou laid'st aright
The uncut gems of Ḥáfiẓ' inmost thought,
And side by side thy sweet care strung the bright
Array of verse on verse—hast thou forgot?

Another beautiful example, in which the poet faces the reality and the mystery of death, is shown in Miss Bell's No. xiv[67]:

The nightingale with drops of his heart's blood
Had nourished the red rose, then came a wind,
And catching at the boughs in envious mood,
A hundred thorns about his heart entwined.
Like to the parrot crunching sugar, good
Seemed the world to me who could not stay
The wind of death that swept my hopes away.

Light of mine eyes and harvest of my heart,
And mine at least in changeless memory!
Ah, when he found it easy to depart,
He left the harder pilgrimage to me!
O Camel-driver, though the cordage start,
For God's sake help me lift my fallen load,
And Pity be my comrade on the road!

My face is seamed with dust, mine eyes are wet.
Of dust and tears the turquoise firmament
Kneadeth the bricks for joy's abode; and yet . . .
Alas, and weeping yet I make lament!
Because the moon her jealous glances set
Upon the bow-bent eyebrows of my moon,
He sought a lodging in the grave—too soon!

I had not castled, and the time is gone.
What shall I play? Upon the chequered floor
Of Night and Day, Death won the game—forlorn
And careless now, Ḥáfiẓ can lose no more.

Mr. K. Sussheim, writing in the *Encyclopædia of Islam*, is of the opinion that "the general line of thought in his poems raises the question whether Ḥáfiẓ's untiring praise of love and wine is to be interpreted in the Ṣúfí fashion as a profession of Muslim pantheism".[68] And his conclusion is that "apart from occasional exceptions the answer is negative".

In his explanation that love is "the supreme principle of Ṣúfí ethics", however, Dr. Nicholson has made the important observation that "what kind of symbolism each mystic will prefer depends on his temperament and character". This he amplifies as follows:

67. Clarke, vol. i, p. 244, and in the ordinary Persian text, No. 132.
68. *Encyclopædia of Islam*, art. "Ḥáfiẓ".

"If he be a religious artist, a spiritual poet, his ideas of reality are likely to clothe themselves instinctively in forms of beauty and glowing images of human love. To him the rosy cheek of the beloved represents the divine essence manifested through its attributes; her dark curls signify the One veiled by the Many; when he says, 'Drink wine that it may set you free from yourself', he means, 'Lose your phenomenal self in the rapture of divine contemplation.'"[69] And his conclusion is that "the love thus symbolized is the emotional element in religion, the rapture of the seer, the courage of the martyr, the faith of the saint, the only basis of moral perfection and spiritual knowledge. Practically, it is self-renunciation and self-sacrifice, the giving up of all possessions—wealth, honour, will, life, and whatever else men value—for the Beloved's sake without any thought of reward."[70]

"The restraints of the ascetic life", as E. H. Palmer has remarked,[71] "seem to have been very little to Ḥáfiẓ's taste, and his loose conduct and wine-bibbing propensities drew upon him the severe censure of his monastic colleagues. In revenge he satirized them unmercifully in his verses, and seldom loses an opportunity of alluding to their hypocrisy." Of this mood to reply to his critics, the following odes afford examples which also show something of his practical ethical principles[72]:

No. 240

That interferer finds fault with me
For profligacy and love,
Who raises objection to mystery,
In occult science found.

Behold the perfection of truth and love,
And not the defect of sin:
For he to whom knowledge is lacking,
The fault alone perceives.

The amorous glance of the *Sáqí*
Did so impress Islam,
That from the red wine, I fear,
Ṣuhaib alone refrained.

The *itr* of the Houri,
In visions given to us,
Makes the dust of this our tavern,
A perfume for the breast.

69. R. A. Nicholson, *The Mystics of Islám*, pp. 103–4.
70. Id., op. cit., p. 107.
71. *Encyclopædia Britannica*, art. "Ḥázfi".
72. These two translations are of odes that occur as Nos. 240 and 430 (cf. Clarke, vol. i, p. 377, and vol. ii, p. 724) in the ordinary Persian text, which is procurable in the bazaars of Teheran, Bombay, Baghdad, Cairo, etc. Those who use the ordinary Persian text, however, will find it an advantage, as Clarke suggests, to insert the numbers of the odes.

The key to the treasure of happiness,
  Is hidden within the heart:
Forbid that in such matters,
  We should hesitate or doubt.

For Moses as a shepherd
  Could only reach his goal,
When years of zealous service
  To Jethro he had given.

At the story now of Ḥáfiẓ,
  His eyes weep tears of blood,
Recalling youthful follies
  In his present feeble years.

No. 430

We try to say nothing bad and wish to do nothing wrong,
To make out that your coat is black and claim that our cloak is blue.

In the Book of Knowledge we hope to enter no mistakes,
Profaning mystery divine with sordid jugglers' tricks.

We do not shame the poor, nor criticize the rich,
For our work with evil is this—to try to avoid it ourselves.

To all wayfarers we show the nature of the world,
Oblivious to the horse's colour and to the saddle's gold.

In spite of the captain's skill the storm destroys his ship;
For on this suspended ocean who can ever depend?

If the Shah disdains to drink the dregs with profligates,
For him we have no wine that's either strained or clear.

Let the friend whom envy wounds be happy and assured,
That heed will not be taken of envy's foolish word.

O Ḥáfiẓ! that foes are false should give you no concern,
But if they speak the truth, the truth you can't oppose.

That Ḥáfiẓ did have serious times, when his heart was moved by fervent religious desire and when his mind sought to make an earnest quest for that which is genuine in man's relation to God, can be shown in many places in his *Díwán*. For example[73]:

No. 150

Unless a soul appreciates the beauty of the Beloved it has no desire for Paradise.
Whoever does not have the one most certainly has not the other.

73. In this and the remaining selections from Ḥáfiẓ, readers who wish to utilize Clarke's translation may note the following references: No. 150 (Clarke, vol. i, p. 326), No. 144 (Clarke, i, p. 312), and No. 487 (Clarke, ii, p. 789).

With no one have I seen the character (*nishání*) of that Heart-ravishing One;
Either I have failed to recognize it or he has had it not.

Every drop of dew on the path is a hundred fiery waves,
Alas that this enigma has neither interpretation nor explanation.

Human effort affords no stage of contentment,
O Camel-driver, let me mount again, for this road has no stopping place.

The curved harp calls you to joy,
But hearken, the counsel of elders will do you no harm.

If your sole companion is a candle, conceal from him the "states",
For that cheerful fellow, with his head cut off, has no brake on his tongue.

A delight like that has no life without the Friend,
And without the Friend life has no delight like that.

The circumstances of the treasure of Qárun, which time dissipated,
Consider with the closed rose-bud, that it keep not its gold hidden.

He whom you call teacher, if you look with care,
Is but a workman, whose work is not accepted.

O Heart, learn the way of profligacy from the Chief of Police!
Drunk is he, though no one suspects such things of him.

No one in the world hath a slave just like Ḥáfiẓ,
And no one in the world hath a King like unto thee!

Another instance of Ṣúfí faith, that is expressed in a more serious strain, may be observed in this ode in which the poet voices feelings of resignation and trust:

No. 144

Would that I could put my hand to something that would bring an end to sorrow!
The solitude of the heart disdains conflict, for only when the demon goes will the angel enter.

The society of princes is a dark winter night,
Seek light from the Sun, perchance it may rise.

Why do you sit waiting at the door of an unmanly potentate, eagerly expecting his eunuch to receive you?
Let the world go, more bitter than poison, for there comes a world more sweet than sugar.

Saliḥ and Ṭáliḥ showed their obedience, to see who will be accepted and whose work recognized.

Nightingale love, ask for life! eventually the garden will be green and the rose will bloom.
Patience and Victory are very old friends, for only after patience does victory come.

The indifference of Ḥáfiẓ in this restricted world is nothing strange;
He who enters the wine-shop becomes unconscious.

Likewise the poet's own feelings of the fleeting nature of life, the intrinsic value of a spirit of gratitude, and the folly of pretending to abstinence are seen in this one ode:

No. 487

I gazed on the green field of the Sky,
And the sickle of the Moon,
And thought of my own sown field,
And the time of the harvest.

I said, "O Fortune, thou hâst been sleeping,
And the Sun is up";
He said, "In spite of all this,
Do not lose hope."

Rely not on the Night-Rover (the Moon),
For this impostor
Seized the crown of Ká'ús
And the girdle of Khusráw.

If you go pure and free to the Sky,
As did the Christ,
From your flame will a hundred rays
Reach unto the Sun.

Invoke the Sky not to sell this glory,
For in love
The crop of the Moon is a grain of barley,
And of the Pleiades two grains.

Though the ear be weighed down with a ring
Of pearls and of rubies,
The season of youth is passing,
So take heed.

Forfending ill fortune, 'twas thy mole,
On the chess-board of beauty,
That moved the pawn that won the game
O'er Moon and Sun.

He who has not made his heart green
   With the seeds of gratitude,
Will face with shame the scant harvest
   He may call his own.

Fast in the circle remain, like the drum-head,
   Enslaved in the tambourine,
Though you need take many a beating,
   From the circle break not away.

The fire of pretending to abstinence
   Will burn the harvest of faith;
O Ḥáfiẓ! discard this woollen cloak
   Of the Ṣúfí, and be gone!

10

MODERN ETHICAL INTERPRETATIONS OF ISLAM

UNDOUBTEDLY THERE is greater freedom in Muslim countries for the consideration of ethical and political problems because of the persistent efforts that were put forth in the nineteenth century by two fugitive reformers. The first of these men was Jamál al-Dín al-Afghání (d. A.D. 1897).[1] He is described by I. Goldziher in the *Encyclopædia of Islam* as "one of the most remarkable figures in the Muslim world in the nineteenth century". This is because of the influence he exerted on the liberationist and constitutional movements in Muhammadan countries. But at the same time, as Professor E. G. Browne considered, he was "at once a philosopher, author, orator, and journalist".[2]

He had the vision of the re-animation of a powerful Muslim Empire, able to resist European exploitation, and united under a single caliphate. He appreciated, however, that the several leading Muslim countries required "independent internal development by the introduction of liberal institutions".

In 1883, while he was living in political exile in Paris, he "carried on a controversy with Ernest Renan in the columns of *Le Journal des Débats* on the subject of 'Islam and Science', the discussions centring about the ability of Islam to reform and adapt itself to modern civilization".[3] And there in Paris, in conjunction with his friend and fellow reformer and exile, Muhammad Abdúh, who served as editor, and with the financial backing of several Indian Muhammadans, he began publishing a paper in Arabic, *al-'Urwat al-Wuthqa* ("The Firm Knot"). Though only eighteen numbers were allowed to appear, and these in the course of eight months, nevertheless this paper exercised considerable influence. In fact it has been spoken of as "the first literary harbinger of the nationalist movements in the Muhammadan territories of England".

When he died in Constantinople, in 1897, it was after a long

1. *Encyclopædia of Islam*, art. "Djamál al-Dín al-Afghání".
2. Professor E. G. Browne, *The Persian Revolution of* 1905–9, Cambridge, 1910.
3. C. C. Adams, *Islam and Modernism in Egypt*, Oxford University Press London, 1933, p. 9.

career of political activity on behalf of Islamic countries, which kept him in and out of Afghanistan, Persia, Turkey, Egypt, and India. His chief aim, as Dr. Adams has stated, "in all his untiring efforts and ceaseless agitation, was the accomplishment of the unification of all Muslim peoples under one Islamic government, over which the one Supreme Caliph should bear undisputed rule, as in the glorious days of Islam before its power had been dissipated in endless dissensions and divisions, and the Muslim lands had lapsed into ignorance and helplessness, to become the prey of Western aggression. The present decadent condition of Muslim countries weighed heavily upon him. He believed that if these countries were once freed from the incubus of foreign domination and interference, and Islam itself reformed and adapted to the demands of present-day conditions, the Muslim peoples would be able to work out for themselves a new and glorious order of affairs, without dependence on, or imitation of, European nations. To him, the religion of Islam was, in all essentials, a world religion and thoroughly capable, by reason of its inner spiritual force, of adaptation to the changing conditions of every age."[4]

In his "Refutation of the Materialists" (*Risálat fí ibṭál madhhab al-dahríyín*), he declared that he had the following main objectives in his teaching and agitation[5]:

1. That the minds of the people should be purified of belief in superstitions and foolish notions. Islam requires this, especially because the doctrine of the Unity of God requires the clarifying of the mind and forbids such foolish and extravagant notions as idolatry, or incarnations and suffering of the deity.

2. That the people should feel themselves capable of attaining the highest levels of nobility of character and should be desirous of doing so. The only thing which cannot be reached by him who desires it is prophecy, which God confers on whomsoever He will. If all the people were persuaded of the possibility of attaining perfection of character they would vie with one another in endeavours to attain it. Islam made possible perfection for all. It is not like Brahminism, which divides men into castes, the limits of which cannot be overstepped. Nor like Judaism, which despised men of other religions and instituted within itself the priesthood as the caste nearest God, without the mediation of which no one could attain nearness to God.

3. That the articles of belief of the religion of the nation should be the first subject taught to the people, and this should be done by teaching also the proper reasons and arguments in support of these beliefs, that the religious beliefs of the people should not rest upon mere acceptance of authoritative teaching (*taqlid*). Guizot, in his work on *Civilization*, shows that the most potent element in the modern progress and civilization of Europe was the appearance of a religious party that claimed the right of investigating the

4. C. C. Adams, *Islam and Modernism in Egypt*, p. 13.
5. Id., op. cit., pp. 15–16.

source of religious belief for themselves, and demanding proof for these beliefs. Islam is almost alone among the religions of the world in addressing itself to man's reason, and demanding that he should accept religious belief only upon the grounds of convincing argument and not of mere claim and supposition. Contrasted with Islam are other religions, such as those that require the belief that one can be more than one and the many can be one, a belief which its professors justify on the ground that it is above reason and cannot be grasped by reason.

4. That in every nation there should be a special class whose function would be the education of the rest of the people, and another class whose function would be the training of the people in morals. One class would combat natural ignorance and the need of instruction, the other would combat the natural passions and the need of discipline. These two provisions, the teacher to perform the work of instruction, and the disciplinarian to command that which is good and to prohibit that which should be avoided, are among the most important provisions of Islam. Islam is thus the only religion by which the happiness of nations can be attained.

If it be objected, "Why then are the Muslims in the evil state in which we find them?" the answer may be given in the words of the Qur'án: "Verily God will not change the state of a people until they change their own state" (Qur'án, xiii. 12).

The second of the two influential reformers who worked of necessity as fugitives from one Muslim country to another was Muhammad Abduh (d. A.D. 1905). When in 1866 he went as a young man to study at the great Azhar Mosque in Cairo, he found that there was a new interest in natural science and history. Influenced as he had been by his grand-uncle, his own object was the study of mysticism, and at first he gave himself assiduously to ascetic practices. But soon he came in contact with Sayyid Jamál al-Dín al-Afghání, who introduced him to translations of books by European writers, and who got him interested in the serious political problems that were facing the Muslims of Egypt. This led eventually to his taking up journalism as a profession.

In 1880 he was appointed to serve as the chief editor of the official gazette, *al-Waqá'i al-Miṣríya*, which soon became the recognized organ of Egypt's liberal party. He was less inclined to be revolutionary than was his friend and teacher Jamál al-Dín. The first great need, he felt, was for a reform of education, with particular regard to moral and religious education. But in 1882, after the rebellion of 'Arábi Pashá had been suppressed, Muhammad Abduh was one of those who were banished from Egypt. He went first to Beirut and then on to Paris, where in 1884 he met his friend Jamál al-Dín and joined him in editing a paper,[6] by which they sought to foster the development of a more self-reliant spirit of nationalism in Muslim countries.

6. This was the *al-'Urwat al-Wuthqa* that is mentioned above.

The following year, when this paper had been suppressed, he returned to Beirut, where he taught and continued his Muslim and Arabic studies. For nearly four years he remained in Beirut, and it was during this time that he translated from the Persian into Arabic Jamál al-Dín's "Refutation of the Materialists", the *Risálat al-Radd 'ala'l-Dahríyín*.

When he returned to Cairo in 1889 he did not resume his teaching, but was appointed as a judge. In ten years time he attained the position of State *mufti*. In this his new work in the courts he had opportunity to assist in necessary legal reforms and also to help in the establishment of the College for Qáḍís.

Then in 1894 a governing body was formed for the "al-Azhar University", and Muhammad Abduh was made one of its members. Owing to his interest and initiative he soon became the leader in the reforms that were instituted. He then resumed his work of teaching and writing. In 1897 he published his book on theology, the *Risálat al-Tawhíd*, then a work on logic in 1898, and a defence of Islam against Christianity in 1902.[7] His commentary on the Qur'án, portions of which had appeared in the magazine *al-Manár*, was revised and completed after his death (in 1905) by his friend and colleague Shaikh Muhammad Raschíd Riḍa.

Muhammad Abduh's biographer in the *Encyclopædia of Islam*, Dr. J. Schacht, has observed that "as an opponent equally of the political control by Europe and of oriental despotism in Muslim lands, he favoured an inner assimilation of Western civilization, without abandoning the fundamental Muslim ideas and a synthesis of the two factors". The definite objectives that he said he had were: (1) to reform the Muslim religion by bringing it back to its original condition, (2) the renovation of the Arabic language, and (3) the recognition of the rights of the people in relation to the government.

While he did not believe that science and religion are necessarily antagonistic, he did feel that these two fields should be kept separate. In the study of the attributes of God, for example, religion recognizes a barrier beyond which human reason may not go. But in natural science no such limits are imposed, and scientific investigators ought not to be inhibited in their efforts by religious intolerance and sectarian bias, as had so frequently occurred in Muslim countries.

This does not mean, however, that he failed to grant to reason its pre-eminent place in religion. He felt that the Qur'án gives to reason "the final decision regarding the matter of happiness, and in the distinction between truth and falsehood, and between what is harmful and what is beneficial".[8] "Thus in requiring faith in the existence

7. This book, first published in *al-Manár*, was entitled *al-Islám wa'l-Naṣráníya ma'a 'l-Ilm wa'l-Madaníya*.

8. C. C. Adams, op. cit., pp. 128–30, with references to the *Risálat*, p. 20, Michel trans., p. 16

and unity of God, Islam depends upon nothing but proof of the reason and human thought, which follows its natural order; it does not astonish you with miracles, nor extraordinary occurrences, nor heavenly voices."[9] So also he was ready to grant "the precedence of reason over the literal meaning of the Divine Law in case of conflict between them". Likewise, in the case of a particular passage in the Qur'án, the apparent sense of which contains what appears to be a contradiction, "reason must believe that the apparent sense was not intended. It is then free to choose between interpreting the passage consistently with the rest of the words of the prophet in whose message the doubtful passage occurs, and between resigning the matter to God and His knowledge."[10] In general, religion may be regarded as a check on human reason, and in this sense it is "to be considered as a friend of science, encouraging the study of the secrets of the universe, summoning to regard for established truths, and requiring dependence upon them in the formation of character and the improvement of actions".[11]

He believed that the recognized laws of society are laws of God, and for Sura xiii. 12, "Verily God does not change the state of a people until they change their own state," he gave this explanation:[12]

> Nations have not fallen from their greatness, nor have their names been wiped off the state of existence, except after they have departed from those laws which God prescribed with supreme wisdom. God will not change the state of a people from might and power and wealth and peace, until that people change their own state of intellectual knowledge, and correctness of thinking and perception, and consideration of the works of God towards previous nations who went astray from the path of God and therefore perished. Ruin overtook them because they turned aside from the law of justice and the path of insight and wisdom . . . and chose to live in falsehood rather than die in the aid of the truth.

Muhammad Abduh did not believe that human society is able to work out its own salvation without divine intervention through the prophets. "In the *Risálat*, emphasis is placed upon love and justice as the bonds which hold human society together. But all men are not actuated by these sentiments, just as all are not actuated by reason. No state of society, therefore, can resist the disintegrating influences of selfishness and injustice. Only the teaching and supernatural personal influence of the prophets can rescue society and restore it to a salutary state."[13]

9. Id., op. cit., p. 129, with references to *al-Islám wa'l-Naṣrániya*, p. 51.
10. Id., op. cit., p. 129, with references to the *Risálat*, p. 143, Michel trans., p. 88.
11. Id., op. cit., p. 135, with references to *al-Manár*, viii. 892.
12. Id., op. cit., p. 141, with references to *Taríkh*, ii, pp. 323–4.
13. Id., op. cit., p. 157, with references to *Risálat*, p. 105, Michel trans., p. 65.

Rational moral approval, as Muhammad Abduh represents it, is a distinction that man has the capacity to make between that which is beautiful and that which is ugly. The following passage from the *Risálat* shows that he was himself familiar with the appeal to reason that had been made by al-Fárábí[14]:

> We find within ourselves a distinction between material things that are beautiful and those that are ugly. Not all persons have the same ideas of beauty and ugliness; yet some things generally excite an impression of beauty, such as flowers. The apprehension of beauty arouses sentiments of pleasure or wonder, and ugliness those of repulsion or fear. This power of distinction is characteristic of man, and even of some animals. Man is sensible of the same distinctions in the world of ideas, although the criteria by which he judges them are different. He finds beauty in the idea of perfection: God as Necessary Existence, for example, or the noble moral qualities of men. On the other hand, defectiveness, in mind or character or will and the like, commonly imparts an impression of ugliness. . . .
>
> Further, some actions that cause pain, like blows and wounds, seem ugly; and others that cause delight, like eating to the man who is hungry, seem beautiful. In making such distinctions man differs little from the higher animals, except in the degree of clearness or keenness with which the distinction is made. Voluntary actions may also be distinguished as beautiful or ugly according to the idea of their utility or harmfulness. Distinctions of this sort are possible only to man. Some actions are pleasurable but are judged to be ugly because of their harmful consequences; for example, excess in eating or drinking which causes harm to body and mind. Some disagreeable actions appear beautiful because of their results, such as fatigue in gaining a livelihood, resistance of passions, and the like. Or again, the hardships which one endures in his efforts to discover truths of the universe hitherto unknown, count for nothing compared with his satisfaction in being assured of the truth. Similarly, appropriation of what belongs to others, and acts of envy, and like actions, are felt to be ugly because of the disturbance which they cause to the general peace and safety, which eventually reacts upon the one who did these things.
>
> All these distinctions the human reason is capable of making. One set of actions it calls doing good, the other doing evil. These distinctions are the basis of the recognition of the differences between the virtues and the vices. The distinctions are drawn more or less closely according to the intelligence of the persons who make them. They are recognized as the causes of happiness or misery in this life, and as the reasons for the progress or decline of civilization, and of the strength or weakness of nations. These things man can discover by his reason, or his senses, without the aid of revelation, as may be determined from the case of children

14. Id., op. cit., p. 165, with references to *Risálat*, pp. 73–9, Michel trans., pp. 46–50.

too young to discern the distinctions of the Law, or from the case of primitive man.

He strongly objects, however, to the idea that such rational distinctions are in any way sufficient to afford the controlling moral force that is required in human society. Here he finds a necessary place for religion: "For religion is the most potent factor in the formation of moral traits, not only for the great mass of people but also for the chosen few; and its authority over their souls is greater than the authority of reason, which is the distinguishing trait of their kind."[15] "The perfect religion," he says elsewhere,[16] "consists of knowledge and experience, intellect and heart, proof and acceptance, thought and emotion. If religion is restricted to one of these two elements, one of its bases has dropped out; and it cannot stand upon the other alone." "The essential morality advocated by Muhammad Abduh may be summed up in the words: 'faith in God alone, and sincerity in the performance of the prescribed religious duties (*'ibádah*); and the mutual aid of all men, one to another, in the day of good, and the prevention of evil in so far as they are able.' This, he says, is the essential message of the one universal religion of God, which is the same in all ages. It is characteristic of all his teaching that he attaches the greatest importance to these three fundamental duties, or rather attitudes, of religion: faith, sincerity, mutual co-operation."[17]

In the opinion of modern Muslim thinkers the fundamental idea in Islam carries with it the gravest ethical responsibility. Man has been granted by Allah what has been described in the Qur'án as *vicegerency*, and it is his moral duty to be appreciative of this his high calling, and to strive to attain to those qualities of character that are recognized in the attributes of Allah himself. Man was made vicegerent (*khalífa*) on the face of the earth (ii. 30–3), and this trust (*imánat*) of vicegerency, refused by the heavens and the earth and the mountains, "man alone undertook to bear" (xxxiii. 72). Such is man's natural place in creation, and on this premise, in so far as Islam makes his duties and privileges explicit, it may be regarded as a religion of Nature. Islam is not confined, however, to natural theology; it is also a religion of revelation. Allah did not leave the human race as his vicegerents without guidance and without provision for the regulation of their conduct:

> Allah it is who hath revealed the word with truth and the Balance (xlii. 17).

15. Id., op. cit., p. 167, with references to *Risálat*, p. 140, Michel trans., p. 86.
16. Id., op. cit., p. 167, with references to *al-Islám wa'l-Naṣráníya*, p. 136.
17. Id., op. cit., p. 168, with references to *al-Islám wa'l-Nasráníya*, p. 47.

The Beneficent God
Hath revealed the Word;[18]
Hath created man;
Hath given him articulate speech.
The Sun and the Moon follow a System,
And the planets and trees bend in adoration,
And the sky, He hath reared it on high,
And *hath set the balance*;
That in the balance ye should not transgress,
But weigh with fairness and not scant the balance (lv. 1–9).

In accord with the lucid explanation that is given by Dr. Sayyid Abdu 'l-Laṭíf,[19] "It is in such figurative language that the Holy Book of Islam points out that the heavens and the earth and whatsoever is between them are not created in sport, but for a serious end, that each object of creation is made subject to the laws intrinsic in its nature in order that it might fulfil its function, and that man, fitted by nature with a sense of balance and discrimination, is to conduct himself in accordance with the laws of his being, and in harmony with the laws governing the rest of creation.

"The primary question with which we have to start is: What position does Islam assign to man in the scheme of divine creation? Does it fit him to translate these beliefs held up for his acceptance into action? The Qur'án does not relegate him to a position of inferiority to any object of creation. He is not inferior in stature in the scale of divine values to the Sun or the Moon or other constellations in the heavens which have formed the objects of worship from a distance in the history of man, or to trees or cattle or fire or water or stones at close range, or again to that body of invisible forces called angels. The Qur'án points out that man is made 'of the goodliest fabric' (xcv. 4), he to whom 'the angels were made to offer obeisance' (vii. 10), and for whom 'whatsoever is in the heavens, and whatsoever is in the earth' are made to do service" (cf. also xlv. 13; cxxxviii. 20; and xvi. 12).

"Thus raised in the scale of creation and placed immediately next to God, man's superiority to the rest of creation is further specified

18. In his translation of *al-kitáb* as "the Word" (in xlii. 17) the author has taken some liberty with the text. The word *al-kitáb* should be translated as "the writing" or "the scripture". Similarly, in his translation of Sura lv. 1, "The Beneficent God hath revealed the Word", the Arabic says rather, "hath revealed the Qur'án" ('allama'l-Qur'án), which may be rendered "the Reading" or "the Reciting". It is important to take note of the special translations, for we find that the author utilizes them to rather beg the question of the identification of the Qur'án with the Logos, with particular reference to the New Testament passage, John i. 1, "In the beginning was the Word, and the Word was with God, and the Word was God."

19. *The Concept of Society in Islam*, and *Prayers in Islam*, by Dr. Sayyid 'Abdu 'l-Laṭíf, pp. 74, Hyderabad Printing Works, 1937, pp. 10–11.

by investing him with the privilege of living on earth as the vicegerent of God Himself" (cf. xx. 30; vi. 166; and xxxviii. 27).

"Such is the position, such the dignity that distinguishes man from the rest of creation. It is with this consciousness that he is required to pursue his path in life. Not merely this, he is made aware of another truth of his nature. The Qur'án declares that man is not born with any stigma attached to his soul. He is not born an untouchable, or handicapped with the pollution of any original sin, committed either by himself in a previous birth of which he has no knowledge or by any of his remote ancestors. He is, as the Qur'án says, born with a balanced soul, without any inherent weaknesses therein, and free from any obligations to suffer for any action except his own. His relation to God is thus equalized amongst his own kind, and no distinction in this respect is made between man and woman."

> Whosoever followeth the right course, it is only for the good of his own soul that he doeth so; and whosoever followeth the wrong course doeth so to his own hurt. No responsible soul shall bear another's responsibility (xvii. 15).

> I will not suffer the work of any among you that worketh, whether male or female, to be lost; the one of you is of the other (iii. 194).

> By the soul of Him who balanced it and infused into the same the sense of discrimination and the power of choosing between the wrong and the right, happy is he who keepeth it pure, and unhappy is he who corrupteth it (xci. 7–10).

This statement by Dr. Laṭíf is an excellent summary of the basic principle of Muslim ethics. The supporting texts from the Qur'án have been judiciously selected, and the argument in general is consistent with the demands of ethical monotheism, whether in Judaism, Christianity, or Islam. It is upon this conception of man's God-intended *vicegerency*, he maintains, that the Qur'án distinguishes right from wrong, and evaluates knowledge and appreciates power.

"His (man's) role of vicegerency", this modern expositor proceeds to show, "is not difficult of comprehension if we refer ourselves to the Islamic concept of God in relation to His attributes. 'Believe and work' is the commandment; work, by 'investing yourself with divine attributes'. And to what end? Here is what the messenger of God himself points out. Says he:

> Respect the ways of Allah, and be affectionate to the family of Allah.

Says he again:

> All creatures of God are His family; and he is the most beloved of God who loveth best His creatures.

"The function of vicegerency has, therefore," as the author

indicates, "to be exercised towards that end, and is to be interpreted in terms of the good that man can offer, not only to his fellow man, but to every living object on earth, who all form together the family of God, every one of whom has a being from their Maker 'unto whom they all will be gathered' (vi. 38).

"Of all the attributes of God with which man should imbue himself in order to fit himself for the task of vicegerency, the primary requisite is the attribute that works for life and movement. It has already been pointed out that the Qur'án makes it explicit that whatsoever is in the heavens and whatsoever is in the earth are intended to subserve to the well-being of man. Only, he is required to reflect over the laws of their nature and make a proper use of them. That is the way of achieving power, and the only means of getting at it is knowledge, the acquisition of which, in the words of the Prophet, 'is a duty on every Muslim'."

The author then quotes the tradition[20] that the Prophet had given command: "Acquire knowledge. It enables the possessor to distinguish right from wrong; it lights the way to heaven; it is our companion when friendless, it guides us to happiness; it sustains us in misery; it is a weapon against enemies and an ornament among friends."

"Such is the distinction," says Dr. Laṭíf, "between right and wrong which the Qur'án keeps before our minds, and which is reflected in the commandment we have already quoted: 'Respect the ways of Allah; and be affectionate to the family of Allah.' All that a Muslim feels or thinks or does should be in pursuance of this commandment; and that is the *right* action. On the other hand, anything that he feels or does in contravention of this commandment is the *wrong* contemplated by the Qur'án. The distinction is thus fixed in the very highest truth of human life, and is manifest in the ethics of Islam, whether it concerns a Muslim's own personal well-being or concerns his relations with his kith and kin, his neighbours, or strangers, or even those who are his enemies, or his conduct towards the dumb creatures. The personal virtues of kindliness, purity, chastity, love, affection, honesty, truth, respect for covenants, forbearance, forgiveness, trustworthiness, justice, mercy, and the like are not mere luxuries to be indulged in at convenience, but are indispensable for right living."

After giving other selected passages from the Qur'án, with his ethical interpretations, the author reaches the conclusion that "the compulsory duties of prayer, fasting, the paying of the poor-due, and the pilgrimage are merely the more important details of this work, and aim at self-discipline and self-purification, and the cultivation of the highest virtues of unselfish service to one's fellow beings, and strengthen the sense of unity and solidarity, first among the members of the faith, and through them among the rest of mankind."[21]

20. Id., op. cit., pp. 33–41.

21. Id., op. cit., p. 43.

The best known of the modern ethical interpretations of Islam by Indian writers is that of the late Dr. Muhammad Iqbál, in his *Reconstruction of Religious Thought in Islam*, where his discussion of man's immortality affords an excellent example of a sincere effort by a modern scholar to interpret the Qur'án to his own satisfaction as a philosopher.[22]

"The Qur'ánic view of destiny," he writes, "is partly ethical, partly biological." The statements of a biological nature, which he says cannot be understood "without a deeper insight into the nature of life", are illustrated by what is revealed in regard to man's first emergence in the spatio-temporal order:

> Now of fine clay have We created man: There We placed him, a moist germ, in a safe abode; then we made the moist germ a clot of blood: then made the clotted blood into a piece of flesh; then made the piece of flesh into bones: and We clothed the bones with flesh: then brought forth man of yet another make (xxiii. 12–14).

These verses make clear the first of three Qur'ánic teachings in regard to man's place in the universe, namely, that "his ego has a beginning in time, and did not pre-exist its emergence in the spatio-temporal order". The second clear teaching is that there is no possibility of man's return to this earth, which is confirmed by reference to verse 102 of Sura xxiii, in which it is represented that on the day of reckoning the godless will beg to be allowed to return to earth to accomplish the good that they have left undone during their lives; but that there is behind them a *barzakh*, which bars the way, "until the day when they shall be raised again". *Barzakh* is a Persian and Arabic word which Zamakhsharí has made equivalent to *ḥá'il*, an obstacle, which he interprets in a moral sense as a divine prohibition. Other commentators explain it as some sort of physical barrier that stands between hell and paradise, or as the grave itself, which lies between this life and the next.[23] Dr. Iqbál interprets it as "a state, perhaps of some kind of suspense between Death and Resurrection".

In this connexion it should be pointed out that he considers that the Qur'án does not base the possibility of resurrection on the evidence of the actual resurrection of an historical person, as does Christianity, but that "he seems to take and argue resurrection as a universal phenomena of life, in some sense true even of birds and animals". For in verse 38 of Sura vi we find this declaration: "No kind of beast is there on earth, nor fowl that flieth with its wings, but is a folk (community) like you: nothing have We passed over in the Book: then unto their Lord shall they be gathered."

The third of these teachings in the Qur'án to which Dr. Iqbál

22. Sir Muhammad Iqbál, *The Reconstruction of Religious Thought in Islam*, Oxford, 1934, pp. 109–12.

23. *Encyclopædia of Islam*, art. "Barzakh", by Baron Carra de Vaux.

ascribes the greatest importance is that man's state of being finite is not a misfortune. Here is taught, as he says, "the irreplaceable singleness" of man's individuality, and that "he is to see for himself the consequences of his past action and to judge the possibilities of his future". Verses 95–6 in Sura xix and verse 14 in Sura xvii are given in evidence: "Verily there is none in the Heavens and in the Earth but shall approach the God of Mercy as a servant. He hath taken note of them with exact numbering: and each of them shall come to Him on the day of resurrection as a single individual." . . . "And every man's fate have We fastened about his neck: and on the Day of Resurrection will we bring forth to him a book which shall be proffered to him wide open: 'Read thy book, there needeth none but thyself to make out an account against thee this day.' "

Here Dr. Iqbál makes the significant comment: "Whatever may be the final fate of man it does not mean the loss of individuality. The Qur'án does not contemplate complete liberation from finitude as the highest state of human bliss. The 'unceasing reward' of man consists in his gradual growth in self-possession, in uniqueness, and in the intensity of his activity as an ego."

In verse 69 of Sura xxxix it is represented that there are those who will be exempt from final destruction: "And there shall be a blast on the trumpet, and all who are in the Heavens and all who are in the Earth shall faint away, *save those in whose case God wills otherwise.*"

"Who can be the subject of this exception?" asks Dr. Iqbál, "but those in whom the ego has reached the very highest point of intensity! And the climax of this development is reached when the ego is able to retain full self-possession, even in the case of a direct contact with the all-embracing Ego. As the Qur'án says of the Prophet's vision of the Ultimate Ego: 'His eye turned not aside, nor did it wander' (lviii. 17).

"This," concludes Dr. Iqbál, "is the ideal of perfect manhood in Islam. Nowhere has it found a better literary expression than in a Persian verse which speaks of the holy Prophet's experience of divine illumination:

> Moses fainted away by a mere surface illumination of Reality:
> Thou seest the very substance of Reality with a smile."

As a mystic Iqbál gave wholesome emphasis to the idea of the "questing God". One of his appreciative critics has expressed his thought in straightforward prose: "God is in search of man even when man forgets Him. When he turns toward God, a state of tense expectancy is created, which is like the tenseness between two positive and negative electric poles brought near each other. The flash of the electric spark is like the sudden splendour of the actual vision. . . . There is something oddly thrilling and attractive about a humanity so gracelessly lost to the sense of its high destiny, that instead of it seeking God it is pursued by a questing God."[24]

The impetus that Iqbál has given to Islamic thought, however, is due mainly to a practical appreciation of daily effort and of continued struggle. "To him the joy of the journey is not in the arrival but in the perpetual tramp, with always the possibility of a new adventure around the corner, and the prospect of the unusual and exciting beyond the hill. Ceaseless effort and not repose is what gives zest to life."[25]

"The moral and religious ideal of man," he writes, "is not self-negation but self-affirmation, and he attains to this ideal by becoming more and more individual, more and more unique. The Prophet said, 'Create in yourselves the attributes of Allah,' and thus man becomes unique by becoming more and more like the most unique Individual."[26]

"In man the centre of life becomes an Ego or Person. Personality is a state of tensions and can continue only if that state is maintained. If the state of tension is not maintained relaxation will ensue. Since personality, or the state of tension, is the most valuable achievement of man, he should see that he does not revert to a state of relaxation. That which tends to maintain the state of tension tends to make us immortal. Thus the idea of personality gives us a standard of value; it settles the problem of good and evil. That which fortifies personality is good, that which weakens it is bad. . . . The ultimate end of all human activity is life—glorious, powerful, exuberant! All human art must be subordinated to this final purpose, and the value of everything must be determined in reference to its life-yielding capacity. The highest art is that which awakens our dormant will-force and nerves us to face the trials of life manfully. All that brings drowsiness and makes us shut our eyes to Reality around, on the mastery of which alone life depends, is a message of decay and death."[27]

It is this philosophy that sustained tension and struggle are essential in human personality that is illustrated by the fable of the ruling tigers and the sheep:

> One of the sheep that was clever and acute,
> Old in years, cunning as a weather-beaten wolf,
> Being grieved at the state of his fellows
> And sorely vexed by the violence of the tigers,
> Made complaint of the course of Destiny,
> And sought by craft to restore his fortunes.

24. *al-Iqbál as a Thinker*, Symposium, Lahore, 1944, pp. 211 and 225.
25. Ibid., p. 225.
26. *Asrár-i-Khudí*, trans. R. A. Nicholson, Introduction, xviii–xix, *The Secrets of the Self*, Macmillan & Co., 1920.
27. Ibid., Introduction, xxi–xxii.

By force we sheep cannot escape from the tiger,
Our legs are silver, his paws are steel.
'Tis not possible, however much one exhorts and counsels,
To create in a sheep the disposition of a wolf.
But to make the ferocious tiger a sheep—that is possible,
To make him unmindful of his nature—that is possible.

Thus it was that "he that used to make sheep his prey now embraced a sheep's religion. The tigers took kindly to a diet of fodder: at length their tigerish nature was broken . . . the wakeful tiger was lulled to slumber by the sheep's charm: he called his decline Moral Culture."[28]

When he was addressing himself to the Muslims of India, who had allowed themselves, as he considered, to become devoid of the active virtues, he wrote[29]:

O thou that hast grown from the earth like a rose,
Thou too art born of the womb of Self.
Do not abandon Self! Persist therein!
Be a drop of water and drink up the ocean!
Glowing with the light of Self as thou art,
Make Self strong, and thou shalt endure.

"The self", as Dr. Ishrat Hasan has indicated,[30] "is at once the starting and the basic point of his thought. It is the self which affords him a highroad to metaphysics, because it is the intuition of the self which makes metaphysics possible for him. Iqbál claims himself to have had this intuition. The Self is a veritable reality. It exists, and exists in its own right. We know by intuition that it is most real. We can intuit its reality directly. Intuition of the self thus gives us a direct and unflinching conviction of the reality of our own experience. And further, intuition not only affirms the reality of the self, but discloses to us its essence and nature also. Self, as revealed in intuition, is essentially directive, free, and immortal."

In comparing the ethical viewpoint of Iqbál with that of Jalál al-Dín Rúmí, Dr. Khalifa 'Abdu 'l-Hakim has written the following suggestive summary[31]:

"Both are poets of Islam. The poetry of both is philosophic. Both, despite being masters of the realms of reason, give preference to experience over reason. Both seek to fortify the Self instead of denying its reality. Both contend that there is no contradiction between the Self and Selflessness if they are rightly understood, that one without the other is indeed vain and meaningless. Both differ with regard to the question of *Taqdír* (or predestination) from the opinions held by

28. *Asrári-i-Khudí*, trans. R. A. Nicholson, pp. 48–55.
29. Ibid., p. 122. Cf. also Shushtery, *Outlines of Islamic Culture*, ii, p. 455.
30. Dr. Ishrat Hasan Enver, *The Metaphysics of Iqbál*, Lahore, 1944, p. 31.
31. *al-Iqbál as a Thinker*, Lahore, 1944. Cf. ch. by Dr. Khalifa 'Abu 'l-Hakim.

the generality of people. Both believe that *Taqdír* does not mean that actions of each individual have been determined by God beforehand, but that *Taqdír* is nothing more than the law of life. Both are evolutionary thinkers. Not only man but rather the whole universe is rising from a lower to a higher level. There is no limit to the progress of man. By the power of his desire and purity of endeavour new worlds may not only be revealed to man but even created by him. Both believe Adam as portrayed in the Holy Qur'án to be the ideal which mankind must strive to realize. Both regard endeavour as life and lack of endeavour as death. Both believe immortality to be determined by endeavour for immortality. Both are completely at home with the body of thought that had been created before them and seek to bring contradictory concepts on to a higher level of thought with a view to discovering or effecting harmony between them. Owing to this natural and inborn similarity between them Iqbál considers himself a disciple of Rúmi."

11

SUMMARY AND APPRAISAL

Moral Stamina of Muhammad's Race. Honour is defined as "high regard or esteem, whether felt, given, or received", and it is said to imply "a sense of what is due or right and fidelity to one's obligations". Thus in the phrase "code of honour" the word connotes "a system of reciprocal rights and obligations".[1]

In the early stages of social development, as among the tribes of pre-Islamic Arabia, the requirements of honour may appear at times to involve a conflict with ethical right. If a man's wife does something to humiliate or taunt him he may think that his honour requires that he should run away and leave her. Or if a neighbour injures him, his retaliation must be of a nature to do more than match the injury. It is easy to see what is meant by the suggestion that "shame is the guardian of honour".[2]

Individuals within a tribe, and also in inter-tribal relationships, conduct themselves as men of honour in expectation of either blame or praise. There is an emotional self-consciousness that accompanies their sense of honour that runs the gamut between a satisfying pride and a mortifying shame. This gave the panegyrics of the early poets significance, and it gave poignancy also to their jibes. The social psychologists tell us that this emotion, which is excited by praise or blame, "is second to none in the extent of its influence upon social behaviour".[3] It is closely related to that recognition of moral approval and moral disapproval on which Westermarck expatiates, and to which he ascribes "all moral concepts which are used as predicates in moral judgements".[4]

While Jewish and Christian ideals of conduct were not entirely unknown in parts of pre-Islamic Arabia, still we recognize that those virtues and vices that are mentioned as most characteristic, e.g. Ḥátim al-Ṭá'ís being generous to the point of prodigality, the clemency of the Banu Ṭamím and the cruel requirements of the vendetta (*th'ár*), all these are representative of a kind of moral stamina in Muhammad's race. Whether for good or for evil, their

1. *Encyclopædia of Religion and Ethics*, vi, p. 771.
2. Haering, *Ethics of the Christian Life*, English trans., p. 257.
3. *E.R.E.*, vi, p. 772; with reference to MacDougall, *Social Psychology*, p. 145.
4. Westermarck, *Christianity and Morals*, p. 6.

qualities of character were staunch and hard, for they were made in the desert. Accustomed to the pinch of famine and the ever-present fact of death, the early Arabs practised infanticide (though this was generally discountenanced by Muhammad's time), and had repeated recourse to raids for plunder. They were a people who were proud and self-reliant, habituated to the use of force, who discriminated instinctively between the status of the master and the slave, the victor and the vanquished. Nevertheless they knew what it was to right wrongs, to show loyalty of friendship at great sacrifice, and to stand in sorrow and in awe at the graves of their loved ones. Such were the people whom Muhammad was to serve as a "prophet of Allah".

Special Privileges of the Quraish. The Quraish, however, Muhammad's own tribe, had become accustomed to the enjoyment of special privileges and to the exercise of authority.[5] A full century before the rise of Islam they had displaced the Banú Khuzá'a as the rulers of Mecca and had secured and maintained the possession of the sanctuary of the Ka'ba. Soon they were divided into ten clans and had established several trading colonies at stopping places on the caravan road to the Indian Ocean. Of these settlements for trading purposes the town of Ṭá'if was the most important, and it was to this town that Muhammad first appealed for refuge when he saw that he would have to flee from Mecca. But the men of Ṭá'if took sides with their fellow Quraish in Mecca, and in consequence of this the banished "prophet" went perforce to Yathrib, a town that did not belong to any of the clans of the Quraish but to the Jewish tribes of Quraiẓa and Naḍír,[6] along with a minority population of non-Jewish Arabs—the Khazrajís and the Awsís.

It is of interest to note that the Quraish of Mecca were renowned for the virtues of rulers and the vices of exploiters. Their *ḥilm* (clemency) is frequently mentioned, a kind of ruling quality or "equilibrium of the intellectual faculties". At the same time, as merchants and as the custodians of the sanctuary, it appears that they were nicknamed "sharks" by the Bedouins. This has been regarded as satire, "directed against the rapacity and aggrandizement of Muhammad's fellow tribesmen". We are told also that they were accustomed to hire Abyssinians to fight for them, and that in the estimation of the nomadic tribes this suggested that their settled life had made them soft and deficient in bravery.[7]

Beliefs Fundamental for the Ethics of Islam. In bold religious proclamations that he declared repeatedly while he was still in Mecca, whether he preached to his own people or to interested groups of

5. *Encyclopædia of Islam*, art. "Ḳuraish".
6. Ya'qúbí (ed. Houtsma, II, pp. 49, 52) gives traditional authority for considering that they were Jewish clans of the Arabic tribe of Djudhám.
7. *Encyclopædia of Islam*, art. "Ḳuraish".

pilgrims, Muhammad made clear three beliefs which came to be regarded as fundamental for the ethics of Islam.

1. *Belief in Allah.* The first of these beliefs is the recognition of Allah as the Creator, whose will is not to be resisted, who sees and hears all that is done by mankind (ii. 233, 237; xxiv. 28), and whose marvellous works must be recognized. A recent Muslim writer has stated,[8] "The Qur'án draws the attention of its readers by pointing to Nature, its laws and phenomena—the gathering of clouds, the fall of rain, the growth of plants, the existence of animal and human life, the movement of the stars, the rise and fall of nations, the change of seasons, life, death, historical events and mythical wonders. In all of these we can detect the same law prevalent: that in all apparent diversity there is a unity of purpose and therefore unity of the originator."

After declaring, "God it is who hath created the heavens and the earth and all that is between them in six days; then He ascended His throne", Muhammad proclaimed, "Save Him ye have no patron, and none to plead for you." Therefore he asked, "Will ye not then reflect?" (xxxii. 3).

Again, after explaining how Allah had shaped man and breathed of His Spirit into him, he said, "and Allah gave you hearing and seeing hearts". This he followed with the challenge, "What little thanks do ye return?" (xxxii. 8).

This argument, or belief, is frequently summarized, as in Sura iii. 188: "Verily, in the creation of the heavens and of the earth, and in the succession of the night and of the day, are signs for men of understanding heart: who, standing, and sitting, and reclining, bear God in mind, and muse on the creation of the heavens and of the earth." Likewise in Sura xl. 66, 67: "It is God who hath given you the earth as a sure foundation, and over it built up the Heaven, and formed you, and made your forms beautiful, and feedeth you with good things. This is God your Lord, Blessed then be God the Lord of the Worlds! He is the Living One. No God is there but He. Call then upon Him and offer Him a pure worship. Praise be to God the Lord of the Worlds!"

2. *Belief in the Day of Judgement.* After death, which men have no power to prevent, Allah will demand of all men an accounting. Thus Muslims are assured in the Qur'án: "Then unto Him shall ye return; and then shall He declare unto you that which ye have wrought" (vi. 60). "When death overtaketh one of the wicked, he saith, 'Lord, send me back again, that I may do the good which I have left undone.' . . . The fire shall scorch their faces and their lips shall quiver therein. 'What! Were not my signs rehearsed unto you? and did ye not treat them as lies?'" (xxiii. 101, 102, 106). "And every man's fate have we fastened about his neck, and on the

8. Shushtery, *Outlines of Islamic Culture*, vol. i, pp. 11 ff.

resurrection will we bring forth to him a book which shall be given to him wide open" (xvii. 24).

3. *Belief in Virtuous Deeds*. The belief that there will be rewards for virtuous deeds is closely connected with the belief in the Day of Judgement, when to each man will be given the "Book of Reckoning" and when his deeds will be weighed in the "Balances". Of the former we are told: "And each shall have his book put into his hand: and thou shalt see the wicked in alarm at that which is therein: and they shall say, 'O woe to us! what meaneth this Book? It leaveth neither small nor great unnoted down!' And they shall find all that they have wrought present to them, and thy Lord will not deal unjustly with anyone" (xviii. 47). Also somewhat more fully we read: "On that day ye shall be brought before Him: none of your hidden deeds shall remain hidden. And he who shall have his book given to him in his right hand will say to his friends, 'Take ye it, read my book; I ever thought that to this my reckoning I should come.' And his shall be a life that shall please him well, in a lofty garden, whose clusters shall be near at hand: 'Eat ye and drink with healthy relish, as the meed of what ye sent on beforehand in the days which are past.' But he who will have his book given into his left hand, will say, 'O that my book had never been given me! And that I had never known my reckoning! O that death had made an end of me! My wealth hath not profited me! My power hath perished from me!' —Lay ye hold on him and chain him, then at the Hell-fire burn him!" (lxix. 18–30).

Of the "Balances" also we learn: "Just balances will we set up for the Day of Resurrection, neither shall any soul be wronged in aught: though, were work but the weight of a grain of mustard seed, we would bring it forth to be weighed: and our reckoning will suffice" (xxi. 48). "And with knowledge will we tell them of their deeds, for we were not absent from them. The weighing on that day, with justice! and they whose balances are heavy, these are they who shall be happy. And they whose balances shall be light, these are they who have lost their souls, for that to our signs they were unjust" (vii. 6–9).[9]

9. The use of the Balances to symbolize the giving of justice on the Day of Judgement, or in the weighing of good deeds, is common in Eastern literature. In the Egyptian "Book of the Dead" there is a picture of the weighing of the heart of a good man against an idol called Má, or Truth. Also from the "Testament of Abraham", which was written first in Egypt and then translated into Greek and Arabic, we find that Abraham is represented as having been allowed to see an amazing sort of man, seated on a throne, and engaged in judging the souls of mankind. There were two angels with him, each of whom was busy writing. The one on the right was recording righteous deeds and the one on the left was marking down deeds that were evil. The book for their final entries was on the Table. "And he that stood before the Table, holding the Balance, was weighing the souls, and the angel holding the fire was passing judgement upon them" (cf. Muir, *The Sources of Islam*, pp. 68 ff.).

The Three Codes. Indications as to what the good deeds are that are to weigh heavy on the day of reckoning are to be found in three codes, each of which occurs in a sura that is said to have been revealed in Mecca. The first of these codes, which somewhat resembles the Decalogue, is in Sura xvii, which is called "The Night Journey" (*isrá*), when shortly before the Migration the Prophet is said to have been transported by night from Mecca to Jerusalem[10]: "Glory be to Him who carried His servant by night from the sacred temple of Mecca to the temple that is more remote" (xvii. 1), and "We ordained the vision which we showed thee" (xvii. 62).

In this *first code* there are four positive commands: to know but one God, to be kind to parents, to give to the poor, and to be moderate in spending. There are also seven definite prohibitions: from the practice of infanticide, from adultery, from killing unjustly, from robbing orphans, from cheating in trade, from believing false reports, and from showing pride.

The *second code*, which is in the Sura *al-Furqán*, "The Distinction" (xxv. 64–75), explains that blessedness is conditional, in that it is for those who are lowly; for those who are discriminating in matters that have to do with spending, killing, or chastity; for those who are penitent; and for those who are truthful.

The *third code*, which is in the sura called *Luqmán* (xxxi. 11–17), gives three injunctions with reference to conduct towards Allah: to have gratitude to Him, to associate no other with Him, and to remember that He brings everything to light. It also gives three injunctions for conduct in human relations: to observe duties to parents; to seek in prayer to be steadfast, reasonable, and patient; and to live so as to avoid pride and ignorance.

The Leader's Decisions in Medina. Gradually there came to be a noticeable change in Muhammad's exhortations. Moral precepts that were of a character to be generally accepted, and lessons that were evolved by recounting "histories" from books that had been previously "sent down", began to give way to the authoritative decisions of the community leader. The issues between those who worshipped idols and those who were ready to submit to Allah and His Apostle had been clearly drawn. Those of his own tribe, the Quraish, and the Jews and Christians who refused to grant to Muhammad the authority of a prophet like Moses, all these unbelievers he continued to warn and to threaten in the name of Allah. But the revelations that came after the great crisis, when his avowed followers had to leave Mecca and go to the Jewish town of Yathrib

10. This is all that the Qur'án has to say about the so-called *isrá* (night journey). It should be remarked that there is difference of opinion among the commentators as to whether the verses of the code (23–41), which are included in Sura xvii, were first revealed in Mecca or in Medina. Most probably they were reiterated in Medina.

(afterwards called al-Medina), these revelations express clearly his reaction to opposition and the resentment he felt when he was ridiculed.

At times we find that the Medina revelations seek to justify or to explain the Prophet's personal conduct. Again they lay down directions for proper procedure in prayer and ceremonial ablutions, or in commercial transactions and in retaliation for injuries. Frequently they simply answer those questions that arose from day to day among the men who looked to him as their leader, questions that had to do with debt, the right of inheritance, giving freedom to slaves, and the value of fasting; whether fighting was permissible in the sacred months of peace, how many wives were allowable to an average man, whether the number of the Prophet's wives should be restricted, and how women who are disobedient should be punished; also the punishments that are to be inflicted upon those men or women who are guilty of theft, of adultery, or of apostasy from the faith.

Development of a Legal System. After the death of the Prophet Muhammad, the Muslims soon felt the need of a comprehensive legal system which their own judges would be capable of administering. They could no longer look to Muhammad himself to make decisions. And in so much as he had claimed to be the last of the prophets it was not to be expected that the caliphs who succeeded him in the right to command should likewise assume his authority as a law-giver. For they would not have the advantage of receiving divine revelations and they might easily make mistakes in their interpretations of the Qur'án.

Moreover, the peoples whom the Muslim armies had conquered were accustomed to regular codes of law. Roman law, through the Justinian Code, which was published in A.D. 529, and which led to the completion of the *Institutes* in A.D. 533, and the imposing *Corpus Juris Civilis* in A.D. 565, had become established in the Near East before Muhammad was born. The Persian Empire also was governed by laws that harped back to the Avesta. In these Zoroastrian laws little distinction was made between moral sins and legal crimes, but we find moral, ritual, civic, and hygienic considerations all mingled together. What is called the "Social Code of the Parsis in Sassanian Times" gives information about slaves, partners and joint proprietors, and "decisions of the leaders of the professions, and agreement and disagreement with their decisions; the laws of property, the income of wives, annuities, mortgages, care and adoption of children, the infallibility of officials, etc."[11] And the Jews, with whom the Muslims first came into conflict in Arabia itself, were established also in all the lands of the expanding Empire. They had an elaborately developed system of law, which was both civil and

11. *E.R.E.*, vii, p. 854.

religious, and all the separate laws that came within it were regarded as divine commands. It was the Jewish system of laws with which Muhammad himself was most familiar, and the desire that the Arabs should have a "Book" such as that of the Jews may have had something to do with the growth of the Qur'án as a series of divine revelations upon which a system of law could be established.

Tafsír, Ḥadíth, and 'Ilm al-Fiqh. But the Jews had also developed what they called the Talmud, which was based on the oral and written teachings that came after the inspired books in their canonical scriptures. This teaching had two general divisions. The instructive and edifying narrative portions were called the *haggádá*, and the legal portion was designated the *halákâ*.

The Muslims came naturally to regard the Qur'án (the "Reading") as their basic revelation, which had to be supplemented, however, when Muhammad was no longer alive to adjudicate their difficulties in person. It was supplemented in the first place by the further knowledge that came from the careful perusal of the Qur'án by commentators, knowledge that was called the science of commentary (*'ilm al-tafsír*); and in the second place by the gradual assembling of oral traditions in regard to actions or sayings of Muhammad, knowledge which they designated the science of tradition (*'ilm al-ḥadíth*). Several hundred years had passed before the Jews felt that it was fitting to reduce the *Halákâ* and the *Haggádá* to writing, and similarly the great majority of the codices of Muslim traditions were not compiled until the third century of Islam.

Two main purposes governed the accumulation of this supplementary information. The first purpose was to discover all that could be known about Muhammad himself, and this biographical material about the Prophet came to be called the *Síra*. The second purpose was to gather together all the case histories that would serve in any way to make the developing legal system of the Muslim Empire more explicit, and this study of the customs (*sunna*) of the Prophet came to be the science of jurisprudence (*'ilm al-fiqh*). The importance of this growth of the *Ḥadíth* for Muslim ethics was great indeed. For the Traditions included what Muhammad is said to have claimed in regard to himself as an ethical example, "I am appointed to perfect moral excellencies." They contained what he declared about the legal side of his service, "I am commissioned to establish justice among you." Among them are utterances that expressed his sympathy for the aspirations of the Ṣúfís, "Whoever of my community perseveres in the state in which ye are, and is satisfied with his condition, he shall be one of my comrades in Paradise." There were also sayings that were obviously patterned after well-known teachings of Jesus, as for example that a man should act "so that his left hand does not know what his right hand hath done".

Growth of the Spirit of Legalism. Once the system of jurisprudence was fully developed, with its four "orthodox schools" (the Hanifites, the Sháfi'ites, the Málikites, and the Ḥanbalites), after considerable controversy as to the importance to be attached to legal opinion (*ra'y*), analogy (*qiyás*), and common consent (*ijmá'*), a high regard came to be placed upon the legality of all actions. Since the Law applied also to religious duties and privileges, as well as to civil rights and obligations, it is easy to understand how Islam, like Judaism, soon had to face the fact that for many of its adherents religion had become little more than a form of legalism, in which compliance with what is stipulated in the letter of the law is thought to be more satisfying than a struggle to meet the demands of its spirit.

It would be unfair to suggest, however, that either Judaism or Islam can be reduced to legalism. They are both monotheistic, and sooner or later monotheism breaks the bonds of legalism. And besides this, they are both ethical, and legalism is merely an external semblance of ethical conduct. But we fear that it may be said with sufficient reason that among the mass of the Jewish peoples and likewise among the mass of the Muslim peoples, "an unintelligent, mechanical, self-interested, and even hypocritical observance of the law is the rule". Undoubtedly it would be wrong to exclude a multitude of Christian people from a like indictment, and that in spite of Jesus' own bold revolt against this spirit of legalism, when he insisted that the true fulfilment of the moral law could only be by love to its Author and by the transformation of mankind into a society of mutual love.

The Inadequacy of Legalism. Judaism, Islam, and Christianity must unite in recognizing that legalism (nomism), the view that moral conduct consists in the observance of a law or body of laws, is opposed to those conceptions of morality which postulate an end to be pursued or an ideal to be realized.[12] Legalism is inadequate to "vicegerency".

The general Muslim conception of virtue is similar to that of Paley (Bk. I, ch. vii), who defined virtue as "doing good to mankind, in obedience to the will of God, and for the sake of everlasting happiness". Ethical criticism suggests that seeking virtue on this basis is ultimately a type of hedonism, which earlier Christian thinkers had abandoned under the influence of the Stoic belief in a moral law that is natural to mankind, the fundamental idea being that "nature was infused with reason, and through the divinely implanted reason within him the natural man was enabled to receive the divine grace" (cf. Knudson, *The Principles of Christian Ethics*, pp. 68–71).

The dangers of legalism, in its positively non-ethical aspects, must be kept clearly in mind. It tends to regard a system of laws as a prescribed programme of conduct, without any effort to discern why or wherefore; and such compliance with authoritarian rules serves to

12. *E.R.E.*, ix, pp. 380 ff.

prevent that higher and better form of obedience that comes only with understanding, approval, and acceptance. From fear of punishment or from the hope of reward the letter of the law may be observed, but that observance may be accomplished without any change in character that is of ethical value. The defect of a system of ethics that is founded upon a doctrine of rewards and punishments is that it "reduces conduct to selfish prudence. All moral differences of character vanished into distinctions of shrewdness. There is no place for moral worth or dignity, but only for hire and salary, loaves and fishes. The individual is no law unto himself and has no law within himself. Sin is a great imprudence because of future retribution, but apart from extrinsic consequences it is not intrinsically bad. Virtue consists in doing the will of God for the sake of everlasting happiness. In such a scheme we miss an essential element of the moral character, namely, the love of goodness for itself and not for its extrinsic or adventitious consequences" (cf. B. P. Browne, *The Principles of Ethics*, pp. 85–6). It is not the compliance and subserviency of slaves that a father wants his sons to have in relation to his will for them, but rather that comprehending obedience and loyalty that comes with their true appreciation of him, and that leads, not to the suppression and cramping of their lives, but to the realization of their highest possible capacities.

The terms "legality" and "morality". Confusion in the employment of these terms should be avoided, for the legality of an action expresses its conformity with judicial or legal requirements, whereas the morality of an agent, in obeying or disobeying laws, depends on whether these laws are ethical and on whether the obedience is ethical. A law-giver may be unethical himself if he gives laws that are unethical, and one who obeys laws may have an utterly unethical motive for so doing. And most assuredly, if in the forum of ethical discussion a particular law-giver makes the claim that his laws have come from God, then it is most important that they should be examined as to their ethical or non-ethical character. For it would be sheer blasphemy to attribute anything non-ethical to God; and there is always the possibility that the human agent in the giving of a law, with its particular prohibitions and stipulated permissions, may have had more concern for some immediate and practical expedient than for the continued ethical validity of his legislation.

For example, the conception of obligations to kith and kin is of primary importance in Muslim ethics. Cutting off relationship (*qaṭ-i-raḥim*) is to be deplored. The emotional life that centres in the family should therefore be maintained at a high level. Whatever tends to discredit or depreciate the worth of its individual members is inimical to its strength and unity. For this reason no self-respecting Muslim will want to give his daughter or his sister to serve as a concubine or to live as a temporary wife. He desires rather that she should have an honourable personal status, with security of tenure, in a family relationship that is accepted and approved, not simply by the letter of a given law, but by the social requirements and ethical demands of the present day and age. It is also coming to be generally recognized that the sentiments of affection and confidence that prevail in a family when it is composed of a father and a mother and their own children are stronger and more enduring than the frequently strained and unnatural relationships that characterize a polygamous household. Notwithstanding sanctions with which they may be familiar in the Qur'án and the Ḥadíth, parents of an educated Muslim girl are naturally averse to making a marriage arrangement for her with a man who has one or two or three other wives.

Legal Decision may be Immoral. The judge who hands down a decision in regard to a particular case will have measured the facts in the light of the existing law. He may be entirely satisfied with the legality of his decision, but at the same time he may be convinced that the law on which it was based was itself unethical. For example, if a modern judge were called upon to pronounce sentences according to laws in the Code of Hammurabi, he would necessarily decree the following punishments by mutilations, and in so doing his decisions would have legality according to this ancient code; but at the same time they would be immoral according to any recognized standard of ethics[13]:

(*a*) a nurse who had substituted another child for one who had died in her care would have her breasts cut off so that she would not be in position to do such a thing again;
(*b*) a son who had struck his father would have his hand amputated so that he would not do so again;
(*c*) and a man who had been hired to work on a farm, and who had stolen wheat and vegetables, was to be condemned if these were found in his hands, to having his hands cut off, so that he would no longer carry any wheat and vegetables with those hands.

Muhammad as a Religious Ideal. The actual claims that Muhammad made for himself, in so far as they can be determined from the Qur'án, are more modest than those of the *walí* of the Súfís or the *imám* of the Shí'ites. But after the former had been given the dignity of "divine men" who were really "one with Allah", and the doctrine of sinlessness had been developed comprehensively so as to include all the prophets and all the imáms, on the theory that indeed they *ought* to be sinless if Allah has chosen them to give guidance to mankind, it is in no way unnatural that the actual Muhammad of the Qur'án should be somewhat obscured. The Prophet is described in the Qur'án, as Professor Nicholson has pointed out, as "no more

13. *E.R.E.*, iv, pp. 259–60.

than a man subject to human weaknesses, who receives at intervals the divine revelation, not from God but from an angel. He has never seen God, he does not share God's secrets, he cannot foretell the future, he can work no miracle: he is only the servant and messenger of Allah."[14] It soon seemed desirable, however, that this restricted status of Muhammad that the Qur'án represented should be radically modified. "This historical Muhammad was incredible even to his contemporaries. They could not understand him when he disclaimed all supernatural powers, and when he died, 'Umar (who afterwards became Caliph) swore that he was not dead and would assuredly return and cut off the hands and feet of the blasphemers."[15] Moreover, as further indicated by Professor Nicholson, "every Ṣúfí who adheres to Islam—and for the present we may ignore the wild pantheists and free-thinking dervishes who reject positive religion altogether—must acknowledge that above the saints, even the most perfect of them, stands the Prophet Muhammad. The religious life in Islam could not find its supreme ideal anywhere but in the person of Muhammad."[16]

At the same time we find that there was at least one outstanding exception in this regard, namely, al-Halláj, who wrote with reference to Jesus, that God "appeared to his creatures visibly in the shape of one who eats and drinks".[17] On this Professor Nicholson has said in comment that "while Halláj asserts the pre-existence of Muhammad as the light from which all prophecy emanates, it is not Muhammad but Jesus in whom he finds the perfect type of the 'deified man', whose personality is not destroyed but essentialized, so that he stands forth as the personal witness and representative of God, revealing from within himself *al-Ḥaqq*, the Creator through whom he exists, the Creative Truth in whom he has all his being. You will agree that this is a singular doctrine on the lips of a Muhammadan. It is entirely opposed to pantheism, for it makes the human nature an image of the divine, though not quite in the same sense that caused Christ to say, 'He that hath seen me hath seen the Father' (John 14. 9). A doctrine that is described, even metaphorically, as *ḥulúl* (incarnation), could not take root in Islam. It perished with Halláj and his immediate disciples. The majority of the later Ṣúfís extol him as a martyr who died on the scaffold because he dared to reveal the divine mystery; but they deny that he taught *ḥulúl* and interpret his *ana'l-Ḥaqq* ('I am the Creative Truth') in a Unitarian or monistic sense; thus giving it a flavour of orthodoxy but altogether disguising the features which make it so remarkable. Hence in the development of his ideas by Ibn al-'Arabí and Jílí the

14. R. A. Nicholson, *The Idea of Personality in Súfism*, p. 58. See the Qur'án, xcvi. 10; xviii. 110; xli. 5; xxi. 35; iii. 138.

15. Id., op. cit., p. 58, with reference to al-Ṭabarí, i. 1815, 14 ff.

16. Id., op. cit., p. 57.

17. Massignon, *Kitáb al-Tawásín*, p. 130.

living clash of personality, divine and human, resolves itself into a logical distinction between God and man as aspects of the One Essence, whose attributes receive their most perfect manifestation in the first created Light of Muhammad, the Prophet of Allah."[18]

It is this unrestrained development of the conception of Muhammad as a religious ideal that does most to alienate Christians from that regard for Islam that they would otherwise have. His conviction, his courage, his devotion, even his career as a reformer and as a prophet are freely respected, on the basis of information that is furnished by the Qur'án, but no credence is given by Christians to either legends or doctrines in regard to Muhammad's pre-existence, or to his sinlessness, or to his journey to Paradise and back again, or to his being more than the Qur'án shows that he claimed to be, an ambitious but God-fearing man.

Importance of "the Historical Muhammad". The student who undertakes to understand the Prophet Muhammad as an ethical ideal will find that it is impossible to ignore the discriminating task of getting acquainted with the historical Muhammad. And in his endeavour to assemble all the information about this great man of Arabia that he can regard as truly historical, he will almost certainly be embarrassed by the conceptions in regard to the Prophet which owe their origin to theological speculation or to pious legend. For one who has been brought up in the Muslim faith anything like clear-cut discrimination in such a study of the life of his Prophet will not be easy. But in ethics it is unsafe to play fast and loose with history. We are unable to determine what really occurred by what we now think ought to have taken place. Ethics is normative and has to do with what ought to be, but it is also realistic when it declares that the conduct of a particular individual was not historically what it ought to have been ethically.

Caution in the Use of Traditions. Here is where the greatest difficulty comes in the study of Islam historically. It is the difficulty of estimating the reliability of information that is gained from the Traditions. How much are we to allow for a narrator's disposition to relate what he was disposed to think should have been the reply given by Muhammad when a particular question arose? And if his narrative has been transmitted orally from one generation to another for nearly two hundred years, even the fact of a presumably creditable line of transmission would not protect it from being exaggerated or minimized according to the personal desire of one or other of the transmitters, perhaps from political or sectarian bias or for polemical convenience. Unfortunately, however, apart from the Qur'án and a few books of pre-Islamic poetry, almost the only sources for the study of the historical biography of Muhammad are these collections of Traditions, with the "histories" that are based upon them.

18. R. A. Nicholson, op. cit., pp. 30–1.

From the strictly ethical viewpoint there is one thing about these early Muslim traditionists to be appreciated, namely that they were not under the necessity of thinking about the approval or disapproval of twentieth-century people. They were not writing to please us, and what measured up to their own ethical standards, say from A.D. 822–922, this they considered sufficient. There are present-day writers, however, both within and without the *dár al-Islám*, who are inclined to disregard the Traditions, as being too unreliable to be considered in serious historical studies. But such a position would be devastating, for so large a proportion of Islamic knowledge is based upon the Traditions that at least their general character, and the lines along which they developed, must be taken into account.

Greek Contributions to Muslim Ethics. The Greek contribution to Muslim thought was scientific, ethical, and religious. The avidity of the Greeks for scientific classification and definition made a tremendous impression upon Muhammadan physicians and philosophers. And in the field of ethics as well, the prevailing method of discussing moral questions soon came to be the Aristotelian way of presenting a whole system of inter-related virtues and vices, each connected with the use or misuse of one or other of the powers of the soul. This undoubtedly brought the advantage of a more rational intellectual scrutiny of moral questions. The reason and purpose for obedience to the moral laws were to be discerned and rationally appreciated, and the Muslims who studied *'ilm al-akhláq* (the science of ethics) found less assurance in the observance of legalistic requirements or in mere compliance with authority.

It must be remembered that even the best of the books of the Greeks had the limitations of pre-Christian sources. The observation made by Illingworth in his *Personality: Human and Divine* (p. 8) is important, that "as a rule it is beyond dispute that neither the *universality* nor the *unity* of personality, its two most obviously essential features, were adequately understood in pre-Christian ages". As evidence of Aristotle's unwillingness to grant the benefits of his conception of personality universally we may instance the fact that he was ready to rule out some men on the ground that they were of barbarous origin, others because they were of slave origin, and women he regarded "as nature's failures in the attempt to produce men". That he was likewise unable to unify human nature is clear from his "unsolved dualism between the soul and its organism", and from the fact that he had "no clear conception of the will, and hardly any of the conscience". And in this connexion Illingworth made the further significant statement that for Aristotle "contemporary society was characterized by a fatal divorce between the various departments of life, the public and the private, the moral and the religious, the intellectual and the sensual: excellence in one region being easily allowed to compensate for license or failure in another".

Moral Law in the Interest of the State. In so far as the Greeks synthesized their moral law in relation to the requirements of the State, it was easy for Muslim teachers of moral philosophy to put the demands of the State foremost. For Islam, like Judaism (at least from the time of Moses until the final destruction of the temple in Jerusalem), was a typical theocracy, with the Shrine, the Book, and the Prophet (or prophets). The guiding principle that resulted from the conception of Islam as a theocracy was that the will of the Prophet of Allah, as expressed in the Qur'án and the Sunna, is the will of Allah. And when after the Prophet's death the Arab tribes began to revolt, then the Islamic State, under the leadership of Abu Bakr, declared as a second principle that force must be employed to constrain believers to maintain the economic status, the religious discipline, and the social unity of the Muslim community. Moreover, when the established theocratic State met with opposition from neighbouring peoples a third principle emerged, that because of its supreme authority from Allah Islam must therefore continue aggressive warfare against other people in the interest of the faith. Thus the world was divided into the *dár al-Islám* (Islamic territory) and the *dár al-ḥarb* (war territory).

In the administration of the conquered countries, however, a measure of concession was made in the general acceptance of the principle that the laws and customs of the subjected peoples should be retained as far as possible in consistency with Islamic supremacy.

Among the great majority of the Muslims themselves this synthesis of the moral law with the interests of Islam as a theocratic State tended to confirm and strengthen the legalistic attitude toward questions of personal conduct. The religious authorities gave the decisions that established the laws, and those decisions were based on the Qur'án and the Sunna. There was in general little inquiry into ethical implications, but the fear of punishment and the hope of reward were presented as the most obviously practical considerations. Because of merit that had been accumulated sins would be forgiven, and sins were failures to comply with the requirements of the *sharia* (the Law)—whether they had to do with ritual and ceremonial duties, with household or tribal matters, or with making the pilgrimage, or with failure to take part in the *Jihád* (warfare for the extension of Islam).

The Rise of Rival Dynasties. Very early in the history of Islam we find that the Muslim State became divided against itself. In matters of political organization, and in the interpretation and administration of the *sharia* (law), there was great divergency of opinion. The ideal of a theocratic *dár al-Islám* was retained, but the only possible course that was open to the average Muslim was to swear fealty to one or other of the rival dynasties that sprang up within the Empire. These dynasties were neither established nor maintained in power without exhausting years of bloodshed, and as happens always in protracted periods of warfare, ethical standards and expectations had been so dishonoured and generally ignored that they would come up for serious reconsideration on the return of peace.

Arabic Books on Ethics. Under the Buwaihids (or Buyids), Ibn Maskawaihi (d. A.D. 1030), who utilized the work of the Syrian Christian translator, Yaḥyá ibn 'Adí (d. A.D. 974), wrote the *Tahdhíb al-Akhláq* ("The Correction of Dispositions"). Didactic and analytical, this book was written on the assumption that there is rational sanction and authority for moral conduct, which is not to be thought of as though it were determined solely by the guidance of commands and prohibitions in the Qur'án, but it is in accord rather with man's essential nature. The development of the capacities of the soul and the healing of the diseases of the soul are the two great functions of ethics.

Under the Seljuqs, the theologian al-Ghazálí (d. A.D. 1111) gave attention to the principles of moral conduct in his massive *Iḥyá' al-'Ulúm al-Dín* ("The Revivification of Religious Sciences"). In the third book of this work, particularly, and in his *Mízán al-'Amal* ("Balance of Conduct"), he has endeavoured to show how changes in the individual's moral condition may be achieved. It is in this connexion that he attributes a degree of freedom of choice to the individual man, pointing out the process of psychological determination that takes place, while at the same time he ascribes to God alone any real power in causation. That man's highest moral development lies in his imitating (*takhalluq*) the qualities (*akhláq*) of Allah he made clear in a book that he called "The Highest Aim in the Explanation of the Excellent Names of Allah" (*al-maqsad al-asná fí sharh 'asmá' al-ḥusná*).

Persian Translations and Revisions. About two generations after the time of al-Ghazálí, there were numerous Shi'ite scholars who took refuge in the mountain fortresses of the Ismá'ílís. They had fled from the persecutions of the later Seljuq rulers, who had proved to be extremely intolerant Sunnis. One of these Shi'ite scholars, a young man, was Naṣír al-Dín al-Ṭúsí (d. A.D. 1274). He was astrologer to the famous Ismá'ílí chieftain 'Alá al-Dín, the very "Old Man of the Mountain" who has been made famous by Marco Polo's description.

But before Naṣír al-Dín Ṭúsí went to serve 'Alá al-Dín he was associated with his subordinate, the governor of the fortress at Sartakht, whose name was Násir al-Dín Mutasham. It was there in Sartakht that he completed the translation into Persian of Ibn Maskawaihi's *Tahdhíb al-Akhláq* ("The Correction of Dispositions"), and he named his finished work, in honour of his patron, the "Ethics of Násir" (*Akhláq-i-Násirí*). It was more than a translation, as it involved revision and further elaboration.

When the Mongols came in hordes from Central Asia, moving

towards Baghdad and carrying destruction with them, Naṣír al-Dín al-Ṭúsí was sent to negotiate terms for the surrender of the Ismá'ílí fortresses. Thus he came in touch with the Moghal leader Khulagu Khan and accompanied him on his expedition to Baghdad. On this expedition he served as astrologer and counsellor, and it was this surging south of the Mongols that ended in the sacking of Baghdad and the overthrow of the Abbasid Caliphate in A.D. 1258.

In Baghdad and later on in Shiráz, Naṣír al-Dín al-Ṭúsí gave his time to astrology and the preparation of astronomical tables. In the religious field his later writings are on Shi'ite and Ṣúfí beliefs, prayers, and traditions. But at present he is remembered more particularly for his early book on ethics.

This book, the *Akhláq-i-Násiri*, held its place in restricted academic circles until the fifteenth century. For after Timur and his Turkomans had swept over Irán and Iráq, mercilessly killing men, women, and children wherever they went, those who survived felt a desperate need to restore a sense of moral values in Muslim society. Again, however, the barbarians who had ravaged their territories accepted their faith, and one of the later Turkoman rulers, Uzun Hasan, gathered about him a circle of Muslim scholars. One of the men in this group of scholars at the court of Uzun Hasan, a man of outstanding literary ability, Jalál al-Dín al-Dawwání (d. A.D. 1501), accepted the commission to revive the study of ethics by writing a new book. His new book, the *Akhláq-i-Jalálí*, which he wrote in Persian and illustrated profusely and appropriately from the Ṣúfí poets, follows the *Akhláq-i-Násiri* very closely. Both of these Persian translations, as well as the original Arabic work of Ibn Maskawaihi, are still read and studied throughout the Muslim world. It may be said that all later books that deal with ethics are based on these three early works.

One of these derived books, a kind of teachers' manual, is the *Akhláq-i-Humayúní*, a manuscript of which is in the Garrett Collection in Princeton University Library. It is of special interest because of its charts and tables, which serve as a summary of the ethics that came to Islam through the Greek philosophers.

Other works, such as the *Akhláq-i-Muhsiní* and the *Miráj al-Sa'ádat*, which are reviewed in the text (ch. vi), and also more recent books of the kind that have been published with the endorsement of the modern bureau of Education in Irán, examples of which are the *Akhláq-i-Rúhí* and the *Akhláq-i-Muḥtashamí*, attempt to embellish and at the same time to simplify the general analysis of virtues and vices that has been handed down throughout the centuries. They add confirming verses from the Qur'án, proverbs and narratives from the Traditions, and pertinent selections from the Ṣúfí poets.

The Subjective Ethics of the Súfís. The moral values in the subjective ethics of Ṣúfism are suggested in the following observations:

1. The quest for inner sincerity in contrast to merely outward conformity is undoubtedly commendable.

2. The belief that there should be a higher motive for human conduct than either fear of punishment or hope of reward is a worthy ethical ideal.

> If it seeks to deny the influence of fears and hopes in the spiritual realm as well as in the material, the realization of this ideal will become vastly more difficult. It will seldom occur in actual individual experience, though there is nothing to prevent the systematic presentation of pious pretensions in this direction.

3. The conception that man has a capacity for spiritual development, with requirements that differ from those of his animal nature, is a fundamental premise of religious faith.

> This spiritual development is explained both as the object of his creation and as the goal of his evolution. It is his spiritual capacity that constitutes man's element of likeness to God, or that degree of moral affinity which makes personal relations to God comprehensible. "Only in so far as personal relations are allowed to exist between the worshipper and his God, can that God be properly described as personal."[19]

4. The doctrine that the right purpose for the purification of the soul is that it may come to know and love God is a teaching that is praiseworthy.

> Its development in Islam is thought to have been considerably influenced by Hellenistic and Christian ideas.[20]

5. The Ṣúfí's knowledge (*ma'rifat*) of God is linked with his love (*mahabbat*) of God. It resembles the gnosis of Hellenistic religion and involves that high degree of self-effacement that leads at times to an ecstatic contemplation of God.

> "It involves the effacement of the individual self and the substitution of divine qualities for human; yet all this is the act of God." And as Professor Nicholson has gone on to explain, "just as St. Paul said to his Galatian converts, 'Now that ye have come to know God, or rather to be known of God', so the Ṣúfí *'árif* or gnostic imputes all his knowledge to Him who by revealing Himself causes the veil of 'otherness' and duality to disappear and the knower to be one with the known."[21]

6. The consciousness of freedom for moral action is made clear in Jalál al-Dín's assertion "that freedom in the full sense of the term belongs only to that man who loves God so perfectly that his will is

19. C. C. J. Webb, *God and Personality*, p. 11, quoted by R. A. Nicholson, op. cit., p. 2.
20. Dr. Margaret Smith, *Early Mysticism in the Near and Middle East*, pp. 98–9 .
21. R. A. Nicholson, op. cit., p. 10.

one with the divine will": and in that unity of feeling the antithesis of freedom and necessity disappears[22]:

> The word "compulsion" makes me impatient for Love's
> sake,
> 'Tis only he who loves not that is fettered by "compulsion".
> This is communion with God, not "compulsion",
> The shining of the moon, not a cloud.
> Or if it be "compulsion", it is not ordinary "compulsion",
> It is not the compulsion exerted by self-will, inciting us to
> sin. (*Masnavi*, Búláq, vol. i, 59.)

7. Appreciation of the significance of man's capacity to receive divine qualities is subject both to the error of neglect (*tafrít*) and to the error of exceeding the bounds (*ifráṭ*). The Ṣúfí conception of *faná'*, as the annihilation of the human personality through absorption in the Divine Being, is in the writer's opinion a clear instance of the error of *ifráṭ* ("exceeding the bounds").

Faná' is described by the Arabian mystic, Ibn al-Faríd (d. A.D. 1235), "as a process wherein the soul is stripped of all its desires, affections, and interests, so that in ceasing to will for itself it becomes an object of the divine will, that is, the beloved of God; and that which loves it and which it loves is now its inward and real self that has 'passed away'. Thus the unified personality finds subject and object of worship in itself:

> "'Both of us are a single worshipper who, in respect of the united state, bows himself to his own essence, in every act of bowing. None prayed to me but myself, nor did I pray to anyone but myself in the performance of every genuflexion.'"[23]

While there were to be found among the Ṣúfís men who were sincere and typical mystics, profound thinkers and inspiring poets, in whose works we find much that is of ethical value, men who made a rightful protest, as Sir Muhammad Iqbál has written,[24] against "the verbal quibbles of our early doctors" and the "dry-as-dust subtleties of contemporary legists", nevertheless, in seeking to make clear what it would mean for mankind to attain unto the very attributes of God, the Ṣúfí saints have failed to observe that discriminating appreciation of human personality that is the basis of ethics. With them "human personality is a transient phenomenon which ultimately disappears in what alone is real—the eternal and everlasting personality of God".[25] We have observed that the Persian Ṣúfí poets represent that this ultimate unity excludes all

22. R. A. Nicholson, op. cit., p. 56.
23. Id., op. cit., pp. 18–19, quoting Ibn al-Faríd, *Tá'iyyatu'l-Kubrá*, vv. 153–4.
24. Sir Muhammad Iqbál, *Reconstruction Religious of Thought in Islam*, p. 143.
25. R. A. Nicholson, op. cit., p. 72.

relations. It is the unity of the raindrop that is lost in the ocean, or of the moth that is consumed in the flame of the candle.

Men of Christian faith can go a long way with the Ṣúfís, in their desire for purified lives and in their eagerness to attain unto the moral qualities that have their ultimate origin and sanction in the attributes of God, but they will stop short of the idea of the negation, annihilation, or obliteration of human personality. That is opposed to the basic fact of historic Christianity. For in the perfection of self-sacrificing love, the Christ of Christianity, when hanging on a cross of moral victory, committed his human spirit to his spiritual "Father". He was never more truly or more triumphantly *personal* than he was at that moment. As has been impressively stated by Illingworth (*Personality: Human and Divine*, p. 40), "Personality, then, lives and grows, but, in so doing, retains its identity; the character in which it issues, however versatile or complex, being never a disconnected aggregate, but always an organic whole. Its unity may seem to vanish in the variety of experience through which it goes, yet only to reappear, enlarged, enriched, developed, or impoverished and degraded, as the case may be, but *self-identical.*"

Men and women who attain unto freedom, according to God's plan and with the help of His grace, do so through the overcoming of self-will, in loving and appreciative obedience to God; but in so doing they are not deprived of any of the properties of personality. On the contrary, it is only in obedience to the divine will that the properties of human personality can be fitly integrated and co-ordinated, so as to work together with freedom and with power. Any religious conception that has for its goal the disintegration or annihilation of human personality, the most amazing and potential of all the marvels of the divine creation, must surely be opposed to the will of "my Father and your Father, my God and your God".[26]

> For we know that the whole creation groaneth and travaileth in pain together until now. . . . For the earnest expectation of the creature waiteth for the manifestation of the sons of God.[27]

Restrictions of Muslim Moral Philosophy. There have been real desires on the part of Muslim philosophers and mystical thinkers to break away at times from the restrictions they have found in accepted doctrines of Islam. But their efforts to work out a system of moral philosophy has met boundaries beyond which they have been unable to advance. One of these boundaries has been the tenaciously held dogma that the Qur'án is the eternal word of Allah, notwithstanding the instances where, from the ethical point of view, its declarations are manifestly unworthy of Allah. Another difficult boundary is the fatalistic half-truth that only what Allah wills comes to pass, which

26. New Testament, John 20. 17.
27. New Testament, Romans 8. 22, 19.

al-Ghazálí tried to qualify and explain, but which has nevertheless remained with all Muslim peoples as the all-sufficing *qismat* (Fate). The third is the prevalent tendency to be satisfied with a legalistic compliance with external requirements, with little consideration of ethical principles. The fourth is the doctrine that the prophet Muhammad is to be regarded as "The Perfect Man" (*al-Insán al-Kámil*), a belief that has served in Islam to delay the acceptance of higher and truer standards of family life. And a fifth boundary is the inadequate conception on the part of the Ṣúfís of the character and significance of human personality.

Restrictions are apparent also in the moral ideal that was developed by Plato and Aristotle, and which has been closely followed in Muslim ethics. In this ideal the true *good* for man was said to lie in the full exercise or realization of the soul's faculties in accordance with its proper excellence. However, as has been clearly indicated by Professor Bowne, "Plato wrote wonderfully about the just and the good; but his theory was compatible in his own mind with infanticide and with the killing off of the old and the helpless. Aristotle's ethics has abiding value for all time, but he viewed slavery as both rational and right. The trouble in these cases was not in their ethical insight, but in their philosophy of man, or in their conception of the worth and destiny of the human person."[28] For in his classical chapter on "Greek and Modern Ideas of Virtue." T. H. Green has conclusively shown that "the conception of these virtues has been enlarged in modern times under the influence of Christianity, and especially by the idea of the brotherhood of men."[29] "The range of faculties called into play in any work of social direction or improvement must be much wider", he says, "when the material to be dealt with consists no longer of supposed chattels but of persons asserting recognized rights, whose welfare forms an integral element in the social good which the directing citizen has to keep in view. Only if we leave long-suffering, considerateness, the charity which 'beareth all things, believeth all things, hopeth all things', with all the art of the moral physician, out of account in our estimate of the realization of the soul's power, can we question the greater fullness of the realization in the present life of Christendom, as compared with the highest life of the ancient world. . . . The qualities of self-adjustment, of sympathy with inferiors, of tolerance for the weak and foolish, which are exercised in it, are very different from the pride of self-sufficing strength which with Aristotle was inseparable from heroic endurance."[30]

A Comparison with Christian Ideals. The implications of belief in the brotherhood of men, in their potential relation to the "Father", as

28. Professor Borden P. Bowne, *Principles of Ethics*, p. 193.
29. T. H. Green, *Prolegomena to Ethics*, Introduction, v.
30. Id., op. cit., sections 258 and 259.

set forth clearly by Jesus, are far more exacting and socially significant than those of either Plato's ideal state or Muhammad's *dár al-Islám*. In ethical philosophy they are made explicit in Kant's categorical imperative, where each and every individual life (without racial, communal, or class distinction) is potentially and ideally a divinely ordered end in itself. Consequently every human self is to be regarded "always as an end and never as a means only".[31] On this basis alone is it possible to conceive of either an international theocracy or the universal brotherhood of mankind.

Kant speaks frequently of the "reverence-arousing idea of personality", and as Dr. Knudsen has remarked in his *Principles of Christian Ethics* (p. 79), "This idea lies at the root of the whole moral life, and without it neither the law of love nor the ideal of human perfection would be invested with the absolute obligation that we ascribe to them. It was Jesus who first brought to light the infinite value of every personality in the sight of God, and in so doing he made his profoundest contribution to ethics."

Muhammad brought to the Arabs a new appreciation of important relations that they had in common—their language, their country, and their faith. Those common relations were natural and significant bonds of sympathy. The Emigrants to Medina, as they arrived in increasing numbers, were enabled to subsist by the pledge of brotherhood that the Prophet encouraged the *Ansár* (or Helpers) to accept. And when the authority of Islam was extended into other countries we observe that the Muslim "brotherhood" was expanded so as to include those who would profess the common faith, with its recognized privileges and obligations. Thus the ideal for Islam also is for a community of mankind that will not be inhibited by racial or national barriers.

As for the Christian conception, it is well known that Jesus' transforming gospel of hope and salvation would make all men and women children of a loving, spiritual Father and therefore heirs of eternal life. For him who follows Jesus as his example, "there is a moral kingdom stretching over all worlds and ages. The moral law is not merely a psychological fact in us, but also an expression of a Holy Will which can be neither defied nor mocked. Hence its triumph is secure. The universe, then, and God within and beyond the universe, are on the side of righteousness."[32] Such a world is accepted in faith as essentially rational and moral, a world in which suffering, disappointment, and sacrifice each find their worthy and logical place in an ideal adjustment between devotion to God, self-realization and the service of mankind.

Efforts to develop institutions in harmony with the conviction of a community of good for all men have shown how frequently, and with

31. *Kant's Theory of Ethics*, trans. Abbot, p. 47.
32. Bowne, op. cit., p. 201.

what facility, practical day-by-day judgements continue to be made without consideration of the moral ideal. A young instructor undertook to settle a quarrel that arose in a students' hostel by reference to the previous week's study of an ethical principle that he thought was applicable. But the students frankly repudiated the suggested standard, saying, "We do not employ ethics in the hostel." This happened in India, but, in a similar way, in so-called Christian countries we see realms in the general community life that are as yet little influenced by the application of a moral ideal that is accepted as good for all men. Too often our moral ideal "makes itself felt", as Green says, "in certain prohibitions, e.g. slavery, but it has no such effect on the ordering of life as to secure for those whom we admit that it is wrong to use as chattels much real opportunity of self-development. They are left to sink or swim in the stream of unrelenting competition, in which we admit that the weaker has not a chance" (*Prolegomena*, set. 245).

However lofty and comprehensive the ideals of moral philosophy, if the primary objectives of individuals are of such a kind that they cannot be enjoyed by all, then social life will continue to be dominated by the slogan of free competition, "let the Devil take the hindmost". The ideal of self-devotion in mutual service must be implemented in practical activities, until it becomes a prevailing public sentiment to judge success in life on the basis of spiritual and ethical values rather than on the materialistic standards of wealth and position.

The moral ideal that is truly Christian is based on principles that enable men to reach their highest capacities. These principles have their place in the essential righteousness of God. They were exemplified and made sacred in the life and death of Jesus. The first is the principle of *love*—to God, to self, and to others[33]: "Thou shalt love the Lord thy God with all thy heart, and with all thy soul, and with all thy mind; and thy neighbour as thyself." . . . "And who is my neighbour?" . . . "In as much as ye have done it unto one of the least of these my brethren, ye have done it unto me." The second is the principle of *perfection*, which is laid down by Jesus' enobling and persuasive injunction, "Be ye therefore perfect, even as your Father which is in heaven is perfect." The goal in view is integrity of character, the attainment of the highest moral values of which mankind are made capable. If the kingdom of God can come only with obedience to the ideal and perfect will of God, then moral perfection must be the ethical goal of the Christian life. There are many New Testament passages to confirm this teaching.[34] In Christian ethics

33. New Testament, Luke 10. 29–36 and Matthew 25. 40.

34. New Testament, Matthew 5. 48; 6. 10; 6. 33; Romans 14. 17; Philippians 3. 12–14; 2 Corinthians 13. 9–11; Ephesians 4. 13; Colossians 1. 28; 4. 12; Hebrews 13. 21; James 1. 4; 1 Peter 5. 10; and 1 John 4. 17.

the acceptance of perfection as a standard is an absolute obligation, for no compromise with right can be ethical. The moral law itself has its source in the perfection and integrity of God's character. "God is thus the norm and ground of moral excellence, and He is also its inspiring source",[35] and it is in no way surprising that "the prophetic vision of Christian centuries is uplifted to the city of God, the holy city, which shall come down out of heaven from God, having the glory of God."[36]

With the Kingdom of God as a standard of perfection, the moral struggle is to bring the earth under the loving authority of those who are seeking to be God's vicegerents. In this high service human appreciation and gratitude become spontaneous and natural, as from children to a Father for the benefits His love provides. It is at the same time a service that calls for renunciation and self-denial, in order that the very best individual characters may be developed, with adequately motivated good-will towards others and loyal devotion to the Kingdom.

One of the chief books of Syriac Christian mysticism was written by Isaac of Nineveh in the latter half of the seventh century. He had resigned his position as the Bishop of Nineveh to devote his time and effort to his "Mystical Treatises", in which he taught that God, as the Creator and Final Cause of all things, is perfect Goodness; and that consequently the way to approach God requires "purification from all defilement for those who would look upon Him as He is", which is in accord with Plotinus' declaration, "Never did the eye see the Sun unless it had first become Sun-like, and never did the soul have vision of the First Beauty unless itself be beautiful" (*Ennead*, i. 9, trans. Mackenna).

However, if the Christian conception of man's ideal place in the Kingdom of God is accepted as the only rational answer to the problem of his moral destiny, a vital question still remains. What is the transforming power by which a weak slave of selfish and unworthy desires can be given freedom for the growth of such ethical consciousness, purpose, and victory? Those who have searched the New Testament to discover what we might call a moral motive power have found that "Jesus' method of making men good was to bring the love of God home to their hearts".[37] He knew that men and women had perverted ideas about God, ideas that they held in ignorance and in fear. In the theism that was taught by Jesus, God is not pure will, divorced from reason and love, but God is above us, with us, and in us—Father, Son, and Holy Spirit.

Accordingly, as Jesus associated with men and women and little children, he brought the good news that every *person* is an object of

35. Professor A. C. Knudsen, *The Principles of Christian Ethics*, p. 140.
36. Newman Smyth, *Christian Ethics*, p. 494.
37. Id., op. cit., p. 486.

God's loving solicitude. Thus it was that Hartmann (*Ethics*, i, p. 55) insisted on this "especially revolutionary factor in Christian ethics", whereby "only through faith in the divine redemptive power can the will be made strong enough to meet the moral tests of life". This is not because of any worthiness that God sees in mankind, but solely because of His inherent love for them. God sees in man the possible self of a vicegerent, as Muslim writers say, or according to Christian belief, of a spiritual son—one who would participate in His qualities, who would strive to obey His will, who would accept His forgiveness, and who would occupy an intended place in His Kingdom.

It was not to a select group of the righteous, however, who would feel that they have need of no physician, that Jesus brought the message of God's love. It was to men and women who knew that they had forsaken their better selves and become depraved, it was to persons who were morally conscious, in that they had realized in their own hearts the degrading nature of sin and shame, it was to a disillusioned and discouraged people that Jesus declared that the great purpose of God's love was that they should be *forgiven*. Forgiveness in the gospels is "a word of healing for soul and body".

As has been well said, "It is the practical, human, ethical side of the truth of God's willingness to forgive sins that is chiefly presented in the words and deeds of Jesus. And what truth lies nearer the springs of new life, what word from God can be so quickly converted under the influence of the Spirit into light and joy, as this truth of the divine forgiveness of sins which is the heart of Jesus' gospel to the world? Men have been lifted up and sent on to new lives of hopeful obedience by this gospel of the divine forgiveness of sins, as they have not been by all the moral philosophies which have been offered for virtue's recovery since the world began."[38]

Those who formed the inner circle of Jesus' associates and disciples were Jews. They were familiar with the Old Testament scriptures, and they understood something of what Jesus meant when he said, "And as Moses lifted up the serpent in the wilderness, even so must the Son of Man be lifted up: that whosoever believeth in him should not perish, but have eternal life" (John 3. 14–15). Their forefathers had suffered punishment for their sins of rebellion, but those who still believed in God, in His justice, and in His mercy, had looked to Him for forgiveness—and the scourge of serpents had ceased. Jesus likewise was to be a Symbol, not of a scourge, but of God's suffering and forgiving love, and those who would look to him would not perish but would have everlasting life. Some had looked to him as a teacher, some had found him to be a shepherd or a healer, then all saw him dying on the cross: "And I, if I be lifted

38. Id., op. cit., p. 490.

up from the earth, will draw all men unto me" (John 12. 32). Those who had learned to love him and to follow him soon came to the conclusion that "God was in Christ, reconciling the world unto himself" (2 Cor. 5. 19).

The thought that there was "no privileged class in the society envisaged by Jesus" raises the question of the possibility of equality among mankind. The answer lies in a positive recognition of essential rights for all—to be well-born, to have a wholesome home environment, to obtain an education, to find employment, to enjoy periods of leisure, and to cherish opportunities for cultural and spiritual development. Men may not be forced to respect and maintain all of their individual rights, there may always be some who will refuse to live up to their highest capacities, but in any social structure that remains Christian in its ideals, such rights for all men are recognized and protected.[39] It is because there are no merely national policies that can come up to this standard, and also because nations are so obviously interdependent, that moral culture and security must be sought on a world basis. The supreme importance of this New Testament teaching is being rediscovered. May it not indeed be true that for the world-wide recognition and protection of essential human rights all mankind are awaiting a fuller understanding and a wider appreciation and application of the ethical ideals of Jesus?

One Muslim writer has suggested that Jesus may be called "Son of God" in a moral and spiritual sense,[40] but he insists that in that sense we are all in some measure equally sons of God. It must be observed, however, that it is only the Jesus of the New Testament who can truly be said to have shown himself to have been the son of God in a moral and spiritual sense. No such moral victory can be attributed to the Jesus of the Qur'án, though singularly enough, in contrast with other "prophets", the Qur'án attributes to Jesus no act of sin. Assuredly, if Muslims would seek to become sons of God in a moral (ethical) and spiritual sense, as exemplified by Jesus, their understanding Christian friends would greet them in the words of a favourite hymn:

> Join hands, then, brothers of the faith,
> What-e'er your race may be.
> Who serves my Father as a son
> Is surely kin to me.

There is a decision for faith and life, "with which Christianity challenges men. It is her faith that the final power in the universe is

39. G. B. Oxnam, *The Ethical Ideals of Jesus*, pp. 30–3.

40. Muhammad Amir Alam, *Islam and Christianity*, Calcutta, 1923: quoted by Professor Arthur Jefferey, *New Trends in Muslim Apologetic*, publ. in Dr. John R. Mott's *The Moslem World of Today*, pp. 305–21.

Spirit, not matter or blind force or impersonal trend: that this Spirit is good in character and purpose, good with the righteousness of mercy revealed in Jesus Christ; and that there is a way of life for men which is according to this Spirit and by which alone man's highest good can be achieved."[41]

41. H. F. Rall, *Christianity: An Inquiry into its Nature and Truth*, p. 260.

BIBLIOGRAPHY

A. GENERAL

Adams, Charles C.: *Islam and Modernism in Egypt*, New York, 1933.

'Ali, Muhammad: *The Religion of Islam*, Aḥmadiyya Press, Lahore, 1936.

'Ali, Sir Saiyid Ameer: *The Spirit of Islam*, London, 1935.

Andrae, Tor: *Mohammed* (trans. by T. Menzel), London, 1936.

Arberry, Dr. Arthur J.: *The Doctrine of the Ṣúfís*, Cambridge, 1935.

——: *Kitáb al-Ṣidq* ("The Book of Truthfulness"), by Abú Sa'íd al-Kharráz. Arabic text, edited with English translation. Oxford Press, 1937.

——: *'Ushsháq-Náma* ("The Song of Lovers"), by Iráqí. Persian text, edited and translated. Oxford Press, 1939.

——: *An Introduction to the History of Súfism*, Longmans, Green and Co., 1942.

Aristotle: *Nichomachean Ethics*, English trans. by F. H. Peters, 10th edit., 1906.

Arnold, T. W.: *The Preaching of Islam*, London, 1935.

——: *The Legacy of Islam*, New York, 1931.

Baring, Evelyn: *Modern Egypt*, 2 vols., New York, 1916.

Becker, C. H.: *Christianity and Islam*, London, 1909.

Bell, Professor Richard: *The Origin of Islam in its Christian Environment*, London, 1926.

de Boer, T. J.: *History of Philosophy in Islam*, trans. by E. R. Jones, Luzac and Co., edit. 1903 and 1933. Cf. art. "Ethics and Morality" (Muslim), in the *Encyclopædia of Religion and Ethics*.

Bolus, E. J.: *The Influence of Islam*, London, 1932.

Brockelmann, C.: *Geschichte der Arabischen Literatur*, Weimar, 1898–1902; also Supplement, 1936–7.

Browne, Rev. L. E.: *The Eclipse of Christianity in Asia*, Cambridge, 1933.

Brunner, Emil: *The Divine Imperative*, trans. by Olive Wyon, Lutterworth Library, vol. vii, 1942.

——: *Revelation and Reason*, trans. by Olive Wyon, London, 1947.

Buhl, F.: *Das Leben Muhammads*, Leipzig, 1930; art. "Muhammad", *Encyclopædia of Islam*.

Burkitt, F. C.: *The History of Early Christianity*, London, 1904.

Cash, W. Wilson: *The Expansion of Islam: An Arab Religion in the Non-Arab World*, London, 1928.

——: *Christendom and Islam*, New York, 1937.

Caussin de Perceval, A. P.: *Essai sur l'histoire des Arabes avant l'Islamisme*, Paris, 1847–8.

Donaldson, Bess A.: *The Wild Rue: Muhammadan Magic and Folklore in Iran*, Luzac and Co., London, 1938.

Donaldson, Dwight M.: *The Shi'ite Religion*, Luzac and Co., London, 1933.

Doughty, C. M.: *Travels in Arabia*, London, 1926.

Encyclopædia Britannica, 11th edit. with supplementary vols. xxx–xxxii, 1922.

Encyclopædia of Islam, 1908–38.

Encyclopædia of Religion and Ethics, ed. Hastings, 1908–22.

Fares, Bichr: *L'Honneur chez les Arabes avant l'Islam*, Paris, 1932.

Field, Claud: *The Confessions of al-Ghazáli*, in the Wisdom of the East Series.

Flewelling, R. T.: *The Survival of Western Culture*, New York, 1943.

Gibb, H. A. R.: *Whither Islam?* London, 1932.
Geiger, Rabbi: *Judaism and Islam*, English trans., S.P.C.K., Madras, 1898.
Goldziher, I.: *Vorlesungen über den Islam*, Heidelberg, 1910.
——: *Muhammedanische Studien*, Halle, 1889.
Guillaume: *The Traditions of Islam*, Oxford, 1924.
——: "Predestination and Free Will in Islam", *J.R.A.S.*, Jan. 1924.
Haering, Theodor: *The Ethics of the Christian Life*, trans. from the German, G. P. Putnam's Sons, New York, 1909.
Hamilton, Charles: *The Hedaya: or A Commentary on the Mussulman Laws*, London, 1791.
Hartmann, Nicolai: *Ethics*, trans. from the German, 3 vols., New York, Macmillan Co., 1932.
Hasan Enver, Dr. Ishrat: *The Metaphysics of Iqbál*, Lahore, 1944.
Henson, H. H.: *Christian Morality*, New York, Oxford Univ. Press, 1936.
Hierotheos: *The Book of the Holy Hierotheos*, edit. and trans. by F. S. Marsh, London, 1927.
Hitti, Philip K.: *History of the Arabs*, Macmillan and Co., London, 1937.
Hocking, W. E.: *Lasting Elements of Individualism*, New Haven, 1937.
Huart, C.: *La Littérature Arabe*, Paris, 1902.
Hughes, T. P.: *A Dictionary of Islam*, London, 1885.
Hurgronje, C. Snouck: *Mohammedanism: Its Origin, Religious and Political Growth, and Present State*, New York, 1916.
Inge, W. R.: *Christian Mysticism*, London, 1899.
International Review of Missions, 2 Eaton Gate, London.
Iqbál, Sir Muhammad: *Reconstruction of Religious Thought in Islam*, New York, 1934.
——: *The Secrets of Self* (*Asrár-i-Khudí*), trans. by R. A. Nicholson, London, 1920.
Isaac of Nineveh: *Mystical Treatises*, trans. by A. Wensinck, Amsterdam, 1924.
Islamic Culture, Hyderabad Journal of, Hyderabad, Deccan, 1930.
Jones, Rev. L. Bevan: *The People of the Mosque*, London, 1932.
Juynboll, A. W. T.: *Handbuch des Islamischen Gesetzes*, Leiden, 1910. Arts. "Hadíth" and "Ibn Hanífa" in the *Encyclopædia of Islam*.
Kant, Immanuel: *Critique of Practical Reason*, English trans. Abbott, 5th edit., 1898.
Knudson, Albert C.: *The Principles of Christian Ethics*, Abingdon Cokesbury Press, New York, 1944.
Lammens, H.: *Islam, Beliefs and Institutions*, New York, 1929.
——: *L'Arabie occidentale avant l'Hégire*, Beirut, 1928.
Lane, E. W.: *Arabic-English Lexicon*, London, 1863–93.
——: *Manners and Customs of the Modern Egyptians*, London, 1923.
——: *Arabian Society in the Middle Ages*, London, 1883.
Lazarus, Moritz: *The Ethics of Judaism*, Pts. i and ii, trans. by Henrietta Szold, 1901.
Lecky, W. E. H.: *History of European Morals*, 2 vols., New York, 1879.
Levy, R.: *Sociology of Islam*, 2 vols., London, 1931–3.
Macdonald, D. B.: *Development of Muslim Theology, Jurisprudence and Constitutional Theory*, New York, 1903.
——: *The Religious Attitude and Life in Islam*, Chicago, 1909.
——: *Aspects of Islam*, New York, 1911.
MacNicol, Nicol: *The Living Religions of the Indian People*, New York, 1934.
Maimonides, Moses: *VIII Centenary Memorial Volume*, ed. Epstein, London, 1935.
Margoliouth, D. S.: *Muhammad and the Rise of Islam*, New York, 1905.
——: *Early Development of Muhammadanism*, New York, 1914.

Massignon, L.: *Essai sur les Origines du Lexique Technique de la Mystique Mussulmane*, Paris, 1922.
Mott, Dr. John R.: *The Moslem World Today*, New York, 1925.
Muir, Sir William: *The Caliphate, its Rise, Decline and Fall*, Edinburgh, 1916.
——: *The Life of Muhammad*, 1 vol., ed. Edinburgh, 1923.
Muslim World, The: edit. S. M. Zwemer and E. E. Calverley, New York, 1911.
Nicholson, Professor R. A.: *Literary History of the Arabs*, London, 1923.
——: *The Mystics of Islam*, London, 1914.
——: *Studies in Islamic Mysticism*, Cambridge, 1921.
——: *The Idea of Personality in Ṣúfism*, Cambridge, 1923.
——: "Origin and Development of Ṣúfism", *J.R.A.S.*, 1906.
Niehbuhr, Rienhold: *An Interpretation of Christian Ethics*, New York, 1935.
Nöldeke-Schwally: *Geschichte des Qorans*, Leipzig, 1909–19.
Nöldeke, Theodor: *Sketches of Eastern History*, London and Edinburgh, 1892.
Patton, W. M.: *Aḥmad b. Hanbal and the Miḥna*, Leiden, 1897.
Pickthall, Md. Marmaduke: *The Cultural Side of Islam*, Madras, 1937.
Plessner, Martin: *Der Oikonomikos der Neupythagoreers 'Bryson' und sein Einfluss auf die islamische Wissenschaft*, Heidelberg, 1928.
Plotinus: *Enneads*, trans. S. Mackenna, London, 1917–30.
Roberts, R.: *Social Law of the Qur'án*, London, 1935.
Sarton, G.: *Introduction to the History of Science* (Carnegie Institution of Washington), 2 vols., Baltimore, 1927–9.
Shah, Sirdar Iqbál 'Ali: *Mohammed, the Prophet*, London, 1934.
Shushtery: *Outlines of Islamic Culture*, 2 vols., Bangalore, 1938.
Silver, Maxwell, D. D.: *The Ethics of Judaism*, Bloch. Publ. Co., New York, 1938.
Smith, Dr. Margaret: *Rábia the Mystic and her Fellow Saints in Islam*, Cambridge, 1928.
——: *Early Mysticism in the Near and Middle East*, London, Sheldon Press, 1931.
——: *An Early Mystic of Baghdad*, London, Sheldon Press, 1935.
——: *al-Ghazálí, The Mystic*, Luzac and Co., 1944.
Sprenger, A.: *Das Leben und die Lehre des Mohammed*, Berlin, 1861–5.
Stanton, H. U. W.: *An Outline of the Religion of Islam*, New York, 1925.
——: *The Teachings of the Qur'án*, S.P.C.K., New York, 1919.
Steinschneider, M.: *Die arabischen Uebersetzungen aus dem Griechischen*, Leipzig, 1893.
Stephanson, J: "The Classification of the Sciences according to Nasir al-Dín Ṭúsí," *Isis*, v, 1923, pp. 329–38.
Subhan, The Rev. Bishop John A.: *Ṣufism: Its Saints and Shrines*, Lucknow, 1938.
Sweetman, Rev. Dr. J. Windrow: *Islam and Christian Theology*, Lutterworth Library, vol. xix, London, 1945, and vol. xx, 1947
Thompson, W. F.: *Practical Philosophy of the Muhammadan People* (*Akhláq-i-Jalálí*), London, 1839.
Titus, Dr. Murray T.: *Indian Islam: A Religious History of Islam in India*, Oxford Univ. Press, New York, 1930.
——: *The Young Moslem Looks at Life*, New York, 1937.
Torrey, Charles C.: *The Jewish Foundation of Islam*, J.I.R. Press, New York, 1933.
Tritton, A. S.: *The Caliphs and their Non-Muslim Subjects*, London, 1930.
——: *Muslim Theology*, London, 1947.
Ueberweg: *A History of Philosophy*, 2 vols.
Umaruddin, M., M.A.: *Some Fundamental Aspects of Imam Ghazzali's Thought*, Aligarh, 1946.

Von Grunebaum, Gustave E.: *Medieval Islam: A Study in Cultural Orientation*, University of Chicago Press, 1946.
Webb, C. C. J.: *God and Personality.*
——: *Contribution of Christianity to Ethics*, New York, 1932.
Wellhausen, J.: *Muhammad in Medina*, Berlin, 1882.
Wensinck, A. J.: *The Book of the Dove*, Leyden, 1909.
——: *A Handbook of Early Muhammadan Traditions*, Leyden, 1927.
——: *The Muslim Creed*, New York, 1932.
Westermarck, Edw.: *The Origin and Development of Moral Ideas*, New York, 1906–8.
——: *Christianity and Morals*, New York, 1939.
Widgery, A. G.: *Christian Ethics in History and Modern Life*, New York, 1940.
Wolfson, H. A.: "The Internal Senses in Latin, Arabic, and Hebrew Philosophical Texts", *Harvard Theological Review*, April 1935.
——: "The Classification of Sciences in Medieval Jewish Philosophy", *H.U.C. Jubilee Volume*, Cincinnati, 1925, pp. 263–315.
Zwemer, Dr. S. M.: *Islam a Challenge to Faith*, New York, 1907.
——: *The Influence of Animism in Islam*, London, 1920.
——: *Across the World of Islam*, New York, 1932.

B. ARABIC, SYRIAC, AND PERSIAN TEXTS AND TRANSLATIONS

Aristotle (Pseudo-): *Kitáb Uthúlújiya Arisṭáṭalís*, ed. F. Dieterici, Leipzig, 1883.
Asadi, 'Ali Akbar: *Catalogue of the Shrine Library of Meshed*, 3 vols., 1927.
'Atáhíya: *Diwán*, Beirut, 1896.
'Attár, Faríd al-Dín: *Tadhkirat al-Awliyá*, ed. R. A. Nicholson, London, 1905.
——: *Le Manticu'ttair ou le Langage des Oiseaux*, trans. by Garcin de Tassey, Paris, 1864.
Barhebraeus, Gregorius Abu'l-Faraj: *Mukhtasar Ta'ríkh al-Duwal*, "Historia Orientalis", ed. Pococke, Oxoniae, 1663; ed. Ṣalihání, Beyrouth, 1890.
——: *The Chronology of Gregorius Abu'l-Faraj*, edit. and trans. by E. A. W. Budge, London, 1932.
——: *Book of the Dove*, with selections from the *Ethicon*, trans. by Wensinck, Leyden, 1919.
——: *The Laughable Stories*, text and English trans. by E. A. W. Budge, Luzac and Co., 1897.
Brockhaus: "*Diwán* of Háfiz," Leipzig, 1854–6.
al-Bukhárí: *al-Ṣaḥíḥ*, ed. L. Krehl, 3 vols., Leiden, 1862–1908.
Cheikho, L.: *Kitáb Shu'ará al-Naṣrániyya*, ed. Beirut, 1891.
Clarke, Col. H. Wilberforce: *Diwán-i-Ḥáfiz*, English trans., 2 vols., Calcutta, 1891; with vol. iii, a précis of the *Awárifu'l-Ma'arif*, by al-Suhrawardi.
al-Dawwání, Md. b. As'ad Jalál al-Dín: *Lawámi'al-Ishráq fí Makárim al-Akhláq*, "Flashes of Splendour Concerning Excellencies of Dispositions", edit. by Md. Kazim Shirází and Major W. G. Grey, Calcutta, 1911. Trans. into English in part by W. F. Thompson, *Practical Philosophy of the Muhammadan People*, London, 1839.
al-Dhahabí: *Tabaqát al-Ḥuffáz*, ed. Westenfeld, Gotha, 1833–4.
al-Dinawárí, Abu Hanifa (d. A.D. 895): *Kitáb al-Akhbár al-Ṭiwál*, ed. Kratchkovsky and Guirgass, 1912.
al-Fárábí: *Maqálát fí Ma'áni al-Aql*, in Dietereci's *al-Fárábí's Philosophische Abhandlungen*, Leiden, 1890.

al-Faraj, Abu (al-Isfaháni) d. A.D. 967: *Kitáb al-Agháni* ("The Book of Songs"), 20 vols., Bulaq edition, A.H. 1285.

Freytaq: *Arabum Proverbia*, 3 vols., Bonn, 1838–43.

Furlani, Giuseppe: art. "L'etica di Ahmad ibn Muhammad ibn Maskawaihi", in *Rivista di Filosofia*, x (1918), pp. 32–47.

al-Ghazálí: *Misán al-'Amal*, Cairo, A.H. 1328.

——: *Ihyá' Ulúm al-Dín*, 4 vols., Cairo, A. H. 1302.

——: *al-Maqsad al-Asná fí Sharh 'Asmá' al-Ḥusná*, Cairo, A.H. 1322.

——: *Risálat al-Laduniyya*, trans. by Margaret Smith, *J.R.A.S.*, 1938.

——: *Maqásid al-Falásifa*, Cairo, A.H. 1331.

——: *Kímiyá al-Sa'áda*, "The Alchemy of Happiness", Persian text, lith. Bombay.

Ḥáfiẓ: *Diwán*, Persian text, lith. Teheran.

——: *Versions from Ḥáfiẓ*, by Walter Leaf, London, 1898.

——: *Poems from the Diwán-i-Ḥáfiẓ*, by Gertrude L. Bell, London, 1897; 2nd edit., 1928.

——: *Diwán-i-Ḥáfiẓ*, English trans. by J. Wilberforce Clarke, 2 vols., Calcutta, 1891; vol. iii with a précis of the *Awárufu'l-Ma'arif*, by Al-Suhrawardi.

Hajji Khalifah: (Kátib Celebi), ed. Fluegel, Leipzig, 1835–58, art. "'ilm al-akhláq". Cf. Arabic text, Bulaq, 1274/1857, of the *Kashf al-Ẓunún 'an Asámu'l-Kutúb wa'l-Funún*, Constantinople text, Maarif Matbassi, 1943.

Ibn Ḥanbal: *Musnad*, 6 vols., Cairo, 1313.

Ibn Ḥishám: *Sirat Sayyidna Muhammad*, ed. Wustenfeld, 2 vols., Goettingen, 1858–60; also Cairo, 4 vols., 1928.

al-Hujwírí: *Kashf al-Maḥjúb*, trans. R. A. Nicholson, Gibb M. Series, vol. xvii.

Ibn Khaldun: *Prolegomena*, Arabic text, edit. Quatremere, 3 vols., Beirut, 1879, 1886, 1900; trans. De Slane, *Notices et extraits*, vols. 19–21.

Ibn Khallikán: *Wafayát al-A'yán*, Cairo, ed. A.H. 1310; trans. de Slane, Paris, 1838–42.

Ibn Maskawaihi: *Tahdhíb al-Akhláq*, text publ. on margin of al-Ṭabarsí's *Makárim al-Akhláq*, Cairo, A.H. 1303; and later, with al-Ghazálí's *Kitáb Adab al-Dín wa'l-Dunyá* on the margin, Cairo, 1317.

——: *Tajárib al-Umam*, ed. Leone Caetani, Gibb M. Series, vii. *Adab al-'Arab wa'l-Furs*, cf. *Le Tableaux de Cébes, version Arabe d'Ibn Miskawaih* (Algiers, 1898), and de Sacy, *Notices et extraits*, x. 95, and *Mémoire de l'Institut*, ix. i ff.

——: *Tahdhíb al-Akhláq*, trans. into Urdu by Hakím Sayyid Zafar Mahdi, *Tahdhíb al-Khaḍa'il wa Tahdhíb al-Faḍa'il*, Bombay, 1885.

Ibn al-Muqaffá': *Kalílah wa Dimnah*, Búláq, A.H. 1249; ed. Beirut, 1912. *al-Adab al-Wajiz li'l-Waladi'l-Saghír*, edit. Abbas Iqbál, A.H.SH. 1312.

Ibn Mutaqqí: *Kanz al-'Ummám fí Sunan al-Aqwál wa'l-Af'ál*, published on the margin of Ibn Hanbal's *Musnad*, Cairo, A.H. 1313.

Ibn al-Nadím: *Fihrist*, ed. Fluegel, 1871–2.

Ibn Qutaiba: *Kitáb al-Ma'árif*, Goettingen, 1850.

——: *Kitáb al-Shi'r wa'l-Shu'ará*, ed. de Goeje. *'Uyún al-Akhbár*, 4 vols., Cairo, 1343/1925, chs. i–iv, edit. by Carl Brockelmann, Berlin, 1900–8.

Ibn Sa'd: *Kitáb al-Tabaqát al-Kabír*, ed. Sachau, Leiden, 1904 sqq., 9 vols.

Ibn Siná: *Rasá'il fí Ḥikmat wa Tabiyát*, Bombay, A.H. 1318.

Ibn Abí Usaibi'a: *'Uyún al-Anbár fí Tabaqát al-Aṭibbá'*, edit. A. Muller, Cairo, 1299/1882.

al-Ibshíhi: *al-Mustatráf*, Cairo, A.H. 1304–8, trans. into French, Paris-Toulon, 1899–1902.

Ivanow, W.: Translation of *Haft Báb-i-Ḅábá Sayyid-i-na*, attributed to Hasan al-Basrí, and other Ismáílí treatises, 1933 ff.

al-Jáhiz: *Bayán wa'l-Tabyín*, Cairo, A.H. 1332.
al-Jámí: *Nafaḥát al-Uns*, ed. W. N. Lees, Calcutta, 1850.
al-Kalabádhí, Abu Bakr: *Kitáb al-Ta'arruf fi Madhhab Ahl al-Tasawwuf*, trans. A. J. Arberry, *The Doctrine of the Ṣúfís*, Cambridge, 1935.
Káshifi, Husain Wá'iz: *Akhláq-Muhsiní*, frequently printed; 20 chs., ed. Ousely, publ. Calcutta, 1850; 15 chs. trans. by Rev. H. G. Keene, London, 1867.
al-Kházimí, al-Háfiz Abí Bakr (d. A.H. 584): *al-I'tibár fi'l-Násikh wa'l-Mansúkh min al-'Athár*, Cairo, A.H. 1346.
al-Kulaini, Md. b. Ya'qub: *al-Káfi fí 'Ilm al-Dín*, lith., 2 vols., Teheran, 1889.
Lichtenstaedter: *Women in the 'Aiyám al-'Arab*, London, 1935.
Loth, Otto: *Das Classenbuch des b. Sa'd*, Leipzig, 1869.
Lyall, Sir Charles: *Mufaḍḍaliyát*, edit. text with English trans., *Anthology of Ancient Arabian Odes*, Oxford, 1918; *Ancient Arabic Poetry*, London, 1885 (trans. from the *Hamasah* and the *Mu'allaqát*).
al-Maidání: *Majma al-Amthál*, Cairo, A.H. 1342.
Mainz, Earnst: "Mutazilitische Ethik", translation from the *Ihyá'* of al-Ghazálí in *Der Islam*, vol. 22 (1935).
Málik b. Anás: *al-Muwaṭṭa'*, Cairo, A.H. 1348.
Massignon, L.: *La Passion d'al-Halláj*, Paris, 1922.
——: *Kitáb al-Tawásín*, ed. Paris, 1913.
Maskawaihi (see Ibn Maskawaihi).
al-Mas'údí: *Murudj al-Dhahab*, *Les Prairies d'Or*, edit. and trans. by S. Barbier de Meynard, 9 vols., Paris, 1861.
al-Máwardí: *Adab al-Dunya wa'l-Dín*, Cairo, A.H. 1315.
Mishkátu'l-Maṣábíh, by Wáliu'l-Dín Abú 'Abd Allah, compilation of A.H. 737, trans. by Captain Matthews, 1809. Cf. *Selections from Muhammadan Traditions*, by Rev. William Goldsack, C.L.S. for India, 1923.
al-Muhásibí: *Muḥasibat al-Nufús*, MS. Brit. Museum, Or. 4026.
——: *Ri'áya*, MS. Oxford, Hunt. 611.
——: *Waṣáyá*, MS. Brit. Museum, Or. 7900. Cf. Margaret Smith, *An Early Mystic of Baghdad*, London, 1935.
Muslim: *Ṣahíh*, 2 vols., Buláq, 1873.
al-Nasá'i: *Sunan*, 2 vols., Cairo, 1894.
al-Násikh wa'l-Mansúkh, by Abu'l-Qasim b. Salama, Cairo, A.H. 1310.
al-Nawbakhtí: *Kitáb Firáq al-Shi'a*, ed. Ritter, Constantinople, 1931.
Nasir-i-Khusraw: *Rawshaná'í Náma* and the *Sa'ádat Náma*, publ. by the Kaviáni Press, Berlin, A.H. 1341; also *Z.D.M.G.*, vols. 33 and 34. *Shahnama*, ed. and trans. by Schefer, Paris, 1881.
Nizám al-Mulk: *Siyását-náma*, edit. Schefer, Paris, 1891.
Nuráqí, Mulla Ahmad (d. A.D. 1128): *Miráj al-Sa'ádat*, lith. Teheran, A.H. 1300.
Palmer, E. H.: *The Koran*, English trans., The World's Classics, Oxford Univ. Press, 1928.
Abu'l-Qasim Hibatullah (d. A.H. 410): *al-Násikh-wa'l-Mansúkh*, Cairo, A.H. 1310. Cf. trans. of selections by Rev. Anvar al-Ḥaqq, *Abrogation in the Koran*, Meth. Publ. House, Lucknow, 1926.
al-Qazwíni, Ahmad (d. A.D. 1185): *Mufíd al-'Ulúm*, Cairo, A.H. 1330.
al-Qiftí: *Ta'ríkh al-Ḥukamá*, ed. Lippirt, Leipzig, 1903.
al-Qúmmi, Shaikh 'Abbas: *Hadayat al-Ahbáb* and *Ḥusn al-Athár min Makárim al Akhláq-i-Saiyid al-Bashar*, Najaf, A.H. 1349. *Kitáb-i-Muqámát-i-'Aliyya*, lith. Najaf, A.H. 1357.
al-Qushayrí, Abú al-Qasim: *Risálá*, Cairo, 1867.
Raḍí, Saiyid (d. 406/1015): *Nahj al-Balagha*, lith. Meshed, 1892.
Rasá'il Ikhwán al-Ṣafá, 4 vols., ed. Cairo, 1928.

al-Rází, Fakr al-Dín: *Jamá'al-'Ulúm.*

Rodwell, James M.: *The Koran*, English trans., E. P. Dutton and Co. (Everyman's Library), 1909.

Rosenzweig-Schwannan, *Der Diwan des grossen lyrischen Dichters Hafis*, Vienna, 1858 (3 vols.).

Rúmí, Jalál al-Dín: *Mathnawí*, abridged trans., E. H. Whinfield, London, 1898. Complete text, edited with English translation and commentary by R. A. Nicholson, Gibb Memorial Series, iv. 1–8, 1934–40.

Sa'di (d. circa 1292): *Translation of the Gulistan of Sa'di*, 2nd edit., by John T. Platts; cf. also trans. of Bks. i–ii, *Kings and Beggars*, by A. J. Arberry, London, 1945.

——: *Bustán*, cf. Graf's edited text, and Levy's translation of selections in *Tales from the Bustán* (Stories of the East Series).

Saná'í, Hakím Abú'l-Majd: *Ḥadíqatu'l-Ḥaqíqat*, Bk. I, edited and translated by Major J. Stephenson, Calcutta, 1910.

Shahrastání (d. 1153): *Kitáb Malal wa'l-Naḥal*, ed. Cureton, 1846. *Kitáb Niháyatu'l-Iqdám fi 'Ilmu'l-Kalam*, edit. by A. Guillaume, Oxford, 1934.

Shiblí, Nu'mání, *Shi'ru'l-'Ajam* (Urdu), 5 vols., A'ẓamgadah, A.H. 1339.

Sukhanán-i-Muhammad, publ. in Persian and in Arabic, Teheran, 1938.

al-Suhrawardi: *'Awárif al-Ma'arif* (on margin of *Iḥyá*), Cairo, A.H. 1272. For précis in English, cf. Clarke's translation of Háfiẓ, vol. iii.

al-Ṭabarí, Abu Ja'far: *Annals* (Arabic text), Leiden, 1879–1901.

al-Tahánawí, Md. Alá b. 'Ali: *Kitáb Kashsháf Iṣṭiláḥát al-Funún*, "Dictionary of the Technical Terms", ed. Sprenger, Calcutta, 1862.

al-Thaalabí (d. A.D. 1035): *Qiṣás al-Anbíyá*, Bombay, 1878.

al-Ṭúsí, Nasír al-Dín: *Akhláq-i-Náṣirí* (cf. Brockelmann, *G.A.L.* i. 510, n. 1; and A. Sprenger, *Z.D.M.G.*, 13 (1849), 540; Lucknow, 1891).

Yahyá ibn 'Adí (d. A.H. 363): *Tahdhíb al-Akhláq*, Cairo, 1630/191.

al-Ya'qúbí, Ibn Wadíh (d. A.D. 900): *Historiae*, ed. Houtsma, Leiden, 1883.

Yáqút: *Irshád al-Aríb ila Ma'rifat al-Adíb*, "Dictionary of Learned Men", Gibb M. Series, vi.

Zamakhshari: *Aṭwáq al-Dhahab*, trans. F. V. Hammer, Vienna, 1835; and by G. Weil, Stuttgart, 1863.

INDEX